Third Edition

GUIDELINES

A Cross-Cultural Reading / Writing Text

W9-CQP-578

RUTH SPACK

CAMBRIDGE
UNIVERSITY PRESS

University Printing House, Cambridge CB2 8BS, United Kingdom

One Liberty Plaza, 20th Floor, New York, NY 10006, USA

477 Williamstown Road, Port Melbourne, VIC 3207, Australia

4843/24, 2nd Floor, Ansari Road, Daryaganj, Delhi – 110002, India

79 Anson Road, #06–04/06, Singapore 079906

Cambridge University Press is part of the University of Cambridge.

It furthers the University's mission by disseminating knowledge in the pursuit of education, learning and research at the highest international levels of excellence.

www.cambridge.org
Information on this title: www.cambridge.org/9780521613019

© Cambridge University Press 2007

This publication is in copyright. Subject to statutory exception and to the provisions of relevant collective licensing agreements, no reproduction of any part may take place without the written permission of Cambridge University Press.

First published 2007
20 19 18 17 16 15 14 13

Printed in Malaysia by Vivar Printing

A catalog record for this publication is available from the British Library.

Library of Congress Cataloging-in-Publication Data
Spack, Ruth.
Guidelines : a cross-cultural reading/writing text / Ruth Spack. – 3rd ed.
p. cm.
Includes biographical references and index.
ISBN 978-0-521-61301-9 (pbk.)
1. English language – Rhetoric. 2. English language – Textbooks for foreign speakers.
3. Pluralism (Social sciences) – Problems, exercises, etc. 4. Report writing – Problems, exercises, etc. 5. Readers – Social sciences. 6. Multicultural education. 7. College readers. I. Title.
PE1408.S659 2006
808' .042–dc22   2006049037

ISBN 978-0-521-61301-9 student's book
ISBN 978-0-521-61302-6 teacher's manual

Cambridge University Press has no responsibility for the persistence or accuracy of URLs for external or third-party internet websites referred to in this publication, and does not guarantee that any content on such websites is, or will remain, accurate or appropriate.

Book design and art direction: Adventure House, NYC
Cover art: Laurence Gartel
Layout services: TSI Graphics, Effingham, IL

Dedicated with love to Norman and Jonathan Spack

and to

Rebecca, Arthur, William, and Zachary Sneider

Brief Contents

Contents

Preface

Guidelines: A Cross-Cultural Reading/Writing Text is designed for composition courses that include multilingual learners and that emphasize the connection between reading and writing.

In *Guidelines*, students are challenged to think critically about what they read and to develop analytical and argumentative strategies that enable them to present and support ideas. In the process, students come to understand that, through their own writing, they are building on and contributing to an existing base of language resources and knowledge. With its multicultural and international scope and its respect for students' experiences and perspectives, *Guidelines* has considerable appeal to a diverse group of readers and writers.

■ The Principles of Guidelines

Guidelines addresses the academic needs of students who can benefit from carefully structured support as they undertake increasingly complex tasks. Guidelines within the text show students ways to integrate new procedures and ideas with previously learned skills and information. These guidelines are based on four basic principles.

- Academic language and literacy are acquired when language is used as a means for understanding and constructing knowledge. Students need to engage with authentic, meaningful, and intellectually challenging content in order to grow as readers and writers.

- Writing generates ideas. Writing gives students time to deliberate and reflect on their thoughts and analyses. This process can lead to insights and understandings that students might otherwise not have had.

- Writing promotes language acquisition. Shaping their ideas in writing before they speak makes it possible for students to consider what they want to say and how they want to say it. Using writing to analyze and interpret what they read leads students to a deeper understanding of the way language generates meaning. Quoting from what they read enables students to incorporate, and ultimately to absorb, new vocabulary.

- Students develop as readers, writers, and learners when they are invited to connect what they already know and have experienced with what they are being asked to learn and to do.

■ The Third Edition of Guidelines

This third edition of *Guidelines* incorporates feedback from numerous students, instructors, reviewers, and editors who have used or evaluated previous editions. It retains the features that are most appreciated, including the integration of reading and writing, a generous selection of diverse and thought-provoking readings, pre-reading and post-reading activities that encourage students to interact with what they read, a variety of tasks that motivate and enable students to write, strategies for fulfilling specific essay and research assignments, guideline boxes that present writing instruction in a format that is easy to understand and use, illustrative examples of student writers at work, and a learner-centered philosophy that encourages students to write from their own perspectives as they analyze and interpret what they read.

New features in the third edition include the following:

- Reorganization of the entire text
- Creation of a separate part on research writing
- Creation of a Handbook for Writing
- Seven new professional readings
- Individualized discussion activities for each reading
- Readings organized according to specific essay assignments
- More specific essay assignments and clearer instructions
- A new Web-based research essay assignment
- Updated information on using Web-based research
- Evaluative criteria for each essay assignment
- A new sample student research essay
- Clearer guidelines overall

■ The Structure of Guidelines

Guidelines has four major divisions: Part One: Responding to Reading, Part Two: Readings and Writing Assignments, Part Three: Research and Writing Assignments, and A Handbook for Writing.

Part One: *Responding to Reading*

Part One consists of one chapter:

Chapter 1 – Strategies for Reading Critically

This chapter provides guidelines for closely examining and reflecting critically on an author's ideas and experiences. Such reading strategies as generating background knowledge, using clues to guess at meaning, annotating, and writing a journal entry on a reading are illustrated with examples of student readers at work. Numerous activities invite students to apply these strategies to the three readings that are included in the chapter.

Part Two: *Readings and Writing Assignments*

Part Two consists of four chapters of readings and guidelines for writing a corresponding essay:

Chapter 2 – Writing from Experience
Chapter 3 – Relating Reading to Experience
Chapter 4 – Analyzing an Argumentative Essay
Chapter 5 – Analyzing Fiction

Many of the readings address the theme of living in multiple worlds: what it means to acquire new ways of communicating across languages and cultures and to adapt to new approaches to learning, literacy, and life. Some of the essays tackle controversial issues related to education: what students should be taught, how they should be taught, and how their learning should be assessed. The fictional pieces, which span more than 100 years, reflect some of the problems and possibilities of living in the United States: what it has meant to live as a slave, immigrant, or exile. Each reading is framed by before-and-after writing and discussion activities that are designed to involve students in active and purposeful engagement with what they read. Within each chapter, guidelines for exploring, focusing, and structuring ideas for the chapter's assigned essay are illustrated with examples of student writers at work.

Part Three: *Research and Writing Assignments*

Part Three consists of two chapters that provide guidelines for writing a research essay:

Chapter 6 – Writing from Field Research

Chapter 7 – Writing from Library and Web-based Research

Strategies for conducting observations, interviews, surveys, library investigations, and Web searches and for synthesizing material drawn from multiple sources are illustrated with examples of student writers at work. Each chapter ends with a sample student research essay.

A Handbook for Writing

A Handbook for Writing consists of four sections of general guidelines for writing:

Section I – Citing, Incorporating, and Documenting Sources

Section II – Drafting, Exchanging Feedback, and Revising

Section III – Locating Errors

Section IV – Correcting Errors

Throughout the handbook, excerpts from student writing illustrate ways to fulfill guidelines for citing, summarizing, paraphrasing, quoting, synthesizing, and documenting sources; for maintaining academic integrity; for testing out ideas on paper and reshaping those ideas in response to oral or written feedback; and for proofreading and editing for error. Numerous activities provide opportunities for students to apply the strategies to their own writing. A sample student essay appears in Section II.

■ The Versatility of Guidelines

Guidelines has grown out of my own teaching experiences. What appears in the text is the result of years of experimenting in the classroom as I tried out new readings, writing assignments, and approaches. For that reason, I do not expect any instructor to use all of the material in this text in one semester. Nor do I expect anyone to use only the material in this book. My goal is to present a versatile text that allows instructors to select whatever seems most productive and to add or substitute other readings and assignments that enrich students' experiences in and out of the classroom.

I expect and hope, too, that instructors will not feel compelled to follow the order of the text. Common themes resonate across readings and writing assignments, making it possible for a reading in one chapter to be used for a writing assignment in another, and vice versa. For me, the long-term success of *Guidelines* is reflected in the work of the hundreds of instructors who, over the years, have experimented with earlier editions of the book in their own classrooms and treated it as a springboard for the creation of their own imaginative and intellectually challenging curricula whose content, texts, and assignments involve students in authentic and meaningful work and thus facilitate their acquisition of language and literacy.

Further ideas for using *Guidelines* can be found in the *Teacher's Manual*.

Acknowledgements

I have many colleagues with whom I share ideas and from whom I garner new approaches to teaching and writing, both at Bentley College and within the larger community of educators, and I deeply appreciate their support of my work. I must give special thanks to my writing partner and friend Vivian Zamel, who has influenced my scholarship and practice in more ways than I can count.

As must be obvious to anyone who reads *Guidelines*, I rely on students' input in order to write about reading and writing. The many students I have taught over the years have experimented with new reading selections and new approaches to writing, appraised early drafts of the book, and contributed their own writing to the project. I will always be grateful for their curiosity, perceptiveness, and willingness to take risks – and for their good humor as they patiently taught me how to teach.

The reviewers for *Guidelines* admirably fulfilled the task of critiquing the text and providing suggestions for revision. What I appreciate most is that they framed their critical commentary with positive reinforcement that helped me see how to preserve the strengths of the previous edition even as I improved upon it. For their thoughtful and encouraging feedback, I thank Vivian Adzaku, Tulane University and Delgado Community College; Michelle Baptiste, University of California at Berkeley; Barbara Berken, SUNY, Albany; Frederick L. De Naples, Bronx Community College; R. Scott Evans, University of the Pacific; Alison Evans, University of Oregon; MaryAnne Ifft, DeAnza College; Stephen R. Jacques, University of Hawaii at Manoa; Patricia Pashby, University of Oregon; Cathy Phelps, University of Oregon; Marjorie Pitts, Ohio Northern University; Gabriela Segade, Contra Costa College; Brad Tucker, Georgia Perimeter College; Belinda Young Davy, University of Oregon; and Dorothy Zemach, Cambridge University Press.

I was fortunate to have the opportunity to work closely with three fine editors at Cambridge University Press. Commissioning Editor Bernard Seal, who has a keen eye for organization and design, showed me how to turn a good book into a better one. Development Editor Phebe Szatmari provided encouragement at precisely the moment I most needed it. Development Editor Karen McAlister Shimoda went above and beyond her editorial role in aiding my writing process, and I am indebted to her for her meticulous approach (I've met my match!), for her insights, and for her generosity. I also want to express my appreciation to editorial assistant Carlos Rountree, copyeditor Linda LiDestri, indexer Heidi Blough, and proofreader Jill Freshney, and to Project Editor Heather McCarron, Publishing Manager Penny Laporte, and Publishing Director Louisa Hellegers, for the part they played in bringing this project to fruition. This remarkable group of people inspired me to strive to meet the highest standards I have ever been asked to reach as a textbook writer. I hope that the resulting book fulfills their expectations.

Ruth Spack

PART ONE
RESPONDING TO READING

Chapter 1

Strategies for Reading Critically

Chapter 1

Strategies for Reading Critically

Reading critically involves reading not only to increase your knowledge but also to develop your own perspective toward the subject matter discussed in a text. The challenges of reading critically include identifying an author's key points, raising questions about what you have read, and determining your own point of view.

Chapter 1 includes a number of guidelines that are designed to help you develop strategies for reading critically. Most of the strategies involve writing, for writing about reading can enable you to discover meaning in a text and to generate your own ideas.

GUIDELINES

Strategies for Reading Critically

Chapter Assignment

In Chapter 1, you will be introduced to a variety of guidelines for reading critically. Together, the guidelines suggest ways to make predictions about a reading's content, to develop reading fluency, to examine an author's ideas and experiences closely, and to capture your own reactions to those ideas and experiences. The reading strategies of three students – Julio, Victoria, and Jaimie – are included to show how they interacted with a particular text. As you apply the guidelines to the reading selections in this chapter, share your reactions and ideas with a partner, in a small group, or with the whole class.

■ Generating Background Knowledge

Generating background knowledge before you begin reading a selection can help you predict what you are about to read and lead you toward a deeper understanding of the text.

Guidelines for Generating Background Knowledge

1. Read the *title* of the reading selection.
2. Read any *background information* that is provided about the reading.
3. Read *headings* or *subheadings* if they are provided.
4. Read words in **boldface** if they are provided.
5. Look at *charts* and *illustrations* if they are provided.

A student reader at work: *Generating background knowledge*

Before reading "What True Education Should Do" by Sydney J. Harris, Julio looked at the title and tried to predict the essay's content. These were his thoughts:

> "Education is the central subject of the essay. And it's going to be about true education or the ideal education. So the title 'What True Education Should Do' probably means that I'm going to read about the author's recommendations for the ideal education."

••• ➡ Your turn: *Generating background knowledge*

Before reading "What True Education Should Do," apply relevant *Guidelines for Generating Background Knowledge* to the reading.

What True Education Should Do

Sydney J. Harris

Sydney J. Harris (1917–1986) was a writer for major newspapers in Chicago, Illinois. His many books include Pieces of Eight *(1982) and* Clearing the Ground *(1986). "What True Education Should Do" was originally published in Harris' syndicated newspaper column, "Strictly Personal," which was published weekly throughout the United States and in several other countries.*

When most people think of the word "education," they think of a pupil as a sort of animate sausage casing. Into this empty casing, the teachers are supposed to stuff "education."

But genuine education, as Socrates knew more than two thousand years ago, is not inserting the stuffings of information *into* a person, but rather eliciting knowledge *from* him; it is the drawing out of what is in the mind.

"The most important part of education," once wrote William Ernest Hocking, the distinguished Harvard philosopher, "is this instruction of a man in what he has inside of him."

And, as Edith Hamilton has reminded us, Socrates never said, "I know, learn from me." He said, rather, "Look into your own selves and find the spark of truth that God has put into every heart, and that only you can kindle to a flame."

In the dialogue called the "Meno," Socrates takes an ignorant slave boy, without a day of schooling, and proves to the amazed observers that the boy really "knows" geometry – because the principles and axioms of geometry are already in his mind, waiting to be called out.

So many of the discussions and controversies about the content of education are futile and inconclusive because they are concerned with what should "go into" the student rather than with what should be taken out, and how this can best be done.

The college student who once said to me, after a lecture, "I spend so much time studying that I don't have a chance to learn anything," was succinctly expressing his dissatisfaction with the sausage-casing view of education.

He was being so stuffed with miscellaneous facts, with such an indigestible mass of material, that he had no time (and was given no encouragement) to draw on his own resources, to use his own mind for analyzing and synthesizing and evaluating this material.

Education, to have any meaning beyond the purpose of creating well-informed dunces, must elicit from the pupil what is latent in every human being – the rules of reason, the inner knowledge of what is proper for men to be and do, the ability to sift evidence and come to conclusions that can generally be assented to by all open minds and warm hearts.

Pupils are more like oysters than sausages. The job of teaching is not to stuff them and then seal them up, but to help them open and reveal the riches within. There are pearls in each of us, if only we knew how to cultivate them with ardor and persistence.

■ Using Clues to Guess at Meaning

Repeatedly using a dictionary as you read can interfere with your reading fluency. You should aim for as full an understanding of a reading as possible, but you do not need to understand every word the first time you read a text. Rereading is a more effective way to develop fluency. As you reread, try *using clues to guess at meaning*. Focus only on the unfamiliar words that seem to hold the key to understanding the passages in which they occur. Then attempt to make sense of the words in the context of the whole passage. The context will not always provide precise meaning, but it may provide enough clues for you to infer the meaning.

Guidelines for Using Clues to Guess at Meaning

1. Read the sentence in which the unfamiliar word or expression appears, as well as the words that immediately precede and follow an unfamiliar word or expression.
2. Try to determine whether the unfamiliar word has a positive or negative connotation or association.
3. Consider how the unfamiliar word or expression fits into the entire text.

A student reader at work: *Using clues to guess at meaning*

In the second paragraph of "What True Education Should Do," Julio underlined the unfamiliar word *eliciting*.

> But genuine education, as Socrates knew more than two thousand years ago, is not inserting the stuffings of information *into* a person, but rather eliciting knowledge *from* him; it is the drawing out of what is in the mind.

Julio then guessed at its meaning by looking at the word in context. He looked at the words that came before *eliciting* ("not inserting . . . information *into* a person") and the words that came after the phrase containing *eliciting* ("it is the drawing out of what is in the mind") and realized from the author's contrast of the two ideas that *eliciting* means the same thing as *drawing out*, or bringing out.

- - -▶ **Your turn:** *Using clues to guess at meaning*

1 Reread "What True Education Should Do."
2 Identify two or three words or expressions whose dictionary definitions you may not know precisely.
3 Using the *Guidelines for Using Clues to Guess at Meaning*, infer the meaning of the words or expressions in the sentences in which they occur. Check your meaning against a dictionary definition of the words.

▮ Annotating

Annotating involves recording your understanding of and reactions to what you read. You can make notes in the margins of the text, within the text, or on a separate sheet of paper.

Guidelines for Annotating
One or more of the following suggestions may be helpful:
1. Create headings or categories to identify different sections.
2. Write brief summaries of different sections.
3. Mark unfamiliar words or phrases.
4. Highlight or underline a passage that you think is significant.
5. Express any emotion you feel in response to what you have just read, for example, pleasure, surprise, anger, or confusion.
6. Recall personal associations with actions or conversations that take place in the reading selection.
7. Make connections with something else you have read, heard, or seen.
8. Ask questions about anything you find confusing.

A student reader at work: *Annotating*

While rereading "What True Education Should Do," Julio created headings in the left-hand margin to identify the topics the author covers. He also highlighted what he thought was the major idea of the first two paragraphs.

1ˢᵗ view of education	When most people think of the word "education," they think of a pupil as a sort of animate sausage casing. Into this empty education casing, the teachers are supposed to stuff "education."
2ⁿᵈ view of education	But genuine education, as Socrates knew more than two thousand years ago, is not inserting the stuffings of information *into* a person, but rather eliciting knowledge *from* him; it is the drawing out of what is in the mind.

▪▪▪▶ Your turn: *Annotating*

Using the *Guidelines for Annotating*, annotate the entire essay, "What True Education Should Do."

■ Clustering Ideas from a Reading

Clustering ideas from a reading is a technique that involves creating a visual pattern in order to show significant relationships among the ideas and details in a reading selection.

Guidelines for Clustering Ideas from a Reading

1. Choose a word or expression that is the central subject of the reading.
2. Write that word or expression in the center of a blank page and circle it.
3. Cluster related words or expressions from the reading around this central word or expression, and circle each of these words.
4. Draw lines to connect the clusters of related words.
5. Draw arrows to connect the central word or expression to each cluster of related words.

A student reader at work: *Clustering ideas from a reading*

To cluster ideas from the first two paragraphs of "What True Education Should Do," Julio wrote the word *Education* in the center of his paper. To the left of the word, he put two phrases that show Harris's view of what true education *is not.* To the right of the word, he put three phrases that show Harris's view of what true education *is.* Julio then drew vertical lines to connect the related phrases. He completed his clustering diagram by drawing arrows from the central word to the two clusters of phrases.

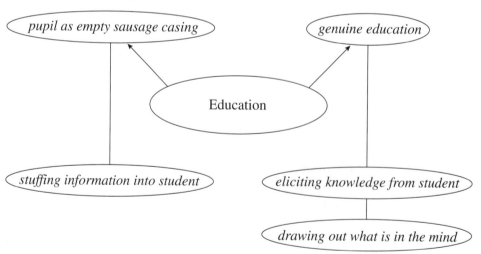

pupil as empty sausage casing   *genuine education*

Education

stuffing information into student   *eliciting knowledge from student*

drawing out what is in the mind

Your turn: *Clustering ideas from a reading*

Using the *Guidelines for Clustering Ideas from a Reading,* create a cluster to show how Sydney J. Harris develops his ideas about education in the rest of his essay.

Making Double-Entry Notes

Making double-entry notes enables you to capture a dual perspective on a reading: the author's ideas and your own ideas. In other words, you summarize what the author is saying and keep it separate from your reactions. You can make double-entry notes by writing in the left- and right-hand margins of the reading selection or on the left and right sides of a sheet of paper folded in two, lengthwise.

Guidelines for Making Double-Entry Notes

1. In the left-hand margin of the reading selection or on the left side of a sheet of paper, write notes that *summarize* the reading to help you understand and focus on what the author is saying. This can be done paragraph by paragraph or in larger chunks.

2. In the right-hand margin of the reading selection or on the right side of a sheet of paper, write notes that *record your reactions* to what you have just read. This can be done paragraph by paragraph or in larger chunks. For example, you can express pleasure, surprise, disagreement, or anger at what you've just read; make connections with something else you've read or seen; recall personal associations; or ask questions.

A student reader at work: *Making double-entry notes*

Victoria made double-entry notes on the first two paragraphs of "What True Education Should Do," summarizing the author's ideas in the left-hand margin and capturing her reactions to these ideas in the right-hand margin.

Here are the notes Victoria wrote in the margins of the reading.

Summary		*Reaction*
Education as sausage casing	When most people think of the word "education," they think of a pupil as a sort of animate sausage casing. Into this empty casing, the teachers are supposed to stuff "education."	*Am I a sausage?*
Education as drawing out	But genuine education, as Socrates knew more than two thousand years ago, is not inserting the stuffings of information *into* a person, but rather eliciting knowledge *from* him; it is the drawing out of what is in the mind.	*Nice, but impossible in college*

Your turn: *Making double-entry notes*

Using the *Guidelines for Making Double-Entry Notes*, make summary and reaction notes on the entire essay, "What True Education Should Do."

■ Taking Notes on a Reading

Taking notes on a reading can help you determine and organize a reading's most important elements. Effective notes show the relationships among the reading's ideas and examples and can help you achieve a clearer understanding of an author's meaning.

Guidelines for Taking Notes on a Reading
1. After you have read the entire piece, reread one section at a time.
2. Determine what you perceive to be the key topic or point of each section.
3. Determine which details or examples illustrate or explain the key topics, points, or arguments.
4. Using phrases rather than full sentences, write down the key topics or points and some of the details and examples that expand on or support them.

A student reader at work: *Taking notes on a reading*

Jaimie took notes on the first two paragraphs of "What True Education Should Do" to show the contrast between the two types of education that Harris discusses.

> *Common view of education:*
> *1. Students as empty sausage casings*
> *2. Students stuffed with education*
> *Genuine education:*
> *1. Not inserting information into students*
> *2. Drawing knowledge from students*

Your turn: *Taking notes on a reading*

Using the *Guidelines for Taking Notes on a Reading*, take notes on the rest of "What True Education Should Do."

■ Writing a Journal Entry on a Reading

One way to capture your reactions to a reading is to make regular entries in a journal. *Writing a journal entry on a reading* provides the opportunity to use written language informally to generate, test out, and communicate ideas. There are no set rules for what a journal entry should look like. How you respond to what you read is shaped by the content and style of the reading selection and by your own experiences, beliefs, and values. And, of course, your response is also shaped by how carefully you have read and how fully you have understood the reading. You may have a lot to say, or you may have very little to say. The first few times you write a journal entry, you may find it difficult to find things to say. You can begin by writing, "I'm not sure what to say about this reading" or "This reading was difficult"; the act of writing itself will probably generate ideas. As you gain experience, you will likely find that you can quickly produce even a lengthy journal entry.

Guidelines for Writing a Journal Entry on a Reading

In your response to the reading, you may write whatever you want or choose among the following suggestions. Incorporate at least one quotation from the reading in your response (see Quoting, pages 245–254).

1. Describe what went through your mind as you were reading.
2. Explore what you like about the reading or what interests you most.
3. Explore what you don't like about the reading or what you find confusing.
4. Explore what you agree or disagree with in the reading.
5. Relate your own experiences or ideas to the reading.
6. Raise questions if you don't understand all or part of the reading.
7. Select a short passage that struck you for some reason, copy the passage, and explain why you chose it.
8. Respond to one or more of the questions in the Discuss After You Read section that follows a reading in this book.

Student readers at work: *Writing a journal entry on a reading*

The following students' journal entries, written in response to Sydney J. Harris's "What True Education Should Do," are reprinted as they were written, with misspellings, errors, and cross-outs, so that you can see that a journal entry does not need to be a polished work.

Journal Entry: Student 1

"There are pearls in each of us, if only we knew how to cultivate them with ardor and persistence."

Even if I hadn't liked the rest of the reading, this concluding phrase would have changed all my feelings. It is so easy to say it but yet so difficult to understand it or even believe it. Most people judge you ~~from the knowledge that~~ without ever trying to reveal what or who you realy are, What you have inside and what you have to offer. That also occurs ~~here specificaly~~ in school. Bad grades mean you are nothing. Not able to understand math? Then you are not someone to ~~to~~ work with. They (most of the times) do not try to see you as a person. ~~but~~ You are a machine to them. A ~~mach~~ computer where they can typewrite their own thoughts and feelings.

Journal Entry: Student 2

In this peace of reading there are things that have made me think about different things and aspects about education. I would like to start talking about the comparisson that we find in the beginning between the human brain, or ability of keeping information to a sausage. If a teacher or instructor thinks that our brain is this "sausage", what's going to happen is what this college student said in the middle of the reading — "I spend so much time studying that I don't have a chance to learn anything" — . This is what would happen to a student if he had a "sausage maker" as a teacher.

In the other hand we can find what Socrates says about eliciting knowledge from a person. Socrates tried to demonstrate that in that dialogue called "Meno". He made a boy with no schooling demonstrate something on geometry. From my point of view we cannot make ourselves Socrates believers because we don't know everything that has happened or it is to come and somebody has to open our "oyster", as the last comparisson made in our reading about knowledge.

What I would say is that we are not either an oyster or a sausage what we need is somebody to teach us and give us information in a way that we have fun receiving this information and we have this energy to keep learning.

Your turn: *Writing a journal entry on "What True Education Should Do"*

Using the *Guidelines for Writing a Journal Entry on a Reading* on page 11, respond to "What True Education Should Do."

Activity: *Applying critical reading strategies*

Select whichever of the reading strategies in this chapter you find most productive and apply them to Reading 1, "Barriers" by Rolando Niella (pages 13–15), or to Reading 2, "Waiting in Line at the Drugstore" by James Thomas Jackson (pages 16–18).

Reading 1

◼ Write Before You Read

Before reading "Barriers" by Rolando Niella, write for several minutes about barriers that inhibit, or block, your own learning.

Barriers

Rolando Niella

Rolando Niella was born and raised in Paraguay. He studied English for several years in Paraguay, for one year as an exchange student in junior high school in the United States, and for a summer just prior to entering college in Massachusetts. Niella now works in the fashion and textile industry and is writing a novel. He wrote this essay to fulfill an essay assignment for a composition course in his first year of college.

A few months ago I decided that I wanted to learn how to play tennis. Today, after much practice and a few classes, I know how to hold the racket and basically how to hit the ball; however, I still can't say that I actually play tennis. It is taking me so long to learn, and it is so difficult! It didn't look that hard when I saw my friends playing it so gracefully. Even so, I am still giving it a try. But to play a sport that I cannot master is becoming a pain. I feel so frustrated sometimes, that I consider forgetting all about tennis. It is hurting my pride.

Today, tennis is not the main source of my frustrations. I have another problem that generates feelings and puts me in moods very similar to those that I experience when I play it. This is daily conversation with people. It may sound bizarre, but it is not. I am a foreign student, and in playing tennis as in speaking English, I am still in the learning process. That is why the best way I can explain these complex feelings created by my communication problem is by associating them with tennis.

One of the most common situations I find myself in, when I play tennis, is that people, either conscious or unconscious of my level, will start the game with a strong service[1] or will answer my weak service with a fast ball which I cannot possibly hit back. Comparable examples are the ladies at the cafeteria telling me about the menu, while speaking at an incredible speed. This is often worsened by their personal style, the Somerville accent. I also encounter the same problem when my roommate speaks with his heavy Massachusetts accent. He is from Peabody, or "PEEb'dy."

Experiences like these are likely to happen when I speak to someone for the first time. Usually, however, once they realize my level, most of them will not

---

[1] *service* or *serve*: the act of putting the ball into play

"serve for the ace."[2] But with those who still do, it is a different story. If, after asking them to repeat their serves many times, and, after repeatedly failing to return their balls, I don't give up, they will find an excuse to leave the court immediately, or they will simply tell me to "forget it." In daily conversation, even my friends will use this phrase when they give up trying to make their point, or to understand my point. I do not blame them sometimes, but this little phrase is one of the most frustrating ones I have heard. It can take away my desire to talk, and discourage me in my efforts to get my ideas across – making me leave the court frustrated and angry. I then isolate myself or look for a friend with whom I can speak a language I don't have to concentrate on, and at which I am very good: Spanish. In like manner, when I am tired of tennis and still want to do some sport, I jog alone or play soccer.

Once a person is aware of my level and tries to go at my pace, I still confront some problems. First, in tennis, if you are a fairly experienced player, you should be familiar with some basic game plans. The way your opponent is sending the balls may lead you to realize which plan he is using to score upon you. In the same way, if in a language you have experience with the cultural patterns of expressing feelings and moods, and you distinguish the different connotations of words, you may understand the point he is trying to make to you. In tennis, I am not very good at predicting what play my opponent is trying to use; and when I do, it is usually too late. Likewise, in conversation, I usually don't react to a joke until it is too late. I also have a hard time realizing how annoyed my roommate gets, because he selects words to make his point; but the connotations of some of them sometimes don't reach me because of my inexperience. I don't know exactly which is worse to him, "mad," "angry," "disturbed," or "pissed off."

Second, in tennis, by observing your opponent's movements, you improve your chances to return the ball and prolong the volley.[3] The swing of his racket, the way he hits the balls, and his position in relation with the net, are good hints for predicting the direction and the power of the ball. I still can't tell precisely how fast the ball is coming, or if I have to return it with a forehand[4] or a backhand shot[5] just by watching my opponent. It is not only that I am unfamiliar with these movements, but I also am too busy analyzing the movements I have done, and the ones I am about to do. At the same time, my opponent can tell very little about my next shot by observing me, because my style is very awkward. When talking to people I also feel the necessity to be familiar with the non-verbal language of Americans. Yesterday, for example, the guy across the hall asked me to turn down my stereo. By the time I had understood what he had said, he was gone. I wasn't sure what his talking from the doorway and the tone of his voice meant. Everything happened so fast, just like a crosscourt backhand. I didn't feel happy with my vague answer, and I am sure he didn't either.

[2] *ace*: a serve the opponent fails to return
[3] *volley*: hitting of the tennis ball before it touches the ground
[4] *forehand shot*: a stroke of the racket made with the palm of the hand moving forward
[5] *backhand shot*: a stroke of the racket made with the back of the hand moving forward

Playing tennis, for me, in general is an uncomfortable situation. I waste too much energy and attention on every single movement of my hand, my racket, my feet, etc., and besides I also have to watch the player at the other side of the net; then I don't enjoy the game. In everyday conversation, it is also very annoying to pay so much attention to things that should be automatic and to give as much thought to almost every word I and the other person are using.

Exposed to so many unfamiliar rules and ways, I easily lose the train of thought in my conversation. I feel that I am not being natural and start questioning the way I communicate and relate with people. I worry so much about the "how to" that conversation is not always as relaxing as it should be. This is a problem from which the only way to escape is by fully experiencing it. As in any sport, if you want to enjoy it, you have to practice until you master it.

So, if you happen to be talking to a foreigner, be aware of this problem. If you are a foreign student yourself, do not feel depressed. I believe that in the long run there will be a reward, a better understanding of ourselves and the vital phenomenon of communication.

■ Write After You Read

1 Write a journal entry in response to "Barriers" using the guidelines on page 11.

2 Summarize in one or two sentences the insight you believe Niella has gained through his experience.

■ Discuss After You Read

1 Does anything in the reading remind you of your own experiences with learning? If so, what is similar?

2 How do the learning experiences Niella describes differ from your own learning experiences? Why do these differences exist?

3 Of the many comparisons Niella makes between learning to play tennis and learning to use a second language, which comparison most effectively explains what it means to be a second language speaker? Which comparison least effectively explains what it means to be a second language speaker? Explain your answers.

4 Which details in the text stand out in your mind, enabling you to see, hear, or feel what happened? How do these details affect your enjoyment and understanding of the experiences described?

Reading 2

■ Write Before You Read

Before reading "Waiting in Line at the Drugstore" by James Thomas Jackson, write for several minutes about a time when you had to wait in line. Why did you have to wait, and how did you react?

Waiting in Line at the Drugstore

James Thomas Jackson

James Thomas Jackson (1925–1985) was born in Texas and grew up at a time when laws restricted where and how African Americans could live, eat, go to school, and travel in the United States. After Jackson became a member of a writers' workshop, he published his work in a variety of newspapers and journals. His writing chronicles his childhood, his years in the U.S. Army in Europe, and his later years, when he practiced his craft. "Waiting in Line at the Drugstore" was originally published in the Los Angeles Times *newspaper.*

I am black. I am a writer and I want to place full credit where it belongs for the direction my life has taken: on a photography studio and a drugstore on Main Street in Houston, Texas.

When I was thirteen, I dropped out of school, bought a bike for $13 (secondhand and innately durable) and went to work as a messenger for the Owl Foto Studio. Each day we processed film which I picked up as raw rolls on my three routes. That was great: a bike and job are supreme joys to a thirteen-year-old.

The Owl Studio, on a nondescript street named Brazos (very Texan), was located in a white stucco building that blended unobtrusively into the rest of the neighborhood, which was mostly residential. The area was predominantly white, and though it did not smack of affluence, it was not altogether poverty stricken either. Six blocks away was the drugstore, where I had to go first thing each morning for coffee, cakes, doughnuts, jelly rolls, milk, cigarettes, whatever – anything the folks at the Owl wanted. My trip amounted to picking up "breakfast" for a crew of six: three printer-developers, one wash man, the roll-film man and the foreman. The drugstore was the biggest challenge of my young life. Being thirteen is doubtless bad enough for white male youths, but for blacks – me in particular – it was pure dee hell. Going to this drugstore each morning was part of my job; it was required of me. With my dropping out of school and all, my parents would have whipped my behind till it roped like okra if I had tried to supply them with reasons for not wanting to go. So, I gritted my teeth and, buoyed by the power of my Western Flyer, rode on down there.

The place had your typical drugstore look: sundries, greeting cards, cosmetics, women's "things," pharmaceuticals – but most instantly fetching was the large, U-shaped lunch counter. White-uniformed waitresses dispensed eats and sweet drinks of varying kinds: from cakes, donuts and pies to cups of the freshest smelling, strongest tasting coffee one could ask for. In the morning, there were countless servings of ham, bacon, sausages and eggs and mounds of hash-brown potatoes. At lunch there was a "Blue Plate Special" – three vegetables and a meat dish. Oh, they were together, no doubt about that.

My beef was that I was forbidden to sit at that counter. If any black wanted service whether for himself or, like me, for those he worked for – he simply had to stand and wait until all the white folks were served. Those blacks who went contrary to this were worked over something fierce, often by those mild-mannered Milquetoasts who looked as if they wouldn't hurt a fly. A fly, no; but an uppity nigger, in a minute.

I had once witnessed the beating of a black brother at the drugstore and heard tales of other beatings elsewhere. Clean and sanitary as the drugstore was, I preferred the ghetto (though we didn't call it that then). There, at least, we had the freedom to roam all over our stretch of black territory and could shuck our feelings of enforced inferiority as soon as we were on common ground.

Yet I went to the drugstore each morning with my order of coffee, cakes and whatever, written out and clutched firmly in my hand. And each time I was confronted with rows of white folks, seated at the counter and clamoring for attention. I did what I was expected to do: I waited, all the while hating it.

Especially that kind of waiting. As those white faces stared at my black face, I stood conspicuously in a spot near the counter, wanting not to be there, to be somewhere else.

My film pickups were not like this at all. I simply went in a store, picked up a small sack of roll film and split. After all, we provided twenty-four-hour service, and every son-of-a-buck and his brother wanted to see how his pictures came out. It was only the drugstore bit that bugged me.

While waiting near the counter one morning, I realized that I was leaning on a bookcase. I had seen it before but had ignored it because I was in a hurry to get served and get the hell out of there. The case was about four feet high and held perhaps six rows of hardcover books. The sign said "Lending Library." I began looking idly at the books, studying the titles and names of authors, so many unfamiliar to me. But the jackets were impressive, alluring, eye-catching.

One book caught my fancy: *Out of the Night*, the bestseller by Jan Valtin. I opened it, glanced at the fly pages and came across a poem by William Ernest Henley:

Out of the night that covers me
Black as the pit from pole to pole
I thank whatever gods may be
For my unconquerable soul.

Then I turned to the beginning of Valtin's narrative, read that first page, and then the second. Eleven pages later, going on twelve, hoping to get to thirteen, I heard the white waitress call my name. My order was ready. I folded a corner of the page and tried to hide the book so no one would take it before I could get back the next day.

I picked up the food and wheeled back to the studio – slowly. My mind was a fog – I had never begun a real book before. All the way back, I felt different from before. Something was happening to me, and I didn't quite know what to make of it. Somehow I didn't feel the "badness" that I usually felt when I returned from the drugstore.

The next day, my usual waiting was not the same. I went from page thirteen to page twenty-seven . . . twenty-eight, pinned a corner down, returned to the studio, delivered my routes, went home, thought and wondered. God, I wondered, when would tomorrow come? The promise of tomorrow, of course, was the difference.

Many mornings later I finished reading Valtin's book. But there was another that looked interesting: *The Grapes of Wrath* by John Steinbeck. (We weren't as poor, I discovered, as those people.) *Then Tobacco Road* by Erskine Caldwell.

A year passed, and I discovered a black library branch at Booker T. Washington High. An elderly friend of mine in the ghetto who had noticed the change in me made a list of things to ask for: Countee Cullen's poem "Heritage," Charles W. Chestnutt's "The Wife of His Youth," Walter White's "Fire in the Flint"; also Frederick Douglass, Paul Laurence Dunbar, Jean Toomer – how was I to read them all?[1]

Find a way, my friend said.

All the while I kept going to the drugstore each morning. I must have read every worthwhile book on that "Lending Library" shelf. But during this period, something strange happened: my waiting time got shorter and shorter each morning. I could hardly get five pages read before my order was handed to me with – of all things – a sense of graciousness from the waitresses. I didn't understand it.

Later on I went off to World War II. My mind and attitudes were primed for the books yet to come and for the words that were to come out of me. I was eighteen then and a drop-out, but I was deep into the wonderful world of literature and life. I found myself, and my niche, in the word. Who would have thought that a drugstore could provide such a vista for anyone? And my waits at the counter? I keep wondering: which way would I have gone had I not waited?

Good question.

◼ Write After You Read

1 Write a journal entry on "Waiting in Line at the Drugstore" using the guidelines on page 11.

2 Summarize in one or two sentences the insight you believe Jackson has gained through his experience.

[1] The authors Jackson refers to in this paragraph were all African American.

■ Discuss After You Read

1 How is Jackson's experience with waiting in line similar to your own experiences with waiting in line?

2 How does Jackson's experience with waiting in line differ from your own experiences with waiting in line? Why do these differences exist?

3 Why do the words or ideas in William Ernest Henley's poem have such an effect on Jackson?

4 Why does Jackson think his waiting time became shorter? Why do you think Jackson's waiting time became shorter?

5 Turn to the footnote of the reading to learn about the authors who appear on the reading list suggested to Jackson by his elderly friend. What do these authors have in common? Why do you think this list is significant for Jackson?

6 Which details in the text stand out in your mind, enabling you to see, hear, or feel what happened? How do these details affect your enjoyment and understanding of the experiences described?

PART TWO
READINGS AND WRITING ASSIGNMENTS

Chapter 2

Writing from Experience

Writing an essay drawn from your own experience involves conveying an insight or expressing a personal viewpoint that grows out of that experience. One of the challenges of composing such an essay is to make your thoughts and experiences clear to others.

Chapter 2 includes five reading selections that demonstrate ways writers can successfully describe experiences and transmit ideas. These reading selections focus on the experience of living in multiple worlds. The experiences in the readings vary widely, for the writers were raised under remarkably different circumstances and in different eras. But their stories share common insights about what it means to acquire new ways of learning, communicating, and writing across languages and cultures.

The guidelines that follow the readings are designed to help you compose your own essay drawn from experience.

Reading 1

■ **Write Before You Read**

Before reading "The School Days of an Indian Girl" by Zitkala-Ša, look carefully at the before-and-after-photographs of three girls on pages 26 and 27, and then write for several minutes about the similarities and differences between the pictures.

The School Days of an Indian Girl
Zitkala-Ša

Zitkala-Ša (1876–1938), also known as Gertrude Simmons Bonnin, was born on an Indian reservation in what is now South Dakota. At age eight, pressured by missionaries, she went to study at a Quaker missionary school in Indiana. Zitkala-Ša was later educated at Earlham College and the New England Conservatory of Music. One of the early Native American writers who recorded the traditions of their people, Zitkala-Ša published most of her work in two books: Old Indian Legends *(1901) and* American Indian Stories *(1921). In addition to being a writer, she was a teacher, violinist, and activist for Native American rights. "The School Days of an Indian Girl," a fictionalized version of Zitkala-Ša's experience, was first published in the* Atlantic Monthly *magazine in 1900. Reprinted here are the first three sections.*

The Land of Red Apples

There were eight in our party of bronzed children who were going East with the missionaries.[1] Among us were three young braves,[2] two tall girls, and we three little ones, Judéwin, Thowin, and I.

We had been very impatient to start on our journey to the Red Apple Country, which, we were told, lay a little beyond the great circular horizon of the Western prairie. Under a sky of rosy apples we dreamt of roaming as freely and happily as we had chased the cloud shadows on the Dakota plains. We had anticipated much pleasure from a ride on the iron horse,[3] but the throngs of staring palefaces[4] disturbed and troubled us.

---

[1] In the nineteenth century, English-only mission boarding schools, such as the one described in this reading selection, educated Native American children for the purpose of replacing Native American languages with English and converting the children to Christianity, even though Native American parents wanted to preserve their own language and culture.
[2] *braves*: males who were old enough to have been initiated into manhood
[3] *iron horse*: train
[4] *palefaces*: white people

On the train, fair women, with tottering babies on each arm, stopped their haste and scrutinized the children of absent mothers. Large men, with heavy bundles in their hands, halted near by, and riveted their glassy blue eyes upon us.

I sank deep into the corner of my seat, for I resented being watched. Directly in front of me, children who were no larger than I hung themselves upon the backs of their seats, with their bold white faces toward me. Sometimes they took their forefingers out of their mouths and pointed at my moccasined feet. Their mothers, instead of reproving such rude curiosity, looked closely at me, and attracted their children's further notice to my blanket. This embarrassed me, and kept me constantly on the verge of tears.

I sat perfectly still, with my eyes downcast, daring only now and then to shoot long glances around me. Chancing to turn to the window at my side, I was quite breathless upon seeing one familiar object. It was the telegraph pole which strode by at short paces. Very near my mother's dwelling, along the edge of a road thickly bordered with wild sunflowers, some poles like these had been planted by white men. Often I had stopped, on my way down the road, to hold my ear against the pole, and, hearing its low moaning, I used to wonder what the paleface had done to hurt it. Now I sat watching for each pole that glided by to be the last one.

In this way I had forgotten my uncomfortable surroundings, when I heard one of my comrades call out my name. I saw the missionary standing very near, tossing candies and gums into our midst. This amused us all, and we tried to see who could catch the most of the sweet-meats. The missionary's generous distribution of candies was impressed upon my memory by a disastrous result which followed. I had caught more than my share of candies and gums, and soon after our arrival at the school I had a chance to disgrace myself, which, I am ashamed to say, I did.

Though we rode several days inside of the iron horse, I do not recall a single thing about our luncheons.

It was night when we reached the school grounds. The lights from the windows of the large buildings fell upon some of the icicled trees that stood beneath them. We were led toward an open door, where the brightness of the lights within flooded out over the heads of the excited palefaces who blocked the way. My body trembled more from fear than from the snow I trod upon.

Entering the house, I stood close against the wall. The strong glaring light in the large whitewashed room dazzled my eyes. The noisy hurrying of hard shoes upon a bare wooden floor increased the whirring in my ears. My only safety seemed to be in keeping next to the wall. As I was wondering in which direction to escape from all this confusion, two warm hands grasped me firmly, and in the same moment I was tossed high in midair. A rosy-cheeked paleface woman caught me in her arms. I was both frightened and insulted by such trifling. I stared into her eyes, wishing her to let me stand on my own feet, but she jumped me up and down with increasing enthusiasm. My mother had never made a plaything of her wee daughter. Remembering this I began to cry aloud.

They misunderstood the cause of my tears, and placed me at a white table loaded with food. There our party were united again. As I did not hush my crying, one of the older ones whispered to me, "Wait until you are alone in the night."

It was very little I could swallow besides my sobs, that evening.

"Oh, I want my mother and my brother Dawée! I want to go to my aunt!" I pleaded; but the ears of the palefaces could not hear me.

From the table we were taken along an upward incline of wooden boxes, which I learned afterward to call a stairway. At the top was a quiet hall, dimly lighted. Many narrow beds were in one straight line down the entire length of the wall. In them lay sleeping brown faces, which peeped just out of the coverings. I was tucked into bed with one of the tall girls, because she talked to me in my mother tongue[5] and seemed to soothe me.

I had arrived in the wonderful land of rosy skies, but I was not happy, as I had thought I should be. My long travel and the bewildering sights had exhausted me. I fell asleep, heaving deep, tired sobs. My tears were left to dry themselves in streaks, because neither my aunt nor my mother was near to wipe them away.

The Cutting of My Long Hair

The first day in the land of apples was a bitter-cold one; for the snow still covered the ground, and the trees were bare. A large bell rang for breakfast, its loud metallic voice crashing through the belfry overhead and into our sensitive ears. The annoying clatter of shoes on bare floors gave us no peace. The constant clash of harsh noises, with an undercurrent of many voices murmuring an unknown tongue, made a bedlam within which I was securely tied. And though my spirit tore itself in struggling for its lost freedom, all was useless.

A paleface woman, with white hair, came up after us. We were placed in a line of girls who were marching into the dining room. These were Indian girls, in stiff shoes and closely clinging dresses. The small girls wore sleeved aprons and shingled hair. As I walked noiselessly in my soft moccasins, I felt like sinking to the floor, for my blanket had been stripped from my shoulders. I looked hard at the Indian girls, who seemed not to care that they were even more immodestly

[5] *mother tongue*: the narrator's first language, Dakota

dressed than I, in their tightly fitting clothes. While we marched in, the boys entered at an opposite door. I watched for the three young braves who came in our party. I spied them in the rear ranks, looking as uncomfortable as I felt.

A small bell was tapped, and each of the pupils drew a chair from under the table. Supposing this act meant they were to be seated, I pulled out mine and at once slipped into it from one side. But when I turned my head, I saw that I was the only one seated, and all the rest at our table remained standing. Just as I began to rise, looking shyly around to see how chairs were to be used, a second bell was sounded. All were seated at last, and I had to crawl back into my chair again. I heard a man's voice at one end of the hall, and I looked around to see him. But all the others hung their heads over their plates. As I glanced at the long chain of tables, I caught the eyes of a paleface woman upon me. Immediately I dropped my eyes, wondering why I was so keenly watched by the strange woman. The man ceased his mutterings, and then a third bell was tapped. Every one picked up his knife and fork and began eating. I began crying instead, for by this time I was afraid to venture anything more.

But this eating by formula was not the hardest trial in that first day. Late in the morning, my friend Judéwin gave me a terrible warning. Judéwin knew a few words of English, and she had overheard the paleface woman talk about cutting our long, heavy hair. Our mothers had taught us that only unskilled warriors who were captured had their hair shingled by the enemy. Among our people, short hair was worn by mourners, and shingled hair by cowards!

We discussed our fate some moments, and when Judéwin said, "We have to submit, because they are strong," I rebelled.

"No, I will not submit! I will struggle first!" I answered.

I watched my chance, and when no one noticed I disappeared. I crept up the stairs as quietly as I could in my squeaking shoes – my moccasins had been exchanged for shoes. Along the hall I passed, without knowing whither I was going. Turning aside to an open door, I found a large room with three white beds in it. The windows were covered with dark green curtains, which made the room very dim. Thankful that no one was there, I directed my steps toward the corner farthest from the door. On my hands and knees I crawled under the bed, and cuddled myself in the dark corner.

From my hiding place I peered out, shuddering with fear whenever I heard footsteps near by. Though in the hall loud voices were calling my name, and I knew that even Judéwin was searching for me, I did not open my mouth to answer. Then the steps were quickened and the voices became excited. The sounds came nearer and nearer. Women and girls entered the room. I held my breath, and watched them open closet doors and peep behind large trunks. Some one threw up the curtains, and the room was filled with sudden light. What caused them to stoop and look under the bed I do not know. I remember being dragged out, though I resisted by kicking and scratching wildly. In spite of myself, I was carried downstairs and tied fast in a chair.

I cried aloud, shaking my head all the while until I felt the cold blades of the scissors against my neck, and heard them gnaw off one of my thick braids. Then I lost my spirit. Since the day I was taken from my mother I had suffered extreme indignities. People had stared at me. I had been tossed about in the air like a wooden puppet. And now my long hair was shingled like a coward's! In my anguish I moaned for my mother, but no one came to comfort me. Not a soul reasoned quietly with me, as my own mother used to do; for now I was only one of many little animals driven by a herder.

The Snow Episode

A short time after our arrival we three Dakotas were playing in the snowdrifts. We were all still deaf to the English language, excepting Judéwin, who always heard such puzzling things. One morning we learned through her ears that we were forbidden to fall lengthwise in the snow, as we had been doing, to see our own impressions. However, before many hours we had forgotten the order, and were having great sport in the snow, when a shrill voice called us. Looking up, we saw an imperative hand beckoning us into the house. We shook the snow off ourselves, and started toward the woman as slowly as we dared.

Judéwin said: "Now the paleface is angry with us. She is going to punish us for falling into the snow. If she looks straight into your eyes and talks loudly, you must wait until she stops. Then, after a tiny pause, say, 'No.'" The rest of the way we practiced upon the little word "no."

As it happened, Thowin was summoned to judgment first. The door shut behind her with a click.

Judéwin and I stood silently listening at the keyhole. The paleface woman talked in very severe tones. Her words fell from her lips like crackling embers, and her inflection ran up like the small end of a switch. I understood her voice better than the things she was saying. I was certain we had made her very impatient with us. Judéwin heard enough of the words to realize all too late that she had taught us the wrong reply.

"Oh, poor Thowin!" she gasped, as she put both hands over her ears.

Just then I heard Thowin's tremulous answer, "No."

With an angry exclamation, the woman gave her a hard spanking. Then she stopped to say something. Judéwin said it was this: "Are you going to obey my word the next time?"

Thowin answered again with the only word at her command, "No."

This time the woman meant her blows to smart, for the poor frightened girl shrieked at the top of her voice. In the midst of the whipping the blows ceased abruptly, and the woman asked another question: "Are you going to fall in the snow again?"

Thowin gave her bad password another trial. We heard her say feebly, "No! No!"

With this the woman hid away her half-worn slipper, and led the child out, stroking her black shorn head. Perhaps it occurred to her that brute force is not the solution for such a problem. She did nothing to Judéwin nor to me. She only returned to us our unhappy comrade, and left us alone in the room.

During the first two or three seasons misunderstandings as ridiculous as this one of the snow episode frequently took place, bringing unjustifiable frights and punishments into our little lives.

Within a year I was able to express myself somewhat in broken English. As soon as I comprehended a part of what was said and done, a mischievous spirit of revenge possessed me. One day I was called in from my play for some misconduct. I had disregarded a rule which seemed to me very needlessly binding. I was sent into the kitchen to mash the turnips for dinner. It was noon, and steaming dishes were hastily carried into the dining room. I hated turnips, and their odor which came from the brown jar was offensive to me. With fire in my heart, I took the wooden tool that the paleface woman held out to me. I stood upon a step, and, grasping the handle with both hands, I bent in hot rage over the turnips. I worked my vengeance upon them. All were so busily occupied that no one noticed me. I saw that the turnips were in a pulp, and that further beating could not improve them; but the order was, "Mash these turnips," and mash them I would! I renewed my energy; and as I sent the masher into the bottom of the jar, I felt a satisfying sensation that the weight of my body had gone into it.

Just here a paleface woman came up to my table. As she looked into the jar she shoved my hands roughly aside. I stood fearless and angry. She placed her red hands upon the rim of the jar. Then she gave one lift and a stride away from the table. But lo! the pulpy contents fell through the crumbled bottom to the floor! She spared me no scolding phrases that I had earned. I did not heed them. I felt triumphant in my revenge, though deep within me I was a wee bit sorry to have broken the jar.

As I sat eating my dinner, and saw that no turnips were served, I whooped in my heart for having once asserted the rebellion within me.

■ Write After You Read

1 Write a journal entry in response to "The School Days of an Indian Girl" using the guidelines on page 11.

2 Summarize in one or two sentences what you believe Zitkala-Ša's narrator has gained through her experience.

■ Discuss After You Read

1   Does anything in the reading remind you of your own early experiences in school? If so, what is similar?

2   How do the early school experiences Zitkala-Ša describes differ from your own early school experiences? Why do these differences exist?

3   Contrast the narrator's present life in school with her past life at home. What are the differences in her relationships with her elders, in her dress style, and in her use of language? What is the significance of these differences?

4   Which details in the text stand out in your mind, enabling you to see, hear, or feel what happened? How do these details affect your enjoyment and understanding of the experiences described?

5   Zitkala-Ša divides her piece into three sections: "The Land of Red Apples," "The Cutting of My Long Hair," and "The Snow Episode." What do you perceive to be the purpose of each section? How do the sections relate to one another?

6   What are the similarities and differences between the learning experiences Zitkala-Ša describes and the learning experiences Niella describes in "Barriers" (pages 13–15)?

Reading 2

■ Write Before You Read

Before reading "My English" by Julia Alvarez, write for several minutes about *your* English.

My English

Julia Alvarez

Julia Alvarez was born in the United States, in New York City, and moved to the Dominican Republic, her parents' homeland, when she was three months old. The family lived there for 10 years but returned to New York when Alvarez's father's life was threatened as a result of his involvement in the underground movement that sought to overthrow the country's dictator. An award-winning author, Alvarez's works include How the Garcia Girls Lost Their Accents *(1991),* In the Time of the Butterflies *(1994),* The Woman I Kept to Myself *(2004), and* Saving the World *(2006). "My English" was first published in the literary journal* Brújula/Compass.

Mami and Papi used to speak it when they had a secret they wanted to keep from us children. We lived then in the Dominican Republic, and the family as a whole spoke only Spanish at home, until my sisters and I started attending the Carol

Morgan School,[1] and we became a bilingual family. Spanish had its many tongues as well. There was the castellano of Padre Joaquin from Spain, whose lisp we all loved to imitate. Then the educated español my parents' families spoke, aunts and uncles who were always correcting us children, for we spent most of the day with the maids and so had picked up their "bad Spanish." Campesinas, they spoke a lilting animated campuno, ss swallowed, endings chopped off, funny turns of phrases. This campuno was my true mother tongue, not the Spanish of Calderón de la Barca or Cervantes or even Neruda,[2] but of Chucha and Iluminada and Gladys and Ursulina from Juncalito and Licey and Boca de Yuma and San Juan de la Maguana. Those women yakked as they cooked, they storytold, they gossiped, they sang – boleros, merengues, canciones, salves. Theirs were the voices that belonged to the rain and the wind and the teeny, teeny stars even a small child could blot out with her thumb.

Besides all these versions of Spanish, every once in a while another strange tongue emerged from my papi's mouth or my mami's lips. What I first recognized was not a language, but a tone of voice, serious, urgent something important and top secret being said, some uncle in trouble, someone divorcing, someone dead. *Say it in English so the children won't understand.* I would listen, straining to understand, thinking that this was not a different language but just another and harder version of Spanish. *Say it in English so the children won't understand.* From the beginning, English was the sound of worry and secrets, the sound of being left out.

I could make no sense of this "harder Spanish," and so I tried by other means to find out what was going on. I knew my mother's face by heart. When the little lines on the corners of her eyes crinkled, she was amused. When her nostrils flared and she bit her lips, she was trying hard not to laugh. She held her head down, eyes glancing up when she thought I was lying. Whenever, she spoke that gibberish English, I translated the general content by watching the Spanish expressions on her face.

Soon, I began to learn more English, at the Carol Morgan School. That is, when I had stopped gawking. The teacher and some of the American children had the strangest coloration: light hair, light eyes, light skin, as if Ursulina had soaked them in bleach too long, to' deteñío. I did have some blond cousins, but they had deeply tanned skin, and as they grew older, their hair darkened, so their earlier paleness seemed a phase of their acquiring normal color. Just as strange was the little girl in my reader who had a *cat* and a *dog*, that looked just like un gatito y un perrito. Her mami was *Mother* and her papi *Father*. Why have a whole new language for school and for books with a teacher who could speak it teaching you double the amount of words you really needed?

[1] *The Carol Morgan School:* a private school in the Dominican Republic that provides instruction, in English, from prekindergarten through grade 12 for students of all nationalities, and offers an English as a Second Language program at the elementary and middle-school levels

[2] *(Pedro) Calderón de la Barca* (1600–1681) and *(Miguel de) Cervantes* (1547–1616) are both writers from Spain, while *(Pablo) Neruda* (1904–1973) is a writer from Chile.

Butter, butter, butter, butter. All day, one English word that had particularly struck me would go round and round in my mouth and weave through all the Spanish in my head until by the end of the day, the word did sound like just another Spanish word. And so I would say, "Mami, please pass la mantequilla." She would scowl and say in English, "I'm sorry, I don't understand. But would you be needing some butter on your bread?"

Why my parents didn't first educate us in our native language by enrolling us in a Dominican school, I don't know. Part of it was that Mami's family had a tradition of sending the boys to the States to boarding school and college, and she had been one of the first girls to be allowed to join her brothers. At Abbot Academy, whose school song was our lullaby as babies ("Although Columbus and Cabot never heard of Abbot, it's quite the place for you and me"), she had become quite Americanized. It was very important, she kept saying, that we learn our English. She always used the possessive pronoun: *your* English, an inheritance we had come into and must wisely use. Unfortunately, my English became all mixed up with our Spanish.

Mix-up, or what's now called Spanglish, was the language we spoke for several years. There wasn't a sentence that wasn't colonized by an English word. At school, a Spanish word would suddenly slide into my English like someone butting into line. Teacher, whose face I was learning to read as minutely as my mother's, would scowl but no smile played on her lips. Her pale skin made her strange countenance hard to read, so that I often misjudged how much I could get away with. Whenever I made a mistake, Teacher would shake her head slowly, "In English, YU – LEE – AH, there's no such word as *columpio*. Do you mean a *swing*?"

I would bow my head, humiliated by the smiles and snickers of the American children around me. I grew insecure about Spanish. My native tongue was not quite as good as English, as if words like *columpio* were illegal immigrants trying to cross a border into another language. But Teacher's discerning grammar-and-vocabulary-patrol ears could tell and send them back.

Soon, I was talking up an English storm. "Did you eat English parrot?" my grandfather asked one Sunday. I had just enlisted yet one more patient servant to listen to my rendition of "Peter Piper picked a peck of pickled peppers" at breakneck pace. "Huh?" I asked impolitely in English, putting him in his place. *Cat got your tongue? No big deal! So there! Take that! Holy Toledo!* (Our teacher's favorite "curse word.") *Go jump in the lake! Really dumb. Golly. Gosh.* Slang, clichés, sayings, hotshot language that our teacher called, ponderously, idiomatic expressions. Riddles, jokes, puns, conundrums. *What is yellow and goes click-click? Why did the chicken cross the road? See you later, alligator.* How wonderful to call someone an alligator and not be scolded for being disrespectful. In fact, they were supposed to say back, *In a while, crocodile.*

There was also a neat little trick I wanted to try on an English-speaking adult at home. I had learned it from Elizabeth my smart-alecky friend in fourth grade, whom I alternately worshiped and resented. I'd ask her a question that required an explanation, and she'd answer, "Because . . ." "Elizabeth, how come you didn't go to Isabel's birthday party?" "Because . . ." "Why didn't you put your name in your reader?" "Because . . ." I thought that such a cool way to get around having to come up with answers. So, I practiced saying it under my breath, planning for the day I could use it on an unsuspecting English-speaking adult.

One Sunday at our extended family dinner, my grandfather sat down at the children's table to chat with us. He was famous, in fact, for the way he could carry on adult conversations with his grandchildren. He often spoke to us in English so that we could practice speaking it outside the classroom. He was a Cornell man, a United Nations representative from our country. He gave speeches in English. Perfect English, my mother's phrase. That Sunday he asked me a question. I can't even remember what it was because I wasn't really listening but lying in wait for my chance. "Because . . . ," I answered him. Papito waited a second for the rest of my sentence and then gave me a thumbnail grammar lesson, *"Because* has to be followed by a clause."
"Why's that?" I asked, nonplussed.
"Because," he winked. "Just because."

A beginning wordsmith, I had so much left to learn; sometimes it was disheartening. Once Tio Gus, the family intellectual, put a speck of salt on my grandparents' big dining table during Sunday dinner. He said, "Imagine this whole table is the human brain. Then this teensy grain is all we ever use of our intelligence!" He enumerated geniuses who had perhaps used two grains, maybe three: Einstein, Michelangelo, da Vinci, Beethoven. We children believed him. It was the kind of impossible fact we thrived on, proving as it did that the world out there was not drastically different from the one we were making up in our heads.
    Later, at home, Mami said that you had to take what her younger brother said "with a grain of salt." I thought she was still referring to Tio Gus's demonstration, and I tried to puzzle out what she was saying. Finally, I asked what she meant. "Taking what someone says with a grain of salt is an idiomatic expression in English," she explained. It was pure voodoo is what it was – what later I learned poetry could also do: a grain of salt could symbolize both the human brain and a condiment for human nonsense. And it could be itself, too: a grain of salt to flavor a bland plate of American food.

When we arrived in New York, I was shocked. A country where everyone spoke English! These people must be smarter, I thought. Maids, waiters, taxi drivers, doormen, bums on the street, all spoke this difficult language. It took some time before I understood that Americans were not necessarily a smarter, superior race. It was as natural for them to learn their mother tongue as it was for a little Dominican baby to learn Spanish. It came with "mother's milk," my mother explained, and for a while I thought a mother tongue was a mother tongue because you got it from your mother's breast, along with proteins and vitamins.

Soon it wasn't so strange that everyone was speaking in English instead of Spanish. I learned not to hear it as English, but as sense. I no longer strained to understand, I understood. I relaxed in this second language. Only when someone with a heavy southern or British accent spoke in a movie, or at church when the priest droned his sermon – only then did I experience that little catch of anxiety. I worried that I would not be able to understand, that I wouldn't be able to "keep up" with the voice speaking in this acquired language. I would be like those people from the Bible we had studied in religion class, whom I imagined standing at the foot of an enormous tower that looked just like the skyscrapers around me. They had been punished for their pride by being made to speak different languages so that they didn't understand what anyone was saying.

But at the foot of those towering New York skyscrapers, I began to understand more and more – not less and less – English. In sixth grade, I had one of the first in a lucky line of great English teachers who began to nurture in me a love of language, a love that had been there since my childhood of listening closely to words. Sister Maria Generosa did not make our class interminably diagram sentences from a workbook or learn catechism of grammar rules. Instead, she asked us to write little stories imagining we were snowflakes, birds, pianos, a stone in the pavement, a star in the sky. What would it feel like to be a flower with roots in the ground? If the clouds could talk, what would they say? She had an expressive, dreamy look that was accentuated by the wimple that framed her face.

Supposing, just supposing . . . My mind would take off, soaring into possibilities, a flower with roots, a star in the sky, a cloud full of sad, sad tears, a piano crying out each time its back was tapped, music only to our ears.

Sister Maria stood at the chalkboard. Her chalk was always snapping in two because she wrote with such energy, her whole habit shaking with the swing of her arm, her hand tap-tap-tapping on the board. "Here's a simple sentence: 'The snow fell.'" Sister pointed with her chalk, her eyebrows lifted, her wimple poked up. Sometimes I could see wisps of gray hair that strayed from under her headdress. "But watch what happens if we put an adverb at the beginning and a prepositional phrase at the end: 'Gently, the snow fell on the bare hills.'"

I thought about the snow. I saw how it might fall on the hills, tapping lightly on the bare branches of trees. Softly, it would fall on the cold, bare fields. On toys children had left out in the yard, and on cars and on little birds and on people out late walking on the streets. Sister Maria filled the chalkboard with snowy print, on and on, handling and shaping and moving the language, scribbling all over the board until English, those verbal gadgets, those tricks and turns of phrases, those little fixed units and counters, became a charged, fluid mass that carried me in its great fluent waves, rolling and moving onward, to deposit me on the shores of my new homeland. I was no longer a foreigner with no ground to stand on. I had landed in the English language.

Write After You Read

1 Write a journal entry in response to "My English" using the guidelines on page 11.

2 Summarize in one or two sentences the insight you believe Alvarez has gained through her experience.

Discuss After You Read

1 Does anything in the reading remind you of your own experiences with language? If so, what is similar?

2 How do the language experiences Alvarez describes differ from your own language experiences? Why do these differences exist?

3 Examine the different languages Alvarez was exposed to as a child – varieties of Spanish, English, and Spanglish – and their different purposes and effects, both in the Dominican Republic and in the United States. What does Alvarez's experience suggest about the process of language acquisition?

4 Which details in the text stand out in your mind, enabling you to see, hear, or feel what happened? How do these details affect your enjoyment and understanding of the experiences described?

5 Alvarez divides her essay into several sections by using a space between each section. What do you perceive to be the purpose of each section? How do the sections relate to one another?

6 What are the similarities and differences between the language learning experiences Alvarez describes and the language learning experiences Niella (pages 13–15) or Zitkala-Ša (pages 24–29) describes?

Reading 3

Write Before You Read

Before reading "College" by Anzia Yezierska, write for several minutes about *your* college experience.

College

Anzia Yezierska

Anzia Yezierska (ca.1883–1970) was born in Plinsk in Russian-occupied Poland. In the late 1890s, she immigrated with her family to the United States, where they settled among other Eastern European Jewish immigrants in New York City's Lower East Side. During the day, Yezierska worked in a sweatshop; in the evening, she studied English. She won a scholarship to Columbia University Teachers College and then taught elementary school in New York for a few years. An award-winning author, Yezierska published several works, including Hungry Hearts

(1920), Children of Loneliness *(1923), and* Red Ribbon on a White Horse *(1950). "College" is excerpted from Yezierska's semi-autobiographical novel,* Bread Givers *(1925).*

That burning day when I got ready to leave New York and start out on my journey to college! I felt like Columbus[1] starting out for the other end of the earth. I felt like the pilgrim fathers[2] who had left their homeland and all their kin behind them and trailed out in search of the New World.

I had stayed up night after night, washing and ironing, patching and darning my things. At last, I put them all together in a bundle, wrapped them up with newspapers, and tied them securely with the thick clothes line that I had in my room on which to hang out my wash. I made another bundle of my books. In another newspaper I wrapped up my food for the journey: a loaf of bread, a herring, and a pickle. In my purse was the money I had been saving from my food, from my clothes, a penny to a penny, a dollar to a dollar, for so many years. It was not much but I counted out that it would be enough for my train ticket and a few weeks' start till I got work out there.

It was only when I got to the train that I realized I had hardly eaten all day. Starving hungry, I tore the paper open. Ach! Crazy-head! In my haste I had forgotten even to cut up the bread. I bent over on the side of my seat, and half covering myself with a newspaper, I pinched pieces out of the loaf and ripped ravenously at the herring. With each bite, I cast side glances like a guilty thing; nobody should see the way I ate.

After a while, as the lights were turned low, the other passengers began to nod their heads, each outsnoring the other in their thick sleep. I was the only one on the train too excited to close my eyes.

Like a dream was the whole night's journey. And like a dream mounting on a dream was this college town, this New America of culture and education.

Before this, New York was all of America to me. But now I came to a town of quiet streets, shaded with green trees. No crowds, no tenements. No hurrying noise to beat the race of the hours. Only a leisured quietness whispered in the air: Peace. Be still. External time is all before you.

Each house had its own green grass in front, its own free space all around, and it faced the street with the calm security of being owned for generations, and not rented by the month from a landlord. In the early twilight, it was like a picture out of fairyland to see people sitting on their porches, lazily swinging in their hammocks, or watering their own growing flowers.

So these are the real Americans, I thought, thrilled by the lean, straight bearing of the passers-by. They had none of that terrible fight for bread and rent that I always saw in New York people's eyes. Their faces were not worn with the hunger

---

[1] *(Christopher) Columbus* (ca. 1451–1506): the Italian explorer who is said to have discovered America

[2] *the pilgrim fathers*: the Puritans who left England to seek a new life and religious freedom and who founded the colony of Plymouth in Massachusetts in 1620

for things they could never have in their lives. There was in them that sure, settled look of those who belong to the world which they were born.

The college buildings were like beautiful palaces. The campus stretched out like fields of a big park. Air – air. Free space and sunshine. The river at dusk. Glimmering lights on passing boats, the floating voices of young people. And when night came, there were the sky and the stars.

This was the beauty for which I had always longed. For the first few days I could only walk about and drink it in thirstily, more and more. Beauty of houses, beauty of streets, beauty shining out of the calm faces and cool eyes of the people! Oh – too cool....

How could I most quickly become friends with them? How could I come into their homes, exchange with them my thoughts, break with them bread at their tables? If I could only lose myself body and soul in the serenity of this new world, the hunger and the turmoil of my ghetto years would drop away from me, and I, too, would know the beauty of stillness and peace.

What light-hearted laughing youth met my eyes! All the young people I had ever seen were shut up in factories. But here were young girls and young men enjoying life, free from the worry for a living. College to them was being out for a good time, like to us in the shop a Sunday picnic. But in our gayest Sunday picnics there was always the under-feeling that Monday meant back to the shop again. To these born lucky ones joy seemed to stretch out for ever.

What a sight I was in my gray pushcart clothes against the beautiful gay colours and the fine things those young girls wore. I had seen cheap, fancy style, Five-and Ten-Cent Store finery. But never had I seen such plain beautifulness. The simple skirts and sweaters, the stockings and shoes to match. The neat finished quietness of their tailored suits. There was no show-off in their clothes, and yet how much more pulling to the eyes and all the senses than the Grand Street[3] richness I knew.

And the spick-and-span cleanliness of these people! It smelled from them, the soap and the bathing. Their fingernails so white and pink. Their hands and necks white like milk. I wondered how did those girls get their hair so soft, so shiny, and so smooth about their heads. Even their black shoes had a clean look.

Never had I seen men so all shaved up with pink, clean skins. The richest store-keepers in Grand Street shined themselves up with diamonds like walking jewellery stores, but they weren't so hollering clean as these men. And they all had their hair clipped so short; they all had a shape to their heads. So ironed out smooth and even they looked in their spotless, creaseless clothes, as if the dirty battle of life had never yet been on them.

I looked at these children of joy with a million eyes. I looked at them with my hands, my feet, with the thinnest nerves of my hair. By all their differences from me, their youth, their shiny freshness, their carefreeness, they pulled me out of my senses to them. And they didn't even know I was there.

I thought once I got into the classes with them, they'd see me and we'd get to know one another. What a sharp awakening came with my first hour!

[3] *Grand Street*: a street on the Lower East Side of New York City where many Jewish immigrants lived

As I entered the classroom, I saw young men and girls laughing and talking to one another without introductions. I looked for my seat. Then I noticed, up in front, a very earnest-faced young man with thick glasses over his sad eyes. He made me think of Morris Lipkin, so I chose my seat next to him.

"What's the name of the professor?" I asked.

"Smith," came from his tight lips. He did not even look at me. He pulled himself together and began busily writing, to show me he didn't want to be interrupted.

I turned to the girl on my other side. What a fresh clean beauty! A creature of sunshine. And clothes that matched her radiant youth.

"Is this the freshman class in geometry?" I asked her.

She nodded politely and smiled. But how quickly her eyes sized me up! It was not an unkind glance. And yet, it said more plainly than words, "From where do you come? How did you get in here?"

Sitting side by side with them through the whole hour, I felt stranger to them than if I had passed them in Hester Street.[4] Wasn't there some secret something that would open us toward one another?

In one class after another, I kept asking myself, "What's the matter with me? Why do they look at me so when I talk with them?"

Maybe I'd have to change myself inside and out to be one of them. But, how? The lectures were over at four o'clock. With a sigh, I turned from the college building, away from the pleasant streets, down to the shabby back alley near the post office, and entered the George Martin Hand Laundry.

Mr. Martin was a fat, easy-going, good-natured man. I no sooner told him of my experience in New York than he took me on at once as an ironer at fifty cents an hour, and he told me he had work for as many hours a day as I could put in.

I felt if I could only look a little bit like other girls on the outside, maybe I could get in with them. And that meant money! And money meant work, work, work!

Till eleven o'clock that night, I ironed fancy white shirtwaists.

"You're some busy little worker, even if I do say so," said Mr. Martin, good-naturedly. "But I must lock up. You can't live here."

I went home, aching in every bone. And in the quiet and good air, I so overslept that I was late for my first class. To make matters worse, I found a note in my mailbox that puzzled and frightened me. It said, "Please report at once to the dean's office to explain your absence from Physical Education I, at four o'clock."

A line of other students was waiting there. When my turn came I asked the secretary, "What's this physical education business?"

"This is a compulsory course," he said, "You cannot get credit in any other course unless you satisfy this requirement."

At the hour when I had intended to go back to Martin's Laundry, I entered the big gymnasium. There was a crowd of girls dressed in funny short black bloomers and rubber-soled shoes.

The teacher blew the whistle and called harshly, "Students are expected to report in their uniforms."

"I have none."

---

[4] *Hester Street*: a street on the Lower East Side of New York City where many Jewish immigrants lived

"They're to be obtained at the bookstore," she said, with a stern look at me, "Please do not report again without it."

I stood there dumb.

"Well, stay for to-day, and exercise as you are," said the teacher, taking pity on me.

She pointed out my place in the line, where I had to stand with the rest like a lot of wooden soldiers. She made us twist ourselves around here and there. "Right face!" "Left face!" "Right about face!" I tried to do as the others did, but I felt like a jumping-jack being pulled this way and that way. I picked up dumbbells and pushed them up and down and sideways until my arms were lame. Then she made us hop around like a lot of monkeys.

At the end of the hour, I was so out of breath that I sank down, my heart pounding against my ribs. I was dripping with sweat worse than Saturday night in the steam laundry. What's all this physical education nonsense? I came to college to learn something, to get an education with my head, and not monkeyshines with my arms and legs.

I went over to the instructor. "How much an hour do we get for this work?" I asked her, bitterly.

She looked at me with a stupid stare. "This is a two-point course."

Now I got real mad, "I've got to sweat my life away enough only to earn a living," I cried. "God knows I exercised enough, since I was a kid – "

"You properly exercised?" She looked at me from head to foot. "Your posture is bad. Your shoulders sag. You need additional corrective exercises outside the class."

More tired than ever, I came to the class next day. After the dumbbells, she made me jump over the hurdles. For the life of me, I couldn't do it. I bumped myself and scratched my knees on the top bar of the hurdle, knocking it over with a great clatter. They all laughed except the teacher.

"Repeat the exercise, please," she said, with a frozen face.

I was all bruises, trying to do it. And they were holding their sides with laughter. I was their clown, and this was their circus. And suddenly, I got so wild with rage that I seized the hurdle and right before their eyes I smashed it to pieces.

The whole gymnasium went still as death.

The teacher's face was white. "Report at once to the dean."

The scared look on the faces of the girls made me feel that I was to be locked up or fired.

For a minute when I entered the dean's grand office, I was so confused I couldn't even see.

He rose and pointed to a chair beside his desk. "What can I do for you?" he asked, in a voice that quieted me as he spoke.

I told him how mad I was, to have piled on me jumping hurdles when I was so tired anyway. He regarded me with that cooling steadiness of his. When I was through, he walked to the window and I waited, miserable. Finally he turned to me again, and with a smile! "I'm quite certain that physical education is not essential in your case. I will excuse you from attending the course."

After this things went better with me. In spite of the hard work in the laundry, I managed to get along in my classes. More and more interesting became the life of the college as I watched it from the outside.

What a feast of happenings each day of college was to those other students. Societies, dances, letters from home, packages of food, midnight spreads and even birthday parties. I never knew that there were people glad enough of life to celebrate the day they were born. I watched the gay goings-on around me like one coming to a feast, but always standing back and only looking on.

One day, the ache for people broke down my feelings of difference from them. I felt I must tear myself out of my aloneness. Nothing had ever come to me without my going out after it. I had to fight for my living, fight for every bit of my education. Why should I expect friendship and love to come to me out of the air while I sat there, dreaming of it?

The freshman class gave a dance that very evening. Something in the back of my head told me that an evening dress and slippers were part of going to a dance. I had no such things. But should that stop me? If I had waited till I could afford the right clothes for college, I should never have been able to go at all.

I put a fresh collar over my old serge dress. And with a dollar stolen from my eating money, I bought a ticket to the dance. As I peeped into the glittering gymnasium, blaring with jazz, my timid fears stopped the breath in me. How the whole big place sang with their light-hearted happiness! Young eyes drinking joy from young eyes. Girls, like gay-coloured butterflies; whirling in the arms of young men.

Floating ribbons arid sashes shimmered against men's black coats. I took the nearest chair, blinded by the dazzle of the happy couples. Why did I come here? A terrible sense of age weighed upon me; yet I watched and waited for someone to come and ask me to dance. But not one man came near me. Some of my classmates nodded distantly in passing, but most of them were too filled with their own happiness even to see me.

The whirling of joy went on and on, and still I sat there watching, cold, lifeless, like a lost ghost. I was nothing and nobody. It was worse than being ignored. Worse than being an outcast. I simply didn't belong. I had no existence in their young eyes. I wanted to run and hide myself, but fear and pride nailed me against the wall.

A chaperon must have noticed my face, and she brought over one of those clumsy, backward youths who was lost in a corner by himself. How unwilling were his feet as she dragged him over! In a dull voice, he asked, "May I have the next dance?" his eyes fixed in the distance as he spoke.

"Thank you. I don't want to dance." And I fled from the place.

I found myself walking in the darkness of the campus. In the thick shadows of the trees I hid myself and poured out my shamed and injured soul to the night. So, it wasn't character or brains that counted. Only youth and beauty and clothes – things I never had and never could have. Joy and love were not for such as me. Why not? Why not?

I flung myself on the ground, beating with my fists against the endless sorrows of my life. Even in college I had not escaped from the ghetto. Here loneliness hounded me even worse than in Hester Street. Was there no escape? Will I never lift myself to be a person among people?

I pressed my face against the earth. All that was left of me reached out in prayer. God! I've gone so far, help me to go on. God! I don't know how, but I must go on. Help me not to want their little happiness. I have wanted their love more than my life. Help me be bigger than this hunger in me. Give me the love that can live without love. . . .

Darkness and stillness washed over me. Slowly I stumbled to my feet and looked up at the sky. The stars in their infinite peace seemed to pour their healing light into me. I thought of the captives in prison, the sick and the suffering from the beginning of time who had looked to these stars for strength. What was my little sorrow to the centuries of pain which those stars had watched? So near they seemed, so compassionate. My bitter hurt seemed to grow small and drop away. If I must go on alone, I should still have silence and the high stars to walk with me.

■ Write After You Read

1 Write a journal entry in response to "College" using the guidelines on page 11.

2 Summarize in one or two sentences the insight you believe Yezierska's narrator has gained through her experience.

■ Discuss After You Read

1 Does anything in the reading remind you of your own experiences in college? If so, what is similar?

2 How do the college experiences Yezierska describes differ from your own college experiences? Why do these differences exist?

3 Note the contrasts Yezierska makes between the narrator's background and the lives of the students at college. How do these differences shape the narrator's college experience?

4 Which details in the text stand out in your mind, enabling you to see, hear, or feel what happened? How do these details affect your enjoyment and understanding of the experiences described?

5 Examine how Yezierska writes about an experience that began with high expectations and resulted in deep disappointment from which the narrator gained insight. Which details reveal the narrator's expectations? Which details suggest that she will be disappointed? At what point does she begin to describe the incidents that opened her eyes? At what point does she discover meaning in her experience? Identify the pages on which these details appear.

6 What are the similarities and differences between the school experiences Yezierska describes and those Zitkala-Ša (pages 24–29) or Alvarez (pages 30–34) describes?

Reading 4

■ Write Before You Read

Before reading "A Book-Writing Venture" by Kim Yong Ik, write for several minutes to answer the following question: If you were to write a book, what would you write about and why?

A Book-Writing Venture

Kim Yong Ik

Kim Yong Ik (1920–1995) was born in Choongmoo, Korea. After being educated at a university in Japan, he went to the United States at the age of 28 to study literature and received a B.A. from Florida Southern College and an M.A. from the University of Kentucky. He later studied creative writing at the Iowa Writers' Workshop. An award-winning author, Kim published several books, including The Happy Days *(1960) and* Love in Winter *(1969). "A Book-Writing Venture" was originally published in* The Writer *magazine.*

In 1948 when I started to write a novel apart from my regular school work at Florida Southern College, Lakeland, Florida, my roommate in the dormitory told me, "If I were you, I wouldn't waste time in this country. I'll give you five hundred dollars if you publish one book in America. Breaking into that racket is nearly impossible even for an American writer who has mastered his own language." I was far from a master of English, but I didn't listen to him inside. I had studied English literature during the Second World War when it was a most unpopular subject to take up in the Orient, but I wanted to study it. Once in America, I wanted to write so much that I refused to accept the fact that my English was far from being adequate to write a novel. I put in three hours early every morning writing a book.

The language problem that I was attacking loomed larger and larger as I began to learn more. When I would describe in English certain concepts and objects enmeshed in Korean emotion and imagination, I became slowly aware of nuances, of differences between two languages even in simple expression. The remark "Kim entered the house" seems to be simple enough, yet, unless a reader has a clear visual image of a Korean house, his understanding of the sentence is not complete. When a Korean says he is "in the house," he may be in his courtyard, or on his porch, or in his small room! If I wanted to give a specific picture of entering the house in the Western sense, I had to say "room" instead of house – sometimes. I say "sometimes" because many Koreans entertain their guests on their porches and still are considered to be hospitable, and in the Korean sense, going into the "room" may be a more intimate act than it would be in the English sense. Such problems! That is merely an example. My Florida friends tried to help.

After three years in Florida, I moved to the University of Kentucky to continue my book-writing venture. During a holiday season when I was hired by the library to wax some leather-bound books, for fifty cents an hour, I often daydreamed that some day I would have my book published and bound in that shining, aromatic leather. I was all by myself in the Precious Books section upstairs. While working with the bindings with my hands full of grease and wax, I would read aloud from a book of poetry open before me. Reading poetry did not require me to turn pages often. I also loved the rhythmical voice in it. Each time my reading was interrupted because with dirty hands I could not turn the page immediately, I was frustrated, as though a phonograph record got stuck in a scratch on a recording of my favorite song. As I was reading Robert Frost's "The Road Not Taken," I saw the librarian in charge of the section standing right behind me. I knew that she would chide me or even dismiss me, for the library was strict about student workers reading during their work hours. I couldn't look up at her to say hello. I saw her dry hand reach for the book, as though she would take it away; instead, her fingers turned the page for me to go on, and she left the room without saying a word! I was deeply moved as I finished the poem – "And that has made all the difference."

I did go on to finish writing my book. In 1953 when I enrolled in the Writers' Workshop of the University of Iowa, I had been writing fiction for six years and had completed one novel. I started to send it to various publishers in New York.

I had to send it by railway express and had to pay return postage. This amounted to nearly five dollars for each mailing. Since it took about a month for the rejected manuscript to reach me, this turned out to be a regular monthly expense. I would walk to the outskirts of Iowa City to the railroad station to save the bus fare that would help pay for mailing the manuscript. The railway express man was quite curious about the mysterious package that kept reappearing, and finally he asked me what was in it.

I explained to him, and he told me there was an old man in Iowa City who kept on mailing his manuscript about every month, just as I did.

Still I appeared so often that finally I was embarrassed whenever I met the express agent. We got to know each other rather well. By this time, he knew that Korean was my mother tongue; Japanese my second (I had learned this under the Japanese occupation);[1] and English my third (I started to learn English during my high school days in Korea). One day I asked him what had become of the old man and his manuscript, and he said "That fellow's manuscript always came back but he is now dead."

I kept up the game of mailing and receiving my novel manuscript, as well as several short stories. I felt I was making some progress in mastering the English language even if my collection of rejection slips seemed to shout otherwise. As days and seasons passed, I became more desperate. I read and wrote harder than before. Even on the train on the way to Maine to work for a family for the summer, I kept up my morning ritual of three hours of writing. By day, I read stories for their children, enjoying the rhythm of the English language. At night, I stayed up late writing. Word got around that the Korean "liked to sleep with his light on."

I returned to school that fall only to write. My landlady in Iowa City would complain that I did not leave the room on the weekend so she could properly clean

[1] Japan occupied Korea from 1910–1945. During that time, Korean citizens were forbidden to use the Korean language in schools and businesses.

my room, and further remarked that she wouldn't like her boy to go abroad just to stay in a room always. I listened to her advice only to learn living language.

I would walk around with a night watchman or with janitors on night duty, and from them I would have free lessons of English – by listening. When I went to work at the University Hospital cafeteria across the Iowa River, I used to copy a poem or two on a slip of paper to read on the way. In the cafeteria I kept the slip of paper hidden under the counter and tried to memorize it while serving food. Of course, I was fired after two weeks.

I actually cared very little about a degree, so there was very small satisfaction in academic success. I wanted to have one story accepted. I was beginning to feel that perhaps this would never happen. I had only my many rejection slips to contemplate – after so many years of labor.

One Saturday it was snowing really hard outside. I was filled with self-doubt and wondered how in the world I had acquired the fantastic idea that I could write the drama of human emotion in fiction in a second language – no, in my third. I was feeling so dejected that I went out and spent nearly all my money on a record player. At least I could have music. Then I borrowed a record of Anthony Vivaldi's *Four Seasons* from the library and played it over and over that day, not even stopping to eat.

As I sat listening and watching the falling snow, I had a strange fantasy. I imagined that I saw a pair of Korean wedding shoes walking away from me in the snow. I followed the shoes in my mind, but I was always behind the figure who wore them, watching the back of the silk brocade shoes and the white muslin socks. The silken wedding shoes walked on and on toward the distant hills. I wanted to discover the person who wore the shoes, but she and her shoes wouldn't turn so I could see her. I heard my heart beat as I ran after the footmarks not to lose sight of the beautiful shoes, fearing that the snow might be wetting the finest silk.

I thought that if only I could see the elusive owner of these shoes, then I could write a real story! I came out of my reverie and got up determined to do just that. I went out.

By then I had begun to feel the effects of my day's fast, so my first stop was the corner grocery store. I went to the back to see the butcher who greeted me with a cheering "Merry Christmas" and a few words of encouragement.

I asked for a few slices of sandwich meat. (After my extravagances with my manuscripts and the impulsive purchase of the record player, there wasn't much left for food.)

I was surprised when the butcher took out a huge hunk of meat, and I reminded him "only a few slices, please." But he quickly wrapped it up and marked it twenty cents. I was sure that this was really about two dollars' worth of meat and I asked, "Is this really only twenty cents?"

He answered, "Yes, sir."

When I went to pay the cashier, she looked closely at package and then at me, but she accepted the twenty cents without comment.

After that, whenever I returned to the butcher, the package of meat seemed to grow even larger but the price was still twenty cents. Because of this kindness of the butcher, I had a high protein diet for the month and a half when I was writing my story of "The Wedding Shoes."

In my story, the butcher in a Korean valley is a very kind man who would give a very generous amount whenever a poor shoemaker's daughter came in with too little money. I wrote the story as if seen through the eyes of the butcher's son. While chasing the coveted shoes in my mind, I tried to capture the rhythm of my own language in English writing and tried not to take a chance of any misunderstanding by putting everything in concrete terms. Whenever I found it difficult to describe a certain scene, I had my usual temptation to delete it. But by this time I knew better than "to glide over" any scene or word that belonged in my work; more often than not, the thorny word or passage that does pose a language problem is the one that breathes pulsing life into the story.

When I completed "The Wedding Shoes," I gave it to Paul Eagle, the director of the Writers' Workshop, but he was busy at the time and gave it to Margarette Young, author of *The Angel of the Forest*. She called me up and said with great enthusiasm, "This is wonderful. You must send this story to *Harper's Bazaar* right away." I did.

A few weeks later I found a letter in my mail box instead of the familiar ugly yellowed package. Alice Morris, the literary editor of *Harper's Bazaar*, wrote me that she wanted to print my story and would pay me $250. It was a time of great joy, but I had no one to share it with.

Soon after my story appeared, *London Bazaar* cabled me: "Offer twenty-five guineas for "The Wedding Shoes."" About the same time, an amateur ballet group in Iowa City planned a ballet based on my story – so, on an electric light pole in front of the grocery store was posted an advertising poster: "A Ballet: The Silken Brocade Shoes."

After my stories had been accepted by the *Mademoiselle, Botteghe Oscure*, and *The New Yorker*, I returned to my homeland after spending ten years in America. Besides my teaching at a university, I continued to write in English as well as in my native tongue. In 1960 I revisited the United States to see my old friends. I was happy to find the librarian at the Precious Books section when I dropped in at the University of Kentucky. She remembered my reading poetry during my work hours and even the incident of turning the page for me. She asked me what I had been doing. When I mentioned what I had written for magazines, that I'd had juvenile books published by Little, Brown, and that an adult novel of mine was to be published by Alfred A. Knopf, she did not believe me until she looked them up in the publication index of the library. Then she was so happy for me that she invited me for dinner in a Chinese restaurant, and later we drove around in that bluegrass country.

That winter, I received a Christmas gift from Little, Brown – a copy of my first juvenile fiction book, written in Florida and Kentucky – *The Happy Days*, bound in beautiful leather.

■ Write After You Read

1 Write a journal entry in response to "A Book-Writing Venture" using the guidelines on page 11.

2 Summarize in one or two sentences the insight you believe Kim has gained through his experience.

■ Discuss After You Read

1 Does anything in the reading remind you of your own experiences with writing? If so, what is similar?

2 How do the writing experiences Kim describes differ from your own experiences with writing? Why do these differences exist?

3 What do Kim's stages of second language acquisition reveal about

  a how language is acquired over time,
  b what learning to write well in a second language entails,
  c what role culture may play in writing,
  d and how rejection or encouragement affects a writer's motivation?

4 Which details in the text stand out in your mind, enabling you to see, hear, or feel what happened? How do these details affect your enjoyment and understanding of the experiences described?

5 Kim writes of his experiences in chronological order – in the order in which events actually happened, one incident after another. Discuss why you think he chose this approach. What other organizational structures might he have chosen and what effect would they have had on his story?

6 What are the similarities and differences between Kim's experiences with writing and the writing experiences Alvarez (pages 30–34) describes?

Reading 5

■ Write Before You Read

Before reading "Mother Tongue" by Amy Tan, write for several minutes about what *mother tongue* means to you.

Mother Tongue

Amy Tan

Amy Tan was born in Oakland, California, after her parents immigrated to the United States from China. Tan earned a B.A. from San Jose State University and an M.A. in English and linguistics from the University of California, Berkeley. She has worked as a language-development specialist for disabled children, a medical journal editor, and a technical writer. An award-winning author, Tan's books include the novels The Joy Luck Club *(1989),* The Bonesetter's Daughter *(2001), and* Saving Fish from Drowning *(2005) and the essay collection,* The Opposite of Fate *(2003). "Mother Tongue" was originally published in the literary journal* The Threepenny Review.

I am not a scholar of English or literature. I cannot give you much more than personal opinions on the English language and its variations in this country or others.

I am a writer. And by that definition, I am someone who has always loved language. I am fascinated by language in daily life. I spend a great deal of my time thinking about the power of language – the way it can evoke an emotion, a visual image, a complex idea, or a simple truth. Language is the tool of my trade. And I use them all – all the Englishes I grew up with.

Recently, I was made keenly aware of the different Englishes I do use. I was giving a talk to a large group of people, the same talk I had already given to half a dozen other groups. The nature of the talk was about my writing, my life, and my book, *The Joy Luck Club*. The talk was going along well enough, until I remembered one major difference that made the whole talk sound wrong. My mother was in the room. And it was perhaps the first time she had heard me give a lengthy speech, using the kind of English I have never used with her. I was saying things like, "The intersection of memory upon imagination" and "There is an aspect of my fiction that relates to thus-and-thus" – a speech filled with carefully wrought grammatical phrases, burdened, it suddenly seemed to me, with nominalized forms, past perfect tenses, conditional phrases, all the forms of standard English that I had learned in school and through books, the forms of English I did not use at home with my mother.

Just last week, I was walking down the street with my mother, and I again found myself conscious of the English I was using, the English I do use with her. We were talking about the price of new and used furniture and I heard myself saying this: "Not waste money that way." My husband was with us as well, and he didn't notice any switch in my English. And then I realized why. It's because over the twenty years we've been together I've often used the same kind of English with him, and sometimes he even uses it with me. It has become our language of intimacy, a different sort of English that relates to family talk, the language I grew up with.

So you'll have some idea of what this family talk I heard sounds like, I'll quote what my mother said during a recent conversation which I videotaped and then transcribed. During this conversation, my mother was talking about a political gangster in Shanghai who had the same last name as her family's, Du, and how the gangster in his early years wanted to be adopted by her family, which was rich by comparison. Later, the gangster became more powerful, far richer than my mother's family, and one day showed up at my mother's wedding to pay his respects. Here's what she said in part:

"Du Yusong having business like fruit stand. Like off the street kind. He is Du like Du Zong – but not Tsung-ming Island people. The local people call putong, the river east side, he belong to that side local people. That man want to ask Du Zong father take him in like become own family. Du Zong father wasn't look down on him, but didn't take seriously, until that man big like become a mafia. Now important person, very hard to inviting him. Chinese way, came only to show respect, don't stay for dinner. Respect for making big celebration, he shows up. Mean gives lots of respect. Chinese custom. Chinese social life that way. If too important won't have to stay too long. He come to my wedding. I didn't see, I heard it. I gone to boy's side, they have YMCA dinner. Chinese age I was nineteen."

You should know that my mother's expressive command of English belies how much she actually understands. She reads the *Forbes* report, listens to *Wall Street Week*, converses daily with her stockbroker, reads all of Shirley MacLaine's books with ease – all kinds of things I can't begin to understand. Yet some of my friends tell me they understand 50 percent of what my mother says. Some say they understand 80 to 90 percent. Some say they understand none of it, as if she were speaking pure Chinese. But to me, my mother's English is perfectly clear, perfectly natural. It's my mother tongue. Her language, as I hear it, is vivid, direct, full of observation and imagery. That was the language that helped shape the way I saw things, expressed things, made sense of the world.

Lately, I've been giving more thought to the kind of English my mother speaks. Like others, I have described it to people as "broken" or "fractured" English. But I wince when I say that. It has always bothered me that I can think of no way to describe it other than "broken," as if it were damaged and needed to be fixed, as if it lacked a certain wholeness and soundness. I've heard other terms used, "limited English," for example. But they seem just as bad, as if everything is limited, including people's perceptions of the limited English speaker.

I know this for a fact, because when I was growing up, my mother's "limited" English limited my perception of her. I was ashamed of her English. I believed that her English reflected the quality of what she had to say. That is, because she expressed them imperfectly her thoughts were imperfect. And I had plenty of empirical evidence to support me: the fact that people in department stores, at banks, and at restaurants did not take her seriously, did not give her good service, pretended not to understand her, or even acted as if they did not hear her.

My mother has long realized the limitations of her English as well. When I was fifteen, she used to have me call people on the phone to pretend I was she. In this guise, I was forced to ask for information or even to complain and yell at people who had been rude to her. One time it was a call to her stockbroker in New York. She had cashed out her small portfolio and it just so happened we were going to go to New York the next week, our very first trip outside California. I had to get on the phone and say in an adolescent voice that was not very convincing, "This is Mrs. Tan."

And my mother was standing in the back whispering loudly, "Why he don't send me check, already two weeks late. So mad he lie to me, losing me money."

And then I said in perfect English, "Yes, I'm getting rather concerned. You had agreed to send the check two weeks ago, but it hasn't arrived."

Then she began to talk more loudly. "What he want, I come to New York tell him front of his boss, you cheating me?" And I was trying to calm her down, make her be quiet, while telling the stockbroker, "I can't tolerate any more excuses. If I don't receive the check immediately, I am going to have to speak to your manager when I'm in New York next week." And sure enough, the following week there we were in front of this astonished stockbroker, and I was sitting there red-faced and quiet, and my mother, the real Mrs. Tan, was shouting at his boss in her impeccable broken English.

We used a similar routine just five days ago, for a situation that was far less humorous. My mother had gone to the hospital for an appointment, to find out about a benign brain tumor a CAT scan had revealed a month ago. She said she had spoken very good English, her best English, no mistakes. Still, she said, the hospital did not apologize when they said they had lost the CAT scan and she had come for nothing. She said they did not seem to have any sympathy when she told them she was anxious to know the exact diagnosis, since her husband and son had both died of brain tumors. She said they would not give her any more information until the next time and she would have to make another appointment for that. So she said she would not leave until the doctor called her daughter. She wouldn't budge. And when the doctor finally called her daughter, me, who spoke in perfect English – lo and behold – we had assurances the CAT scan would be found, promises that a conference call on Monday would be held, and apologies for any suffering my mother had gone through for a most regrettable mistake.

I think my mother's English almost had an effect on limiting my possibilities in life as well. Sociologists and linguists probably will tell you that a person's developing language skills are more influenced by peers. But I do think that the language spoken in the family, especially in immigrant families which are more insular, plays a large role in shaping the language of the child. And I believe that it affected my results on achievement tests, IQ tests, and the SAT. While my English skills were never judged as poor, compared to math, English could not be considered my strong suit. In grade school I did moderately well, getting perhaps B's, sometimes B-pluses, in English and scoring perhaps in the sixtieth or seventieth percentile on achievement tests. But those scores were not good enough to override the opinion that my true abilities lay in math and science, because in those areas I achieved A's and scored in the ninetieth percentile or higher.

This was understandable. Math is precise; there is only one correct answer. Whereas, for me at least, the answers on English tests were always a judgment call, a matter of opinion and personal experience. Those tests were constructed around items like fill-in-the-blank sentence completion, such as, "Even though Tom was _____ , Mary thought he was _____ ." And the correct answer always seemed to be the most bland combinations of thoughts, for example, "Even though Tom was shy, Mary thought he was charming," with the grammatical structure "even though" limiting the correct answer to some sort of semantic opposites, so you wouldn't get answers like, "Even though Tom was foolish, Mary thought he was ridiculous." Well, according to my mother, there were very few limitations as to what Tom could have been and what Mary might have thought of him. So I never did well on tests like that.

The same was true with word analogies, pairs of words in which you were supposed to find some sort of logical, semantic relationship – for example, "*Sunset* is to *nightfall* as _____ is to _____ ." And here you would be presented with a list of four possible pairs, one of which showed the same kind of relationship: *red* is to *stoplight, bus* is to *arrival, chills* is to *fever, yawn* is to *boring*. Well, I could never think that way. I knew what the tests were asking, but I could not block out of my mind the images already created by the first pair, "*sunset* is to *nightfall*" – and I would see a burst of colors against a darkening sky, the moon rising, the lowering of a curtain of stars. And all the other pairs of words – red, bus, stoplight, boring – just threw up a mass of confusing images, making it impossible for me to sort out something as logical as saying: "A sunset precedes nightfall" is the same as "a chill precedes a fever." The only way I would have gotten that answer right would have been to imagine an associative situation, for example, my being disobedient and staying out past sunset, catching a chill at night, which turns into feverish pneumonia as punishment, which indeed did happen to me.

I have been thinking about all this lately, about my mother's English, about achievement tests. Because lately I've been asked, as a writer, why there are not more Asian Americans represented in American literature. Why are there few Asian Americans enrolled in creative writing programs? Why do so many Chinese students go into engineering? Well, these are broad sociological questions I can't begin to answer. But I have noticed in surveys – in fact, just last week – that Asian students, as a whole, always do significantly better on math achievement tests than in English. And this makes me think that there are other Asian-American students whose English spoken in the home might also be described as "broken" or "limited." And perhaps they also have teachers who are steering them away from writing and into math and science, which is what happened to me.

Fortunately, I happen to be rebellious in nature and enjoy the challenge of disproving assumptions made about me. I became an English major my first year in college, after being enrolled as pre-med. I started writing nonfiction as a freelancer the week after I was told by my former boss that writing was my worst skill and I should hone my talents toward account management.

But it wasn't until 1985 that I finally began to write fiction. And at first I wrote using what I thought to be wittily crafted sentences, sentences that would finally prove I had mastery over the English language. Here's an example from the first draft of a story that later made its way into *The Joy Luck Club*, but without this line: "That was my mental quandary in its nascent state." A terrible line, which I can barely pronounce.

Fortunately, for reasons I won't get into today, I later decided I should envision a reader for the stories I would write. And the reader I decided upon was my mother, because these were stories about mothers. So with this reader in mind – and in fact she did read my early drafts – I began to write stories using all the Englishes I grew up with: the English I spoke to my mother, which for lack of a better term might be described as "simple"; the English she used with me, which for lack of a better term might be described as "broken"; my translation of her Chinese, which could certainly be described as "watered down"; and what I imagined to be her translation of her Chinese if she could speak in perfect English, her internal language, and for that I sought to preserve the essence, but neither an English nor a Chinese structure. I wanted to capture what language ability tests can never reveal: her intent, her passion, her imagery, the rhythms of her speech and the nature of her thoughts.

Apart from what any critic had to say about my writing, I knew I had succeeded where it counted when my mother finished reading my book and gave me her verdict: "So easy to read."

■ Write After You Read

1 Write a journal entry in response to "Mother Tongue" using the guidelines on page 11.

2 Summarize in one or two sentences the insight you believe Tan has gained through her experience.

■ Discuss After You Read

1 How are the cross-cultural or cross-linguistic experiences Tan describes similar to or different from your own experiences? Why do these similarities or differences exist?

2 Do you use "different Englishes" or different variations of another language? If so, how does each variation relate to your identity?

3 What does this reading say or imply about the following?
   a The nature of speaking a second language
   b The relationship between speaking a second language and reading in a second language

4 Which details in the text stand out in your mind, enabling you to see, hear, or feel what happened? How do these details affect your enjoyment and understanding of the experiences described?

5 Tan divides her essay into three sections by using a space between each section. What do you perceive to be the purpose of each section? How do the sections relate to one another?

6 What are the similarities and differences between Tan's experiences with writing and the writing experiences Alvarez (pages 30–34) or Kim (pages 42–45) describes?

GUIDELINES

Writing from Experience

Essay Assignment

Write an essay in which you describe an experience – or series of related experiences – that has led you to a new insight or point of view. Provide details and examples that enable readers to see, hear, and feel what happened. Your purpose is to find meaning in what you have experienced. The exploratory writing of one student, Rolando Niella, is included in the following guidelines to show how he developed ideas for an essay based on his own experience. His completed essay, "Barriers," appears on pages 13–15.

■ Exploring a Topic

Exploring a topic before you begin writing an essay can lead you to produce a more fully developed piece of writing. If you have not yet thought of an experience to write about, or if you have thought of one but don't know what to say about it, the following exploratory strategies may help you get started. These strategies represent ways of thinking on paper. Since exploratory writing is primarily for your own eyes, you do not need to be concerned with grammatical correctness at this stage.

Making a List

Making a list can be a valuable first step in writing. If it works for you, it can help you find a topic to write about as well as details to include in your own writing.

Guidelines for Making a List

1. Make a list of possible topics for your essay.
2. Choose one of the topics and then make a list of related details, which may include the following:
   - Where, when, why, and over what period of time events took place
   - Who was involved
   - What you or other people did
   - What you or other people said
3. Look for a pattern or repeated theme that might help you discover the significance of these details.

A student writer at work: *Making a list*

In preparation for his essay, Rolando made a list of several problems he had experienced or was experiencing and put an asterisk next to related topics that he thought could be turned into an essay.

> * *Culture shock*
> * *Making friends*
>   *Problems in my family*
>   *Problems in adolescence*
>
> * *Defining my friends*
>   *Taking tests*
>   *Christian problem*
>   *good problems*

Your turn: *Making a list*

Using the *Guidelines for Making a List*, list possible topics and related details for your own essay.

Freewriting

Freewriting is a writing activity in which you write whatever comes into your mind about a topic. In other words, you talk to yourself on paper as a way to get started on your writing and find something to say about your topic. If this technique works for you, it can help you find out what is really on your mind.

Guidelines for Freewriting

1. Write a topic at the top of a blank sheet of paper.
2. Write whatever comes into your mind about the topic.
3. Write for several minutes on the topic.
4. Don't focus on grammar, punctuation, or spelling.

A student writer at work: *Freewriting*

Even after he had made his list of problems (see page 53), Rolando was still not sure what to write about in his essay. He began to freewrite to discover which problem was most important to him, and the problem of culture shock eventually emerged as the most important thing on his mind.

> *I have to start writing. I just thought . . . I don't have other problems. There must be some other problems that I'm not aware of, but I can't think. I think it's because there is one problem that takes so much time and space in my head. THE CULTURE SHOCK. Well that's a problem, to have a problem that goes around your head night and day and wears your brain away. What to do. I don't know. Well, there are some problems in my family, but they are so complicated. I have to look for some other problem not so complicated – what could it be? I don't really know. What else is a problem in the past, problem in the past . . . define my friends . . . problem in the past was to . . . I don't know. Well, I guess I'm running out of ideas about problems. Come on problems, come to my mind. I don't know. What a problem not to know.*

Your turn: *Freewriting*

Using the *Guidelines for Freewriting* on page 53, write for five to ten minutes to find or develop a topic for your essay.

Looping

Looping is a writing activity in which you loop, or join, two or more freewriting passages and then reflect on what you have written. If this technique works for you, it will help you explore a topic in some depth.

Guidelines for Looping
1. Freewrite on a topic for several minutes.
2. Stop and read what you have just written.
3. Find an idea in your freewriting that you want to pursue.
4. Write that idea in a new sentence.
5. Freewrite on that idea.
6. Repeat steps 2 through 6 once or twice.

A student writer at work: *Looping*

After freewriting, Rolando realized that the number one problem in his mind was the culture shock he was experiencing by living in the United States. He began to explore this subject by looping. Rolando wrote freely for several minutes, using the word *problem* as his topic.

> *I have of course many problems in my life like everybody has, but right now I am feeling new problems like the cultural shock. I got out of my country and came to study in the U.S.A. One of the biggest problems is to make friends, to make or have the good old friends I have back home. It's so hard here — you don't know how to act, whether you should ask them their telephone number or wait for them to do it, whether you should call them very often or not. Are they bothered by my language problem? Can they not carry on a conversation with me because they always talk about local or national subjects about which I am not informed? This is really hard and sometimes makes me feel like a stranger in a group where everybody is laughing and talking and they supposedly were my friends.*

Rolando then stopped writing and read what he had just written. He found an idea he wanted to pursue and wrote that idea in a new sentence.

> *Sometimes I feel like a stranger.*

Rolando then began to freewrite on the idea in that sentence.

> *Sometimes I feel like a stranger.*
>
> *Yes, this is true, so I start wondering if my feelings are part of my imagination or not. I try to put myself into the same position — my having a foreign kid as a friend in Paraguay — and I realize that sometimes you just can't explain everything even though you still care for the person. I really care about my friends. I mean, whenever they know I like to be their friend, I care a lot about them. But I wonder, are these new friends like that? Is that the way they act but not what they mean? I know what the solution is: get together with the Latin people; but I don't want that. I don't want to be part of a minority and limit my circle of friends. I want to meet a lot of people.*

Rolando then repeated steps 2–4 and came up with a new idea he wanted to pursue, this time creating two sentences: *I don't want to limit my circle of friends. I want to meet a lot of people.* He then began to freewrite on the idea.

> *I don't want to limit my circle of friends. I want to meet a lot of people.*
>
> *This is a hard experience. I don't know the solution for this problem. Otherwise I would have solved it already. But it seems to me that the only thing I can do is keep trying — try to get close to people very carefully — try to learn, not only the way they act, but their language and their culture. But there is so much to learn. I have to wait — I think waiting is the best thing — and be very observant and careful. But I have to watch out and not become paranoid and over-analyze every single aspect of what happens between me and my friends. I don't know if I am going to write about this problem. It seems so confusing that I don't even know if a good paper will come out of it. The least it could show is the total confusion I have in my head.*

Rolando read over everything that he had written and decided that the problem that most affected him was communicating in a second language because it interfered with his ability to make new friends.

Your turn: *Looping*

Using the *Guidelines for Looping* on page 54, explore a topic for your essay.

Cubing

Cubing is a writing activity that allows you to explore a specific topic from six different perspectives. Imagine that your topic is inside a cube and that you are looking at it through each of the six sides. Move quickly from one viewpoint to another, writing down whatever each perspective suggests to you about your subject. If this technique works for you, it can help you find a way to approach your topic.

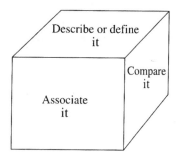 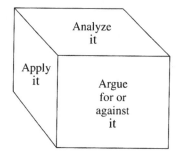

Guidelines for Cubing

Explore a topic through these six perspectives:

1. Describe or define what it is.
2. Compare and contrast what it is similar to or different from.
3. Associate it with other things that come to mind.
4. Analyze its various parts and their relationships to one another.
5. Apply it to other situations.
6. Argue for *and* against it.

A student writer at work: *Cubing*

To explore his topic, which he now called "The Language Barrier," Rolando used the cubing activity and then underlined the ideas he decided to focus on in his essay.

Rolando first *described* his topic.

> The language barrier is the idealistic or imaginary barrier that you feel
> in a country or groups of people that speak a different language than
> you do. You feel that barrier because even though you can speak the
> language and you can make yourself understand, you can't get your
> ideas across. You are speaking but you <u>feel your words disintegrate
> before reaching their effect</u>. You feel continuously that <u>you have to
> think about every word you are saying when the natural thing is just
> to let your spirit express without thinking</u>. <u>You doubt yourself</u>; you feel
> <u>insincere</u>; you feel <u>insecure</u>; you feel <u>false</u> because you are choosing
> your words so much. But when you use them just like that you are
> misunderstood.

He then *compared* it with other things.

> It is hard to compare, but it is like you reach a point where you feel
> you are in a theater rehearsing where everybody is talking in a way
> that deep inside is not natural, that all talking doesn't belong to reality.
> It's like seeing a poem but you don't know its meaning. It's like when
> you have to write a letter and you don't have the paper to write on, or
> even you write but you don't know the zip code so you don't send your
> letter. It's like talking to yourself.

He *made associations*.

> It reminds me of reading a very hard book and not understanding the
> meaning but yes the words. It's like being in a band and not singing
> with the group. Every time I feel the barrier of language, I feel how far
> I am from home and how necessary are cultures. <u>Feeling the language
> barrier is like when I play tennis. I can't get a serve in and sometimes I
> can't even answer the ball. You don't know how to say what you want
> to say</u>. Pain. Frustration.

He *analyzed* his topic.

> Well . . . there are two sides, and you are trying to go over it, to make
> your ball go over the net . . . There are two parts: (a.) Make yourself
> understood and (b.) understand the others.
> a. <u>You are always choosing the words</u>.
>   <u>You don't know the words</u>.
>   <u>You just shut up</u>.
> b. They talk and you can't understand because of so many reasons. So
>   they give up or they tell you "<u>forget it</u>," "it doesn't matter." This is the
>   terrible part because these are the things that really enable you to
>   <u>participate</u>, <u>share</u>, that make you feel part of the team, of a system
>   of that "<u>functioning</u>" or "<u>belongness</u>" you were used to.

He tried to *apply* it.

> What do you mean by "apply it"? It [the language barrier] is applied
> to me by force, because of you.
>
> • When they tell jokes
> • When they talk slowly
> • When they say something good to you and you have to ask again
> • When they complain to you
> • When they give "trivial comments" that will help you
> • When you want to express your inner feelings, being mean but
>   nice, etc.

Finally, he *argued for* and *against* it.

> • For: because it makes you aware of everything, of every word;
>   develops your senses; gives an idea of how important language is
> • Against: frustrated, bad complex, unhappiness, paranoia, anxiety,
>   wastes your time

After Rolando had covered all of the perspectives, he read what he had written.
He decided that he would try to write an essay comparing learning how to play
tennis with learning a new language.

■■▶ **Your turn:** *Cubing*

Using the *Guidelines for Cubing* on page 57, explore a topic from several perspectives. Spend only a few minutes on each perspective.

Clustering Ideas for Writing

Clustering ideas for writing involves creating a visual pattern of words that may appear in your essay. If this technique works for you, it can help you focus on your topic and see relationships among the ideas and examples.

Guidelines for Clustering Ideas for Writing

1. Choose a word or expression that might become the central subject of your essay.
2. Write that word or expression in the center of a blank page and circle it.
3. Cluster related words and expressions around this central word or expression, and circle each of these words.
4. Draw lines to connect clusters of related words.
5. Draw arrows to connect the central word or expression to each cluster of related words.

A student writer at work: *Clustering ideas for writing*

In the following example, the central subject is *Language Barrier*; all of the other words are taken from Rolando's exploratory writing.

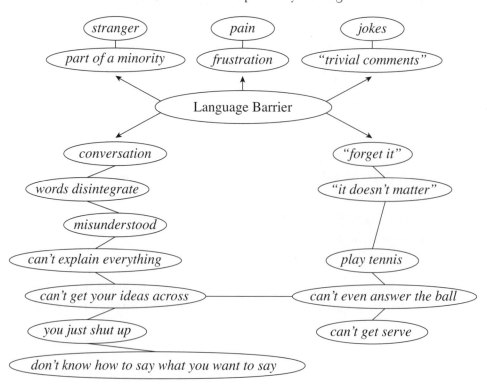

Your turn: *Clustering ideas for writing*

Using the *Guidelines for Clustering Ideas for Writing*, create a cluster of words that are related to the topic of your essay.

■ Focusing Ideas

When you engage in exploratory writing, you generate ideas to develop your own understanding of a topic. When you write an essay, you share your understanding with others, *focusing ideas* for your readers.

Guidelines for Focusing Ideas

1. Reread whatever you have written about your chosen topic.
2. Determine what overall idea or theme ties everything together.
3. Ask yourself: "What do I want to show in my essay?" Answer this question by writing a sentence or two that establishes the idea you want to focus on in your essay.
4. If you are not yet ready to establish a focal point, use the drafting process to discover what you want to show in your essay (see Drafting, pages 274–275).

A student writer at work: *Focusing ideas*

Rolando generated many ideas about the language barrier in his exploratory writing. He now needed to turn his explorations into a focused idea that he could share with readers. He started several different sentences until he settled on one.

> *Learning a foreign language as a means of integration into a new culture is like learning how to play tennis.*

As you can see by looking at his final essay, "Barriers" (pages 13–15), Rolando did not repeat the exact wording of this sentence in his essay. But this sentence did act as a focal point, guiding him as he drafted his essay.

Your turn: *Focusing ideas*

Using the *Guidelines for Focusing Ideas*, create a focal point for your essay.

■ Structuring the Essay

Structuring the essay that is drawn from experience involves moving readers toward some insight into the experience. Such essays have a basic, three-part organizational framework: a *beginning*, a *middle*, and an *ending*.

The following flow charts may help you visualize various ways to structure your essay. You can use the drafting process to experiment with organization; your early efforts can be revised later (see Drafting, pages 274–275, and Revising, pages 278–282).

Organizational Pattern 1

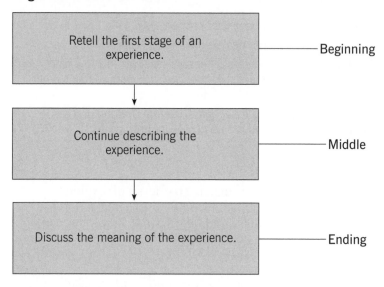

Organizational Pattern 2

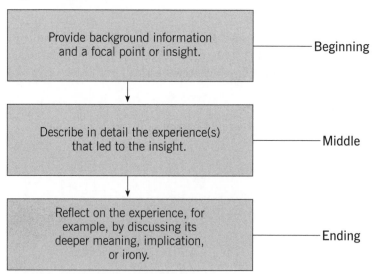

Organizational Pattern 3

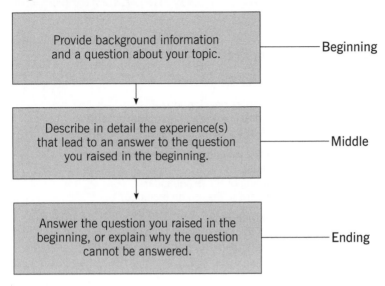

Provide background information and a question about your topic. — Beginning

Describe in detail the experience(s) that lead to an answer to the question you raised in the beginning. — Middle

Answer the question you raised in the beginning, or explain why the question cannot be answered. — Ending

Your turn: *Structuring the essay*

Create a flow chart to show what you might include in the beginning, middle, and ending of your essay. You may follow one of the three organizational patterns just listed.

■ Writing the Essay

Writing the essay can be accomplished most effectively by going through the processes of drafting, receiving feedback, and revising (see Section II of A Handbook for Writing, pages 274–284). Use the checklist on page 64 to see if your essay fulfills readers' expectations for writing from experience. The checklist may be used for self-evaluation or for evaluation of your essay by another reader.

		Evaluative Criteria for Writing an Essay from Experience

YES   NO

☐   ☐   **1 Is the focus of the essay clear?**
              If yes, what is the focus?
              If no, how can the focus be clarified?

☐   ☐   **2 Do the details and examples develop ideas?**
              If yes, which details and examples help to clarify a point?
              If no, where can details and examples be added or changed?

☐   ☐   **3 Does the essay reveal the meaning of the experience: an insight shared with readers?**
              If yes, what is the meaning of the experience?
              If no, where or how might the insight be included?

☐   ☐   **4 Is the essay logically structured?**
              If yes, what makes the structure logical?
              If no, how could the essay be more logically structured?

■ Completing the Essay

Completing the essay involves proofreading and editing your final draft as well as preparing a clear final copy to hand in to your instructor for evaluation. See Sections II and III of A Handbook for Writing, pages 282–288.

Chapter 3

Relating Reading to Experience

Writing an essay relating reading to experience involves testing an author's ideas against your own experiences. One of the challenges of composing such an essay is to determine the truth, or validity, of the author's ideas.

Chapter 3 includes four reading selections that can become sources for your essay. These reading selections focus on communicating across languages and cultures and adapting to new approaches to learning and literacy. The authors consider their topics from different angles, drawing their conclusions from their own research, reading, or experience.

The guidelines that follow the readings are designed to help you compose an essay relating reading to experience.

Reading 1

▇ Write Before You Read

Before reading "Intercultural Communication Stumbling Blocks" by LaRay M. Barna, write for several minutes about what you believe are the most challenging stumbling blocks, or barriers, to communication across cultures.

Intercultural Communication Stumbling Blocks

LaRay M. Barna

LaRay M. Barna, Associate Professor Emerita, Department of Speech Communication at Portland State University in Oregon, wrote "Intercultural Communication Stumbling Blocks" to report on her research undertaken with U.S. and international students in her own intercultural communication course. "Intercultural Communication Stumbling Blocks" was originally published in Kentucky Speech Arts Journal, *a scholarly journal for professionals in the field of communication.*

Introduction

There are many viewpoints regarding the practice of intercultural communication but a familiar one is that "people are people," basically pretty much alike; therefore increased interaction through travel, student exchange programs, and other such ventures should result in more understanding and friendship between nations. Others take a quite different view, particularly those who have done research in the field of speech communication and are fully aware of the complexities of interpersonal interaction, even *within* cultural groups. They do not equate contact with communication, do not believe that the simple experience of talking with someone insures a successful transfer of meanings and feelings. Even the basic commonalities of birth, hunger, family, death, are perceived and treated in vastly different ways by persons with different backgrounds (Singer; Hall, "Hidden"). If there is a universal, it might be that each has been so subconsciously influenced by his own cultural upbringing that he assumes that the needs, desires, and basic assumptions of others are identical to his own (Hall, "Silent").

It takes a long time of noninsulated living[1] in a new culture before a foreigner can relax into new perceptions and nonevaluative thinking so that he can adjust his reactions and interpretations to fit what's happening around him. The few who achieve complete insight and acceptance are outstanding by their rarity.

---

[1] *noninsulated living*: participating socially

After nine years of monitoring dyads[2] and small group discussions between U.S. and international students, this author, for one, is inclined to agree with Charles Frankel, who says: "Tensions exist within nations and between nations that never would have existed were these nations not in such intense cultural communication with one another" (1). The following typical reactions of three foreign students to one nonverbal behavior that most Americans expect to bridge gaps – the smile – may serve as an illustration:

Japanese student: On my way to and from school I have received a smile by nonacquaintance American girls several times. I have learned they have no interest for me; it means only a kind of greeting to a foreigner. But if someone smiles at a stranger in Japan, especially a girl, she can assume he is either a sexual maniac or an impolite person.

Korean student: An American visited me in my country for one week. His inference was that people in Korea are not very friendly because they didn't smile or want to talk with foreign people. That's true because most Korean people take time to get to be friendly with people. We never talk or smile at strangers.

Vietnamese student: The reason why certain foreigners may think that Americans are superficial – and they are, some Americans even recognize this – is that they talk and smile too much. For people who come from placid cultures where nonverbal language is more used, and where a silence, a smile, a glance have their own meaning, it is true that Americans speak a lot. The superficiality of Americans can also be detected in their relations with others. Their friendships are, most of the time, so ephemeral compared to the friendships we have at home. Americans make friends very easily and leave their friends almost as quickly, while in my country it takes a long time to find out a possible friend and then she becomes your friend – with a very strong sense of the term. Most Americans are materialistic and once they are provided with necessities, they don't feel the need to have a friend. Purposes of their friendships are too clear, and you can hardly find a friendship for friendship's sake.

An American girl in the same class gives her view:

In general it seems to me that foreign people are not necessarily snobs but are very unfriendly. Some class members have told me that you shouldn't smile at others while passing them by on the street. To me I can't stop smiling. It's just natural to be smiling and friendly. I can see now why so many foreign people stick together. They are impossible to get to know. It's like the Americans are big bad wolves. How do Americans break this barrier? I want friends from all over the world but how do you start to be friends without offending them or scaring them off – like sheep?

One reason for the long delay in tackling the widespread failure to achieve understanding across cultures might be that it is not readily apparent when there has been miscommunication at the interpersonal level. Unless there is overt reporting of assumptions[3] such as in the examples above, which seldom happens

---

[2] *dyads:* groups of two people
[3] *overt reporting of assumptions:* open explanations of basic beliefs and practices

in normal settings, there is no chance for comparing impressions. The foreign visitor to the United States nods, smiles, and gives affirmative comments, which the straightforward, friendly American confidently translates as meaning that he has informed, helped, and pleased the newcomer. It is likely, however, that the foreigner actually understood very little of the verbal and nonverbal content and was merely indicating polite interest or trying not to embarrass himself or his host with verbalized questions. The conversation may even have confirmed his stereotype that Americans are insensitive and ethnocentric.

In a university classroom, U.S. students often complain that the international members of a discussion or project seem uncooperative or uninterested. The following is a typical statement from the international point of view:

> I had difficulty with the opinion in the class where peoples in group discuss about subject. I was surrounded by Americans with whom I couldn't follow their tempo of discussion half of the time. I have difficulty to listen and speak, but also with the way they handle the group. I felt uncomfortable because sometimes they believe their opinion strongly. I had been very serious about the whole subject but I was afraid I would say something wrong. I had the idea but not the words.

Typically, the method used to improve chances for successful intercultural communication is to gather information about the customs of the other country and a smattering of the language. The behaviors and attitudes are sometimes researched, but almost always from a secondhand source. The information is seldom sufficient and may or may not be helpful. Knowing "what to expect" too often blinds the observer to all but what is confirmatory to his image or preconception. Any contradictory evidence that does filter through is likely to be treated as an exception (Bem 9).

A better approach is to study the history, political structure, art, literature, and language of the country if time permits. But more important, one should develop an investigative nonjudgmental attitude[4] and a high tolerance for ambiguity[5] – which means lowered defenses. Margaret Mead suggests sensitizing persons to the kinds of things that need to be taken into account instead of developing behavior and attitude stereotypes, mainly because of the individual differences in each encounter and the rapid changes that occur in a culture pattern. Edward Stewart concurs with this view (*American* 14).

The Stumbling Blocks

Language
One way to reach an improved state of awareness and sensitivity to what might go wrong is to examine five variables in the communication process that seem to be

---

[4] *investigative nonjudgmental attitude*: the objective position a researcher attempts to take toward a research subject

[5] *high tolerance for ambiguity*: willingness to accept uncertainty and complexity

major stumbling blocks when the dyad or small group is cross-cultural. The first is so obvious it hardly needs mentioning – *language*. Vocabulary, syntax, idioms, slang, dialects, and so on, all cause difficulty, but the person struggling with a different language is at least aware when he's in this kind of trouble. A worse language problem is the tenacity with which someone will cling to *"the"* meaning of a word or phrase in the new language once he has grasped one regardless of connotation or context. The infinite variations, especially of English, are so impossible to cope with that they are waved aside. The reason the problem is "worse" is because each thinks he understands. The nationwide misinterpretation of Khrushchev's sentence "We'll bury you"[6] is a classic example. Even "yes" and "no" cause trouble. When a Japanese hears, "Won't you have some tea?" he listens to the literal meaning of the sentence and answers, "No," meaning that he wants some. "Yes, I won't" would be a better reply because this tips off the hostess that there may be a misunderstanding. In some cultures, also, it is polite to refuse the first or second offer of refreshment. Many foreign guests have gone hungry because their U.S. hostess never presented the third offer.

Nonverbal Signs and Symbols

Learning the language, which most foreign visitors consider their only barrier to understanding, is actually only the beginning. As Frankel says, "To enter into a culture is to be able to hear, in Lionel Trilling's phrase, its special 'hum and buzz of implication'" (103). This brings in *nonverbal areas* and the second stumbling block. People from different cultures inhabit different nonverbal sensory worlds. Each sees, hears, feels, and smells only that which has some meaning or importance for him. He abstracts whatever fits into his personal world of recognitions and then interprets it through the frame of reference[7] of his own culture.

An Oregon girl in an intercultural communication class asked a young man from Saudi Arabia how he would signal nonverbally that he liked her. His response was to smooth back his hair which, to her, was just a common nervous gesture signifying nothing. She repeated her question three times, He smoothed his hair three times and, finally realizing that she was not recognizing this movement as his reply to her question, automatically ducked his head and stuck out his tongue slightly in embarrassment. This behavior *was* noticed by the girl, and she interpreted it as the way he would express his liking for her.

The lack of comprehension of obvious nonverbal signs and symbols such as gestures, postures, and vocalizations is a definite communication barrier, but it is possible to learn the meaning of these messages (once they are perceived) in much the same way as a verbal language is learned. It is more difficult to correctly note the unspoken codes of the other culture that are further from awareness, such as the handling of time and spatial relationships, subtle signs of respect or formality, and many others.

---

[6] *"We'll bury you"*: Nikita Krushchev, leader of the Soviet Union from 1953 to 1964, directed these words to the people of the United States. He was referring to *economic* competition with the West, but Americans misunderstood it as a *military* boast.

[7] *frame of reference*: a set or system of beliefs against which other ideas are tested

Preconceptions and Stereotypes

The third stumbling block is the presence of *preconceptions* and *stereotypes*. If the label "inscrutable" has preceded the Japanese guest, it is thus we explain his constant and inappropriate smile. The stereotype that Arabs are "inflammable" causes U.S. students to keep their distance when an animated and noisy group from Libya is enjoying lunch in the cafeteria. A professor who "knows" of the bargaining habits of natives of certain countries may unfairly interpret a hesitation by one of his foreign students as a move to "squirm out" of a commitment. Stereotypes help do what Ernest Becker says the anxiety-prone human race *must* do, and that is to reduce the threat of the unknown by making the world predictable (84–89). Indeed, this is one of the basic functions of culture: to lay out a predictable world in which the individual is firmly oriented. Stereotypes are overgeneralized beliefs that provide conceptual bases from which to "make sense" out of what goes on around us. In a foreign land they increase our feeling of security and are psychologically necessary to the degree that we cannot tolerate ambiguity or the sense of helplessness resulting from inability to understand and deal with people and situations beyond our comprehension.

Stereotypes are stumbling blocks for communicators because they interfere with objective viewing of stimuli.[8] Unfortunately, they are not easy to overcome in others or in ourselves by demonstrations of the "truth," hoping to teach a lesson of tolerance or cultural relativity.[9] They persist because they sometimes rationalize prejudices or are firmly established as myths or truisms by one's own national culture. They are also sustained and fed by the tendency to perceive selectively only those pieces of new information that correspond to the image. The Asian or African visitor who is accustomed to privation and the values of denial and self-help cannot fail to experience American culture as materialistic and wasteful. The stereotype for him turns into a concrete reality.

The Tendency to Evaluate

Another deterrent to an understanding between persons of differing cultures or ethnic groups is the *tendency to evaluate*, to approve or disapprove, the statements and actions of the other person or group rather than to try to completely comprehend the thoughts and feelings expressed. Each person's culture, his own way of life, always seems right, proper, and natural. This bias prevents the open-minded attention needed to look at the attitudes and behavior patterns from the other's point of view. A midday siesta changes from a "lazy habit" to a "pretty good idea" when someone listens long enough to realize the midday temperature in that country is 115° Fahrenheit.

The communication cut-off caused by immediate evaluation is heightened when feelings and emotions are deeply involved; yet this is just the time when listening with understanding is most needed. It takes both awareness of the tendency to close our minds and courage to risk change in our own values and perceptions to dare to comprehend why someone thinks and acts differently from us. As stated by Sherif, Sherif, and Nebergall, "A person's commitment to his

[8] *objective viewing of stimuli*: the ability to look at things without making judgments about them
[9] *cultural relativity*: the evaluation of a custom in relation to other customs of a particular group

religion, politics, values of his family, and his stand on the virtue of his way of life are ingredients in his self-picture – intimately felt and cherished" (vi). It is very easy to dismiss strange or different behaviors as "wrong," listen through a thick screen of value judgments, and therefore fail miserably to receive a fair understanding. The impatience of the American public over the choice of the shape of the conference table at the Paris Peace Talks[10] and their judgment of a "poor reception" for the President of the United States because there were no bands or flag-waving throngs waiting for Nixon as he was driven through towns in New China on his historic visit[11] are two examples.

The following paragraph written by an international student from Korea illustrates how a clash in values can lead to poor communication and result in misunderstanding and hurt feelings:

> When I call on my American friend, he had been studying his lesson. Then I said, "May I come in?" He said through window, "I am sorry. I have no time because of my study." Then he shut the window. I thought it over and over. I couldn't understand through my cultural background. In our country, if someone visits other's house, house owner should have welcome visitor whether he likes or not and whether he is busy or not. Then next, if the owner is busy, he asks to visitor, "Would you wait for me?" Also the owner never speaks without opening his door.

This example also illustrates how difficult it is to bring one's own cultural norm[12] into awareness. It is unlikely the "American friend" ever knew that he insulted the young Korean.

High Anxiety

The fifth stumbling block is *high anxiety*, separately mentioned for the purpose of emphasis. Unlike the other four (language, illusive nonverbal cues, preconceptions and stereotypes, and the practice of immediate evaluation), the stumbling block of anxiety is not distinct but underlies and compounds the others. The presence of high anxiety/tension is very common in cross-cultural experiences because of the uncertainties present. An international student says it well:

> During those several months after my arrival in the U.S.A., every day I came back from school exhausted so that I had to take a rest for a while, stretching myself on the bed. For all the time, I strained every nerve in order to understand what the people were saying and make myself understood in my broken English. When I don't understand what American people are talking about and why they are laughing, I sometimes have to pretend to understand by smiling, even though I feel alienated, uneasy and tense.

[10] *Paris Peace Talks*: talks between Vietnamese and United States representatives in the early 1970s whose purpose was to end the Vietnam War

[11] *Nixon's historic visit*: Richard Nixon was the first United States president to visit the People's Republic of China (1972).

[12] *cultural norm*: a standard regarded as typical or appropriate for a specific cultural group

In addition to this, the difference in culture or customs, the way of thinking between two countries, produces more tension because we don't know how we should react to totally foreign customs or attitudes, and sometimes we can't guess how the people from another country react to my saying or behavior. We always have a fear somewhere in the bottom of our hearts that there are much more chances of breakdown in intercultural communication than in communication with our own fellow countrymen.

The native of the country is uncomfortable when talking with a foreigner because he cannot maintain the normal flow of verbal and nonverbal interaction to sustain the conversation. He is also threatened by the unknown other's knowledge, experience, and evaluation – the visitor's potential for scrutiny and rejection of himself and his country. The inevitable question, "How do you like it here?" which the foreigner abhors, is the host's quest for reassurance, or at least the "feeler" that reduces the unknown and gives him ground for defense if that seems necessary.

The foreign member of the dyad is under the same threat, with the added tension of having to cope with the differing pace, climate, and culture. The first few months he feels helpless in coping with messages that swamp him and to which his reactions may be inappropriate. His self-esteem is often intolerably undermined when be employs such defenses as withdrawal into his own reference group[13] or into himself, screening out or misperceiving stimuli, rationalizing, overcompensating, even hostility – none of which leads to effective communication.

Conclusion

Since all of the communication barriers mentioned are hard to remove, the only simple solution seems to be to tell everybody to stay home. This advice obviously is unacceptable, so it is fortunate that a few paths are being laid around the obstacles. Communication theorists are continuing to offer new insights and are focusing on problem areas of this complex process (see Ruesch and Bateson). Educators and linguists are improving methods of learning a second language. The nonverbal area, made familiar by Edward T. Hall in his famous books *The Silent Language* and *The Hidden Dimension,* is getting a singular amount of attention (see, for example, Mehrabian). The ray of hope offered by Hall and others is that nonverbal cues, culturally controlled and largely out-of-awareness, can be discovered and even understood when the communicator knows enough to look for them, is alert to the varying interpretations possible, and is free enough from tension and psychological defenses to notice them.

In addition, textbooks are appearing and communication specialists are improving means for increasing sensitivity to the messages coming from others in an intercultural setting (see, for eample, Stewart, "Simulation"; Kraemer; Hoopes).

---

[13] *reference group:* the group of people with whom one has something in common, such as nationality or native language

Professional associations are giving increased amounts of attention to intercultural communication, and new societies such as the Society for Intercultural Education, Training and Research are being developed. The International and Intercultural Communication Annual has a complete listing of these (Speech Communication Assn.).

What the interpersonal intercultural communicator must seek to achieve can be summarized by two quotations: The first is by Roger Harrison, who says:

> The communicator cannot stop at knowing that the people he is working with have different customs, goals, and thought patterns from his own. He must be able to feel his way into intimate contact with them and within them, neither losing his own values in the confrontation nor protecting himself behind a wall of intellectual detatchment (4).

Robert T. Oliver phrases it thus: "If we would communicate across cultural barriers, we must learn what to say and how to say it in terms of the expectations and predispositions of those we want to listen" (154).

Works Cited

Becker, Ernest. *The Birth and Death of Meaning*. New York: Free Press, 1962.

Bem, Daryl J. *Beliefs, Attitudes, and Human Affairs*. Belmont, CA: Brooks / Cole, 1970.

Frankel, Charles. *The Neglected Aspect of Foreign Affairs*. Washington, D.C.: Brookings Inst., 1965.

Hall, Edward T. *The Hidden Dimension*. New York: Doubleday, 1966.

————. *The Silent Language*. Greenwich, CT: Fawcett, 1959.

Harrison, Roger. "The Design of Cross-Cultural Training: An Alternative to the University Model." *Explorations in Human Relations Training and Research*. Bethesda, MD: Natl Training Laboratories, 1966.

Hoopes, David, ed. *Readings in Intercultural Communication*. Vol. 1–4. Pittsburgh, PA: U. of Pittsburgh, Regional Council Intl. Educ., 1975.

International and Intercultural Communication Annual. Vol. 1. New York: Speech Communication Assoc., 1974.

Kraemer, Alfred J. *The Development of Cultural Self-Awareness: Design of a Program of Instruction*. Washington, D.C.: GWU. HR Research Office, 1969.

Mead, Margaret. "The Cultural Perspective." *Communication or Conflict*. Ed. Mary Capes. New York: Association Press, 1960.

Mehrabian, Albert. *Silent Messages*. Belmont, CA: Wadsworth, 1971.

Oliver, Robert T. *Culture and Communication: The Problem of Penetrating National and Cultural Boundaries*. Springfield, IL: Charles C. Thomas, 1962.

Ruesch, Jurgen, and Gregory Bateson. *Communication: The Social Matrix of Psychiatry*. New York: Norton, 1968.

Sherif, Carolyn W., Musafe Sherif, and Roger E. Nebergall. *Attitude and Attitude Change*. Philadelphia: Saunders, 1965.

Singer, Marshall R. "Culture: A Perceptual Approach." Hoopes. Vol. 1.

Stewart, Edward C. *American Cultural Patterns: A Cross-Cultural Perspective*. Pittsburgh, PA: Univ. of Pittsburgh, Regional Council Intl. Educ., 1971.

————."The Simulation of Cultural Differences." *The Journal of Communication* 16 (1966).

▓ Write After You Read

1. Write a journal entry in response to "Intercultural Communication Stumbling Blocks" using the guidelines on page 11.

2. Summarize the reading in one or two sentences by explaining what you perceive to be Barna's main point.

▓ Discuss After You Read

1. Define in your own words each of the five major stumbling blocks that Barna identifies as interfering with successful communication across cultures. Then describe any experiences you have had with these stumbling blocks:

   a Language
   b Nonverbal signs and symbols
   c Preconceptions and stereotypes
   d The tendency to evaluate
   e High anxiety

2. Do any of your experiences contradict what Barna is saying, or do you disapprove of the way she has presented the ideas and experiences? Explain.

3. Has Barna neglected to discuss other common cross-cultural communication barriers? If so, what are they?

4. What are Barna's solutions to the problem of intercultural communication? Do you believe her solutions will be successful? Based on your own experience, can you provide other solutions?

5. Examine how Barna structures her essay. Compare and contrast the introduction with the conclusion. Which ideas are similar? Which ideas are different? What purpose does the middle of the essay serve? How does this structure help you to follow Barna's ideas?

6. How does Barna's discussion of intercultural communication help to explain the experiences in Zitkala-Ša's "School Days of an Indian Girl" (pages 24–29), Alvarez's "My English" (pages 30–34), Yezierska's "College" (pages 35–41), or Tan's "Mother Tongue" (pages 46–51)?

Reading 2

■ Write Before You Read

Before reading "Social Time: The Heartbeat of Culture" by Robert Levine, write for several minutes about the role that time plays in your life or culture.

Social Time: The Heartbeat of Culture

Robert Levine, with Ellen Wolff

Robert Levine, professor of psychology at California State University at Fresno, collaborated with Ellen Wolff, a freelance writer, to write "Social Time: The Heartbeat of Culture." Levine is also the author of A Geography of Time: The Temporal Misadventures of a Social Psychologist, or How Every Culture Keeps Time Just a Little Bit Differently *(1997) and* The Power of Persuasion: How We're Bought and Sold *(2003). "Social Time: The Heartbeat of Culture" was originally published in* Psychology Today, *a monthly magazine that presents research findings to a nonprofessional audience.*

"If a man does not keep pace with his companions, perhaps it is because he hears a different drummer." This thought by Thoreau strikes a chord in so many people that it has become part of our language. We use the phrase "the beat of a different drummer" to explain any pace of life unlike our own. Such colorful vagueness reveals how informal our rules of time really are. The world over, children simply "pick up" their society's time concepts as they mature. No dictionary clearly defines the meaning of "early" or "late" for them or for strangers who stumble over the maddening incongruities between the time sense they bring with them and the one they face in a new land.

I learned this firsthand, a few years ago, and the resulting culture shock led me halfway around the world to find answers. It seemed clear that time "talks." But what is it telling us?

My journey started shortly after I accepted an appointment as visiting professor of psychology at the federal university in Niteroi, Brazil, a midsized city across the bay from Rio de Janeiro. As I left home for my first day of class, I asked someone the time. It was 9:05 A.M., which allowed me time to relax and look around the campus before my 10 o'clock lecture. After what I judged to be half an hour, I glanced at a clock I was passing. It said 10:20! In panic, I broke for the classroom, followed by gentle calls of "Hola,[1] professor" and "Tudo bem,[2] professor?" from unhurried students, many of whom, I later realized, were my own. I arrived breathless to find an empty room.

Frantically, I asked a passerby the time. "Nine forty-five" was the answer. No, that couldn't be. I asked someone else. "Nine fifty-five." Another said: "Exactly 9:43." The clock in a nearby office read 3:15. I had learned my first lesson about Brazilians: Their timepieces are consistently inaccurate. And nobody minds.

[1] *Hola:* "Hi" in Portuguese
[2] *Tudo bem:* "Is everything OK?" in Portuguese

My class was scheduled from 10 until noon. Many students came late, some very late. Several arrived after 10:30. A few showed up closer to 11. Two came after that. All of the latecomers wore the relaxed smiles that I came, later, to enjoy. Each one said hello, although a few apologized briefly, none seemed terribly concerned about lateness. They assumed that I understood.

The idea of Brazilians arriving late was not a great shock. I had heard about "manhã," the Portuguese equivalent of "mañana" in Spanish. This term, meaning "tomorrow" or "the morning," stereotypes the Brazilian who puts off the business of today until tomorrow. The real surprise came at noon that first day, when the end of class arrived.

Back home in California, I never need to look at a clock to know when the class hour is ending. The shuffling of books is accompanied by strained expressions that say plaintively, "I'm starving. . . . I've got to go to the bathroom. . . . I'm going to suffocate if you keep us one more second." (The pain usually becomes unbearable at two minutes to the hour in undergraduate classes and five minutes before the close of graduate classes.)

When noon arrived in my first Brazilian class, only a few students left immediately. Others slowly drifted out during the next 15 minutes, and some continued asking me questions long after that. When several remaining students kicked off their shoes at 12:30, I went into my own "starving/bathroom/suffocation" routine.

I could not, in all honesty, attribute their lingering to my superb teaching style. I had just spent two hours lecturing on statistics in halting Portuguese. Apparently, for many of my students, staying late was simply of no more importance than arriving late in the first place. As I observed this casual approach in infinite variations during the year, I learned that the "manhã" stereotype oversimplified the real Anglo/Brazilian differences in conceptions of time. Research revealed a more complex picture.

With the assistance of colleagues Laurie West and Harry Reis, I compared the time sense of 91 male and female students in Niteroi with that of 107 similar students at California State University in Fresno. The universities are similar in academic quality and size, and the cities are both secondary metropolitan centers with populations of about 350,000.

We asked students about their perceptions of time in several situations, such as what they could consider late or early for a hypothetical lunch appointment with a friend. The average Brazilian student defined lateness for lunch as $33\frac{1}{2}$ minutes after the scheduled time, compared to 19 minutes for the Fresno students. But Brazilians also allowed an average of about 54 minutes before they'd consider someone early, while the Fresno students drew the line at 24.

Are Brazilians simply more flexible in their concepts of time and punctuality? And how does this relate to the stereotype of the apathetic, fatalistic and irresponsible Latin temperament? When we asked students to give typical reasons for lateness, the Brazilians were less likely to attribute it to a lack of caring than the North Americans were. Instead, they pointed to unforeseen circumstances that the person couldn't control. Because they seemed less inclined to feel personally responsible for being late, they also expressed less regret for their own lateness and blamed others less when they were late.

We found similar differences in how students from the two countries characterized people who were late for appointments. Unlike their North American counterparts, the Brazilian students believed that a person who is consistently late is probably more successful than one who is consistently on time. They seemed to accept the idea that someone of status is expected to arrive late. Lack of punctuality is a badge of success.

Even within our own country, of course, ideas of time and punctuality vary considerably from place to place. Different regions and even cities have their own distinct rhythms and rules. Seemingly simple words like "now," snapped out by an impatient New Yorker, and "later," said by a relaxed Californian, suggest a world of difference. Despite our familiarity with these homegrown differences in tempo, problems with time present a major stumbling block to Americans abroad. Peace Corps volunteers told researchers James Spradley of Macalester College and Mark Phillips of the University of Washington that their greatest difficulties with other people, after language problems, were the general pace of life and the punctuality of others. Formal "clock time" may be a standard on which the world agrees, but "social time," the heartbeat of society, is something else again.

How a country paces its social life is a mystery to most outsiders, one that we're just beginning to unravel. Twenty-six years ago, anthropologist Edward Hall noted in *The Silent Language* that informal patterns of time "are seldom, if ever, made explicit. They exist in the air around us. They are either familiar and comfortable, or unfamiliar and wrong." When we realize we are out of step, we often blame the people around us to make ourselves feel better.

Appreciating cultural differences in time sense becomes increasingly important as modern communications put more and more people in daily contact. If we are to avoid misreading issues that involve time perceptions, we need to understand better our own cultural biases and those of others.

When people of different cultures interact, the potential for misunderstanding exists on many levels. For example, members of Arab and Latin cultures usually stand much closer when they are speaking to people than we usually do in the United States, a fact we frequently misinterpret as aggression or disrespect. Similarly, we assign personality traits to groups with a pace of life that is markedly faster or slower than our own. We build ideas of national character, for example, around the traditional Swiss and German ability to "make the trains run on time." Westerners like ourselves define punctuality using precise measures of time: 5 minutes, 15 minutes, an hour. But according to Hall, in many Mediterranean

New York, New York: Pounding the pavement at a pretty pace.

Tokyo, Japan: Lead, follow, or get out of the way.

Arab cultures there are only three sets of time: no time at all, now (which is of varying duration) and forever (too long). Because of this, Americans often find difficulty in getting Arabs to distinguish between waiting a long time and a very long time.

According to historian Will Durant, "No man in a hurry is quite civilized." What do our time judgments say about our attitude toward life? How can a North American, coming from a land of digital precision, relate to a North African who may consider a clock "the devil's mill"?

Each language has a vocabulary of time that does not always survive translation. When we translated our questionnaires into Portuguese for my Brazilian students, we found that English distinctions of time were not readily articulated in their language. Several of our questions concerned how long the respondent would wait for someone to arrive, as compared with when they hoped for arrival or actually expected the person would come. In Portuguese, the verbs "to wait for," "to hope for" and "to expect" are all translated as "esperar." We had to add further words of explanation to make the distinction clear to the Brazilian students.

To avoid these language problems, my Fresno colleague Kathy Bartlett and I decided to clock the pace of life in other countries by using as little language as possible. We looked directly at three basic indicators of time: the accuracy of a country's bank clocks, the speed at which pedestrians walked and the average time it took a postal clerk to sell us a single stamp. In six countries on three continents, we made observations in both the nation's largest urban area and a medium-sized city: Japan (Tokyo and Sendai), Taiwan (Taipei and Tainan), Indonesia (Jakarta and Solo), Italy (Rome and Florence), England (London and Bristol) and the United States (New York City and Rochester).

What we wanted to know was: Can we speak of a unitary concept called "pace of life"? What we've learned suggests that we can. There appears to be a very

Florence, Italy: Living at a leisurely pace, particularly at the post office.

strong relationship (see chart on page 81) between the accuracy of clock time, walking speed and postal efficiency across the countries we studied.

We checked 15 clocks in each city, selecting them at random in downtown banks and comparing the time they showed with that reported by the local telephone company. In Japan, which leads the way in accuracy, the clocks averaged just over half a minute early or late. Indonesian clocks, the least accurate, were more than three minutes off the mark.

I will be interested to see how the digital-information age will affect our perceptions of time. In the United States today, we are reminded of the exact hour of the day more than ever, through little symphonies of beeps emanating from people's digital watches. As they become the norm, I fear our sense of precision may take an absurd twist. The other day, when I asked for the time, a student looked at his watch and replied, "Three twelve and eighteen seconds."

"'Will you walk a little faster?' said a whiting to a snail. 'There's a porpoise close behind us, and he's treading on my tail.'"

So goes the rhyme from *Alice in Wonderland*, which also gave us that famous symbol of haste, the White Rabbit. He came to mind often as we measured the walking speeds in our experimental cities. We clocked how long it took pedestrians to walk 100 feet along a main downtown street during business hours on clear days. To eliminate the effects of socializing, we observed only people walking alone, timing at least 100 in each city. We found, once again, that the Japanese led the way, averaging just 20.7 seconds to cover the distance. The English nosed out the Americans for second place – 21.6 to 22.5 seconds – and the Indonesians again trailed the pack, sauntering along at 27.2 seconds. As you might guess, speed was greater in the larger city of each nation than in its smaller one.

Solo, Indonesia: Volleyball, anyone? There's always time for a friendly game.

Our final measurement, the average time it took postal clerks to sell one stamp, turned out to be less straightforward than we expected. In each city, including those in the United States, we presented clerks with a note in the native language requesting a common-priced stamp. . . . They were also handed paper money, the equivalent of a $5 bill. In Indonesia, this procedure led to more than we bargained for.

At the large central post office in Jakarta, I asked for the line to buy stamps and was directed to a group of private vendors sitting outside. Each of them hustled for my business: "Hey, good stamps, mister!" "Best stamps here!" In the smaller city of Solo, I found a volleyball game in progress when I arrived at the main post office on Friday afternoon. Business hours, I was told, were over. When I finally did get there during business hours, the clerk was more interested in discussing relatives in America. Would I like to meet his uncle in Cincinnati? Which did I like better: California or the United States? Five people behind me in line waited patiently: Instead of complaining, they began paying attention to our conversation.

When it came to efficiency of service, however, the Indonesians were not the slowest, although they did place far behind the Japanese postal clerks, who averaged 25 seconds. That distinction went to the Italians, whose infamous postal service took 47 seconds on the average.

"A man who wastes one hour of time has not discovered the meaning of life. . . ."

That was Charles Darwin's belief, and many share it, perhaps at the cost of their health. My colleagues and I have recently begun studying the relationship between pace of life and well-being. Other researchers have demonstrated that a chronic sense of urgency is a basic component of the Type A, coronary-prone personality. We expect that future research will demonstrate that pace of life is related to rate of heart disease, hypertension, ulcers, suicide, alcoholism, divorce and other indicators of general psychological and physical well-being.

THE PACE OF LIFE IN SIX COUNTRIES			
	Accuracy of Bank Clocks	Walking Speed	Post Office Speed
Japan	1	1	1
United States	2	3	2
England	4	2	3
Italy	5	4	6
Taiwan	3	5	4
Indonesia	6	6	5

Numbers (1 is top value) indicate the comparitive rankings of each country for each indicator of time sense.

As you envision tomorrow's international society, do you wonder who will set the pace? Americans eye Japan carefully, because the Japanese are obviously "ahead of us" in measurable ways. In both countries, speed is frequently confused with progress. Perhaps looking carefully at the different paces of life around the world will help us distinguish more accurately between the two qualities. Clues are everywhere but sometimes hard to distinguish. You have to listen carefully to hear the beat of even your own drummer.

■ Write After You Read

1 Write a journal entry in response to "Social Time: The Heartbeat of Culture" using the guidelines on page 11.

2 Summarize the reading in one or two sentences by explaining what you perceive to be Levine's main point.

■ Discuss After You Read

1 Have you experienced a difference in time sense (e.g., punctuality) in adapting to a new culture or place? If so, explain how the time sense is different by contrasting specific examples from each culture or place. Have these experiences affected your attitude or behavior?

2 Have you experienced a different pace of life (e.g., pace of walking) in adapting to a new culture or place? If so, explain how the pace of life is different by contrasting specific examples from each culture or place. Have these experiences affected your attitude or behavior?

3 Do any of your experiences contradict what Levine is saying, or do you disapprove of the way he has presented the ideas and experiences? Explain.

4 Has reading this article helped you understand your own culture or influenced the way you perceive people from a different cultural background? Explain.

5 Examine how Levine and Wolff structure their article. Note when the authors switch back and forth from making a point to sharing personal experience to reporting on research findings. How do they make the transition from one style to another? Which words give cues to readers that the style will change? What effect do these changes have on you as a reader?

6 How does Barna's discussion of nonverbal communication on pages 66–74 help to explain Levine's examples of nonverbal communication?

Reading 3

■ Write Before You Read

Before reading "Creativity in the Classroom" by Ernest L. Boyer, write for several minutes about your definition of creativity in the classroom.

Creativity in the Classroom

Ernest L. Boyer

Ernest L. Boyer (1928–1995) helped to shape education in the United States as Chancellor of the State University of New York, as U.S. Commissioner of Education, and as President of the Carnegie Foundation for the Advancement of Teaching. His publications include School Reform: A National Strategy *(1989) and* The Basic School: A Community for Learning *(1995). "Creativity in the Classroom" is the ninth chapter of Boyer's book,* College: The Undergraduate Experience in America, *a report on research sponsored by the Carnegie Foundation for the Advancement of Teaching, which included numerous team visits to public and private colleges and universities.*

At a freshman psychology lecture we attended, 300 students were still finding seats when the professor started talking. "Today," he said into the microphone, "we will continue our discussion of learning." He might as well have been addressing a crowd in a Greyhound bus terminal. Like commuters marking time until their next departure, students in this class alternately read the newspaper, flipped through a paperback novel, or propped their feet on the chairs ahead of them, staring into space. Only when the professor defined a term which, he said, "might appear on an exam" did they look up and start taking notes.

What we found in many classrooms was a mismatch between faculty and student expectations, a gap that left both parties unfulfilled. Faculty, concerned with scholarship, wanted to share ideas with students, who were expected to appreciate what professors do. This appreciation might exist in graduate or upper-division courses, where teachers and students have overlapping interests, but we found that often this was not the case in lower-division courses.

"If you're batting .666 in attendance, you're doing well," one faculty member complained, implying that if only two out of three students attend a class, it was a success. Another asserted: "Students don't seem to have the attention span they used to. It's hard to hold their interest. You practically have to do a song and dance, and I won't do that." An English teacher described the learning climate on his campus as one of "intellectual meekness."

As for students, they are remarkably conscious of grades, willing to conform to the formula for success. A sophomore in a pre-med program said she wanted her courses to be spelled out "with no surprises. My goal is to get a good background so I can pass the MCAT [Medical College Admission Test] and I'm not interested in hearing about the professor's Ph.D. dissertation."

"A college degree isn't enough," said one honors student. "You've got to have a good GPA to get into graduate school, or get a first-rate job." Another commented: "People at this college are very résumé-conscious. Undergraduates are afraid of controversy. They hesitate to participate in vigorous give and take on any topic. The main thing is to prepare for the exam."

If faculty and students do not see themselves as having important business to do together, prospects for effective learning are diminished. If students view teachers as distant and their material as irrelevant, what could be a time of exciting exploration is reduced to a series of uninspired routines.

The most discouraging comment came from a professor who said he *liked* the passivity of students. "With these students, not everything has to be proven. . . . Some people say this is a return to the fifties. Perhaps, and that isn't all bad. . . . We didn't feel we knew it all and neither do they. For the first time in a while, I don't feel a generation gap" (Yaffe 7).

This "no hassle" attitude was vividly revealed in the classroom at a prestigious Northeast college. Students in a Gothic fiction course had been asked to read all of Peter Straub's novel *Ghost Story*. When they assembled the following Monday morning, only six of the sixty students in a large lecture hall raised their hands when asked who had done the reading. A few volunteered that they were halfway through the novel, but most admitted that they hadn't cracked the book. The professor then took all of his ninety-minute lecture to review the plot. Some students took notes. At the end of class he apologized: "I'm sorry if I spoiled the finish for those of you who haven't gotten there yet." But no one looked disappointed. They'd just received all the information they needed for an upcoming test and wouldn't have to read.

A science professor stated this frustration: "How am I to cover difficult and important material when students are unwilling to really work? Sure, they'll cram for tests but they want to be spoon-fed, and when I try to get them interested in more substantial matters only a few respond. I'm pretty discouraged with students."

Students are just as quick to switch the blame to their professors. One student said, "Why should I be interested in the class if the professor acts bored?" Another student agreed and added, "There's nothing worse than my biology professor, who acts as though he's doing us a big favor by teaching us about photosynthesis. Believe me, he's not doing me a favor." Still another student said, "Most of my professors are great. But I have one who makes it clear that he'd rather be in his laboratory conducting research than standing in front of two hundred students."

At a large university with many teaching assistants who handle labs and discussion sections, students resent the lack of attention from the professor, suspecting (correctly) that only the T.A. will see and grade their work during the course of the quarter. In particular departments, foreign teaching assistants are a problem. Mathematicians, according to the arts and science dean, are "hard to hire in this city, unless they're foreign students who can barely speak English."

Students are quick to praise their teachers, too. One said, "I love my history professor. I don't even like history but he makes it so interesting that I really want to go to class." Another said, "I like the professors who have a sense of humor. They come into class, joke around a little, and then start the lecture." Students also praise their professors for being available after class. Another student: "The professors here will go out of their way to find time to see if you need help or want to discuss something." Said another: "This college has a good academic reputation. So, I knew the classes were going to be hard. I didn't know they were going to be as hard as they are, though. Still, that's why I'm here."

One sophomore said, "My biology teacher is the worst. He is all biology. He comes in and starts talking. It's like he's not even human." She continued, "But my French teacher is great. He comes into class, talks informally with us before he begins the lecture. I feel like he really gets to know his students." A senior engineering major said, "The best teachers are those that really care about their students. I've never had a professor who wouldn't find time to talk with you after class, but some professors really make an effort to get to know their students. I also like professors who act like they're interested in what they're teaching."

This mixed response, the ambivalence we found to teaching and learning, was reinforced in our national survey. Most students are quite satisfied with the teaching on their campus, but the pressure to get good grades diminishes their enthusiasm. Almost two-thirds say they are under great pressure to get high grades; about one-third feel it is difficult to get good grades and still "really learn something." Forty-three percent of today's undergraduates also say that many students at their institutions succeeded by "beating the system" rather than by studying. The cheating on assignments, the term papers students buy, the shortcuts to duplicating homework assignments – all enhance the cynicism of students and erode the quality of education.

Do professors take a personal interest in the academic progress of their students? At liberal arts colleges 73 percent of the students feel they do. The proportion dropped to 59 percent when all institutions were counted. On the matter of classroom participation, we found that 81 percent of liberal arts college students feel they are encouraged to "discuss their feelings about important issues"; but that's true for only 66 percent of the total sample. Students at liberal arts colleges are also far more satisfied with the teaching they receive. And a higher percentage of these students believe their teachers look out for their interests.

On a nonacademic level, students at liberal arts colleges are more inclined to seek personal advice from professors than are students at all institutions. When asked whether professors encourage them to participate in classroom discussion, 91 percent of the students at liberal arts colleges said yes – 10 percent more than undergraduates at all colleges and universities.

Class size, like so many other aspects of teaching and learning, varies from one type of institution to another. Twenty-nine percent of the students at research universities report that "most" or "all" of their classes have more than one hundred students enrolled; at liberal arts colleges only 1 percent of the students report having most or all classes of this size. At the other end, only 5 percent of students at research universities said they had no classes larger than one hundred students. At liberal arts colleges, it was 80 percent.

We also discovered that, for most undergraduates, the freshman and sophomore classes (often the general education sections) are the ones most likely to be overloaded. Further, we found that at large institutions these classes are often taught by graduate assistants or junior professors. Forty-one percent of the students we surveyed report that "general education courses are rarely taught by the best faculty members in the departments in which they are given." And 37 percent said, "General education courses reflect the interests of the faculty" rather than of the students.

We concluded that one important way to measure a college's commitment to undergraduate education is to look at class size in general education. Do these courses enroll hundreds of students? Are they taught by senior professors? Do students have an opportunity to meet with their teachers? A college or university that does not give top priority to the basic undergraduate courses is not fully committed to excellence in education.

A significant number of students we interviewed said they had no objection to being in a large lecture course; others, however, strongly favored small classes that allow discussion. A math professor in a small university went so far as to say that if he had been introduced to mathematics in the kind of large, distracting lecture hall he himself was teaching in, he would never have continued to study the subject. We strongly urge, therefore, that the finest teachers should teach freshmen, and that undergraduate classes should he small enough for students to have lively intellectual interaction with teachers and fellow students.

In the early American college the primary method of instruction was recitation, a process in which students repeated from memory, often verbatim, textbook assignments. For disputation, students defended or attacked a proposition in Latin, the required language both in and out of class (Levine 171). By the mid-eighteenth century, the lecture by teachers occasionally supplemented student recitations. Lectures were, however, a talking textbook as instructors read slowly and students copied down what was said, word for word.

The lecture slowly replaced recitation and disputations. There was new knowledge to be conveyed, and it became more difficult to call on all students in the enlarged classes. Another sign of the times: The blackboard was first used by a teacher at Bowdoin College in about 1823 (Levine 173). And experiments with the seminar, a German import, were introduced in the mid-nineteenth century. According to Arthur Levine, in his significant *Handbook on Undergraduate Curriculum*, it was in 1869 that Charles Kendall Adams tried the seminar at The University of Michigan. "Seven years later it became a staple in the curriculum at Johns Hopkins. . . . A discussion class, designed to supplement lecture instruction originally called the 'conference quiz section,' was created at Harvard in 1904" (173).

Today, the lecture method is preferred by most professors. With few exceptions, when we visited classes, the teacher stood in front of rows of chairs and talked most of the forty-five or fifty minutes. Information was presented that often students passively received. There was little opportunity for positions to be clarified or ideas challenged.

There are times, of course, when lecturing is necessary to convey essential issues and ideas and also to handle large numbers of students. At other times, such a procedure seems inappropriate, especially when the class is small and much of the material being presented is available in the text.

When discussion did occur in classes we visited, a handful of students, usually men, dominated the exchange. We were especially struck by the subtle yet significant differences in the way men and women participated in class. This situation persists despite the ascendancy of female enrollments on most campuses.

Women now make up over half of all undergraduate enrollments and they get the majority of bachelor's and master's degrees. In 1963 about half of all women undergraduates majored in education. In 1983 only 15 percent were doing so. They receive 32 percent of the academic doctorates awarded, 25 percent of those in medicine, and 33 percent in law (Hacker 7).

Still, in many classrooms women are overshadowed. Even the brightest women students often remain silent. They may submit excellent written work, and will frequently wait until after class to approach a teacher privately about issues raised in the discussion. But it is the men who seem most often to be recognized and talk most in class. Not only do men talk more, but what they say often carries more weight. This pattern of classroom leaders and followers is set very early in the term (see Hall and Sandler 7–8).

We agree with Mortimer Adler's conclusion that "all genuine learning is active, not passive. It involves the use of the mind, not just the memory. It is a process of discovery in which the student is the main agent, not the teacher" (23). And all students, not just the most aggressive or most verbal, should be actively engaged. It is unacceptable for a few students to participate in the give and take with teachers while others are allowed to be mere spectators.

On a related matter, we frequently were struck by the competitive climate in the classroom. Since as a democracy we are committed to equality of opportunity, and since in a vital society we need some way of bringing talent forward, we use, both on and off the campus, the calculus of competition to stimulate ambition and achievement. We must do this, or else we lack essential leadership in all areas of life.

However, if democracy is to be well served, cooperation is essential too. And the goal of community, which is threaded throughout this report, is essentially related to the academic program, and, most especially, to procedures in the classroom. We urge, therefore, that students be asked to participate in collaborative projects, that they work together occasionally on group assignments, that special effort be made, through small seminar units within large lecture sections, to create conditions that underscore the point that cooperation is as essential as competition in the classroom.

The undergraduate experience, at its best, means active learning and disciplined inquiry that leads to the intellectual empowerment of students. Professor Carl Schorake, at Princeton University, says that the test of a good teacher is "Do you regard 'learning' as a noun or a verb? If as a noun, as a thing to be possessed and passed along, then you present your truths, neatly packaged, to your students. But if you see 'learning' as a verb! – the process is different" (McCleery 106).

While the college teaching we observed was often uninspired, we still found exciting examples of outstanding teaching at many institutions. One professor of English spoke to our site visitor as follows: "At this college there's a lot of emphasis on teaching and there's a lot of good teaching. I like that because teaching is my real vocation. I feel most strongly about that." Another professor also enthusiastically endorsed his role as teacher: "This college is not filled with many academic bright lights. Students work hard and they really care about their studies. The fact that many are 'average' doesn't bother me. My favorite image of a teacher is that of the midwife encouraging students, coaching them. What you really do in the classroom is help students come to know their own mind – become independent thinkers. These students have potential, but they have to have more confidence academically. It's our job to bring it out of them."

One Monday morning, at a New England college, we visited an "Introduction to Philosophy" course. The subject for the day was a problem from Thomas Aquinas: If God is all-powerful and all-good, how can there be evil in the world? The students offered answers: because salvation must be achieved through suffering, because Adam's sin produced suffering, because God just set the world in motion and didn't know how everything would turn out. "You're revising the premise," the professor responded to the last answer. "Your God is not all-powerful, he's only good-intentioned."

A student asked: "Why would you worship a God who is not all-powerful?" "Why not?" asked another. And so it went, with many hands raised and ideas flowing so fast that the professor had to intervene often to sort out key points and keep the discussion on course. "Today's students are poorly equipped to deal with questions about ethics," he told us later. "I think they're unaccustomed to reasoning." Yet, he persisted in engaging students in active forms of inquiry, providing them experience in addressing questions of ethics and challenging them to learn.

At a public institution in the West, we visited a mid-afternoon class in European history, with about one hundred students. The day's lecture was on the influence of the writings of the French philosophers on the enlightened despots of the eighteenth century. "Did Voltaire and Diderōt favor a radical reconstruction of society?" the professor asked.

"No, they just wanted to reform society in some ways," a student answered.

"What ways?" the professor probed.

"To make it more rational."

"How can people be made more rational?"

"Through education."

"Did the Enlightenment writers want to introduce mass public education?"

"No, they still favored the aristocracy."

"Why was that?"

This exchange continued through a discussion of how uniform legal codes developed. The professor lectured briefly, highlighting key themes, but he never stopped asking penetrating questions – and expecting thoughtful answers.

In an upper-division constitutional law class the professor used the "case method." Each student had been assigned to read summaries of a series of cases dealing with the president, Congress, and the courts. Guiding the discussion, the teacher would name a case and tell a student to give him "the principles we can take from this example." The classroom discussion was lively, with the instructor making it a point to call on different students instead of waiting for them to respond. He occasionally digressed from the set format with interesting historical asides, discussing, for example, Earl Warren's role in the internment of Japanese citizens during World War II. He also tried, when possible, to tell students what was going on in the Supreme Court right now that related to the issues and cases they discussed.

In a class in the history of modern music, we watched the instructor, through a combination of knowledge, enthusiasm, humor, recordings, and exercises, keep the class engaged – even excited – through a ninety-minute session on the early technique in the music of Arnold Schönberg. In a freshman chemistry class, the professor spent the entire period on problem-solving techniques, hoping to break students of the habit of "looking for plug-in formulas" to solve problems.

In a seminar called "Women in Literature," some students who were obviously not impressed with *Jane Eyre* were kept intellectually engaged through a compelling and at times humorous lecture style. "So she faints. Why? Look, you can't have a nineteenth-century novel without somebody fainting. All right? All right." Then: "Okay, let's go through some of your objections to the novel. The diction is first on the list, right?"

At a New England college, we visited a course in French literature conducted entirely in French. The seventeen students enrolled had read Rousseau's *Discourse on the Origin of Inequality* for homework. In class, the professor asked questions about the style and substance of the work: What does Rousseau say is the basis of human inequality? How would people label Rousseau were he to present his ideas today? What was the source of evil for Rousseau? For whom was he writing? What was his tone? Students seemed generally comfortable with discussing the work in French and were able to pinpoint passages from the text to illustrate their answers.

The professor corrected their grammar and pronunciation from time to time. One student, for example, spoke as if *l'amour du bien-être* – love of comfort – were the same as *l'amour* – love. The professor asked her to translate the words literally into English, and she figured out her mistake for herself. But the professor's main emphasis was at least as much on creativity, on original thinking, as on the mastery of French.

The central qualities that make for successful teaching can be simply stated: command of the material to be taught, a contagious enthusiasm for the play of ideas, optimism about human potential, the involvement with one's students, and – not least – sensitivity, integrity, and warmth as a human being. When this combination is present in the classroom, the impact of a teacher can be powerful and enduring.

Works Cited

Adler, Mortimer J. *The Paideia Proposal: An Educational Manifesto*. New York: Macmillan, 1982.

Hacker, Andrew. "The Decline of Higher Learning." *New York Review of Books* 13 Feb. 1986: 7.

Hall, Roberta M., and Bernice R. Sandler. *The Classroom Climate: A Chilly One for Women?* Washington: Assoc. Amer. Coll., 1982.

Levine, Arthur. *Handbook on Undergraduate Curriculum*. San Francisco: Jossey-Bass, 1978.

McCleery, William. *Conversations on the Character of Princeton*. Princeton: Princeton UP, 1986.

Yaffe, Elaine. "What Are Today's Students Really Like?" *Colorado College Bulletin* Feb. 1985: 7.

▓ Write After You Read

1 Write a journal entry in response to "Creativity in the Classroom" using the guidelines on page 11.

2 Summarize the reading in one or two sentences by explaining what you perceive to be Boyer's main point.

▓ Discuss After You Read

1 How have your experiences with college lectures been similar to or different from Boyer's descriptions of college lectures? Provide specific examples in your response.

2 How have your experiences with active learning been similar to or different from Boyer's descriptions of active learning? Provide specific examples in your response.

3 What problem does Boyer identify, and what reasons does he provide to explain why the problem exists? Can you think of other reasons that might explain these circumstances?

4 What is Boyer's solution to the problem he identifies? Do you agree with his solution? Explain.

5 Examine how Boyer structures his chapter. What kind of information or ideas are provided in the opening paragraphs? What kind of details and examples are provided in the middle paragraphs? What information or ideas are provided in the ending? How does this structure help you to follow Boyer's thinking?

6 How might Boyer evaluate the teachers in Zitkala-Ša's "The School Days of an Indian Girl" (pages 24–29), Yezierska's "College" (pages 35–41), or Alvarez's "My English" (pages 30–34)?

Reading 4

▇ Write Before You Read

Before reading "The Art of Reading" by Lin Yutang, write for several minutes about one or more of the following topics: (1) your earliest memory of reading or being read to, (2) your most positive experience with reading, (3) your most negative experience with reading.

The Art of Reading

Lin Yutang

Lin Yutang (1895–1976) was born in Amory, Fukien Province, China. He attended English-language schools, graduated from St. John's University in Shanghai, and received a master's degree in literature from Harvard University and a Ph.D. in linguistics from the University of Leipzig. Later, Lin became a college professor at Peking National University and dean of humanities at Hsiamun University. He also lived in the United States and France. A writer in both Chinese and English, Lin wrote the novels A Moment in Peking *(1939) and* Chinatown Family *(1948) and the nonfiction works* My Country and My People *(1935) and* Chinese Theory of Art *(1967). "The Art of Reading" was originally published in Lin's book of essays,* The Importance of Living.

Reading or the enjoyment of books has always been regarded among the charms of a cultured life and is respected and envied by those who rarely give themselves that privilege. This is easy to understand when we compare the difference between the life of a man who does no reading and that of a man who does. The man who has not the habit of reading is imprisoned in his immediate world, in respect to time and space. His life falls into a set routine; he is limited to contact and conversation with a few friends and acquaintances, and he sees only what happens in his immediate neighborhood. From this prison there is no escape. But the moment he takes up a book, he immediately enters a different world, and if it is a good book, he is immediately put in touch with one of the best talkers of the world. This talker leads him on and carries him into a different country or a different age, or unburdens to him some of his personal regrets, or discusses with him some special line or aspect of life that the reader knows nothing about. An ancient author puts him in communion with a dead spirit of long ago, and as he reads along, he begins to imagine what that ancient author looked like and what type of person he was. Both Mencius and Ssemna Ch'ien, China's greatest historian, have expressed the same idea. Now to be able to live two hours out of twelve in a different world and take one's thoughts off the claims of the immediate present is, of course, a privilege to be envied by people shut up in their bodily prison. Such a change of environment is really similar to travel in its psychological effect.

But there is more to it than this. The reader is always carried away into a world of thought and reflection. Even if it is a book about physical events, there is a difference between seeing such events in person or living through them, and reading about them in books, for then the events always assume the quality of a spectacle and the reader becomes a detached spectator. The best reading is therefore that which leads us into this contemplative mood, and not that which is merely occupied with the report of events. The tremendous amount of time spent on newspapers I regard as not reading at all, for the average readers of papers are mainly concerned with getting reports about events and happenings without contemplative value.

The best formula for the object of reading, in my opinion, was stated by Huang Shanku, a Sung poet and friend of Su Tungp'o. He said, "A scholar who hasn't read anything for three days feels that *his talk has no flavor* (becomes insipid), *and his own face becomes hateful to look at* (in the mirror)." What he means, of course, is that reading gives a man a certain charm and flavor, which is the entire object of reading, and only reading with this object can be called an art. One doesn't read to "improve one's mind," because when one begins to think of improving his mind, all the pleasure of reading is gone. He is the type of person who says to himself: "I must read Shakespeare, and I must read Sophocles, and I must read the entire Five Foot Shelf of Dr. Eliot, so I can become an educated man." I'm sure that man will never become educated. He will force himself one evening to read Shakespeare's *Hamlet* and come away, as if from a bad dream, with no greater benefit than that he is able to say that he has "read" *Hamlet*. Anyone who reads a book with a sense of obligation does not understand the art of reading. This type of reading with a business purpose is in no way different from a senator's reading up of files and reports before he makes a speech. It is asking for business advice and information, and not reading at all.

Reading for the cultivation of personal charm of appearance and flavor in speech is then, according to Huang, the only admissible kind of reading. This charm of appearance must evidently be interpreted as something other than physical beauty. What Huang means by "hateful to look at" is not physical ugliness. There are ugly faces that have a fascinating charm and beautiful faces that are insipid to look at. I have among my Chinese friends one whose head is shaped like a bomb and yet who is nevertheless always a pleasure to see. The most beautiful face among Western authors, so far as I have seen them in pictures, was that of G. K. Chesterton. There was such a diabolical conglomeration of mustache, glasses, fairly bushy eyebrows and knitted lines where the eyebrows met! One felt there were a vast number of ideas playing about inside that forehead, ready at any time to burst out from those quizzically penetrating eyes. That is what Huang would call a beautiful face, a face not made up by powder and rouge, but by the sheer force of thinking. As for flavor of speech, it all depends on one's way of reading. Whether one has "flavor" or not in his talk, depends on his method of reading. If a reader gets the flavor of books, he will show that flavor in his conversations, and if he has flavor in his conversations, he cannot help also having a flavor in his writing.

Hence I consider flavor or taste as the key to all reading. It necessarily follows that taste is selective and individual, like the taste for food. The most hygienic way of eating is, after all, eating what one likes, for then one is sure of his digestion. In reading as in eating, what is one man's meat may be another's poison. A teacher cannot force his pupils to like what he likes in reading, and a parent cannot expect his children to have the same tastes as himself. And if the reader has no taste for what he reads, all the time is wasted. As Yüan Chunglang says, "You can leave the books that you don't like alone, *and let other people read them.*"

There can be, therefore, no books that one absolutely must read. For our intellectual interests grow like a tree or flow like a river. So long as there is proper sap, the tree will grow anyhow, and so long as there is fresh current from the spring, the water will flow. When water strikes a granite cliff, it just goes around it; when it finds itself in a pleasant low valley, it stops and meanders there a while; when it finds itself in a deep mountain pond, it is content to stay there; when it finds itself traveling over rapids, it hurries forward. Thus, without any effort or determined aim, it is sure of reaching the sea some day. There are no books in this world that everybody must read, but only books that a person must read at a certain time in a given place under given circumstances and at a given period of his life. I rather think that reading, like matrimony is determined by fate or *yinyüan*. Even if there is a certain book that every one must read, like the *Bible*, there is a time for it. When one's thoughts and experience have not reached a certain point for reading a masterpiece, the masterpiece will leave only a bad flavor on his palate. Confucius said, "When one is fifty, one may read the *Book of Changes*," which means that one should not read it at forty-five. The extremely mild flavor of Confucius' own sayings in the *Analects* and his mature wisdom cannot be appreciated until one becomes mature himself.

Furthermore, the same reader reading the same book at different periods, gets a different flavor out of it. For instance, we enjoy a book more after we have had a personal talk with the author himself, or even after having seen a picture of his face, and one gets again a different flavor sometimes after one has broken off friendship with the author. A person gets a kind of flavor from reading the *Book of Changes* at forty, and gets another kind of flavor reading it at fifty, after he has seen more changes in life. Therefore, all good books can be read with profit and renewed pleasure a second time. I was made to read *Westward Ho!* and *Henry Esmond* in my college days, but while I was capable of appreciating *Westward Ho!* in my 'teens, the real flavor of *Henry Esmond* escaped me entirely until I reflected about it later on, and suspected there was vastly more charm in that book than I had then been capable of appreciating.

Reading, therefore, is an act consisting of two sides, the author and the reader. The net gain comes as much from the reader's contribution through his own insight and experience as from the author's own. In speaking about the Confucian *Analacts*, the Sung Confucianist Ch'eng Yich'uan said, "There are readers and readers. Some read the *Analects* and feel that nothing has happened, some are pleased with one or two lines in it, and some begin to wave their hands and dance on their legs unconsciously."

I regard the discovery of one's favorite author as the most critical event in one's intellectual development. There is such a thing as the affinity of spirits, and among the authors of ancient and modern times, one must try to find an author whose spirit is akin to his own. Only in this way can one get any real good out of reading. One has to be independent and search out his masters. Who is one's favorite author, no one can tell, probably not even the man himself. It is like love at first sight. The reader cannot be told to love this one or that one, but when he has found the author he loves, he knows it himself by a kind of instinct. We have such famous cases of discoveries of authors. Scholars seem to have lived in different ages, separated by centuries, and yet their modes of thinking and feeling were so akin that their coming together across the pages of a book was like a person finding his own image. In Chinese phraseology, we speak of these kindred spirits as re-incarnations of the same soul, as Su Tungp'o was said to be re-incarnation of Chuangtse or T'ao Yüanming, and Yüan Chunglang was said to be the re-incarnation of Su Tungp'o. Su Tungp'o said that when he first read Chuangtse, he felt as if all the time since his childhood he had been thinking the same things and taking the same views himself. When Yüan Chunglang discovered one night Hsü Wench'ang, a contemporary unknown to him, in a small book of poems, he jumped out of bed and shouted to his friend, and his friend began to read it and shout in turn, and then they both read and shouted again until their servant was completely puzzled. George Eliot described her first reading of Rousseau as an electric shock. Nietzsche felt the same thing about Schopenhauer, but Schopenhauer was a peevish master and Nietzsche was a violent-tempered pupil, and it was natural that the pupil later rebelled against the teacher.

It is only this kind of reading, this discovery of one's favorite author, that will do one any good at all. Like a man falling in love with his sweetheart at first sight, everything is right. She is of the right height, has the right face, the right color of hair, the right quality of voice and the right way of speaking and smiling. This author is not something that a young man need be told about by his teacher. The author is just right for him; his style, his taste, his point of view, his mode of thinking, are all right. And then the reader proceeds to devour every word and every line that the author writes, and because there is a spiritual affinity, he absorbs and readily digests everything. The author has cast a spell over him, and he is glad to be under the spell, and in time his own voice and manner and way of smiling and way of talking become like the author's own. Thus he truly steeps himself in his literary lover and derives from these books sustenance for his soul. After a few years, the spell is over and he grows a little tired of this lover and seeks for new literary lovers, and after he has had three or four lovers and completely eaten them up, he emerges as an author himself. There are many readers who never fall in love, like many young men and women who flirt around and are incapable of forming a deep attachment to a particular person. They can read any and all authors, and they never amount to anything.

Such a conception of the art of reading completely precludes the idea of reading as a duty or as an obligation. In China, one often encourages students to "study bitterly." There was a famous scholar who studied bitterly and who stuck an awl in his calf when he fell asleep while studying at night. There was another scholar who had a maid stand by his side as he was studying at night, to wake him up every time he fell asleep. This was nonsensical. If one has a book lying before him and falls asleep while some wise ancient author is talking to him, he should just go to bed. No amount of sticking an awl in his calf or of shaking him up by a maid will do him any good. Such a man has lost all sense of the pleasure of reading. Scholars who are worth anything at all never know what is called "a hard grind" or what "bitter study" means. They merely love books and read on because they cannot help themselves.

With this question solved, the question of time and place for reading is also provided with an answer. There is no proper time and place for reading. When the mood for reading comes, one can read anywhere. If one knows the enjoyment of reading, he will read in school or out of school, and in spite of all schools. He can study even in the best schools. Tseng Kuofan, in one of his family letters concerning the expressed desire of one of his younger brothers to come to the capital and study at a better school, replied that: "If one has the desire to study, he can study at a country school, or even on a desert or in busy streets, and even as a woodcutter or a swineherd. But if one has no desire to study, then not only is the country school not proper for study, but even a quiet country home or a fairy island is not a proper place for study." There are people who adopt a self-important posture at the desk when they are about to do some reading, and then complain they are unable to read because the room is too cold, or the chair is too hard, or the light is too strong. And there are writers who complain that they cannot write because there are too many mosquitos, or the writing paper is too shiny, or the noise from the street is too great. The great Sung scholar, Ouyang Hsiu, confessed to "three on's" for doing his best writing: on the pillow, on horseback and on the toilet. Another famous Ch'ing scholar, Ku Ch'ienli, was known for his habit of "reading Confucian classics naked" in summer. On the other hand, there is a good reason for not doing any reading in any of the seasons of the year, if one does not like reading:

To study in spring is treason;

And summer is sleep's best reason;

If winter hurries the fall,

Then stop till next spring season.

What, then, is the true art of reading? The simple answer is to just take up a book and read when the mood comes. To be thoroughly enjoyed, reading must be entirely spontaneous.

■ Write After You Read

1 Write a journal entry on "The Art of Reading" using the guidelines on page 11.

2 Summarize in one or two sentences what you perceive to be Lin's main point.

■ Discuss After You Read

1 According to Lin, what is the first major advantage a reader has over a person who does not read? Explain why you agree or disagree with him.

2 Why does Lin think that reading newspapers is "not reading at all" (page 91)? Explain why you agree or disagree with him.

3 According to Lin, what should be the prime reason for reading? Explain why you agree or disagree with him. What other reasons for reading exist?

4 Why does Lin think it is so important for readers to discover their favorite authors? Explain why you agree or disagree with him. Do you have a favorite author? If so, who is the author and why does this author appeal to you?

5 What is the meaning of the phrase "bitter study" (page 94)? Have you ever experienced such bitterness? How does Lin evaluate this method of reading? Explain why you agree or disagree with him.

6 How might Lin analyze the reading experiences described in Jackson's "Waiting in Line at the Drugstore" (pages 16–18) or Kim's "A Book-Writing Venture" (pages 42–45)?

GUIDELINES

Relating Reading to Experience

Essay Assignment

Write an essay in which you compare the ideas and experiences discussed in one or more readings to your own experiences and attitudes. Show how the generalizations, theories, or experiences of another writer correspond to or contradict your own background knowledge and experience. Your purpose is to test the truth, or validity, of the author's ideas. To accomplish this goal, you will need to incorporate ideas and details from the reading into your own essay (see Section I of A Handbook for Writing, pages 236–273). The exploratory writing of one student, Doxis Doxiadis, is included in the following guidelines to show how he developed ideas for an essay relating a reading to his own experience.

■ Exploring a Topic

Exploring a topic for an essay relating reading to experience may involve using some of the exploratory strategies described in Chapter 2 on pages 52–61. In addition, to evaluate what you have read, you will need to incorporate direct references to the reading. The strategies that follow suggest approaches you can take to fulfill the assignment.

Selecting a Reading

Selecting a reading is the first step in writing an essay that relates reading to experience.

Guidelines for Selecting a Reading

1. Skim all of the assigned readings.
2. Review whatever you have written about the reading selections, for example, your annotations (see page 7), clustering (see page 8), double-entry notes (see page 9), journal entries (see page 11), or any notes you may have taken during class discussions.
3. Determine which reading interests you most and will be the source for your essay.

A student writer at work: *Selecting a reading*

After reviewing his own writing, Doxis decided to write about LaRay Barna's "Intercultural Communication Stumbling Blocks" (pages 66–74). Here is

Doxis's explanation for how his journal entry helped him choose to write about Barna's article.

> "My journal reminded me that I thought the article was interesting. But also, my journal didn't say enough. I wanted to think more about what Barna was saying. Is it true? Is it complete?"

Your turn: *Selecting a reading*

Using the *Guidelines for Selecting a Reading*, decide which of the readings will be the source for your own essay.

Taking Notes on a Reading

Taking notes on a reading can help you understand an author's purpose, for example, by listing the author's main ideas or facts or by copying significant passages. Another way to achieve that goal is to create an outline of the author's key topics or points and the examples that illustrate those topics or points. The following template for outlining may be helpful.

   I. Key topic or point
      A. Example
      B. Example
   II. Key topic or point
      A. Example
      B. Example

Add further topics or points as necessary.

A student writer at work: *Taking notes on a reading*

Doxis took notes on "Intercultural Communication Stumbling Blocks," listing some of the key information from Barna's article that he thought he might want to use in his essay.

- *Americans behave too friendly – smile a lot – superficial*
- *Problems with language – misunderstanding*
- *People offended (foreigners) by American actions*
- *Different customs/values*
- *Stereotypes*
- *Different ideas, behaviors, and likings*
- *Anxiety*

Doxis also listed some quotations from Barna's article that he thought he might want to use.

> QUOTATIONS:
> - "The reason why certain foreigners may think that Americans are superficial — and they are, some Americans even recognize this — is that they talk and smile too much." (page 67)
> - "Stereotypes are stumbling blocks for communicators because they interfere with objective viewing of stimuli." (page 70)
> - "Another deterrent to an understanding between persons of differing cultures or ethnic groups is the tendency to evaluate . . . rather than to try to completely comprehend the thoughts and feelings expressed." (page 70)
> - "a clash of values can lead to poor communication and result in misunderstanding and hurt feelings." (page 71)
> - "The presence of high anxiety/tension is very common in cross-cultural experiences because of the uncertainties present." (page 71)

Your turn: *Taking notes on a reading*

Using the *Guidelines for Taking Notes on a Reading* in Chapter 1 on page 10 or the template for outlining on page 97, take notes on your selected reading.

Selecting Experiences That Relate to a Reading

Selecting experiences that relate to a reading is one way to develop evidence to support or challenge an author's statements.

Guidelines for Selecting Experiences that Relate to a Reading

One or more of the following suggestions may be helpful:

1. Use one or more of the exploratory strategies described in Chapter 2 – such as freewriting, looping, and cubing – or any strategy that helps you to remember experiences of your own that relate to a reading.

2. Review the discussion questions following the reading, and write down answers to the most relevant questions.

3. Speak to someone who may have had similar experiences. You may use someone else's experiences or reactions to emphasize a point you want to make as long as you credit that person as the source of the information.

4. Make a list showing the relationship between the parts of the reading you will refer to and the specific experiences you will describe.

A student writer at work: *Selecting experiences that relate to a reading*

Doxis first made a list of his own intercultural communication problems.

- *learning idioms*
- *understanding pronouns*
- *being on time*
- *their personal questions*
- *their jokes*
- *making friends – Americans avoid foreign students (but they act friendly)*
- *different habits*

Doxis then added to the list and omitted items that did not seem important. He went back to his reading notes and found some quotations that could fit into his essay. Doxis also took points from the article, under which he listed related personal experiences. Finally, he made a list of points not mentioned in Barna's article.

I. language problem
  – idioms/expressions
      "beat it"
      "hot dog"
      pronunciation
II. language not the only problem
  – values/habits
      personal questions
      Americans superficial
  – hurt feelings and misunderstanding
      Saudi Arabia/soles of feet
      jokes/insults
III. things not developed enough by Barna
      Americans avoid foreigners
      pace of life/Levine's essay

···▶ **Your turn:** *Selecting experiences that relate to a reading*

Using the *Guidelines for Selecting Experiences That Relate to a Reading* on page 98, select experiences of your own that correspond to the generalizations, theories, or experiences discussed in the reading you have selected.

▓ Focusing Ideas

To fulfill the goal of *focusing ideas* for your readers, you need to determine your overall perspective on the relationship between the reading and your experience, and write a sentence or two that can serve as the focal point of your essay.

A student writer at work: *Focusing ideas*

Doxis wanted to support Barna's ideas with examples from his own experience. He also wanted to discuss issues that he thought Barna did not adequately cover. He created two sentences to establish the ideas he wanted to focus on in his essay.

> *The problems discussed in "Intercultural Communication Stumbling Blocks" are experienced by most international students, to different extents. But Barna's article leaves out some important things.*

···▶ **Your turn:** *Focusing ideas*

Using the *Guidelines for Focusing Ideas* on page 61, create a focal point for your essay.

▓ Structuring the Essay

Structuring the essay that relates reading to experience involves moving readers toward determining the validity of the ideas in the reading. Such essays have a basic, three-part organizational framework: a beginning, a middle, and an ending. These sections of an academic essay are also referred to as the *introduction*, the *body*, and the *conclusion*.

The following flow chart may help you visualize an overall structure for an essay relating reading to experience.

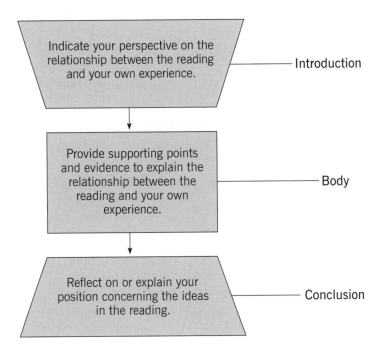

The Introduction

The *introduction* to an essay relating reading to experience provides a focal point that reveals your perspective on the relationship between the ideas in the reading and your own experiences.

Guidelines for Writing the Introduction

The introduction will usually accomplish the following goals in one or two paragraphs:

1. Involve readers in your topic at the very beginning. For example, if it is relevant to your topic, you can tell a poignant story, relate a humorous anecdote, quote an inspirational passage, state a shocking fact, or ask a thought-provoking question.

2. Provide *general* background information on the topic. For example, you can explain the topic's thematic, philosophical, political, or historical context.

3. Indicate the *specific* focus of the essay to help readers understand your perspective. You can directly state your perspective on the topic, or you can raise or imply a question about the topic.

If these guidelines do not suit your essay, discuss alternatives with your instructor.

Activity: *Evaluating introductions*

The following passages are introductions to student essays relating reading to experience. Evaluate two or more of the introductions by answering the following questions.

1 Does the introduction involve you in the topic and make you want to read the rest of the essay? Explain.

2 Can you tell, at the beginning of the essay, what the general subject of the essay is?

3 Can you tell which reading the student writer is focusing on?

4 Can you determine the student writer's perspective on the relationship between the ideas in the reading and the student's experience?

5 If you think the introduction should be revised, what suggestions do you have for the student writer?

Student A

> My first visit in the U.S. was quite a disappointment. I expected to find a lot of new friends in this country, but I soon realized that this would not be so easy. A number of problems, generated from the first minute I stepped into this country, did not allow me to fulfill my expectations and forced me to seek the company of other foreigners with similar cultural backgrounds to my own. These problems, discussed in LaRay Barna's article "Intercultural Communication Stumbling Blocks," are experienced, to different extents, by most international students and force them to form groups among themselves in order to find shelter where their problems can be shared and understood.
> – Doxis

Student B

> My first picture of America was the beginning of my cultural shock when I stepped on to the floor of Kennedy Airport in New York. I was eight years old and my eyes were too little to grasp the gigantic hallways and the endless piles of luggage that was higher than me. I looked around and saw so many different faces. For the first time I saw babies being carried like backpacks, I saw men with cellular phones and kids stuffing their faces with what looked like crunchy greasy sticks which I later found to be the very famous McDonald's French fries. What really stood out in my mind was a man who was wearing shorts and sandals when the weather outside was biting cold. He looked very relaxed and casually walked out of the sliding doors like it was summer and he was heading for the beach. I thought this was peculiar because in the Ukraine when it was cold outside people bundled up and wore pants. All I could think about was him freezing and getting pneumonia. I couldn't understand how he was so calm about wearing shorts when my teeth were chattering. For the man it was perfectly normal to wear shorts but I thought he was crazy to do it.

Intercultural communication begins by the transfer of ideas into language, which is then decoded by the other person. Communication occurs only when people are comfortable using a specific language and can easily absorb and respond to the person talking to them. If a person cannot maneuver the language then that creates difficulties on a social level and a personal level with issues such as self-esteem, giving up hope or staying in a native shell. People who immigrate to America tend to go through difficulties with language because their whole lives they spoke their native tongue and now in America they've had a change in language with an addition of a cultural shock. The bilingual person is going to have a distinct way of communicating when compared to a native speaker; he or she may have an accent, grammatical errors or practice their cultural beliefs. They are going to view Americans through a different set of eyes because they cannot relate to them; thus they need to feel trust and sensitivity in order to assimilate. **– Irina**

Student C

When I first came to college in the United States, all I could think of was how I would get along with American students. But soon I found out that I was facing a new problem: time synchronization. I couldn't understand how it was possible for professors and students to be so exact about time when I had always lived in a country where five minutes more or less would not mean a thing. Reading Robert Levine's article, "Social Time: The Heartbeat of Culture," was very interesting to me, for I saw my own problem through the eyes of a man who had the exact experience as I had trying to adjust to the time sense of another society. **– Patricia**

Student D

Reading has always been a challenge for me. I simply don't like to read. Even if someone hands me a good book, I will probably toss it aside, and let the book sit there for days before I will ever pick it up. Maybe it's not that I don't like to read, but I'm just not in the mood to read at all most of the time. I read books that were assigned to me in high school, and there were some books that I quite enjoyed. However, it seems as though someone needs to force or assign me to read the first page of a book before I can actually get started. I have tons of books at home but I have never read any of them. The reason is because no one ever tells me to read so I never bother. Last year, I bought a Japanese study guidebook so I could learn the language by myself. Today, the book still resides at the bottom drawer of my desk. I think that I only skimmed through the first few pages, and then placed it back inside the drawer. I have to admit that I am a very lazy person, and waste a lot of time doing nothing. Many people will read a book during such times, but not I. I, on the other hand, will just watch TV or

continued

go to sleep. My whole point here is that I'm losing faith in myself to ever pick up a book and read it on my own.

Before reading "The Ingrate" by Paul Laurence Dunbar, "Waiting in Line at the Drugstore" by James Thomas Jackson, and "The Art of Reading" by Lin Yutang, my thoughts of reading were fairly negative. Many people like to read fictional books, but what is the point of reading them? I used to think that a person doesn't really get anything out of reading fictional books because the settings in the books are not real. A person cannot really put himself/herself in the same situation as the main character in the book because it's all fictional. I used to argue that the only enjoyment out of a fictional book is the emotional feeling generated by the reading. If a story has a happy ending, then a person will feel happy after reading it. If the story has a sad ending, then the person will feel sad. If the ending is a mystery, then it will leave the reader curious as to what has happened. However, these feelings are only temporary, and will disappear after a few hours or maybe days. What does stay is the feeling whether the person liked the book or not. If a person spends days reading a certain book, and later finds out that the book made absolutely no sense, then that would just be a complete waste of time. The only books that I like to read are ones that are beneficial to me after reading them. That is, I will learn something or gain some knowledge after completing the book. That is why the only books that I ever bought are the Japanese guidebook and the computer book purchased at the library book sale. I also brought an accounting book because I thought it would be useful for me in the future since I am planning to major in accounting. This is how I used to view reading. I used to believe that the sole purpose of reading was to benefit a reader's interest. By reading such reference books, the knowledge gained is permanent, and would stay within a person for years not days. However, after reading Dunbar, Jackson, and Lin, and a lengthy consideration, my thoughts on reading changed. – **Sam**

The Body

The *body* of an essay that relates reading to experience provides evidence to explain your perspective on the relationship between the ideas in the reading and your own experience. It should include paraphrased or quoted passages from the reading as well as descriptions of your experiences.

Guidelines for Structuring the Body Paragraphs

The body of an essay will usually fulfill the following goals:

1. For each paragraph or set of paragraphs, provide at least one supporting point that relates to and expands on the specific topic that you focused on in the introduction.
2. Within each paragraph, include details, examples, and quotations that serve as evidence to illustrate or substantiate the supporting point (see Paraphrasing, Quoting, and Synthesizing, pages 241–258).
3. Comment on each quotation to clarify its meaning and to make its significance clear (see Quoting, pages 274–275).

The following suggestions offer three possibilities for structuring the body paragraphs of an essay relating reading to experience. You can use the drafting process to experiment with the organization of the body; your early efforts can be revised later (see Drafting, pages 274–275, and Revising, pages 278–282).

1. Explore several ideas from the reading one by one, devoting at least one paragraph to each idea.
    a. Explain an idea from the reading and indicate your perspective on the idea.
    b. Describe at least one experience in detail to show how it relates to the idea.
    c. Explain another idea from the reading, indicate your perspective on that idea, and describe at least one experience in detail to show how it relates to the idea.
    d. Repeat this process for each idea you want to discuss.
    e. Present the ideas in a logical order. For example, you could
        - begin with the least important idea and end with the most important, or
        - first discuss the ideas that your experiences support, then discuss the ideas that your experiences contradict.
2. Explore one major idea from the reading.
    a. Explain the major idea you are focusing on.
    b. Describe an experience in detail to show how it supports or challenges the reading's major idea.
    c. Then describe another experience in detail to show how it supports or challenges the reading's major idea.
    d. Continue this process for each experience you want to discuss.
    e. Throughout the body, include periodic references to the reading, through paraphrase or quotation, so that you don't lose your focus on the connection between the reading and your own experiences.

3. Explore several ideas from the reading, and then explore one or more ideas that the reading does not develop enough or neglects altogether.

   a. In the first half of the body, explain an idea from the reading, indicate your perspective on that idea, and then describe your experiences in detail to show how they support or challenge that idea. Repeat this process for each idea you want to discuss.

   b. In the second half of the body, state an idea that the reading ignores and then provide your own specific, detailed information to explain your idea. Repeat this process for each idea you want to discuss.

Activity: *Evaluating body paragraphs*

The following passages are body paragraphs from student essays relating reading to experience. Evaluate two or more of the paragraphs by answering the following questions.

1 How well does the student writer explain the idea from the reading that is the focus of the paragraph?

2 Can you determine the student writer's perspective on the idea from the reading?

3 Does the student writer adequately show how a personal experience supports or challenges the idea from the reading?

4 If you think the paragraph should be revised, what suggestions do you have for the student writer?

Student A

> However, as Barna points out, language is not the only problem an international student will face. When I first came to the U.S., I found out that my values, preferences, and habits were totally different from those of Americans. I thought that people here were ruder according to my standards. I could never ask someone the personal – and maybe too friendly – questions they asked me from the very first minute of our acquaintance. I remember that I couldn't understand why all the students were smiling and greeting me. My roommates behaved as though I was a long lost friend of theirs; and such friendliness embarrassed me since I could not, or thought I did not, respond accordingly. This behavior seemed to me quite shallow, and I don't think that this impression was mine alone. As a Vietnamese student says in the Barna article, "foreigners . . . think that Americans are superficial" (p. 67). In the eyes of a foreigner, Americans look like happy fools even though, as I found out, this is certainly not true. However, the first impression of Americans will make most foreigners avoid them and they won't therefore find their true self.
> – Doxis

Student B

Bilingual students in America are faced with the challenge of separating ideas and concepts in their cultural background from the new ideas they are developing because they are learning a new language and a new way of life. For some people adapting is natural and easy while for others it's a struggle that takes time and never reaches the final stage of assimilation. It is difficult for foreigners to adapt when they feel certain vibes from Americans. For example, Barna quotes a student as saying, "'Americans make friends easily and leave their friends almost as quickly, while in my country it takes a long time to find out a possible friend and then she becomes your friend – with a very strong sense of the term'" (p. 67). In the foreign student's culture making friends is not as simple as in American culture. Thus, a new student in America will eventually have to learn how to make fast friends because that's how the social circle runs unless the foreign student decides to stay with his or her own people. Then there is a barrier that can never be torn down. Are cultures not meant to mix or are people so used to their ways of life that they are blind to everything else? – **Irina**

Student C

Teachers can have a very powerful influence on students' desire to learn and use the English language. In "My English," Julia Alvarez writes about a teacher who showed great passion toward the language. This teacher helped her to improve upon her writing skills and open her imagination to all of the possibilities that English can provide. I was fortunate enough to have one such teacher that instilled in her students her love of the English language. Because of this one experience with my Creative Writing teacher I am always thinking of more creative ways to express myself and of different experiences that could be made into a story, and I always to try to write to the best of my ability. Writing is something that takes years to master, and only practice will help. – **Katie**

Student D

Entering college exposed me to a whole new world of English. Many more factors influenced my language. There was an influence from school but also a more social language: a language that consisted of phrases and words I'd use with friends and family talking on the phone, communicating through instant messenger, writing notes, writing in a diary, and everyday slang. This is where I stand today. I have many different forms of English that I use to communicate, and it has been confusing at times to distinguish where and when to use which forms. I find that in all situations of writing and speaking, "I use them all – all the Englishes I grew up with" (Tan, p. 47). – **Sara**

The Conclusion

The *conclusion* to an essay relating reading to experience establishes or emphasizes your perspective on the truth, or validity, of the author's ideas. Having shown the similarities and differences between the author's ideas and your own experience, you can now discuss the implications of what you have written.

Guidelines for Writing the Conclusion

The conclusion of an essay will usually fulfill the following goals:

1. Briefly remind your readers of the main focus of your essay and make a strong statement that aims to convince them of the validity of your point of view.

2. Discuss the implications of what you have written in the body of the essay. For example, you can offer a solution to a problem, raise or answer a question, make a recommendation, predict a future possibility or consequence, suggest a future area of exploration, or apply the insight you gained from your reading and writing to your own experience.

Your turn: *Structuring the essay*

Using the *Guidelines for Writing the Introduction* on page 101, the *Guidelines for Structuring the Body Paragraphs* on page 105, and the *Guidelines for Writing the Conclusion* on page 108, create a flow chart such as the one on page 101 to show what ideas and specifics you might include in your essay.

Writing the Essay

Writing the essay can be accomplished most effectively by going through the processes of drafting, receiving feedback, and revising (see Section II of A Handbook for Writing, pages 274–284). Use the checklist on the next page to see if your essay fulfills readers' expectations for relating reading to experience. The checklist may be used for self-evaluation or for evaluation of your essay by another reader.

Evaluative Criteria for an Essay Relating Reading to Experience

YES	NO	
☐	☐	**1 Does the opening of the essay provide general background information on the topic?** If yes, what is the general background? If no, what background information might be relevant?
☐	☐	**2 Does the essay make clear, at any point, which reading is the source for comparison between ideas and experiences?** If yes, which reading is the source for comparison? If no, where might the name of the author and title of the reading be included?
☐	☐	**3 Does the essay provide a specific focus that reveals a perspective on the relationship between ideas in the reading and personal experience?** If yes, what is the perspective? If no, how could the focus be clarified?
☐	☐	**4 Does the essay provide sufficient paraphrased and quoted references to the reading?** If yes, which references present the reading's ideas? If no, where could references be added or changed?
☐	☐	**5 Does the essay provide sufficient and relevant experiences to support or challenge points made about the reading?** If yes, which experiences help to clarify a point? If no, what kind of experiences would help to clarify a point?
☐	☐	**6 Does the conclusion discuss the implications of what is written in the body of the essay?** If yes, what are the implications? If no, what might the implications be?
☐	☐	**7 Is the essay logically structured?** If yes, what makes the structure logical? If no, how could the essay be more logically structured?

▧ Completing the Essay

Completing the essay involves proofreading and editing your final draft as well as preparing a clear final copy to hand in to your instructor for evaluation. See Sections II and III of A Handbook for Writing, pages 282–288.

Chapter 4

Analyzing an Argumentative Essay

Writing an essay analyzing argumentative writing involves determining how effectively a writer makes an argument. One of the challenges of composing such an essay is to represent the author's ideas fairly and accurately, whether or not you agree with the author's point of view.

Chapter 4 includes five reading selections that can become sources for your essay. These reading selections focus on controversial issues related to education: what students should be taught, how they should be taught, and how their learning should be assessed. The authors' arguments may be flawed, but like all writers of argumentative essays, they aim to influence readers to believe what they believe.

The guidelines that follow the readings are designed to help you compose an essay analyzing an argument.

READINGS

Reading 1

■ Write Before You Read

Before reading "We Should Cherish Our Children's Freedom to Think" by Kie Ho, work in a team or small group to write brief notes identifying the following people, places, and items of which you have some knowledge. Then compare your results with those of the rest of the class. What do the results reveal about the knowledge level of the class?

a Mussolini	k the author of *The Canterbury Tales*
b Dostoevski	l Romeo and Juliet
c Belgrade	m *Donkey Kong*
d Prague	n Shakespeare
e Kabul	o Lyndon Johnson
f Karachi	p Ho Chi Minh
g Hamlet	q Hirohito
h Buenos Aires	r Periodic Table
i tacos	s Richard Pryor
j two rivers in Brazil	t Ku Klux Klan

We Should Cherish Our Children's Freedom to Think

Kie Ho

Kie Ho was born and raised in Indonesia and became a business executive in the United States. "We Should Cherish Our Children's Freedom to Think" originally appeared in the Los Angeles Times *newspaper.*

Americans who remember "the good old days" are not alone in complaining about the educational system in this country. Immigrants, too, complain, and with more up-to-date comparisons. Lately I have heard a Polish refugee express dismay that his daughter's high school has not taught her the difference between Belgrade and Prague. A German friend was furious when he learned that the mathematics test given to his son on his first day as a freshman included multiplication and division. A Lebanese boasts that the average high-school graduate in his homeland can speak fluently in Arabic, French and English. Japanese businessmen in Los Angeles send their children to private schools staffed by teachers imported from Japan to learn mathematics at Japanese levels, generally considered at least a year more advanced than the level here.

But I wonder: If American education is so tragically inferior, why is it that this is still the country of innovation?

I think I found the answer on an excursion to the Laguna Beach Museum of Art, where the work of schoolchildren was on exhibit. Equipped only with colorful yarns, foil paper, felt pens and crayons, they had transformed simple paper lunch bags into, among other things, a waterfall with flying fish, Broom Hilda the witch and a house with a woman in a skimpy bikini hiding behind a swinging door. Their public school had provided these children with opportunities and direction to fulfill their creativity, something that people tend to dismiss or take for granted.

When I was 12 in Indonesia, where education followed the Dutch system, I had to memorize the names of all the world's major cities, from Kabul to Karachi. At the same age, my son, who was brought up a Californian, thought that Buenos Aires was Spanish for good food – a plate of tacos and burritos, perhaps. However, unlike his counterparts in Asia and Europe, my son had studied *creative* geography. When he was only 6, he drew a map of the route that he traveled to get to school, including the streets and their names, the buildings and traffic signs and the houses that he passed.

Disgruntled American parents forget that in this country their children are able to experiment freely with ideas; without this they will not really be able to think or to believe in themselves.

In my high school years, we were models of dedication and obedience: we sat to listen, to answer only when asked, and to give the only correct answer. Even when studying word forms, there were no alternatives. In similes pretty lips were *always* as red as sliced pomegranates, and beautiful eyebrows were *always* like a parade of black clouds. Like children in many other countries in the world, I simply did not have a chance to choose, to make decisions. My son, on the contrary, told me that he got a good laugh – and an A – from his teacher for concocting "the man was as nervous as Richard Pryor at a Ku Klux Klan convention."

There's no doubt that American education does not meet high standards in such basic skills as mathematics and language. And we realize that our youngsters are ignorant of Latin, put Mussolini in the same category as Dostoevski, cannot recite the Periodic Table by heart. Would we, however, prefer to stuff the developing little heads of our children with hundreds of geometry problems, the names of rivers in Brazil and 50 lines from *The Canterbury Tales*? Do we really want to retard their impulses, frustrate their opportunities for self-expression?

When I was 18, I had to memorize Hamlet's "To be or not to be" soliloquy flawlessly. In his English class, my son was assigned to write a love letter to Juliet, either in Shakespearean jargon or in modern lingo. (He picked the latter; his Romeo would take Juliet to an arcade for a game of *Donkey Kong*.)

Where else but in America can a history student take the role of Lyndon Johnson in an open debate against another student playing Ho Chi Minh? It is unthinkable that a youngster in Japan would dare to do the same regarding the role of Hirohito in World War II.

Critics of American education cannot grasp one thing, something that they don't truly understand because they are never deprived of it: freedom. This most important measurement has been omitted in the studies of the quality of education in this century, the only one, I think, that extends even to children the license to freely speak, write and be creative. Our public education certainly is not perfect, but it is a great deal better than any other.

▪ Write After You Read

1 Write a journal entry in response to "We Should Cherish Our Children's Freedom to Think" using the guidelines on page 11.

2 Summarize in one sentence what you perceive to be the major point of Ho's argument.

▪ Discuss After You Read

1 Which of Ho's ideas or examples correspond to what you have experienced or what you know about education? Explain.

2 Which of Ho's ideas or examples conflict with what you have experienced or what you know about education? Explain.

3 Analyze the strengths and weaknesses of the evidence Ho provides to support his argument.

  a Which supporting points or examples best clarify Ho's main argument? Explain.

  b Which supporting points or examples are least convincing? Explain.

4 What additional evidence might strengthen Ho's argument?

5 What evidence or counterarguments might challenge Ho's argument?

6 Is the language Ho uses likely to convince teachers or students that his preferred approach is the best one?

  a If yes, which specific words or phrases are most likely to appeal to teachers? Which specific words or phrases are most likely to appeal to students? Explain your answers.

  b If no, which specific words or phrases are most likely to offend teachers? Which specific words or phrases are most likely to offend students? Explain your answers.

7 How might Ho respond to Harris's "What True Education Should Do" (page 5)? Create a dialogue between the two authors to illustrate your response.

Reading 2

▦ Write Before You Read

Before reading "Teach Knowledge, Not 'Mental Skills'" by E. D. Hirsch, write for several minutes about what you perceive to be the difference between *knowledge* and *mental skills*.

Teach Knowledge, Not "Mental Skills"

E. D. Hirsch

E. D. (Eric Donald) Hirsch is a professor of English at the University of Virginia. Among his many books are The Aims of Interpretation (1976) *and* Cultural Literacy: What Every American Needs to Know (1987). *Hirsch gained recognition with* Cultural Literacy: What Every American Needs to Know, *in which he identified 5,000 names, dates, facts, and concepts that he claimed every educated person should know in order to function effectively in society. "Teach Knowledge, Not 'Mental Skills'" originally appeared in the* New York Times *newspaper on the opinion page.*

The children at Public School 67 in the South Bronx[1] are all African-American or Hispanic, and all are poor enough to qualify for free lunch. In the late '80s, the school was so ineffective that the district board was about to shut it down.

But in 1991 a new principal, Jeff Litt, introduced a grade-by-grade "core knowledge" curriculum. The students' academic performance has risen so dramatically – their reading scores, for instance, were up 13.5 percent last year – that Mr. Litt has had to limit the flow of curious visitors to his school.

The curriculum was developed by the Core Knowledge Foundation, a nonprofit group I founded that advises public schools free of charge. Mr. Litt became an enthusiast of the grade-by-grade sequence after visiting the Three Oaks School in Lee County, Fla., the country's first core-knowledge school. This year the Bronx will get two more core-knowledge schools, joining about 100 others across the nation.

What's the secret of their success? About 50 percent of classroom time is spent teaching each student a core of knowledge that is the same material offered to every other child in the same grade throughout the school.

To understand why this plan has contributed to strong academic improvement, consider how rare such common sense is.

Typically, school guidelines are couched in terms of learning skills, rather than the content of learning. For example, school guidelines might say, "First graders develop map skills" and "learn about plants." In contrast, the Core Knowledge guidelines specify that first graders will "identify the seven continents" and "learn the difference between evergreen and deciduous trees."

---

[1] *South Bronx:* The Bronx is a borough of New York City.

Because guidelines are so vague in skill-oriented curriculums, huge variations occur in the content of what is learned from one class to another. A Connecticut mother wrote me that her young twins, who were in separate classrooms at the same school, were learning totally different things.

Because there's no consistency in what children were taught in previous grades, teachers have to make a disastrous compromise: either they fill in knowledge gaps for all students in the class, making progress excruciatingly slow, or they go forward at a pace suited to the more prepared students, leaving others behind.

Such a hit-or-miss approach does the most harm to disadvantaged students, who usually depend on school alone for access to academic knowledge. But even advantaged students are hurt by being left with huge knowledge gaps or by being bored with repetition.

That problem is avoided in the best and fairest school systems in Europe and Asia, which offer programs similar to the core-knowledge schools. Since students have learned the same things, teachers can build on that shared foundation and bring the whole class forward.

It is a promising sign that the Clinton[2] Administration's new education bill employs the resonant new phrase "content standards." Nonetheless, most educational reformers continue to emphasize skills and scornfully dismiss the teaching of "mere facts," which they claim are destined for quick obsolescence.

Hearing few contrary voices, well-intentioned philanthropists and politicians echo such slogans as "learning-to-learn skills," "critical-thinking skills" and "problem-solving skills."

Yes, problem-solving skills are necessary. But they depend on a wealth of relevant knowledge. Meanwhile, street-smart children in the Bronx and elsewhere demonstrate outside school that they already possess higher-order thinking skills. As Jeff Litt has shown, what these students lack is not critical thinking but academic knowledge.

Contrary to proponents' claims, emphasizing all-purpose mental skills to "prepare children for the 21st century" is not new. The tired slogans have dominated U.S. educational discourse for over 40 years, and are a chief cause of the curricular chaos.

Leaving such slogans behind, and following the lead of effective systems in Europe and Asia, P.S. 67 demonstrates how we can achieve excellence and fairness for all.

■ Write After You Read

1 Write a journal entry in response to "Teach Knowledge, Not 'Mental Skills'" using the guidelines on page 11.

2 Summarize in one sentence what you perceive to be the major point of Hirsch's argument.

---

[2] Bill Clinton was president of the United States from 1993–2001.

■ Discuss After You Read

1 Which of Hirsch's ideas or examples correspond to what you have experienced or what you know about education? Explain.

2 Which of Hirsch's ideas or examples conflict with what you have experienced or what you know about education? Explain.

3 Analyze the strengths and weaknesses of the evidence Hirsch provides to support his argument.

   a Which supporting points or examples best clarify Hirsch's main argument? Explain.

   b Which supporting points or examples are least convincing? Explain.

4 What additional evidence might strengthen Hirsch's argument?

5 What evidence or counterarguments might challenge Hirsch's argument?

6 Is the language Hirsch uses likely to convince teachers or students that his program is the best approach?

   a If yes, which specific words or phrases are most likely to appeal to teachers? Which specific words or phrases are most likely to appeal to students? Explain your answers.

   b If no, which specific words or phrases are most likely to offend teachers? Which specific words or phrases are most likely to offend students? Explain your answers.

7 How might Hirsch's ideas support or challenge the ideas in Harris's "What True Education Should Do" (page 5) or Ho's "We Should Cherish Our Children's Freedom to Think" (pages 112–114)? Create a dialogue between Hirsch and one of the other authors to illustrate your response.

Reading 3

■ Write Before You Read

Before reading "Grades and Self-Esteem" by Randy Moore, write for several minutes about what you perceive to be the relationship between grades and self-esteem.

Grades and Self-Esteem

Randy Moore

Randy Moore is a professor of biology at the University of Minnesota in Minneapolis. Moore has published numerous scientific articles and is the author of The Living Desert *(1991),* Evolution in the Courtroom *(2002),* Biology Laboratory Manual *(2004), and several biology textbooks. "Grades and Self-Esteem" first appeared as an editorial in the journal* The American Biology Teacher.

If you're around teachers long enough, the conversation will inevitably get around to "today's under-prepared students." We complain endlessly that students don't know anything, don't want to know anything, can't write well and can't think critically. Our complaints are supported by much evidence, including firsthand observations and declining scores on objective tests (e.g., SAT, ACT). Indeed,

- Only 11% of eighth-graders in California's public schools can solve seventh-grade math problems.

- More than 30% of U.S. 17-year-olds don't know that Abraham Lincoln wrote the Emancipation Proclamation. Almost half do not know who Josef Stalin was, and 30% can't locate Britain on a map of Europe.

Employers echo our complaints: 58% of Fortune 500 companies cannot find marginally competent workers, and the CEOs of major companies report that four of 10 entry-level workers cannot pass seventh-grade exams. Does all of this make a difference? Yes. For example, several major corporations now ship their paperwork to countries such as Ireland because U.S. workers "make too many mistakes."

We have many prepackaged excuses for our failures, some of which are partly valid and others that are self-delusion: I argue that a major reason for our failures is that the primary mission of many schools has shifted from education to "building self-esteem."

Disciples of the self-esteem mission for schools preach that we should take seriously – even praise – all self-expression by students, regardless of its content, context, accuracy or worth. This, the disciples claim, "humanizes" education and makes our courses "nonjudgmental." Everyone is right! Everyone's opinion has equal value! I'm OK, you're OK! Don't worry about learning, thinking or communicating; the important thing is to feel good about ourselves.

Of course, when we assign grades we become *very* judgmental. This upsets teachers who feel bad about holding students accountable to any kind of grading standards. To avoid feeling bad, these teachers lower their standards so that virtually all students meet them, regardless of the students' performance. There are many subtle examples of this: eliminating (or not recording) failing grades, allowing students to withdraw from courses when faced with making a poor grade, "dumbing down" our courses so that everyone "earns" an A or B, and renaming sub-remedial courses to make them appear to be academically viable. All of this produces grade inflation. Consider these facts:

- In 1966, high school teachers gave twice as many C's as A's. By 1978, the proportion of A's exceeded that of C's. In 1990, more than 20% of all students entering college had an A *average* for their entire high school career.

- In the 1980s, almost three-fourths of grades at Amherst, Duke, Hamilton, Haverford, Pomona, Michigan, North Carolina and Wisconsin were A or B. At Harvard, the average grade is now B–; at Princeton, 80% of undergraduates get *only* A's or B's.

- In some colleges, the *average* undergraduate is an "honors" student.

Many teachers have lowered their standards so far that most of their students – the same ones we claim cannot think critically and who employers know are unprepared for entry-level jobs – are A or B students. These teachers apparently think that our students, like the children at Lake Wobegon,[1] are all above average.

The belief that self-esteem is a precondition to learning is now dogma that few teachers question. However, this confuses cause and effect. Granted, people who excel at what they do usually feel better about themselves than do frauds or convicted felons. But does high self-esteem *cause* success? To many educators, it apparently does: These people claim that self-esteem precedes performance, not vice versa. I argue that self-esteem is *earned* and that schools, despite their good intentions, cannot dispense it as a prepackaged handout. We should avoid the "Wizard of Oz"[2] syndrome in which we merely dispense substitutes for brains, bravery and hearts. We should insist on the real thing.

Despite having lowered our standards to new depths, many self-esteem crusaders claim that we've not lowered our standards far enough. For example, high school seniors in some states must pass a ninth-grade-level test before they can get their diploma. When some students failed the test repeatedly and were told they would not graduate, the self-esteem gurus immediately jumped to their defense. "Outrageous!" they claimed. "If students failed, the tests must be flawed!" One educator even proclaimed that the students "would be stigmatized the rest of their lives because they don't have a diploma." Of course, asking the students to work harder, repeat a grade or achieve a meaningful goal is out of the question because such requests could damage the students' self-esteem. The result? Students who could not pass the ninth-grade test "graduated" and received a "diploma of attendance" (ironically, the fact that many of the students *didn't* attend classes was the basis for their problem). I'm sure that employers – people who care less about "self-esteem" than integrity and productivity – will be *very* impressed by a "diploma of attendance."

The delusion that results from our current emphasis on self-esteem rather than education is best shown by the results of an international study of 13-year-olds that found that Koreans ranked first in math and Americans ranked last. Only 23% of Korean youngsters claimed that they were "good at mathematics," as compared to a whopping 68% of U.S. youngsters. Apparently, self-esteem has little to do with one's ability to do math.

The products of our current emphasis on "self-esteem" – that is, grade inflation, lowered standards, meaningless diplomas and an ignorance of important skills – greatly compromise our work: We cheat students out of a quality education and give parents false hopes about their child's intellectual skills. Moreover, our teaching convinces students that achievement is an entitlement that is given, not earned. Luckily, life is not that way.

---

[1] *Lake Wobegon*: a fictional town created by popular radio show host and author Garrison Keillor
[2] *Wizard of Oz*: a novel by L. Frank Baum (later made into a popular film) in which a fake wizard gives a cowardly lion a badge to show he is brave, a tin man a heart to show he is kind, and a scarecrow a diploma to show he is smart

We cannot continue to equate higher self-esteem with lowered standards. If we do, we'll not only produce students who can't think, but also students who don't know what thinking *is*. At that point, self-esteem won't matter all that much.

We'll improve students' self-esteem most by helping and motivating our students to exceed *higher* standards. Only then will our students have accomplished something meaningful and will we have excelled at our work.

▥ Write After You Read

1 Write a journal entry in response to "Grades and Self-Esteem" using the guidelines on page 11.

2 Summarize in one sentence what you perceive to be the major point of Moore's argument.

▥ Discuss After You Read

1 Which of Moore's ideas or examples correspond to what you have experienced or what you know about grades? Explain.

2 Which of Moore's ideas or examples conflict with what you have experienced or what you know about grades? Explain.

3 Analyze the strengths and weaknesses of the evidence Moore provides to support his argument.

   a Which supporting points or examples best clarify Moore's main argument? Explain.

   b Which supporting points or examples are least convincing? Explain.

4 What additional evidence might strengthen Moore's argument?

5 What evidence or counterarguments might challenge Moore's argument?

6 Is the language Moore uses likely to convince teachers or students to change their behavior?

   a If yes, which specific words or phrases are most likely to appeal to teachers? Which specific words or phrases are most likely to appeal to students? Explain your answers.

   b If no, which specific words or phrases are most likely to offend teachers? Which specific words or phrases are most likely to offend students? Explain your answers.

7 Discuss the similarities and differences between Moore's essay and Ho's "We Should Cherish Our Children's Freedom to Think" (pages 112–114). How might one author's ideas support or challenge the other's?

Reading 4

▓ Write Before You Read

Before reading "Confusing Harder with Better" by Alfie Kohn, write for several minutes to answer the following question: If school is harder for students, does that make it better?

Confusing Harder with Better

Alfie Kohn

Alfie Kohn has been a teacher, a journalist, and a researcher. He now writes and speaks widely on human behavior, education, and parenting. Among his books are The Schools Our Children Deserve: Moving Beyond Traditional Classrooms and "Tougher Standards" *(1999) and* Unconditional Parenting: Moving from Rewards and Punishments to Love and Reason *(2005). "Confusing Harder with Better" originally appeared in* Education Week, *a newspaper published by Editorial Projects in Education Inc., a nonprofit organization whose primary mission is to help professionals and the public understand important issues in American education.*

Never underestimate the power of a catchy slogan and a false dichotomy. When a politician pronounces himself a supporter of "law and order" or "a strong defense," you may protest that it's not that simple, but even as you start to explain why, you've already been dismissed as soft on crime or unwilling to defend Our Way of Life.

People who attend to nuance have long been at a disadvantage in politics, where spin is out of control. Never before, however, has the same been quite so true of the public conversation about education, which is distinguished today by simplistic demands for "accountability" and "raising the bar." Not only public officials but business groups and many journalists have played a role in reducing the available options to two: Either you're in favor of higher standards or you are presumably content with lower standards. Choose one.

These days almost anything can be done to students and to schools, no matter how ill-considered, as long as it is done in the name of raising standards. As a result, we are facing a situation in this country that can be described without exaggeration as an educational emergency: The intellectual life is being squeezed out of classrooms, schools are being turned into giant test-prep centers, and many students – as well as some of our finest educators – are being forced out.

Part of the problem is that the enterprise of raising standards in practice means little more than raising the scores on standardized tests, many of which are norm-referenced, multiple-choice, and otherwise flawed. The more schools commit themselves to improving performance on these tests, the more that meaningful opportunities to learn are sacrificed. Thus, high scores are often a sign of *lowered* standards – a paradox rarely appreciated by those who make, or report on, education policy.

Compounding the problem is a reliance on the sort of instruction that treats children as passive receptacles into which knowledge or skills are poured. "Back to basics" education – a misnomer, really, because most American schools never left it – might be described as outdated except for the fact that there never was a time when it worked all that well. Modern cognitive science just explains more systematically why this approach has always come up short. When you watch students slogging through textbooks, memorizing lists, being lectured at, and working on isolated skills, you begin to realize that nothing bears a greater responsibility for undermining educational excellence than the continued dominance of traditional instruction. Shrill calls for "accountability" usually just produce an accelerated version of the same thing.

Underlying the kind of pedagogy and assessment associated with the tougher-standards movement is an assumption that has rarely been identified and analyzed – namely, that the main thing wrong with the schools today is that kids get off too easy. Texts and tests and teaching have been "dumbed down," it is alleged. At the heart of metaphors like *raising* standards (or the bar) is the premise that harder is better.

Now, the first and most obvious thing to be said in response is that assignments and exams can be too difficult just as they can be too easy. If the latter can leave students insufficiently challenged, the former can make them feel stupid, which, in turn, can lead them to feel alienated, to lose interest in the subject matter, and sometimes to misbehave. (It's usually less threatening for kids to be seen as incorrigible than as inadequate.) Anyone can ask students questions that are laughably easy *or* impossibly difficult. "The trick," observed Jerome Bruner, "is to find the medium questions that can be answered and that take you somewhere." In short, maximum difficulty isn't the same as optimal difficulty.

But let's delve a little deeper. Maybe the issue isn't whether harder is always better so much as why we focus so much attention on the whole question of difficulty.

John Dewey reminded us that the value of what students do "resides in its connection with a stimulation of greater *thoughtfulness*, not in the greater strain it imposes." If you were making a list of what counts in education – that is, the criteria to use in judging whether students would benefit from what they were doing – the task's difficulty level would be only one factor among many, and almost certainly not the most important. To judge schools by how demanding they are is rather like judging an opera on the basis of how many notes it contains that are hard for singers to hit. In other words, it leaves out most of what matters.

Here's what follows from this recognition: If homework assignments or exams consist of factual-recall questions, it really doesn't make all that much difference whether there are 25 tough questions or 10 easy ones. Similarly, a textbook does not become a more appropriate teaching tool just because it is intended for a higher grade level. Some parents indignantly complain that their kids are bored and can complete the worksheets without breaking a sweat. They ought to be complaining about the fact that the teacher is relying on worksheets at all. Likewise, some teachers disdain any colleague who spoon-feeds information, insisting (often with a tone of self-congratulation) that in *their* classrooms, students have to *work*! But the latter may not be any better than the former, and the two together constitute a false dichotomy. We have to look at the whole method of instruction, the underlying theory of learning, rather than just quibbling about how hard the assignment is or how much the students must strain.

One reason a back-to-basics curriculum fits perfectly with the philosophy of prizing hard work is that it *creates* hard work – often unnecessarily. It's more difficult to learn to read if the task is to decode a string of phonemes than if it is to make sense of interesting stories. It's more exhausting to memorize a list of scientific vocabulary words than it is to learn scientific concepts by devising your own experiment. If kids are going to be forced to learn facts without context, and skills without meaning, it's certainly handy to have an ideology that values difficulty for its own sake. To be sure, learning often requires sustained attention and effort. But there's a vital difference between that which is rigorous and that which is merely onerous.

Other words are similarly slippery. Do we want students to be "challenged" more, or to live up to "higher expectations" in a school that stands for "excellence"? It all depends on how these words are being defined. If they signify a deeper, richer, more engaging curriculum in which students play an active role in integrating ideas and pursuing controversial questions, then you can count on my support. But if these terms are used to justify memorizing more state capitals, or getting a student to bring up her grades (a process that research has shown often undermines the quality of learning), then it's not so clear that rigor and challenge and all the rest of it are worth supporting.

If these distinctions are missed by some parents and teachers, they are systematically ignored by the purveyors of tougher standards. Recently, my own state introduced a test that students will soon have to pass in order to receive a high school diploma. It requires them to acquire a staggering number of facts, which allowed policymakers to claim proudly that they had raised the bar. After new proficiency exams were failed by a significant proportion of students in several other states, education officials there responded by making the tests even harder the following year. The commissioner of education for Colorado offered some insight into the sensibility underlying such decisions: "Unless you get bad results," he declared, "it is highly doubtful you have done anything useful with your tests. Low scores have become synonymous with good tests." Such is the logic on which the tougher-standards movement has been built.

But how many adults could pass these exams? How many high school teachers possess the requisite stock of information outside their own subjects? How many college professors, for that matter, or business executives, or state legislators could confidently write an essay about Mayan agricultural practices or divergent plate boundaries? We would do well to adopt (Deborah) Meier's Mandate: *No student should he expected to meet an academic requirement that a cross section of successful adults in the community cannot.*

(In the same spirit, I propose Kohn's Corollary to Meier's Mandate: All persons given to pious rhetoric about the need to "raise standards" and produce "world-class academic performance for the 21st century" not only should be required to take these exams themselves but must agree to have their scores published in the newspaper.)

Beyond the issue of how many of us could meet these standards is an equally provocative question: How many of us *need* to know this stuff – not just on the basis of job requirements but as a reflection of what it means to be well-educated? Do these facts and skills reflect what we honor, what matters to us about schooling and human life? Often, the standards being rammed into our children's classrooms are not merely unreasonable but irrelevant. It is the kinds of things students are being forced to learn, and the approach to learning itself, that don't ring true. The tests that result – for students and sometimes for teachers – are not just ridiculously difficult but simply ridiculous.

"It is not enough to be busy," Henry David Thoreau once remarked. "The question is, what are we busy about?" If our students are memorizing more forgettable facts than ever before, if they are spending their hours being drilled on what will help them ace a standardized test, then we may indeed have raised the bar – and more's the pity. In that case, school may be harder, but it sure as hell isn't any better.

▇ Write After You Read

1 Write a journal entry in response to "Confusing Harder with Better" using the guidelines on page 11.

2 Summarize in one sentence what you perceive to be the major point of Kohn's argument.

▇ Discuss After You Read

1 Which of Kohn's ideas or examples correspond to what you have experienced or what you know about the college experience? Explain.

2 Which of Kohn's ideas or examples conflict with what you have experienced or what you know about the college experience? Explain.

3 Analyze the strengths and weaknesses of the evidence Kohn provides to support his argument.

   a Which supporting points or examples best clarify Kohn's main argument? Explain.

   b Which supporting points or examples are least convincing? Explain.

4 What additional evidence might strengthen Kohn's argument?

5 What evidence or counterarguments might challenge Kohn's argument?

6 Is the language Kohn uses likely to convince educators to change their behavior?

   a If yes, which specific words or phrases are most likely to appeal to educators? Explain.

   b If no, which specific words or phrases are most likely to offend educators? Explain.

7 How might Kohn respond to Moore's "Grades and Self-Esteem" (pages 117–120)? Create a dialogue between the two authors to illustrate your response.

Reading 5

■ Write Before You Read

Before reading "The Commencement Speech You'll Never Hear" by Jacob Neusner, write for several minutes about what you expect a commencement speaker to say at a college graduation.

The Commencement Speech You'll Never Hear

Jacob Neusner

Jacob Neusner was a professor and distinguished scholar at Brown University in Rhode Island when he wrote this essay. His numerous books include How to Grade Your Professors, and Other Unexpected Advice *(1984),* Judaism and Christianity in the First Century *(1990), and* World Religions in America *(2003). As the title suggests, "The Commencement Speech You'll Never Hear" was not delivered at a college graduation, but it was published in the Brown University campus newspaper, the* Daily Herald.

We the faculty take no pride in our educational achievements with you. We have prepared you for a world that does not exist, indeed, that cannot exist. You have spent four years supposing that failure leaves no record. You have learned at Brown that when your work goes poorly, the painless solution is to drop out. But starting now, in the world to which you go, failure marks you. Confronting difficulty by quitting leaves you changed. Outside Brown, quitters are no heroes.

   With us you could argue about why your errors were not errors, why mediocre work really was excellent, why you could take pride in routine and slipshod presentation. Most of you, after all, can look back on honor grades for most of what you have done. So, here grades can have meant little in distinguishing the excellent from the ordinary. But tomorrow, in the world to which you go, you had best not defend errors but learn from them. You will be ill-advised to demand praise for what does not deserve it, and abuse those who do not give it.

For years we created an altogether forgiving world, in which whatever slight effort you gave was all that was demanded. When you did not keep appointments, we made new ones. When your work came in beyond the deadline, we pretended not to care.

Worse still, when you were boring, we acted as if you were saying something important. When you were garrulous and talked to hear yourselves talk, we listened as if it mattered. When you tossed on our desks writing upon which you had not labored, we read it and even responded, as though you earned a response. When you were dull, we pretended you were smart. When you were predictable, unimaginative and routine, we listened as if to new and wonderful things. When you demanded free lunch, we served it. And all this why?

Despite your fantasies, it was not even that we wanted to be liked by you. It was that we did not want to be bothered, and the easy way out was pretense: smiles and easy Bs.

It is conventional to quote in addresses such as these. Let me quote someone you've never heard of: Prof. Carter A. Daniel, Rutgers University (*Chronicle of Higher Education*, May 7, 1979):

> College has spoiled you by reading papers that don't deserve to be read,
> listening to comments that don't deserve a hearing, paying attention even to
> the lazy, ill-informed and rude. We had to do it, for the sake of education. But
> nobody will ever do it again. College has deprived you of adequate preparation
> for the last 50 years. It has failed you by being easy, free, forgiving, attentive,
> comfortable, interesting, unchallenging fun. Good luck tomorrow.

That is why, on this commencement day, we have nothing in which to take much pride.

Oh, yes, there is one more thing. Try not to act toward your coworkers and bosses as you have acted toward us. I mean, when they give you what you want but have not earned, don't abuse them, insult them, act out with them your parlous relationships with your parents. This too we have tolerated. It was, as I said, not to be liked. Few professors actually care whether or not they are liked by peer-paralyzed adolescents, fools so shallow as to imagine professors care not about education but about popularity. It was, again, to be rid of you. So go, unlearn the lies we taught you. To Life!

■ Write After You Read

1 Write a journal entry in response to "The Commencement Speech You'll Never Hear" using the guidelines on page 11.

2 Summarize in one sentence what you perceive to be the major point of Neusner's argument.

■ Discuss After You Read

1 Which of Neusner's ideas or examples correspond to your own experience at college? Explain.

2 Which of Neusner's ideas or examples conflict with your own experience at college? Explain.

3 Analyze the strengths and weaknesses of the evidence Neusner provides to support his argument.

   a Which supporting points or examples best clarify Neusner's main argument? Explain.

   b Which supporting points or examples are least convincing? Explain.

4 What additional evidence might strengthen Neusner's argument?

5 What evidence or counterarguments might challenge Neusner's argument?

6 Is the language Neusner uses likely to convince teachers or students to change their behavior?

   a If yes, which specific words or phrases are most likely to appeal to teachers? Which specific words or phrases are most likely to appeal to students? Explain your answers.

   b If no, which specific words or phrases are most likely to offend teachers? Which specific words or phrases are most likely to offend students? Explain your answers.

7 Discuss the similarities and differences between Neusner's argument and Harris's argument in "What True Education Should Do" (page 5), Moore's in "Grades and Self-Esteem" (pages 117–120), or Kohn's in "Confusing Harder with Better" (pages 121–124). How might one author's ideas support or challenge the other's?

GUIDELINES

Analyzing an Argumentative Essay

Essay Assignment

Write an essay in which you analyze the strengths and weaknesses of another writer's argument. Explain what the author says, how well the author's points are made, and what points the author may have overlooked. Your purpose is to establish and support your own position agreeing or disagreeing with – or taking a mixed position toward – the author's viewpoint. To accomplish this goal, you will need to incorporate ideas and details from the reading into your own essay (see Section I of A Handbook for Writing, pages 236–273). You may write about more than one reading, for example, by using evidence provided by one writer to refute an argument presented by another writer. The exploratory writing of one student, Ida Timothee, is included in the following guidelines to show how she developed ideas for an essay that analyzes an argument.

■ Exploring a Topic

Exploring a topic for an essay analyzing an argument may involve using some of the exploratory strategies described in Chapters 2 and 3. In addition, you need to analyze the strengths and weaknesses of an author's arguments and determine why you agree or disagree with certain points. The strategies that follow suggest approaches you can take to fulfill the assignment.

Selecting a Reading

Selecting a reading is a first step in analyzing an argumentative essay. You can accomplish this goal by skimming the readings, reviewing whatever you have written about them, and then deciding which argumentative essay you want to analyze.

A student writer at work: *Selecting a Reading*

After skimming the readings, Ida decided she wanted to write about Jacob Neusner's essay "The Commencement Speech You'll Never Hear" (pages 125–126). This is what Ida said about why she chose Neusner's essay:

> "I was shocked when I read this article. Really shocked. It's so . . . cold, so rude, what's the word I want . . . pessimistic. This essay really made me mad."

Your turn: *Selecting a reading*

Using the *Guidelines for Selecting a Reading* on page 96, choose an argumentative essay to analyze.

Taking Notes on a Reading

Taking notes on a reading can help you understand the reasons for an author's argument before you make any judgment. One way to achieve that goal is to create an outline of the author's main argument, supporting points, and evidence. The following template for outlining an argumentative essay may be helpful.

> I. Main argument
>> A. Supporting point
>>> 1. Evidence
>>> 2. Evidence
>> B. Supporting point
>>> 1. Evidence
>>> 2. Evidence
>> (Add further supporting points and evidence as necessary.)
> II. Conclusion

A student writer at work: *Taking notes on a reading*

As Ida reread Neusner's essay, she underlined some of his key points. Then she organized those points in a list. She did not list his supporting evidence because the examples made her angry: "I was trying to concentrate on his major points so that I could argue logically with him, without too much angry emotion."

> 1. College = forgiving world
> 2. Preparation for a world that is not real
> 3. Failure at college leaves no record
> 4. Teachers are concerned about being liked by students
> 5. College is "easy, free . . . unchallenging" etc.
> 6. College offers "painless solutions" to problems

Your turn: *Taking notes on a reading*

Using the *Guidelines for Taking Notes on a Reading* on page 10, or the template for outlining an argumentative essay, take notes on your selected reading.

Evaluating Evidence

Evaluating evidence is necessary for determining whether an argument is strong or weak. This process requires reading critically, which involves not just identifying what the author is saying but also determining whether the author has argued convincingly or effectively.

Guidelines for Evaluating Evidence

Answers to some or all of the following questions may help you evaluate the strength of the evidence the author provides to support an argument:

1. Has the author provided evidence fairly by presenting more than one side of the issue, or has the author provided only a one-sided argument?
2. Has the author provided carefully reasoned evidence to support key points?
3. Has the author provided faulty or misleading evidence?
4. Has the author omitted key evidence that could counter the argument?
5. If the author has included other people's opinions on the subject, do those people have some expertise or trustworthy knowledge of the subject?
6. Is the author's use of language appropriate to the content, or is the language slanted in some way, for example, in exaggeration or cruel attack?

A student writer at work: *Evaluating evidence*

As Ida evaluated the evidence in Neusner's essay, she came to the conclusion that the author had presented a one-sided argument. Here is what Ida had to say after assessing Neusner's evidence:

> "Neusner did not present the students' side of the issue. He just attacked us. So I want my essay to give the other side – to give some balance. I know I have to be careful not to be one-sided myself."

Your turn: *Evaluating evidence*

Using the *Guidelines for Evaluating Evidence*, evaluate the evidence in the essay you are analyzing.

Identifying Points of Agreement and Disagreement

Identifying points of agreement and disagreement can help you to find a pattern in your own reactions to another writer's argument.

Guidelines for Identifying Points of Agreement and Disagreement

1. Make a list of points of agreement between the author and yourself.
2. Make a list of points of disagreement between the author and yourself.
3. Review your lists to see if you can find a pattern in your reactions, which may help you organize your own essay. For example,
   - you may disagree with everything the author says,
   - you may agree on one point but disagree on others,
   - you may agree and disagree on an equal number of points, or
   - you may agree with the author's viewpoint but disapprove of the way the author has presented it.

A student writer at work: *Identifying points of agreement and disagreement*

In rereading the article, Ida recognized a pattern in her thinking:

> "I realized that I <u>completely</u> disagreed with Neusner. I couldn't see his side at all. So I knew that in my essay I would disagree. I looked back at my reading notes and chose three of Neusner's points that I wanted to write about in my paper."

- *Preparation for a world that is not real*
- *Failure leaves no record*
- *College is "easy, free . . . unchallenging"*

Your turn: *Identifying points of agreement and disagreement*

Using the *Guidelines for Identifying Points of Agreement and Disagreement*, determine which of the author's points you will discuss in your own essay.

Determining Reasons for Agreement or Disagreement

Determining reasons for agreement or disagreement can lead you to provide the necessary evidence to support your own argument. It is not enough in an academic essay to simply say "I agree" or "I disagree." You need to explain your reasons fully by giving examples, relating experiences, or referring to other relevant readings or information.

| Guidelines for Determining Reasons for Agreement or Disagreement |

Guidelines for Determining Reasons for Agreement or Disagreement

One or more of the following suggestions may help you determine why you agree or disagree with the author:

1. Use one or more of the exploratory strategies described in Chapter 2 – such as making a list, freewriting, looping, cubing – or any strategy that helps you to generate reasons for agreeing or disagreeing with the author.
2. Review the discussion questions following the reading, and write down answers to the most relevant questions.
3. Discuss the reading with a friend. You may use your friend's examples or experiences as evidence in your essay, but be sure to credit the friend as the source of the information.

A student writer at work: *Determining reasons for agreement or disagreement*

Ida now had a list of Neusner's points that she wanted to debate (see page 131). Her next step was to think of ways to support her ideas. She decided to do some freewriting, and this process led her to create a list of reasons to explain her position in relation to Neusner's ideas.

Here are three points that Ida disagreed with in Neusner's essay, along with her reasons.

> 1. Preparation for a world that is not real
>   - we learn to be independent
>   - learn to budget time and money
>   - learn from diverse student body
>   - we learn to be tolerant
> 2. Failure leaves no record
>   - if you fail a test or a course, teacher won't change the grade
>   - drop a class — you'll have to take more courses next semester
>   - low GPA — no graduate school
> 3. College is "easy, free . . . unchallenging"
>   - living in triple
>   - one-day reading period
>   - work load

Your turn: *Determining reasons for agreement or disagreement*

Using the *Guidelines for Determining Reasons for Agreement or Disagreement*, generate reasons to explain why you agree or disagree with the author's argument.

◼ Focusing Ideas

To fulfill the goal of *focusing ideas* for your readers, you need to determine your position in relation to the author's argument, and write a sentence or two that can serve as the focal point of your essay.

A student writer at work: *Focusing ideas*

This is what Ida reported about the process of creating a focal point for her essay:

> "I knew why I thought Neusner was wrong, but I had to think about making my points clear. I looked at my list to try to decide what idea tied everything together. I wanted to think about what is really wrong with Neusner's essay. So I wrote a sentence that I thought would tell anyone who read my essay what I wanted to say: 'College is not as easy and perfect for the student as Neusner presents it.' The funny thing is that I didn't use this sentence in my paper. I was thinking about it when I started writing, but I got so excited that I forgot about my readers. So when my classmates read my paper, they got really confused. It was a good thing I could revise."

▪▪▶ Your turn: *Focusing ideas*

Using the *Guidelines for Focusing Ideas* on page 61, create a focal point for your essay.

◼ Structuring the Essay

Structuring the essay that analyzes an argument involves moving readers toward an understanding of the strengths and weaknesses of the argument. Such essays have a basic, three-part organizational framework: an *introduction*, a *body*, and a *conclusion*.

The flow chart on page 134 may help you visualize an overall structure for an essay analyzing an argumentative essay.

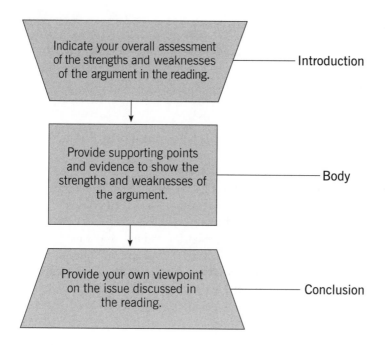

Indicate your overall assessment of the strengths and weaknesses of the argument in the reading. — Introduction

Provide supporting points and evidence to show the strengths and weaknesses of the argument. — Body

Provide your own viewpoint on the issue discussed in the reading. — Conclusion

The Introduction

The *introduction* to an essay that analyzes an argumentative essay summarizes the gist of the author's argument and provides a focal point that reveals your overall position toward the argument. You should make clear whether you agree with, disagree with, or have a mixed position toward the ideas in the reading. (See also *Guidelines for Writing the Introduction* on page 101.)

Activity: *Evaluating introductions*

The passages on the following page are introductions to student essays analyzing argumentative essays. Evaluate two or more of the introductions by answering the following questions.

1 Does the introduction involve you in the topic and make you want to read the rest of the essay? Explain.

2 Can you tell, at the beginning of the essay, what the general subject of the essay is?

3 Can you tell which reading the student writer is analyzing?

4 Has the student writer accurately summarized the gist of the author's argument in his or her own words?

5 Can you determine the student writer's perspective toward the author's argument?

6 If you think the introduction should be revised, what suggestions do you have for the student writer?

Student A

In "The Commencement Speech You'll Never Hear," Jacob Neusner argues that we have been made to believe, according to our college experience, that "failure leaves no record" (p. 125) and that things can be easily achieved. It seems to Neusner that college is not a good preparatory school for life because it is making us ready "for a world that does not exist" (p. 125).

There's no doubt that Neusner should have taken a closer look at what college life is really like before formulating such a strong opinion about it. He is completely ignoring all the pressures and hard times students go through to make it at college. It is not the way he describes it at all. – **Ida**

Student B

In the article "What True Education Should Do," author Sydney J. Harris states that good education does not bombard the child with information; instead the teacher should try to extract the knowledge from the student. He argues that students who were besieged with information had no time to express their own thoughts and to use their mind for "analyzing and synthesizing and evaluating the material" (p. 5). I agree with the author, but I think a little improvement can be made. I believe that the author is too one-sided. Sometimes not everything is black and white; there are always some gray areas in life. – **David**

Student C

Kie Ho states that the public education in the States is "certainly not perfect, but it is a great deal better than any other" (p. 114). I cannot take a stand on this statement because there are aspects that I do not agree with and some I do. It is not necessarily true that the education is "a great deal better," but certainly it is, in a way, "better." – **Stephanie**

Student D

In his essay, "We Should Cherish Our Children's Freedom to Think," Kie Ho supports the American system of education. He expresses disappointment with the Indonesian way of teaching that he had experienced. As he points out, American schools tend to teach students how to develop their creativity more, rather than try to stuff their heads with knowledge. Ho always had to memorize things and to acquire as much knowledge as he could from books, while his son in California learned practical things through experience. Ho admires the approach of his son's school. But I hesitate to endorse it. – **Sophia**

The Body

The *body* of an essay analyzing an argument provides evidence to explain your position toward the author's argument. It should include paraphrased and quoted passages from the reading as well as your reasons for agreeing with, disagreeing with, or having a mixed position toward the author's ideas. (See also *Guidelines for Structuring the Body Paragraphs* on page 105.)

The following suggestions offer three possibilities for structuring the body paragraphs of an essay analyzing an argument. You can use the drafting process to experiment with the organization of the body; your early efforts can be revised later (see Drafting, pages 274–275, and Revising, pages 278–282).

1. Analyze several ideas from the reading one by one, devoting at least one paragraph to each idea.
   a. State the author's idea, and explain it.
   b. Provide evidence to explain why you agree or disagree with this idea.
   c. Repeat this process for each idea you want to discuss.
   d. Present the ideas in a logical order. For example, you could
      - begin with the least important idea and end with the most important; or
      - first discuss the ideas that you support, then discuss the ideas that you challenge; or
      - first discuss the author's ideas, then discuss the opposing viewpoint.

2. Analyze one major idea from the reading.
   a. Explain one of the author's major ideas.
   b. Provide evidence in different paragraphs to explain why you agree or disagree with this idea.
   c. Throughout the body, include periodic references to the reading selection through paraphrase or quotation to show the connection between the author's points and your analysis.

3. Analyze several ideas from the reading, and then explore one or more ideas that the reading does not develop enough or neglects altogether.
   a. In the first half of the body, state and explain an idea from the reading, then explain why you agree or disagree with this idea. Repeat this process for each idea you want to discuss.
   b. In the second half of the body, state an idea that the reading ignores, then explain why that idea is important to consider. Repeat this process for each idea you want to discuss.

Activity: *Evaluating body paragraphs*

The passages on the following pages are body paragraphs from student essays analyzing argumentative essays. Evaluate two or more of the paragraphs by answering the following questions.

1 How well does the student writer explain the author's argument?
2 Can you determine the student writer's perspective on the author's argument?

3 Does the student writer provide relevant and sufficient evidence to explain the reasons for agreeing or disagreeing with the author's argument?

4 If you think the paragraph should be revised, what suggestions do you have for the student writer?

Student A

Neusner believes that in college we are trained to think that "failure leaves no record" because we can supposedly get way with mistakes easily. Well, I have news for him. If you fail a test, you can't take it again or the teacher won't erase the grade even if he thinks you will hate him for the rest of your life. If you drop out of a class, next semester you will have to take more courses. If you get low grades, your chances of getting into a fine graduate school are almost none. If your G.P.A. is not reasonably high for a number of classes, you just don't get your degree. When mid-terms and finals come, no one can avoid taking them. When the going gets tough, the tough have to get down to work because, unlike what Neusner believes, college does not give "painless" solutions to mistakes (p. 125). It is not "an altogether forgiving world," and by no means have teachers "pretended not to care" (p. 126) when deadlines are not kept, or when things aren't done at the time they are supposed to be. – **Ida**

Student B

Ho connects this focus on creativity and practicality with the country's strength. He asks why so many people complain about the American education system, since America is "the country of innovation" (p. 113). This innovativeness is tied to the fact that the public schools provide children with the opportunity to be creative:

> I think I found the answer on an excursion to the Laguna Beach Museum of Art, where the work of school children was on exhibit . . . they had transformed simple paper lunch bags into, among other things, a waterfall with flying fish. (p. 113)

I have to agree that Ho's observation is true. The opportunity for creativity impressed me, too, when I first went to an American high school. I admired how much attention the teachers gave to students' work and talents. I was impressed by the programs the school offered, the many different opportunities they gave students to do whatever they wanted, no matter how different and unique it was. I noticed that the students were always involved in activities, competitions, and exhibitions that are connect with their classes at school. That is a way of learning that Ho supports. – **Sophia**

Student C

Sydney J. Harris quotes a college student who says, "I spend so much time studying that I don't have a chance to learn anything" (p. 5). Harris says this student is "succinctly expressing his dissatisfaction with the sausage casing view of education" (p. 5). I like this section because I believe it is true. Some teachers want to finish a lot of work in a little time in order to keep up with the syllabus. I don't think anyone will benefit from this. It's liking giving someone twenty new vocabulary words to memorize in one day. The person will not be able to memorize them, and even if he did he'll only have them memorized for the quiz and then they'll all be forgotten. – **Adam**

Student D

Students should be allowed to be creative and not just memorize. In other words, we should give the opportunity to students to fulfill their creativity. As Kie Ho says in his essay, "We Should Cherish Our Children's Freedom to Think," children will not really be able to think or believe in themselves without experimenting freely with ideas. He also claims that if we force children to memorize, we will "retard their impulses" and prevent them from self-expression (p. 113). Sydney J. Harris, in "What True Education Should Do," makes the same point. According to Harris, the best way to educate is to elicit knowledge, not "stuff" it into a person's head (p. 5). – **Lisa**

The Conclusion

The *conclusion* to an essay analyzing an argument emphasizes the validity of your point of view. Having established what the author has said, analyzed how well the author's points are made, and explained why you agree or disagree with those points, you can now discuss the implications or consequences of accepting or rejecting the author's point of view. (See also *Guidelines for Writing the Conclusion*, page 108).

Your turn: *Structuring the essay*

Using the *Guidelines for Writing the Introduction* on page 101, the *Guidelines for Structuring the Body Paragraphs* on page 105, and the *Guidelines for Writing the Conclusion* on page 108, create a flow chart such as the one on page 134 to show what ideas and specifics you might include in your essay.

■ Writing the Essay

Writing the essay can be accomplished most effectively by going through the processes of drafting, receiving feedback, and revising (see Section II of A Handbook for Writing, pages 274–284). Use the checklist on the next page to see if your essay fulfills readers' expectations for analysis of an argument. The checklist may be used for self-evaluation or for evaluation of your essay by another reader.

Evaluative Criteria for an Essay Analyzing an Argument

YES **NO**

☐ ☐ **1 Does the opening of the essay provide general background information on the topic?**
If yes, what is the general background?
If no, what background information might be relevant?

☐ ☐ **2 Does the essay make clear which argumentative essay is being analyzed?**
If yes, which argumentative essay is being analyzed?
If no, where might the name of the author and title of the argumentative essay be included?

☐ ☐ **3 Does the essay provide a specific focus that reveals a position toward the author's argument?**
If yes, what is the position?
If no, how can the focus be clarified?

☐ ☐ **4 Does the essay clearly state and explain the author's arguments?**
If yes, which explanations help to clarify the author's arguments?
If no, how might the arguments be clarified?

☐ ☐ **5 Does the essay provide sufficient paraphrased and quoted references to the reading?**
If yes, which references present the reading's ideas?
If no, where might references be added or changed?

☐ ☐ **6 Does the essay provide sufficient and relevant evidence to support or challenge points made about the reading?**
If yes, which evidence helps to clarify a point?
If no, what kind of evidence would clarify a point?

☐ ☐ **7 Does the conclusion discuss the implications of what is written in the body of the essay?**
If yes, what are the implications?
If no, what might the implications be?

☐ ☐ **8 Is the essay logically structured?**
If yes, what makes the structure logical?
If no, how could the essay be more logically structured?

■ Completing the Essay

Completing the essay involves proofreading and editing your final draft as well as preparing a clear final copy to hand in to your instructor for evaluation. See Sections II and III of A Handbook for Writing, pages 282–288.

Chapter 5

Analyzing Fiction

Writing an essay analyzing fiction involves developing an interpretation that grows out of the details of a story. One of the challenges of composing such an essay is to infer the author's meaning, for fictional works are drawn from writers' imaginations and do not directly state main ideas.

Chapter 5 includes five short stories that can become sources for your essay. These reading selections, spanning more than one hundred years, focus on some of the problems and possibilities of living in the United States of America. The authors take readers inside the minds of their characters to show what it means for them to live as slaves, immigrants, and exiles.

The guidelines that follow the readings are designed to help you compose an essay analyzing fiction.

Reading 1

The Ingrate

Paul Laurence Dunbar

Paul Laurence Dunbar (1872–1906) was born in the United States, in Dayton, Ohio, the son of former slaves. His father escaped from enslavement in Kentucky and served in the Massachusetts 55th Regiment during the Civil War. Despite a distinguished high school record, Dunbar was unable to find meaningful work because of the racial discrimination of the era. Already a published poet, he continued to read extensively and began to write and publish fiction. Widely admired, Dunbar was the first African American to make a living as a professional writer. Among his many books are eleven volumes of poetry, including Lyrics of Lowly Life *(1896) and* Howdy, Honey, Howdy *(1905), and the novels* The Uncalled *(1898) and* The Sport of the Gods *(1902). "The Ingrate" was originally published in the* New England Magazine *in 1899.*

1

Mr. Leckler was a man of high principle. Indeed, he himself had admitted it at times to Mrs. Leckler. She was often called into counsel with him. He was one of those large-souled creatures with a hunger for unlimited advice, upon which he never acted. Mrs. Leckler knew this, but like the good, patient little wife that she was, she went on paying her poor tribute of advice and admiration. Today her husband's mind was particularly troubled – as usual, too, over a matter of principle. Mrs. Leckler came at his call.

"Mrs. Leckler," he said, "I am troubled in my mind. I – in fact, I am puzzled over a matter that involves either the maintaining or relinquishing of a principle."

"Well, Mr. Leckler?" said his wife, interrogatively.

"If I had been a scheming, calculating Yankee,[1] I should have been rich now; but all my life I have been too generous and confiding. I have always let principle stand between me and my interests." Mr. Leckler took himself all too seriously to be conscious of his pun, and went on: "Now this is a matter in which my duty and my principles seem to conflict. It stands thus: Josh has been doing a piece of plastering for Mr. Eckley over in Lexington,[2] and from what he says, I think that city rascal has misrepresented the amount of work to me and so cut down the pay for it. Now, of course, I should not care, the matter of a dollar or two being nothing to me; but it is a very different matter when we consider poor Josh."

[1] *Yankee*: a native or inhabitant of a northern state in the United States, where slavery was no longer legal
[2] *Lexington*: a city in the southern U.S. state of Kentucky

There was deep pathos in Mr. Leckler's tone. "You know Josh is anxious to buy his freedom, and I allow him a part of whatever he makes; so you see it's he that's affected. Every dollar that he is cheated out of cuts off just so much from his earnings, and puts further away his hope of emancipation."

If the thought occurred to Mrs. Leckler that, since Josh received only about one-tenth of what he earned, the advantage of just wages would be quite as much her husband's as the slave's, she did not betray it, but met the naïve reasoning with the question, "But where does the conflict come in, Mr. Leckler?"

"Just here. If Josh knew how to read and write and cipher – "

"Mr. Leckler, are you crazy!"

"Listen to me, my dear, and give me the benefit of your judgment. This is a very momentous question. As I was about to say, if Josh knew these things, he could protect himself from cheating when his work is at too great a distance for me to look after it for him."

"But teaching a slave – "

"Yes, that's just what is against my principles. I know how public opinion and the law look at it. But my conscience rises up in rebellion every time I think of that poor black man being cheated out of his earnings. Really, Mrs. Leckler, I think I may trust to Josh's discretion, and secretly give him such instructions as will permit him to protect himself."

"Well, of course, it's just as you think best," said his wife.

"I knew you would agree with me," he returned. "It's such a comfort to take counsel with you, my dear!" And the generous man walked out onto the veranda, very well satisfied with himself and his wife, and prospectively pleased with Josh. Once he murmured to himself, "I'll lay for Eckley next time."

Josh, the subject of Mr. Leckler's charitable solicitations, was the plantation plasterer. His master had given him his trade, in order that he might do whatever such work was needed about the place; but he became so proficient in his duties, having also no competition among the poor whites, that he had grown to be in great demand in the country thereabout. So Mr. Leckler found it profitable, instead of letting him do chores and field work in his idle time, to hire him out to neighboring farms and planters. Josh was a man of more than ordinary intelligence; and when he asked to be allowed to pay for himself by working overtime, his master readily agreed – for it promised more work to be done, for which he could allow the slave just what he pleased. Of course, he knew now that when the black man began to cipher this state of affairs would be changed; but it would mean such an increase of profit from the outside, that he could afford to give up his own little peculations. Anyway, it would be many years before the slave could pay the two thousand dollars, which price he had set upon him. Should he approach that figure, Mr. Leckler felt it just possible that the market in slaves would take a sudden rise.

When Josh was told of his master's intention, his eyes gleamed with pleasure, and he went to his work with the zest of long hunger. He proved a remarkably apt pupil. He was indefatigable in doing the tasks assigned him. Even Mr. Leckler, who had great faith in his plasterer's ability, marveled at the speed which he had acquired the three R's. He did not know that on one of his many trips a free negro had given Josh the rudimentary tools of learning, and that ever since the slave had been adding to his store of learning by poring over signs and every bit of print that he could spell out. Neither was Josh so indiscreet as to intimate to his benefactor that he had been anticipated in his good intentions.

It was in this way, working and learning, that a year passed away, and Mr. Leckler thought that his object had been accomplished. He could safely trust Josh to protect his own interests, and so he thought that it was quite time that his servant's education should cease.

"You know, Josh," he said, "I have already gone against my principles and against the law for your sake, and of course a man can't stretch his conscience too far, even to help another who's being cheated; but I reckon you can take care of yourself now."

"Oh, yes, suh, I reckon I kin," said Josh.

"And it wouldn't do for you to be seen with any books about you now."

"Oh, no, suh, su't'n'y not." He didn't intend to be seen with any books about him.

It was just now that Mr. Leckler saw the good results of all he had done, and his heart was full of a great joy, for Eckley had been building some additions to his house, and sent for Josh to do the plastering for him. The owner admonished his slave, took him over a few examples to freshen his memory, and sent him forth with glee. When the job was done, there was a discrepancy of two dollars in what Mr. Eckley offered for it and the price which accrued from Josh's measurements. To the employer's surprise, the black man went over the figures with him and convinced him of the incorrectness of the payment – and the additional two dollars were turned over.

"Some o' Leckler's work," said Eckley, "teaching a nigger to cipher! Close-fisted old reprobate – I've a mind to have the law on him." Mr. Leckler heard the story with great glee. "I laid for him that time – the old fox." But to Mrs. Leckler he said: "You see, my dear wife, my rashness in teaching Josh to figure for himself is vindicated. See what he has saved for himself."

"What did he save?" asked the little woman indiscreetly.

Her husband blushed and stammered for a moment, and then replied, "Well, of course, it was only twenty cents saved to him, but to a man buying his freedom every cent counts; and after all, it is not the amount, Mrs. Leckler, it's the principle of the thing."

"Yes," said the lady meekly.

2

Unto the body it is easy for the master to say, "Thus far shalt thou go, and no farther." Gyves, chains, and fetters will enforce that command. But what master shall say unto the mind, "Here do I set the limit of your acquisition. Pass it not"? Who shall put gyves upon the intellect, or fetter the movement of thought? Joshua Leckler,[3] as custom denominated him, had tasted of the forbidden fruit,

[3] *Joshua Leckler*: Slaves were commonly assigned the surnames of their owners.

and his appetite had grown by what it fed on. Night after night he crouched in his lonely cabin, by the blaze of a fat pine brand, poring over the few books that he had been able to secure and smuggle in. His fellow servants alternately laughed at him and wondered why he did not take a wife. But Joshua went on his way. He had no time for marrying or for love; other thoughts had taken possession of him. He was being swayed by ambitions other than the mere fathering of slaves for his master. To him his slavery was deep night. What wonder, then, that he should dream, and that through the ivory gate should come to him the forbidden vision of freedom? To own himself, to be master of his hands, feet, of his whole body – something would clutch at his heart as he thought of it; and the breath would come hard between his lips. But he met his master with an impassive face, always silent, always docile; and Mr. Leckler congratulated himself that so valuable and intelligent a slave should be at the same time so tractable. Usually intelligence in a slave meant discontent; but not so with Josh. Who more content than he? He remarked to his wife: "You see, my dear, this is what comes of treating even a nigger right."

Meanwhile the white hills of the North were beckoning to the chattel, and the north winds were whispering to him to be a chattel no longer. Often the eyes that looked away to where freedom lay were filled with a wistful longing that was tragic in its intensity, for they saw the hardships and the difficulties between the slave and his goal and, worst of all, an iniquitous law[4] – liberty's compromise with bondage, that rose like a stone wall between him and hope – a law that degraded every free-thinking man to the level of a slave-catcher. There it loomed up before him, formidable, impregnable, insurmountable. He measured it in all its terribleness, and paused. But on the other side there was liberty; and one day when he was away at work, a voice came out of the woods and whispered to him "Courage!" – and on that night the shadows beckoned him as the white hills had done, and the forest called to him, "Follow."

"It seems to me that Josh might have been able to get home tonight," said Mr. Leckler, walking up and down his veranda; "but I reckon it's just possible that he got through too late to catch a train." In the morning he said: "Well, he's not here yet; he must have had to do some extra work. If he doesn't get here by evening, I'll run up there."

In the evening, he did take the train for Joshua's place of employment, where he learned that his slave had left the night before. But where could he have gone? That no one knew, and for the first time it dawned upon his master that Josh had run away. He raged; he fumed; but nothing could be done until morning, and all the time Leckler knew that the most valuable slave on his plantation was working his way toward the North and freedom. He did not go back home, but paced the floor all night long. In the early dawn he hurried out, and the hounds were put on the fugitive's track. After some nosing around they set off toward a stretch of woods. In a few minutes they came yelping back, pawing their noses and rubbing their heads against the ground. They had found the trail, but Josh had played the

---

[4] *law*: The Fugitive Slave Act of 1850 stated that any person aiding a runaway slave was liable to imprisonment and a $1,000 fine, and that a person suspected of being a runaway slave could be arrested without warrant or trial and turned over to a slave owner.

old slave trick of filling his tracks with cayenne pepper. The dogs were soothed, and taken deeper into the wood to find the trail. They soon took it up again, and dashed away with low bays. The scent led them directly to a little wayside station about six miles distant. Here it stopped. Burning with the chase, Mr. Leckler hastened to the station agent. Had he seen such a negro? Yes, he had taken the northbound train two nights before.

"But why did you let him go without a pass?" almost screamed the owner.

"I didn't," replied the agent. "He had a written pass, signed James Leckler, and I let him go on it."

"Forged, forged!" yelled the master. "He wrote it himself."

"Humph!" said the agent. "How was I to know that? Our niggers round here don't know how to write."

Mr. Leckler suddenly bethought him to hold his peace. Josh was probably now in the arms of some northern abolitionist,[5] and there was nothing to be done now but advertise; and the disgusted master spread his notices broadcast before starting for home. As soon as he arrived at his house, he sought his wife and poured out his griefs to her.

"You see, Mrs. Leckler, this is what comes of my goodness of heart. I taught that nigger to read and write, so that he could protect himself – and look how he uses his knowledge. Oh, the ingrate, the ingrate! The very weapon which I give him to defend himself against others he turns upon me. Oh, it's awful – awful! I've always been too confiding. Here's the most valuable nigger on my plantation gone – gone, I tell you – and through my own kindness. It isn't his value, though, I'm thinking so much about. I could stand his loss, if it wasn't for the principle of the thing, the base ingratitude he has shown me. Oh, if I ever lay hands on him again!" Mr. Leckler closed his lips and clenched his fist with an eloquence that laughed at words.

Just at this time, in one of the underground railway[6] stations, six miles north of the Ohio, an old Quaker[7] was saying to Josh: "Lie still – thee'll be perfectly safe there. Here comes John Trader, our local slave catcher, but I will parley with him and send him away. Thee need not fear. None of thy brethren who have come to us have ever been taken back to bondage – Good-evening, Friend Trader!" and Josh heard the old Quaker's smooth voice roll on, while he lay back half smothering in a bag, among other bags of corn and potatoes.

It was after ten o'clock that night when he was thrown carelessly into a wagon and driven away to the next station, twenty-five miles to the northward. And by such stages, hiding by day and traveling by night, helped by a few of his own people who were blessed with freedom, and always by the good Quakers wherever found, he made his way into Canada. And on one never-to-be-forgotten morning he stood up, straightened himself, breathed God's blessed air, and knew himself free!

---

[5] *abolitionist*: a member of a movement organized to end slavery

[6] *underground railway*: a network of paths formed by those interested in ending slavery to provide hiding and transportation for slaves to escape to the North

[7] *Quaker*: Members of the Religious Society of Friends, which was active in the abolitionist movement, are called Quakers. Quakers used the words *thee* for *you* and *thy* for *your*.

3

To Joshua Leckler this life in Canada was all new and strange. It was a new thing for him to feel himself a man and to have his manhood recognized by the whites with whom he came into free contact. It was new, too, this receiving the full measure of his worth in work. He went to his labor with a zest that he had never known before, and he took a pleasure in the very weariness it brought him. Ever and anon there came to his ears the cries of his brethren in the South. Frequently he met fugitives who, like himself, had escaped from bondage; and the harrowing tales that they told him made him burn to do something for those whom he had left behind him. But these fugitives and the papers he read told him other things. They said that the spirit of freedom was working in the United States, and already men were speaking out boldly in behalf of the manumission of the slaves; already there was a growing army behind that noble vanguard, Sumner, Phillips, Douglass, Garrison. He heard the names of Lucretia Mott and Harriet Beecher Stowe,[8] and his heart swelled, for on the dim horizon he saw the first faint streaks of dawn.

So the years passed. Then from the surcharged clouds a flash of lightning broke, and there was the thunder of cannon and the rain of lead[9] over the land. From his home in the North he watched the storm as it raged and wavered, now threatening the North with its awful power, now hanging dire and dreadful over the South. Then suddenly from out the fray came a voice like the trumpet tone of God to him: "Thou and thy brothers are free!" Free, free, with the freedom not cherished by the few alone, but for all that had been bound. Free, with the freedom not torn from the secret night, but open to the light of heaven.

When the first call for colored soldiers came, Joshua Leckler hastened down to Boston, and enrolled himself among those who were willing to fight to maintain their freedom. On account of his ability to read and write and his general intelligence, he was soon made an orderly sergeant. His regiment had already taken part in an engagement before the public roster of this band of Uncle Sam's niggers, as they were called, fell into Mr. Leckler's hands. He ran his eye down the column of names. It stopped at that of Joshua Leckler, Sergeant, Company F. He handed the paper to Mrs. Leckler with his finger on the place.

"Mrs. Leckler," he said, "this is nothing less than a judgment on me for teaching a nigger to read and write. I disobeyed the law of my state and, as a result, not only lost my nigger, but furnished the Yankees with a smart officer to help them fight the South. Mrs. Leckler, I have sinned – and been punished. But I am content, Mrs. Leckler; it all came through my kindness of heart – and your mistaken advice. But, oh, that ingrate, that ingrate!"

---

[8] *(Charles) Sumner, (Wendell) Phillips, (Frederick) Douglass,* and *(William) Garrison* were American abolitionists. *Lucretia Mott* was an American social reformer. *Harriet Beecher Stowe* was an American novelist and reformer and author of *Uncle Tom's Cabin* (1852), which was influential in promoting the abolitionist movement.

[9] *the thunder of cannon and the rain of lead*: the Civil War (1861–1865), fought between northern and southern states, which led to the end of slavery in the United States

Write After You Read

1 Write a journal entry in response to "The Ingrate" using the guidelines on pages 11.

2 Summarize the story in a few sentences by explaining the key events, the main conflict, and the final outcome.

Discuss After You Read

1 What is the reason Mr. Leckler gives his wife for Josh's lessons? What is the real reason?

2 What is the reason Mr. Leckler gives Josh for ending the instruction? What is the real reason?

3 Examine closely the conversations that take place between Mr. Leckler and his wife. On the basis of these conversations, how would you characterize their marriage?

4 Compare and contrast Josh's behavior in the presence of Mr. Leckler in part 1 of the story to his behavior when he is alone in part 2. What do the similarities or differences suggest about Josh's personality and character?

5 What do you perceive to be the significance of the story's title?

6 Compare and contrast the experience of being oppressed in Dunbar's "The Ingrate" with the oppressive experience in Zitkala-Ša's "The School Days of an Indian Girl" (pages 24–29).

Reading 2

In the Land of the Free

Sui Sin Far

Sui Sin Far (1865–1914) was born Edith Maud Eaton in England to a Chinese mother and an English father. Her family moved to Montreal, Canada, when she was seven. As an adult, she lived in the United States and Canada. Sui Sin Far was the first person of Chinese ancestry to publish stories in the United States that were focused on Chinese-American experiences. Two years before her death, thirty-seven of her stories were collected in the book Mrs. Spring Fragrance. *When Sui Sin Far died in Montreal, the Chinese community erected a monument to her memory. "In the Land of the Free" was originally published in the magazine* Independent *in 1909.*

1

"See, little one – the hills in the morning sun. There is thy home for years to come. It is very beautiful and thou wilt be very happy there."

The Little One looked up into his mother's face in perfect faith. He was engaged in the pleasant occupation of sucking a sweetmeat; but that did not prevent him from gurgling responsively.

"Yes, my olive bud; there is where thy father is making a fortune for thee. Thy father! Oh, wilt thou not be glad to behold his dear face. 'Twas for thee I left him."

The Little One ducked his chin sympathetically against his mother's knee. She lifted him on to her lap. He was two years old, a round, dimple-cheeked boy with bright brown eyes and a sturdy little frame.

"Ah! Ah! Ah! Ooh! Ooh! Ooh!" puffed he, mocking a tugboat steaming by.

San Francisco's waterfront was lined with ships and steamers, while other craft, large and small, including a couple of white transports from the Philippines, lay at anchor here and there off shore. It was some time before the *Eastern Queen* could get docked, and even after that was accomplished, a lone Chinaman who had been waiting on the wharf for an hour was detained that much longer by men with the initials U.S.C. on their caps, before he could board the steamer and welcome his wife and child.

"This is thy son," announced the happy Lae Choo.

Hom Hing lifted the child, felt of his little body and limbs, gazed into his face with proud and joyous eyes; then turned inquiringly to a customs officer at his elbow.

"That's a fine boy you have there," said the man. "Where was he born?"

"In China," answered Hom Hing, swinging the Little One on his right shoulder, preparatory to leading his wife off the steamer.

"Ever been to America before?"

"No, not he," answered the father with a happy laugh.

The customs officer beckoned to another.

"This little fellow," said he, "is visiting America for the first time."

The other customs officer stroked his chin reflectively.

"Good day," said Hom Hing.

"Wait!" commanded one of the officers. "You cannot go just yet."

"What more now?" asked Hom Hing.

"I'm afraid," said the customs officer, "that we cannot allow the boy to go ashore. There is nothing in the papers that you have shown us – your wife's papers and your own – having any bearing upon the child."

"There was no child when the papers were made out," returned Hom Hing. He spoke calmly; but there was apprehension in his eyes and in his tightening grip on his son.

"What is it? What is it?" quavered Lae Choo, who understood a little English.

The second customs officer regarded her pityingly.

"I don't like this part of the business," he muttered.

The first officer turned to Hom Hing and in an official tone of voice, said:

"Seeing that the boy has no certificate entitling him to admission to this country you will have to leave him with us."

"Leave my boy!" exclaimed Hom Hing.

"Yes; he will be well taken care of, and just as soon as we can hear from Washington he will be handed over to you."

"But," protested Hom Hing, "he is my son."

"We have no proof," answered the man with a shrug of his shoulders; "and even if so we cannot let him pass without orders from the Government."

"He is my son," reiterated Hom Hing, slowly and solemnly. "I am a Chinese merchant and have been in business in San Francisco for many years. When my wife told to me one morning that she dreamed of a green tree with spreading branches and one beautiful red flower growing thereon, I answered her that I wished my son to be born in our country, and for her to prepare to go to China. My wife complied with my wish. After my son was born my mother fell sick and my wife nursed and cared for her; then my father, too, fell sick, and my wife also nursed and cared for him. For twenty moons my wife care for and nurse the old people, and when they die they bless her and my son, and I send for her to return to me. I had no fear of trouble. I was a Chinese merchant and my son was my son."

"Very good, Hom Hing," replied the first officer. "Nevertheless, we take your son."

"No, you not take him; he my son too."

It was Lae Choo. Snatching the child from his father's arms she held and covered him with her own.

The officers conferred together for a few moments; then one drew Hom Hing aside and spoke in his ear.

Resignedly Hom Hing bowed his head, then approached his wife. "'Tis the law," said he, speaking in Chinese, "and 'twill be but for a little while – until tomorrow's sun arises."

"You, too," reproached Lae Choo in a voice eloquent with pain. But accustomed to obedience she yielded the boy to her husband, who in turn delivered him to the first officer. The Little One protested lustily against the transfer; but his mother covered her face with her sleeve and his father silently led her away. Thus was the law of the land complied with.

2

Day was breaking. Lae Choo, who had been awake all night, dressed herself then awoke her husband.

"'Tis the morn," she cried. "Go, bring our son."

The man rubbed his eyes and arose upon his elbow so that he could see out of the window. A pale star was visible in the sky. The petals of a lily in a bowl on the windowsill were unfurled.

"'Tis not yet time," said he, laying his head down again.

"Not yet time. Ah, all the time that I lived before yesterday is not so much as the time that has been since my Little One was taken from me."

The mother threw herself down beside the bed and covered her face. Hom Hing turned on the light, and touching his wife's bowed head with a sympathetic hand inquired if she had slept.

"Slept!" she echoed, weepingly. "Ah, how could I close my eyes with my arms empty of the little body that has filled them every night for more than twenty moons! You do not know – man – what it is to miss the feel of the little fingers and the little toes and the soft round limbs of your little one. Even in the darkness his darling eyes used to shine up to mine, and often have I fallen into slumber with his pretty babble at my ear. And now, I see him not; I touch him not; I hear him not. My baby, my little fat one!"

"Now! Now! Now!" consoled Hom Hing, patting his wife's shoulder reassuringly; "There is no need to grieve so; he will soon gladden you again. There cannot be any law that would keep a child from its mother!"

Lae Choo dried her tears.

"You are right, my husband," she meekly murmured. She arose and stepped about the apartment, setting things to rights. The box of presents she had brought for her California friends had been opened the evening before; and silks, embroideries, carved ivories, ornamental lacquer-ware, brasses, camphorwood boxes, fans, and chinaware were scattered around in confused heaps. In the midst of unpacking the thought of her child in the hands of strangers had overpowered her, and she had left everything to crawl into bed and weep.

Having arranged her gifts in order she stepped out on to the deep balcony.

The star had faded from view and there were bright streaks in the western sky. Lae Choo looked down the street and around. Beneath the flat occupied by her and her husband were quarters for a number of bachelor Chinamen, and she could hear them from where she stood, taking their early morning breakfast. Below their dining-room was her husband's grocery store. Across the way was a large restaurant. Last night it had been resplendent with gay colored lanterns and the sound of music. The rejoicings over "the completion of the moon," by Quong Sum's firstborn, had been long and loud, and had caused her to tie a handkerchief over her ears. She, a bereaved mother, had it not in her heart to rejoice with other parents. This morning the place was more in accord with her mood. It was still and quiet. The revellers had dispersed or were asleep.

A roly-poly woman in black sateen, with long pendant earrings in her ears, looked up from the street below and waved her a smiling greeting. It was her old neighbor, Kuie Hoe, the wife of the gold embosser, Mark Sing. With her was a little boy in yellow jacket and lavender pantaloons. Lae Choo remembered him as a baby. She used to like to play with him in those days when she had no child of her own. What a long time ago that seemed! She caught her breath in a sigh, and laughed instead.

"Why are you so merry?" called her husband from within.

"Because my Little One is coming home," answered Lae Choo. "I am a happy mother – a happy mother."

She pattered into the room with a smile on her face.

The noon hour had arrived. The rice was steaming in the bowls and a fragrant dish of chicken and bamboo shoots was awaiting Hom Hing. Not for one moment had Lae Choo paused to rest during the morning hours; her activity had been ceaseless. Every now and again, however, she had raised her eyes to the gilded clock on the curiously carved mantelpiece. Once, she had exclaimed: "Why so long, oh! why so long?" Then, apostrophizing herself: "Lae Choo, be happy. The Little One is coming! The Little One is coming!" Several times she burst into tears, and several times she laughed aloud.

Hom Hing entered the room; his arms hung down by his side.

"The Little One!" shrieked Lae Choo.

"They bid me call tomorrow."

With a moan the mother sank to the floor.

The noon hour passed. The dinner remained on the table.

3

The winter rains were over: the spring had come to California, flushing the hills with green and causing an ever-changing pageant of flowers to pass over them. But there was no spring in Lae Choo's heart, for the Little One remained away from her arms. He was being kept in a mission. White women were caring for him, and though for one full moon he had pined for his mother and refused to be comforted he was now apparently happy and contented. Five moons or five months had gone by since the day he had passed with Lae Choo through the Golden Gate; but the great Government at Washington still delayed sending the answer which would return him to his parents.

Hom Hing was disconsolately rolling up and down the balls in his abacus box when a keen-faced young man stepped into his store.

"What news?" asked the Chinese merchant.

"This!" The young man brought forth a typewritten letter. Hom Hing read the words:

"Re Chinese child, alleged to be the son of Hom Hing, Chinese merchant, doing business at 425 Clay Street, San Francisco.

"Same will have attention as soon as possible."

Hom Hing returned the letter, and without a word continued his manipulation of the counting machine.

"Have you anything to say?" asked the young man.

"Nothing. They have sent the same letter fifteen times before. Have you not yourself showed it to me?"

"True!" The young man eyed the Chinese merchant furtively. He had a proposition to make and was pondering whether or not the time was opportune.

"How is your wife?" he inquired solicitously – and diplomatically Hom Hing shook his head mournfully.

"She seems less every day," he replied. "Her food she takes only when I bid her and her tears fall continually. She finds no pleasure in dress or flowers and cares not to see her friends. Her eyes stare all night. I think before another moon she will pass into the land of spirits."

"No!" exclaimed the young man, genuinely startled.

"If the boy not come home I lose my wife sure," continued Hom Hing with bitter sadness.

"It's not right," cried the young man indignantly. Then he made his proposition.

The Chinese father's eyes brightened exceedingly.

"Will I like you to go to Washington and make them give you the paper to restore my Son?" cried he. "How can you ask when you know my heart's desire?"

"Then," said the young fellow, "I will start next week. I am anxious to see this thing through if only for the sake of your wife's peace of mind."

"I will call her. To hear what you think to do will make her glad," said Hom Hing.

He called a message to Lae Choo upstairs through a tube in the wall. In a few moments she appeared, listless, wan, and hollow-eyed; but when her husband told her the young lawyer's suggestion she became electrified; her form straightened, her eyes glistened; the color flushed to her cheeks.

"Oh," she cried, turning to James Clancy. "You are a hundred man good!"

The young man felt somewhat embarrassed; his eyes shifted a little under the intense gaze of the Chinese mother.

"Well, we must get your boy for you," he responded. "Of course" – turning to Hom Hing – "it will cost a little money. You can't get fellows to hurry the Government for you without gold in your pocket."

Hom Hing stared blankly for a moment. Then: "How much do you want, Mr. Clancy?" he asked quietly.

"Well, I will need at least five hundred to start with."

Hom Hing cleared his throat.

"I think I told to you the time I last paid you for writing letters for me and seeing the Custom boss here that nearly all I had was gone!"

"Oh, well then we won't talk about it, old fellow. It won't harm the boy to stay where he is, and your wife may get over it all right."

"What that you say?" quavered Lae Choo.

James Clancy looked out of the window.

"He says," explained Hom Hing in English, "that to get our boy we have to have much money."

"Money! Oh, yes."

Lae Choo nodded her head.

"I have not got the money to give him."

For a moment Lae Choo gazed wonderingly from one face to the other; then, comprehension dawning upon her, with swift anger, pointing to the lawyer, she cried: "You not one hundred man good; you just common white man."

"Yes, ma'am," returned James Clancy, bowing and smiling ironically.

Hom Hing pushed his wife behind him and addressed the lawyer again: "I might try," said he, "to raise something; but five hundred – it is not possible."

"What about four?"

"I tell you I have next to nothing left and my friends are not rich."

"Very well!"

The lawyer moved leisurely toward the door, pausing on its threshold to light a cigarette.

"Stop, white man; white man, stop!"

Lae Choo, panting and terrified, had started forward and now stood beside him, clutching his sleeve excitedly.

"You say you can go to get paper to bring my Little One to me if Hom Hing give you five hundred dollars?"

The lawyer nodded carelessly; his eyes were intent upon the cigarette which would not take the fire from the match.

"Then you go get paper. If Hom Hing not can give you five hundred dollars – I give you perhaps what more that much."

She slipped a heavy gold bracelet from her wrist and held it out to the man. Mechanically he took it.

"I go get more!"

She scurried away, disappearing behind the door through which she had come.

"Oh, look here, I can't accept this," said James Clancy, walking back to Hom Hing and laying down the bracelet before him.

"It's all right," said Hom Hing, seriously, "pure China gold. My wife's parent give it to her when we married."

"But I can't take it anyway," protested the young man.

"It is all same as money. And you want money to go to Washington," replied Hom Hing in a matter-of-fact manner.

"See, my jade earrings – my gold buttons – my hairpins – my comb of pearl and my rings – one, two, three, four, five rings; very good – very good – all same much money. I give them all to you. You take and bring me paper for my Little One."

Lae Choo piled up her jewels before the lawyer.

Hom Hing laid a restraining hand upon her shoulder. "Not all, my wife," he said in Chinese. He selected a ring – his gift to Lae Choo when she dreamed of the tree with the red flower. The rest of the jewels he pushed toward the white man.

"Take them and sell them," said he. "They will pay your fare to Washington and bring you back with the paper."

For one moment James Clancy hesitated. He was not a sentimental man; but something within him arose against accepting such payment for his services.

"They are good, good," pleadingly asserted Lae Choo, seeing his hesitation.

Whereupon he seized the jewels, thrust them into his coat pocket, and walked rapidly away from the store.

4

Lae Choo followed after the missionary woman through the mission nursery school. Her heart was beating so high with happiness that she could scarcely breathe. The paper had come at last – the precious paper which gave Hom Hing and his wife the right to the possession of their own child. It was ten months now since he had been taken from them – ten months since the sun had ceased to shine for Lae Choo.

The room was filled with children – most of them wee tots, but none so wee as her own. The mission woman talked as she walked. She told Lae Choo that little Kim, as he had been named by the school, was the pet of the place, and that his little tricks and ways amused and delighted every one. He had been rather difficult to manage at first and had cried much for his mother; "but children so soon forget, and after a month he seemed quite at home and played around as bright and happy as a bird."

"Yes," responded Lae Choo. "Oh, yes, yes!"

But she did not hear what was said to her. She was walking in a maze of anticipatory joy.

"Wait here, please," said the mission woman, placing Lae Choo in a chair. "The very youngest ones are having their breakfast."

She withdrew for a moment – it seemed like an hour to the mother – then she reappeared leading by the hand a little boy dressed in blue cotton overalls and white-soled shoes. The little boy's face was round and dimpled and his eyes were very bright.

"Little One, ah, my Little One!' cried Lae Choo.

She fell on her knees and stretched her hungry arms toward her son.

But the Little One shrunk from her and tried to hide himself in the folds of the white woman's skirt.

"Go 'way, go 'way!" he bade his mother.

■ Write After You Read

1   Write a journal entry in response to "In the Land of the Free" using the guidelines on page 11.

2   Summarize the story in a few sentences by explaining the key events, the main conflict, and the final outcome.

■ Discuss After You Read

1   Examine the opening scene and analyze why Hom Hing and Lae Choo behave as they do with the officers.

a   What does this scene suggest about the relationship between Chinese immigrants and government officials in this era?

b   What does this scene suggest about the relationship between males and females in this era?

2   What do you learn about Chinese culture in part 2 of the story? What might be the author's purpose in providing these details?

3   Compare and contrast Lae Choo's behavior in part 3 to her behavior in part 1. What do the similarities or differences suggest about her personality and character?

4   Examine the child's experience in the school in parts 3 and 4. What does the experience suggest about the relationship between the government and missionaries and between the missionaries and immigrants?

5 What do you perceive to be the significance of the story's title?

6 Compare the experience of being oppressed in Sui Sin Far's "In the Land of the Free" with the oppressive experience in Zitkala-Ša's "The School Days of an Indian Girl" (pages 24–29) or Dunbar's "The Ingrate" (pages 142–147).

Reading 3

America

Arthur Schnitzler

Arthur Schnitzler (1862–1931) was born in Vienna, Austria, where he lived his entire life. For many years, he had a dual career as a physician and writer, but he abandoned medicine after the success of his first play. Schnitzler wrote more than thirty plays and numerous prose works, including Anatol *(1893),* The Road into the Open (Der Weg ins Freie, *1908), and* The Comedy of Seduction (Komödie der Verführung, *1924). "America" was published in 1889 and translated from the German by Tom J. Lewis and Robert E. Jungman.*

The ship is docking; I am setting my foot on the new world . . .

The gray autumn morning overshadows sea and land; everything under me is still swaying; again and again I feel the unquiet rolling of the waves . . . Out of the fog rises the city. . . Next to me, with open eyes, lively, the crowd is hurrying along. Not something strange do they see, but only something new. I listen, as one or the other whispers to himself, "America" – as if he just wanted to impress on himself that he were now really here, so far away!

I am standing alone on the shore. Not about the new America am I thinking, from which I am going to have to claim the happiness that my homeland denied me – I am thinking about a different one.

I see that little room; so clearly do I see it that it seems as if I had left it yesterday instead of many years ago. On the table is the lamp with the green shade, the embroidered armchair in the corner. Copper-engravings hang on the wall; their images swim away into the shadows. Anna is next to me. She is lying at my feet, her head with its curly hair propped against my knee. I have to bend over, in order to look into her eyes.

We have stopped talking; the evening progresses, and it's quiet in the room. Outside it is beginning to rain. We hear the drops, slow and heavy, beat against the windowpane. She smiles, and I bend over to reach her mouth. I kiss her lips, her forehead, and her eyes, which she has closed. My fingers play with the fine, golden hair, which is curled behind her ear.

I push it back and kiss her on this sweet, white patch of skin behind her ear. She looks up again and laughs. "Something new," she whispers, as if amazed. I hold my lips firmly pressed behind her ear. Then I say smiling, "Yes, we have discovered something new!" She bursts out laughing, and like a child she calls out happily, "America."

How funny it was then. So crazy and so silly I see her face before me, as she looked up at me with those roguish eyes and "America" echoed from her lips. How we laughed then, and how the fragrance intoxicated me, which streamed out of her hair over this America . . .

And this splendid name remained. At first we always called it out, if, of our innumerable kisses, one strayed behind the ear; then we whispered it – then we just thought it. But always it came into our consciousness.

A profusion of memories rise up in me. How once we saw a large ship pictured on an advertising billboard and, having stepped nearer, read: "From Liverpool to New York – From Bremen to New York." We burst out laughing, in the middle of the street, and she asserted quite loudly, while people were standing nearby, "Hey, we're going to travel to America today!" The people stared at her in complete amazement, especially a young man with a blond mustache, who also smiled. That annoyed me very much, and I thought, "'Yes, he'd probably like to come along."

Then we were sitting once in the theatre (I no longer remember any more at which play), when someone on the stage spoke of Columbus. It was a piece in iambics, and I recall the line, "and when Columbus stepped out on the bridge." Anna pressed her arm softly against mine; I looked at her and understood her disparaging glance. Poor Columbus, as if he had discovered the true America! After the play, when we were sitting in a cafe, we spoke a great deal about the good man who had prided himself so much on his poor America. We were actually sorry for him. For a long time, I was unable to imagine him any other way than standing with a sorrowful glance on the coast of his new part of the world, oddly enough with a top-hat and a very modern overcoat, and shaking his head disappointedly. Once we drew him together on the marble surface of a coffee house table and added some new details. She insisted that he had to be smoking a cigar; in our picture, moreover, the good explorer was carrying an umbrella, and his top-hat was crushed, naturally, by the mutineers. So Columbus became for us the humorous symbol of the history of the whole world. How crazy! How silly! . . .

And now I'm standing in the middle of a large, cold city. I'm in the false America and dreaming about my sweet, fragrant America over there. And how long ago that was! Many, many years. A pain, a madness comes over me that something has so irrevocably been lost. That I don't even know where a message from me, where a letter could reach her. That I know nothing, absolutely nothing any more about her . . .

My way takes me further along into the city, and my porter follows me. I stop a moment, close my eyes, and through a strange, deceiving game of the senses the same fragrance embraces me that wafted over me from Anna's hair when we first discovered America.

▇ Write After You Read

1 Write a journal entry in response to "America" using the guidelines on page 11.

2 Summarize the story in a few sentences by explaining the key events, the main conflict, and the final outcome.

▇ Discuss After You Read

1 Contrast the words the narrator associates with America before and after his arrival. What do these contrasting images suggest about the narrator's view of America and his state of mind before and after his arrival?

2 What is the significance of Columbus to the narrator's experience and attitude?

3 What has been lost and what has been gained as a result of the narrator's emigration?

4 What is the significance of the "fragrance" that wafts over the narrator in the last line of the story?

5 What do you perceive to be the significance of the story's title?

6 Compare the immigrant experience in Schnitzler's "America" with the immigrant experience in Yezierska's "College" (pages 35–41) or Sui Sin Far's "In the Land of the Free" (pages 148–155).

Reading 4

Tito's Good-bye

Cristina Garcia

Cristina Garcia was born in Havana, Cuba, and moved to the United States with her parents when she was two years old. She grew up in New York City, and prior to becoming a novelist, she worked as a political journalist for Time *magazine. An award-winning writer, Garcia has published three novels,* Dreaming in Cuban *(1992),* The Aguero Sisters *(1997), and* Monkey Hunting *(2003). "Tito's Good-bye" was originally published in* Iguana Dreams: New Latino Fiction.

Agustin "Tito" Ureña thought at first that the massive heart attack that would kill him in a matter of seconds was just a bad case of indigestion. He had eaten spareribs with pork fried rice, black beans, and a double side order of sweet plantains at a new Cuban-Chinese cafeteria on Amsterdam Avenue the night before and he hadn't felt quite right all day. "Okay, okay, I hear you!" he lamented aloud, rubbing his solar plexus and dropping his fourth pair of antacid tablets in the dirty glass of water on his desk. He remembered with longing the great spits of suckling pigs dripping with fragrant juices back in Cuba, the two inches of molten fat beneath their crispy skins.

"Coño!"[1] Tito Ureña protested as a violent spasm seized his heart then squeezed it beyond endurance. He stood up, suddenly afraid, and with a terrible groan he slumped forward, his arms swimming furiously, and swept from his oversized metal desk a half-eaten bag of candy corn, the citizenship papers of a dozen Central American refugees, his Timex travel clock in its scuffed plastic case, and the stout black rotary telephone he tried in vain to reach.

It was late Friday afternoon and Tito told his secretary to leave after lunch because it had started to snow and she lived in Hoboken, but mostly because he could deduct the eighteen dollars from her weekly pay. His law office, a squalid room over a vegetable market in Little Italy, was convenient to the federal courts downtown, his prime hunting grounds for the illegal immigrants who made up the bulk of his clients. Tito's specialties were self-styled – forging employment records, doctoring birth certificates, securing sponsors, thwarting deportation, applying for political asylum. Only rarely did he achieve the ultimate, the most elusive victory: procuring a legitimate green card.

Tito worked with the poorest of New York City's immigrants, uneducated men and women from the Dominican Republic, Mexico, El Salvador, Peru, Guatemala, Panama. He impressed them with his deliberate, florid Spanish, with the meaningful pauses and throat clearing they had come to expect from important men. In reality Tito Ureña's qualifications, elaborately set out and framed on the wall behind his secondhand executive chair, came from a correspondence school in Muncie, Indiana. This did not deter him, however, from charging many thousands of dollars, payable in monthly installments ("I'm not an unreasonable man," he protested again and again, his arms outstretched, palms heavenward, when his clients balked or appeared uncertain), for his dubious efforts.

Occasionally Tito Ureña would come by small-time jobs for the mob, defending lowlifes fingered to take the rap for their bosses. These cases paid handsomely and required virtually no work. Tito only had to be careful that his "defense" went off without a hitch and the saps went directly to jail. It helped take the pressure off the mob's local operations. Last year, flush with cash from two such cases, Tito bought sixty seconds of air time on late-night Spanish television to advertise his legal services. With his thick mustache and broad reassuring smile, he received over four hundred calls on the toll-free hotline in less than a week. The only trouble was that his wife, who was something of a night owl, also saw him on TV. Haydée called his office, posing as a rich widow from Venezuela, and made an appointment with her husband the following day. It took Tito months to cover his tracks again.

Tito Ureña had been separated from Haydée for nearly sixteen years and in all that time she had steadfastly refused to divorce him. Whenever she located her husband, Haydée managed to wring from him considerable sums of money to maintain, she said, the lifestyle to which she had grown accustomed as a descendant of the Alarcón family, the greatest sugarcane dynasty in Trinidad,

[1] *coño*: an offensive word in Spanish

Cuba. Tito insisted that Haydée could smell his cash three miles away in her tiny apartment on Roosevelt Island, even on the hottest days of summer when the stench from the East River and all that was buried there would have stopped a bloodhound dead in its tracks with confusion.

For a while Tito skittered from place to place in the vast waterfront complexes of apartment buildings near Wall Street which, during a down turn in the economy, were offering three months' free rent with every two-year lease. Tito rented beige furniture, always beige (he preferred its soothing neutrality), and lived high above the river, face-to-face with the lights of the city in his glass box suites in the sky.

It snowed hard the night Tito Ureña died of a heart attack in his office in Little Italy. Nine inches fell in the space of twelve hours. It continued to snow the next day, blanketing the city's rooftops and fire escapes, its parks and delivery trucks, awnings and oak trees with a deceptive peacefulness, and it snowed the day after that. It snowed on the black veiled hat Haydée had stolen from Bloomingdale's that very afternoon and which she would later come to interpret as a premonition of her husband's death.

It snowed on the sliver of concrete she called a balcony, decorated with a life-sized plastic statue of Cinderella. It snowed on Tito's daughter's brick Colonial house in western Connecticut, across from the country club with its own riding stable. Inés Ureña had married a Yale-trained cardiologist the year before and devoted her days to mastering the baroque recipes in *Gourmet* magazine. It snowed especially hard in Prospect Park, near where her older brother, Jaime, had rented a room and plastered his walls with posters of Gandhi, Beethoven, and Malcolm X.

Tito lay dead in his office all weekend as it snowed, well preserved by the freezing temperatures. His mistress, Beatrice Hunt, called him Saturday night from Antigua, where she had returned to visit her family for an extended holiday. She cut her trip short when a policeman, who had found her number in Tito's wallet, called her in St. Johns. Beatrice, dressed in her Sunday finery, went to claim her lover's body at the Manhattan city morgue. After four days, nobody else had come.

If Tito Ureña had had the chance, if he had known that only a few moments remained of his life and that it was neither indigestion nor an incipient ulcer that was causing his gastric discomfort, he might have permitted himself the brief luxury of nostalgia. He would have remembered the warmth of his mother's cheek, smelling faintly of milk, and her face the last time he saw her (Tito was only nine when she died), or the sight of his father's hands – enormous hands with stiff hairs sprouting near the knuckles – stroking the doves that roosted in his study. He would have remembered the girl he loved madly when he was seven years old and in a moment of melancholy would profess to love still.

And since these would be the very last moments of his life, Tito might even have permitted himself the memory of his first glimpse of Haydée at sixteen, riding her thoroughbred, English style, along the road which marked the southern boundary of her father's vast plantation. She was a magnificent sight – so small, so white, a china doll. How afraid he was of breaking her on their wedding night! He would have remembered too, her belly, swelling with his child, and the pride he felt strolling with her through the Plaza Mayor. This was long before the problems began, long before they'd sent their son to the orphanage in Colorado to save him from the Communists, who, it was rumored, were planning to ship Cuba's children to boarding schools in the Ukraine. Jaime was still healthy and without rancor then, and Tito's daughter, Inés, danced to please him, clapping her dimpled hands.

It was that life that Tito Ureña would have remembered if he had had the opportunity, a life richly marred by ignorance.

But he had no time to reminisce when his heart attack came. No time to save the Salvadorans from deportation or to pick up the dry cleaning Beatrice Hunt had forgotten on Broadway and 74th Street. No time to call his brothers, whom he hadn't seen in five years, or his sister, Aurora, in New Jersey, who'd announced her determination to save his soul. No time to have dinner with his daughter, Inés, estranged from him in her brick Colonial house in western Connecticut (Tito had missed her fancy wedding and she never forgave him). No time to apologize to his son, if he could have even worked up the courage, or to earn enough money to finally keep Haydée happy. No time to visit his father in Cuba or to plant jonquils on his mother's sad grave. No, Tito no longer had time even to hope. When his hour came on that snowy winter afternoon in Little Italy, all Tito had time to do was say *coño*.

■ Write After You Read

1 Write a journal entry in response to "Tito's Good-bye" using the guidelines on page 11.

2 Summarize the story in a few sentences by explaining the key events, the main conflict, and the final outcome.

■ Discuss After You Read

1 Examine closely how Tito treats his secretary and his clients.

　a What is the reason Tito gives his secretary for sending her home early? What is the real reason?

　b How did Tito qualify for his position as a lawyer? How does he attract his clients? What does he do for them?

　c What do your answers suggest about Tito's character?

2 Contrast the family's present life with their past life in Cuba.

　a Characterize Tito's past and present living conditions.

　b Characterize the past and present living conditions of Tito's wife, Haydée, and his children, Inés and Jaime.

　c Characterize Tito's past and present relationships with his wife and children.

　d What is the significance of these contrasts?

3 What role does politics play in the personal lives of these characters?

4 What does the narrator say Tito's last thoughts might have been? What are Tito's actual last thoughts? What is the significance of this difference?

5 What do you perceive to be the significance of the story's title?

6 Compare the experience of being an exile in Garcia's "Tito's Good-bye" with the immigrant experience in Sui Sin Far's "In the Land of the Free" (pages 148–155) or Schnitzler's "America" (pages 156–157).

Reading 5

Albert and Esene

Frances Khirallah Noble

Frances Khirallah Noble received her JD degree from the University of Southern California Law School. She left the practice of law to write fiction full time and is the author of the short-story collection, The Situe Stories: A Century of Arab Americans (2000), *the title of which refers to the Arabic word used in Lebanon for "grandmother," or "aunt" in some cases. "Albert and Esene" was originally published in* The Situe Stories.

They sat side by side in the living room of the small duplex, their short, white legs without demarcation for ankle or calf – identical legs, except that one pair was plump and the other, thin – hanging over the side of the couch. Their feet barely grazed the floor. In a rare convergence, they had agreed that the occasion called for their good black dresses Amelia and Safiyah, in dignity and forbearance, visiting Esene.

The husband of Esene had died two weeks before. His sisters, also widows, had come to console. And to have lunch. Already the smells for which Esene was known floated from her kitchen to reassure her neighbors that she was recovered enough to cook.

Esene carried two mugs of coffee into the living room.

"Did you put cream and sugar?" asked Saliyah.

"I know how you like it," answered Esene.

"I don't see how you can drink coffee in this heat," complained Amelia, her vast and magnificent bosom rising like bread dough above her dropped neckline. "Usually it wakes me up, but in this heat, it makes me so tired."

"If anyone should be tired," Safiyah said, "it should be me. I drove us all the way up here."

"You slam on the brakes every time you see a car," Amelia accused, and she inclined toward Esene, pretending to be confidential. "People were honking and shouting at us the whole trip and she didn't notice. Stop. Start. Stop. Start. She stops twenty feet before every intersection." Then she turned to Safiyah. "This is the last time I let you drive me anywhere."

"He who digs a pit is likely to fall into it," Safiyah answered, subsiding into her sweetened coffee. "Who'll drive you if I don't?" And she clutched the cup with her bony hands, her perfect red fingernails, like pyracantha berries blazing against the white glass, her diamond rings weighting her fingers.

"At any rate," Amelia began again, "now we're all the same. Floating in the same boat, eh, Esene? Safiyah and I, we can tell you what it's like to be a widow."

Esene. Who'd taken the armchair by the window, stepping past the pile of unfolded newspapers and untouched magazines that tilted against the leg of the television. Esene. Crocheting. Cream thread growing into a doily. Defeating Amelia's attempts to encircle her with her defeating smile.

For sixty-two years, Esene had paid little attention to her sisters-in-law. This, on the advice of her husband when she'd asked how to approach the women into whose family she had intruded. "Don't get drawn into it," he'd said. "It's the only way they know how to speak. If you say little," Albert wisely counseled in the face of their outstretched arms, the imbroglio of their embraces, the Sunday feasts, the shirts off their backs, "and act less, they'll think you agree with them. No one will argue. There'll be no one to convince. Or if you prefer," he brushed his luxuriant black mustache with the tip of his finger, "I'll do the talking for both of us."

Which is what he did.

"She's like a silent child," his family said. "Not a thought in her head. It's probably a good thing they have no children." This was Esene's only real sadness. Not that Albert wasn't vigorous and passionate in bed. Not that Esene didn't respond, urging him. Everyone in Albert's family blamed Esene. Her family, distant by the width of a country, ceased to think about faraway grandchildren, until Esene existed for them primarily as the exotic aunt in California who mailed five-dollar bills in Christmas cards written in pencil in her large, coarse script.

For Albert (whom they had met but once) had taught her to read and write.

At first he had merely read to her every night from the evening papers, adjusting the position of his magnifying glass for the Arabic or English letters, railing against the injustices reported from around the world. Esene sat like a cat on the rug next to his chair, her head pressing against his knee.

One night he proclaimed, "Esene, I'm going to teach you to read!"

"Albert," she laughed. "Why?"

"The women in this country read."

With the same fervor that led him to stock his tiny Arabic grocery store with Coca-Cola, American cigarettes and magazines and candy, and to encourage his customers to speak English on the premises (if they could) every other Monday, he set out to teach Esene to read. She was thirty-five years old and much younger than he.

"At . . . bat . . . cat . . . This is so silly."

"Here, Esene, smoke, if it helps you relax . . ."

Shades drawn. Front door locked. To prevent discovery, because Albert wanted it to be a surprise, his surprise to unveil like a repainted statue. It was not to humiliate his sister, Amelia, who had received their mother's recipes, wordlessly, by watching and doing; who handed over to her husband without a glance all written matter; and who argued day and night with that husband over what her mother said, his sister said, what they should do, where they should go, while she expanded and puffed up until he resentfully wondered how much larger she could grow. Nor to spite Safiyah: wealthy by marriage, with her diamonds and her sheared fox wrap, whose empty head held jet stones in place of eyes and whose teeth clenched its own paws in a ring around Safiyah's elegant neck. It was certainly not to defy Albert's mother, Hasna – no, he was her favorite and he basked in her affectionate glow.

When Esene asked again, "Why, Albert?" he merely laughed and pushed her nose in to a book. "Our secret," he reminded her.

Esene pronounced "tin, fin . . . bob, cob . . ." from lists of Albert's devising. Then words from a child's book that Albert searched for in the library, a book that would not cause Esene to bristle with impatience.

"You must be diligent," he instructed. "You must work every day."

"I will not miss my programs," she snapped, leaving the theme book, the pencils adrift on the couch with elaborate indifference. For one day, then two, while she expanded her radio listening to cover every available hour.

"But how will you be ready?" Albert asked. "Christmas is coming and you won't be ready. What about our plan – "

" – Your plan, Albert!"

" – to send out American Christmas cards for the first time. In your hand. Which you will write. You'll surprise them all, Esene. . . . Please."

But, for the time being, Esene said, she wanted to revive her afternoon card games with her friends, who'd wondered at her unavailability – that is, if she still had any friends, she said to him morosely; if they hadn't disappeared in the labyrinth of her many absences.

"But, Esene, you only study in the evening. You've had plenty of time for your friends."

"You don't know what I do all day," Esene sobbed. And she gathered herself to parade down the sidewalk, past the small, respectable house of Albert's mother, Safiyah's large two-story house, and Amelia's white frame cottage, nestled in a court of six equivalent structures – without a glance in their direction – to social events to which they were not invited.

"She looks different coming and going," said Safiyah.

"Less steady on her feet," Amelia observed.

"Slower."

"Drunk."

"Albert indulges her."

"Is ruled by her, you mean."

If Albert came home early, he tucked her in bed himself tasting the lovely bourbon on her lips (which the women around the card table sipped from crystal shot glasses), slipping off her navy dress, unrolling her stockings, sliding his hands over her olive-skinned body, releasing the combs in her hair. He pulled down the shades; he loved her easily and languorously, so that before they'd finished, she was nearly asleep. Afterward, he lay on his back in their mahogany bed and pulled the covers over his face. It was the way he always slept.

As December approached, Albert increased the pace of the lessons: three- and four-syllable words in sentences, the use of the comma, the closing of a letter.

"All you need to know is enough to sign the Christmas cards," he badgered impatiently. "And write a short message." Esene adamantly refused to use a pen; they smeared and could not be erased. Albert shopped for cards they could afford, with space enough to accommodate Esene's expansive script.

As for Esene, even though she didn't love to study, even though Albert pushed and prodded her, she began to realize the power of what she was doing. She could hardly keep quiet. Words she knew floated all around her – in shop windows, on street signs, in magazines, newspapers, on packages, at church. Words she could read sat on the tip of her tongue, ready to leap off at any moment. What could she do? Deny what she knew? What was becoming automatic? Almost beyond her control? Esene's secret knowledge had begun to burn like a hot potato in her stomach; like a fox gnarling.

Albert tried to remind her: "Remember, it's our secret for now."

"Yes, yes, Albert. I know. I know."

Still, Esene stuffed magazines at the top of her shopping bag, allowing the corner fringes to peek over the edges. She asked out loud in front of Safiyah and Amelia, "Where is your Sunday paper?" Adding, after a moment's taunting silence, "For Albert."

On an evening several days before the cards were to be written and mailed, retrieved from the safety of their hiding place in the space under the kitchen sink, Esene said to old Nasef, Albert's father, who was deaf and nearly blind, "Would you like me to read you a story?" Then she turned to Albert, whose heart had made an invisible leap, and said, "Did I startle you?"

One morning soon after, the family set out to visit an ailing third cousin who'd arrived from Boston to winter in the paradise that was Los Angeles – warm, uncluttered, like the old country, healing to the joints and lungs, where the familiarity of oranges, grapes, and dates grew along the streets and in the vast spaces between buildings. Everyone disembarked from the streetcar. They shook out wrinkled skirts. The younger men placed dark hats on dark-haired heads. Dried sleep was cleaned from the corner of a child's eye. They gathered on the sidewalk to decide which way to walk: Hasna and Nasef; Albert and Esene; Safiyah and Amelia and their husbands and children.

"What street are we trying to find, for God's sake?" asked Amelia's husband.

"Hancock Street," answered Safiyah impatiently.

"Here we are then," Esene called out boldly, pointing to a street sign a few yards away.

A simple slip. A flick of the serpent's tongue, Esene's eyes opened wide, beseeching Albert.

"What did you say, Esene?" asked Amelia, slightly out of breath from the exertion of lowering herself from the platform of the streetcar.

"I said," Esene looked at her evenly, "'Here . . . we . . . are . . . then.'"

"What does she mean, Albert?" asked Safiyah as she joined arms with her husband.

While the children explored the sidewalk ahead of them, Albert's mother, his sisters, their husbands drew sharply toward him. His father, unaware, stood apart, left behind.

"This is the New World," Albert said softly.

"You're responsible for this?" Safiyah asked.

"The cat is out of the bag," said Esene.

The group shifted toward Esene.

"Arabic, too?" Safiyah asked.

"No. Only English."

"Can you write?"

"Yes."

Amelia burst into tears. When Albert looked at his mother, he saw a hint of surprise behind her solid deference. Albert's father, in his old man's sweater, stood holding his lightly crushed brown hat in both hands, uncaring, impassive, waiting to be urged in the right direction by a son-in-law's hands.

"How could you do this? Keep such a secret from your family?"

Albert answered, "Not a secret. A surprise."

It took some time for Albert's family to accustom itself to the sight of Esene's reading whatever came in front of her. When she was silent, they suspected she was reading and looked around the room to determine the object of her attention. After the first set of Christmas cards (Albert had chosen a Madonna and Child), Safiyah and Amelia invited Father Nicholas to Safiyah's prosperous home for coffee and cakes and steered the conversation to the great sin of pride, which caused the downfall of the favorite angel of God.

At Easter, an old woman was called in on the pretext of having lunch. Through her fingers she sifted the sand she'd brought in the broad flat brass box. "From the old country," she assured them, referring to the sand. Her eyes traveled over the ridges, which she leveled and created again according to a plan Esene didn't divine. "Beware," she finally told Esene, lifting her fortune from the sifting grains, and it was clear from the tone of her voice that it pained her to deliver the message. "The consequences of a life of following your own inclinations are not easy to control."

When the men argued American politics in Arabic and the children who went to American schools played outdoors, the women, including Esene, sat on Hasna's porch on hard-backed chairs carried from the kitchen. If Esene walked past the living room, the men's mouths snapped shut like empty purses. Even Albert's exhortations to Esene to join them did not revive their powers of speech. "They're old-fashioned," Albert would say later. "They're not the beginning and the end." Still, it bored him to sit on the porch with the women. To have to listen to Safiyah say, "You need more lemon in your tabbouleh, Esene." Or to hear Amelia add, "If I were you, I'd increase the cinnamon in the rice," as though a woman who read and had no children could expect nothing else.

The evening of the day she had read that first word out loud before Albert's family, Esene had breathed into his ear, "Oh, Albert, I didn't mean to."

"Our secret – ," he began,

"What did you expect?" Esene wailed. "The words became automatic. They were swirling around in front of my eyes, in my head. it was only a matter of time before they flew out my mouth."

After dinner, Albert had walked back to his shop and rearranged everything on the shelves. He smoked. He drank a little whiskey. He sat alone while Esene, remorseful and fearful, read the evening papers. For most of one month he worked late, missing dinner at home. One night, Esene packed food and took it to the grocery.

"Give me a drink," she said, as she unwrapped the food. "You always like the taste of bourbon in my mouth."

The lights in the shop attracted an older man, a regular customer. "Something wrong?" he asked when he reached the door. "No, come in. Talk with us," Albert said in English. Esene listened this night and many of the others. When Albert decided to extend the hours of the shop into the evening, Esene joined him and the small circle of men – never more than four or five – for conversation and coffee. She began coming earlier in the afternoon, carrying their dinner so they didn't have to break away until they finally locked the door.

Albert and Esene grew old. It was his idea that Esene should learn to cook American food, and when he found a cooking class at the local adult school, and when he bought their car, he drove her every evening, reading his newspaper in the front seat while she was inside, and taking her home again when she came out.

It was her idea to get a library card.

"I need to be able to explain why I say what I say," she told Albert.

And so Esene walked stiffly up the imposing steps of the main library downtown and through the majestic double-glass doors and asked the librarian for an application. And in response to the librarian's request, on this day and this day only, Esene wrote in ink.

Albert and Esene continued to send Christmas cards each year. Albert chose them and Esene wrote them at their small kitchen table: salutations, season's greetings, expressions of love from her and Albert, and, more often than not, her opinions on the world in general or certain issues in particular, quotations from favorite articles, wise sayings, bits of advice. All in pencil in her childlike script. Esene, unfinished, yet whole; Albert, quite pleased.

▥ Write After You Read

1 Write a journal entry in response to "Albert and Esene" using the guidelines on page 11.

2 Summarize the story in a few sentences by explaining the key events, the main conflict, and the final outcome.

▓ Discuss After You Read

1 Examine the opening scene and analyze the family interactions and their thoughts about one another. What does this scene reveal about the relationships between the women in the family, between the siblings, and between the husband and wife?

2 What does Albert teach Esene and why does he do it? What does Albert's decision to teach Esene suggest about his values?

3 Why is it so important to Albert that the lessons be kept secret? Why does his family react the way they do when they learn about the lessons?

4 What effect do the lessons have on Albert and Esene's marriage? On Esene's life experience? On Esene's sense of self? Explain your answers.

5 What do you perceive to be the significance of the story's title?

6 Compare the experiences of living in two cultures in Noble's "Albert and Esene" with Sui Sin Far's "In the Land of the Free" (pages 148–155), Garcia's "Tito's Good-bye" (pages 158–161), or any of the readings in Chapter 2.

GUIDELINES

Analyzing Fiction

> ### Essay Assignment
>
> Write an essay in which you analyze a work of fiction. Closely examine the story's elements, such as its characters or setting, or their relationship to each other. Your purpose is to interpret the story, that is, to explain what you believe to be the story's deeper meaning. To accomplish this goal, you will need to incorporate details and quotations from the story into your essay (see Section I of A Handbook for Writing, pages 236–273). You may write about more than one story, for example, by comparing characters and themes from different stories. The exploratory writing of one student, Shinya Nagase, is included in the following guidelines to show how he developed ideas for an essay that analyzes a short story.

▪ Exploring a Topic

Exploring a topic for an essay analyzing fiction may involve using some of the exploratory strategies described in Chapters 2, 3, or 4. In addition, you need to select evidence for literary analysis of the story. The strategies that follow suggest approaches you can take to fulfill the assignment.

Selecting a Reading

Selecting a Reading is a first step in analyzing fiction. You can accomplish this goal by skimming the stories, reviewing whatever you have written about them, and then deciding which story you want to discuss in depth.

A student writer at work: *Selecting a reading*

After reading his journal entries, Shinya decided he wanted to write an essay on Cristina Garcia's short story, "Tito's Good-bye," because he had a question he wanted to explore:

> "In my journal entry I wrote that the Cuban revolution was the reason why Tito's marriage failed. But, after our class discussion, I began to wonder if there was another reason. So I decided that in my essay I would try to find the answer."

▪▪▪➤ **Your turn:** *Selecting a reading*

Using the *Guidelines for Selecting a Reading* on page 96, choose a short story to analyze.

Examining Elements of Fiction

Examining elements of fiction within the story – including plot, character, setting, point of view, imagery, and symbolism – provides clues that can help you interpret a story.

Guidelines for Examining Elements of Fiction

1. Summarize the *plot* to determine what happened and why. (See Summarizing Fiction, pages 239–241.)

2. Analyze each *character* to determine that character's appearance, behavior, inner thoughts, and values.
   - How is each character described?
   - What does the character do, say, and think? Are the character's actions, words, and thoughts consistent, or are they contradictory?
   - What do other characters say and think about the character, and how do they react to the character?
   - What choices does the character make?
   - What changes, if any, does the character undergo?

3. Analyze the *setting* to determine how it might relate to the characters' emotional state.
   - Where does the story take place?
   - When does the story take place? In what period of history? Over what period of time? During what season? At what time of day as revealed, for example, in descriptions of light, darkness, or shadows?
   - What is the social environment: the manners, customs, rules, moral codes, or socioeconomic level of the society in which the story is set?
   - What is the physical environment as revealed, for example, in descriptions of nature, objects, clothing, food, rooms, or weather?

4. Analyze the *point of view* to determine the narrative perspective from which the story is told.
   - Is the narrator a character in the story?
   - If the narrator is not a character in the story, how much does the narrator know about the events and characters?
   - Does the narrator merely describe events and characters, or does the narrator comment on them?
   - Is the narrator reliable? Does the author reveal the narrator's limitations?
   - What is gained or lost by the author's choice to create this type of narrator?

5. Analyze the *imagery*, the mental pictures created by words, and *symbolism*, the physical images that represent abstract ideas or emotions, to determine a pattern of images and ideas.
   - What image or images appeal to your senses of sight, sound, taste, smell, or touch?
   - What is the literal, factual, or dictionary definition or meaning of the image?
   - Does the image have a universal meaning – that is, a meaning that might be recognized worldwide, for example, rain after a drought symbolizing rebirth, renewal, or regeneration?
   - Does the image have a culturally specific meaning in the context of the story?

A student writer at work: *Examining elements of fiction*

As he analyzed the family relationships in "Tito's Good-bye," Shinya was interested in comparing the family's living conditions in Cuba with their living conditions in the United States. Here is an excerpt from his list of details related to the physical environment in the two countries.

In Cuba:	*In the United States:*
"vast plantation"	"squalid room"
	"tiny apartment"
	"glass box suites"
	"brick Colonial house"

Your turn: *Examining elements of fiction*

Using the *Guidelines for Examining Elements of Fiction*, analyze various elements of the story you have selected.

Discovering a Theme

Discovering a theme involves uncovering a truth that a story reveals. Through the creation of a fictional world, authors reveal what they believe to be true about the real world. Fiction writers rarely state a theme directly, however. Instead, readers discover a theme, inferring meaning from the story's details by exploring an abstract concept such as love, freedom, or communication; a recurring pattern of behavior such as dishonesty, secrecy, or rebellion; or a repeated image such as a wall, cloud, or newspaper.

A theme may grow out of a conflict: a dramatic struggle between two or more forces in a story. A conflict may be internal, involving a character's inner psychological struggle. Or a conflict may be external, involving a struggle between the characters or between the characters and their physical, social, political, economic, or spiritual environment.

A theme is not a moral of a story. A *moral* is a statement or lesson that teaches right and wrong behavior, for example: "Never tell a lie." Fiction writers rarely tell people how to behave; rather, they show how people do behave. The authors of the short stories in this chapter create characters to examine their behavior and motivation, revealing why human beings are the way they are or why things happen as they do.

Guidelines for Discovering a Theme

1. Answer the questions in the *Guidelines for Examining Elements of Fiction* on page 170 and look for an abstract concept, a recurring pattern of behavior, or a repeated image. For example, if physical details such as doors or walls hint at a lack of communication and the characters in the story have trouble communicating, you can focus on the connection between the setting and the concept of communication.

2. Answer whichever of the following questions is relevant to your selected story:
   - What is the main character's inner psychological struggle?
   - What is the source of the conflict between two or more characters?
   - Why is there a conflict between the characters and their physical, social, political, economic, or spiritual environment?

A student writer at work: *Discovering a theme*

As Shinya examined various elements of the story, "Tito's Good-bye," he noticed a recurring pattern of behavior that suggested to him that Tito's conduct, not just the Cuban Revolution, was responsible for the disintegration of the family. This is what Shinya had to say about the pattern:

> "The author shows that Tito keeps deceiving and cheating people, so I think the theme of deception or dishonesty may be important. That kind of behavior ends up hurting Tito."

Your turn: *Discovering a theme*

Using the *Guidelines for Discovering a Theme*, look for an abstract idea, recurring pattern of behavior, repeated image, or significant conflict in the short story you have selected to analyze.

Selecting Relevant Evidence

Selecting relevant evidence from a story enables you to support the points you make about the story. You should be careful not to ignore details that may contradict your points, however. And you should be careful not to create details that do not appear in the story. To interpret a story, you need to read "between the lines," but you should analyze only the lines that the author provides.

> ## Guidelines for Selecting Relevant Evidence
>
> One or more of the following suggestions may help you infer meaning from evidence:
>
> 1. Review the questions that follow the story, and write down responses that may help you develop a theme.
> 2. Annotate the story (see page 7), cluster ideas from the story (see page 8), or make double-entry notes on the story (see page 9).
> 3. Copy what you perceive to be significant passages and note why you think they are important.
> 4. List key scenes or details and then group them under specific categories. For example, if you are writing about the setting, you can make separate lists for animate objects and inanimate objects.

A student writer at work: *Selecting relevant evidence*

Among the many notes Shinya took to prepare for his essay, he made two lists to show the difference between Tito's family relationships before and after they left Cuba. In making the lists, Shinya saw that the evidence he had gathered showed that the family had disintegrated.

In Cuba (before)	*In the United States* (after)
Married	Separated
Rich wife	Wife always wants money from him
Healthy son	Son has "rancor"
Happy daughter	Daughter is "estranged"

Your turn: *Selecting relevant evidence*

Using the *Guidelines for Selecting Relevant Evidence*, select evidence to support an analysis of the story you have selected.

■ Focusing Ideas

To fulfill the goal of *focusing ideas* for your readers, you need to identify a recurring theme in the story, such as an abstract concept or pattern of behavior, and write a sentence or two that can serve as the focal point of your essay.

A student writer at work: *Focusing ideas*

Shinya planned to focus on the theme of Tito's deception and decided to put his focal point in the form of a question that he wanted to answer in his essay: *Why did Tito's family fall apart?*

Your turn: *Focusing ideas*

Using the *Guidelines for Focusing Ideas* on page 61, create a focal point for your essay.

■ Structuring the Essay

Structuring the essay that analyzes fiction involves moving readers toward an interpretation of the story. Such essays have a basic, three-part organizational framework: an *introduction*, a *body*, and a *conclusion*.

The following flow chart may help you visualize an overall structure for an essay analyzing fiction.

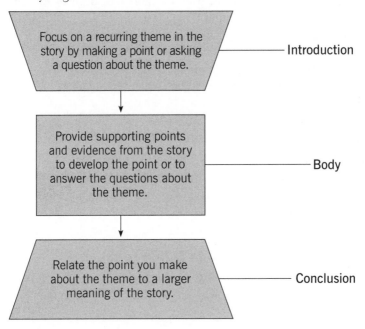

Focus on a recurring theme in the story by making a point or asking a question about the theme. —— Introduction

Provide supporting points and evidence from the story to develop the point or to answer the questions about the theme. —— Body

Relate the point you make about the theme to a larger meaning of the story. —— Conclusion

The Introduction

The *introduction* to an essay that analyzes fiction provides a focal point that reveals a recurring theme. (See also *Guidelines for Writing the Introduction* on page 101.)

Activity: *Evaluating introductions*

The passages on the following page are introductions to student essays analyzing fiction. Evaluate two or more of the introductions by answering the following questions.

1   Does the introduction involve you in the topic and make you want to read the rest of the essay? Explain.

2   Do you learn, at the beginning of the essay, some general background information related to the story that the student writer is analyzing?

3   Can you tell which story the student writer is analyzing?

4   Can you determine what point the student writer will prove or what question the student writer will answer about a theme of the story?

5   If you think the introduction should be revised, what suggestions do you have for the student writer?

Student A

In 1959, Fidel Castro, a communist, led a revolution in Cuba. At the same time, many Cubans fled the country and entered the United States. In "Tito's Good-bye," Cristina Garcia tells of a family who fell apart after their exile. After I read the story, I began to question who was responsible for the disintegration of Tito's family. – **Shinya**

Student B

During our lifetime, what are the most important goals we want to accomplish? Is it having wealth and power or simply having a happy life with a loving family? In the story of "Tito's Good-bye" by Cristina Garcia, Tito chooses wealth over family. At the end, he had a heart attack and died as an unhappy man. He did not even have time to regret. All he had time for was a swear word in Spanish. After he died, no one from his family came to his funeral. If he were given a chance to start over, would he make his life a little better? – **David**

Student C

The Chinese Exclusion Act of 1882 limited the number of Chinese people who could come into the United States. The act was supposed to end in ten years but the government added ten more years to it and then it did not end until 1943. This act had an impact on many Chinese families. For example, men would be in the United States but their family would not. "In the Land of the Free" by Sui Sin Far takes place in the time of the Chinese Exclusion Act. The author shows how it separated the family and tore up the relationships between the husband and the wife and the parents and the child. – **Donny**

Student D

In the late nineteenth century, many Americans thought that God gave them "manifest destiny," so they believed they were superior to other people with different cultures and religions. For that reason, they tried to force others to give up their own culture and accept the American one. Chinese in "In the Land of the Free" and Native Americans in "The School Days of an Indian Girl" are such victims. The two authors, Sui Sin Far and Zitkala-Ša, give us stories of their own people that defend the Chinese and Native Americans in America and counter beliefs widely held at the time that they are inferior and morally corrupt. – **Wai Yam**

The Body

The *body* of an essay analyzing fiction provides evidence to support your interpretation of the story. It should include details and quotations from the story. (See also *Guidelines for Structuring the Body Paragraphs* on page 105.)

The following suggestions offer three possibilities for structuring the body paragraphs of an essay analyzing fiction. You can use the drafting process to experiment with the organization of the body; your early efforts can be revised later (see Drafting, pages 274–275, and Revising, pages 278–282).

1. Present relevant evidence from different scenes chronologically, in the order in which the scenes occur in the story, devoting at least one paragraph to each scene.

   a. Begin at the beginning of the story, make a point about the beginning, and then provide evidence to support the point.

   b. Then make a point about the next scene, and provide evidence to support that point.

   c. Continue this process until you reach the end of the story.

2. Present relevant evidence from different scenes in order of importance, according to your view of what is important, devoting at least one paragraph to each scene.

   a. Select a scene from any part of the story that you think is significant to your topic, make a point about the scene, and provide evidence to support the point.

   b. Then move to another scene in the story, make a point about the scene, and provide evidence to support it.

3. Present relevant evidence according to a set of categories that you determine, devoting at least one paragraph to each category. For example, you might analyze different aspects of a character's behavior or personality in different paragraphs. Or you might explore related themes such as restriction and freedom, expectation and disillusionment, illusion and reality, greed and generosity, or love and jealousy.

   a. Make a point about the story that is related to your chosen category, and provide evidence to support it.

   b. Then make another point that is related to one of your chosen categories, and provide evidence to support it.

   c. Continue this process until you have discussed all of your categories.

   d. Throughout the body of the essay, show how the different categories are connected or follow logically from one another.

Activity: *Evaluating body paragraphs*

The following passages are body paragraphs from student essays analyzing fiction. Evaluate two or more of the paragraphs by answering the following questions.

1 Can you determine, at the beginning of the paragraph, the point the student writer is making about the story?

2 Does the student writer provide sufficient and appropriate details and quotations from the story to support the point?

3 Does the student writer clarify the meaning of selected quotations and make their significance clear?

4 If you think the paragraph should be revised, what suggestions do you have for the student writer?

Student A

From my point of view, there was nothing wrong in Tito's family before Castro came to Cuba. Tito was married to Haydée who came from a wealthy family. Tito met Haydée when she was "sixteen, riding her thoroughbred, English style, along the road which marked the southern boundary of her father's vast plantation" (p. 160). He fell in love with her at that moment. After the marriage, Jaime and Inés were born. Jaime was a healthy and carefree boy and Inés made her father happy by dancing and clapping. Tito's family was having a wonderful time there. Then Tito heard a rumor that children might be sent away to the Ukraine, and so Tito quickly sent Jaime to school in Colorado in the United States. After the communists took over the country, and Jaime had gone to the United States, their family started to disintegrate. – **Shinya**

Student B

In my opinion, I think Tito was a very selfish man. He did not care about his family. The only thing he thought about was how to make enough money. Tito thought of many ways to save his money. Before his death, he told his secretary to go home early because there was a snowstorm. This would seem like a good and caring act, but, in reality, Tito was thinking about himself. He was thinking that he could save himself money by cutting a portion of his secretary's paycheck. I truly believe that if Tito was generous enough, he would not have died the way he did. At the moment of his heart attack, if his secretary had been there, she could have helped him to the emergency room. However, because of his greed, he was left alone in his office and suffered a painful death. – **David**

Student C

> Hom Hing had missed his wife when he was in the United States. Once they saw each other, they were filled with joy. However, because their child did not have the papers to get in, the customs officers took him away. This made Lae Choo really upset and she started to yell, but Hom Hing told her to be quiet. The man was the one in charge and the wife had to listen to what he said. When their child was away, Hom Hing was not comforting his wife. Months passed and their child was not back yet. The lawyer came by one day and said the same old things. The lawyer said it would cost them money for him to go to Washington to get the papers. They were short of money, but Lae Choo wanted her child back. So she would give him everything and was getting emotional. The husband was trying to make her be quiet, but she did not obey and started to yell at the lawyer, "'You are not one hundred man good; you just a common white man'. . . . Hom Hing pushed his wife behind him. . . . 'See my jade earrings – my gold buttons'" (p. 154). This shows she was getting impatient with her husband for what he was doing to get their child. You can say she was disobeying but it was worth it. **– Donny**

Student D

> In "The School Days of an Indian Girl," the Indian children in the story, like the Little One in "In the Land of the Free," were removed from their parents and sent to a mission school for an extended period of time: "There were eight in our party of bronzed children who were going east with the missionaries" (p. 24). The Americans in both of these stories impose their own culture on other people. The Americans in the boarding school don't give a choice to the Indian girl. They force her to do different actions: cut her hair, change her garments and moccasins, and speak English. All of these actions were stripping her of anything that she had grown to know and forcing her to change into something she wasn't (an American). This situation is similar to the Little One who is forced to accept an American identity. The Americans do such actions without true consideration for the Indian girl's emotions and feeling: "I lost my spirit. Since the day I was taken from my mother I had suffered extreme indignities" (p. 28). Through the Indian girl, the audience realizes that America can be a place where people are exploited. **– Wai Kam**

The Conclusion

The *conclusion* to an essay analyzing fiction establishes your interpretation of the story: what you believe to be the story's larger meaning. For example, you can explain how the story reveals the author's view of society or human behavior; how it illuminates a philosophical, ethical, or psychological concept; or how it relates to an important issue in today's world. (See also *Guidelines for Writing the Conclusion* on page 108.)

■➤ Your turn: *Structuring the essay*

Using the *Guidelines for Writing the Introduction* on page 101, the *Guidelines for Structuring the Body* on page 105, and the *Guidelines for Writing the Conclusion* on page 108, create a flow chart such as the one on page 174 to show what ideas and specifics you might include in your essay.

■ Writing the Essay

Writing the essay can be accomplished most effectively by going through the processes of drafting, receiving feedback, and revising (see Section II of A Handbook for Writing, pages 274–284). Use the following checklist to see if your essay fulfills readers' expectations for an analysis of fiction. The checklist may be used for self-evaluation or for evaluation of your essay by another reader.

Evaluative Criteria for an Essay Analyzing Fiction		

YES **NO**

☐ ☐ **1 Does the opening of the essay provide general background information about the topic?**
If yes, what is the general background?
If no, what background information might be relevant?

☐ ☐ **2 Does the essay make clear, at any point, which story is being analyzed?**
If yes, which story is being analyzed?
If no, where might the name of the author and title of the story be included?

☐ ☐ **3 Does the essay focus on a recurring theme in the story?**
If yes, what is the theme?
If no, how can the focus be clarified?

☐ ☐ **4 Does the essay provide sufficient and relevant evidence from the story to support points or answer questions about the theme?**
If yes, which evidence helps to explain the points or answer the questions?
If no, which evidence could help explain the points or answer the questions?

☐ ☐ **5 Does the conclusion provide an interpretation of the story?**
If yes, what is the story's larger meaning?
If no, how might the story be interpreted?

☐ ☐ **6 Is the essay logically structured?**
If yes, what makes the structure logical?
If no, how could the essay be more logically structured?

■ Completing the Essay

Completing the essay involves proofreading and editing your final draft as well as preparing a clear final copy to hand in to your instructor for evaluation. See Sections II and III of A Handbook for Writing, pages 282–288.

PART THREE
RESEARCH AND WRITING ASSIGNMENTS

Chapter 6

Writing from Field Research

Chapter 7

Writing from Library and Web-Based Research

Chapter 6

Writing from Field Research

Writing an essay drawn from field research involves gathering information primarily through observations, interviews, or surveys. One of the challenges of composing such an essay is to formulate your own generalization or theory about the issue you have chosen to research.

Chapter 6 includes guidelines that are designed to help you conduct field research and develop your essay. The guidelines for different methods of conducting research are presented separately, for clarity. In the course of doing the research, however, you may want to combine methodologies, for example, observe *and* interview or observe *and* survey.

GUIDELINES

Writing from Field Research

Essay Assignment

Write an essay in which you draw from field research to investigate an issue that is addressed in this book, such as communicating across languages and cultures, adapting to new approaches to learning and literacy, or evaluating teaching and learning. Alternatively, you may investigate another issue that you want to learn more about. Gather information about your chosen topic through observations, interviews, or surveys, or a combination of these methods. Your purpose is to develop a generalization or theory about the issue you are investigating. To accomplish this goal, you will need to analyze and interpret the information you gather. The exploratory writing of one student, Ayse Yeyinmen, is included in the following guidelines to show how she developed ideas for an essay drawn from field research. Her completed essay, "The Relationship Between International and U.S.-Born Students: Two Perspectives," appears on pages 199–203.

■ Selecting a Field Research Topic

Selecting a field research topic that you want to explore provides the opportunity to find an answer to a question triggered by your reading or experience. As you consider which issue you want to investigate, remember that, because field research involves human subjects, you may need to receive approval for your project and written permission from the participants.

Guidelines for Selecting a Field Research Topic

1. Skim this book to remind yourself of the issues that have been addressed, or use some of the exploratory writing strategies described in Chapter 2 on pages 52–61 to discover an issue of interest to you.
2. Consider whether the issue lends itself to field research. Ask yourself: "Can I gather enough information and ideas on this issue by observing, interviewing, or conducting a survey?"
3. Formulate a preliminary question about the issue that your field research project will be designed to answer, with the understanding that the question may change as your research proceeds.

A student writer at work: *Selecting a field research topic*

Ayse wanted to research the experiences of international students in U.S. colleges, an issue that is discussed in LaRay M. Barna's "Intercultural Communication Stumbling Blocks" (pages 66–74). Her preliminary question was: *How do international students see themselves fitting into the college community?*

▪▪▪▶ **Your turn:** *Selecting a field research topic*

Using the *Guidelines for Selecting a Field Research Topic*, choose an issue that you can investigate through field research.

▪ Gathering Background Information

Gathering background information before you observe, interview, or conduct a survey provides the opportunity to become more fully informed about the issue you have chosen to research. For example, you can speak informally to a knowledgeable person or collect relevant materials from college departments, organizations, libraries, or the Internet.

Guidelines for Gathering Background Information

The following sources may provide relevant background information on your research topic:

1. **Academic departments.** Consult a faculty member or administrator who can provide material related to a particular field of interest.
2. **Offices.** Check a college catalog for a listing of offices, such as Admissions or a Dean's office, that can provide material on relevant topics.
3. **Organizations.** Check with a student activities office for a listing of campus or community organizations that can provide material on specific areas of interest.
4. **Libraries.** Consult a reference librarian for help in finding material related to your research topic. See Chapter 7: *Library and Web-Based Research*, pages 208–214, for further information.
5. **The Internet.** Conduct a Web-based search to find material related to your research topic. See Chapter 7, pages 214–215, for further information.

A student writer at work: *Gathering background information*

To research the experiences of international students on her campus, Ayse went to the International Center to gather documents. She collected several copies of the Center newsletter and a pamphlet describing the International Club. In addition, Ayse reread and took notes on LaRay M. Barna's "Intercultural Communication Stumbling Blocks" (pages 66–74).

▪▪▪▶ **Your turn:** *Gathering background information*

Using the *Guidelines for Gathering Background Information*, find material on your chosen research topic.

■ Observing

Observing people in action enables you to gain first-hand knowledge of the issue you are investigating. For such research to be meaningful, it should be conducted as systematically as possible.

Guidelines for Observing

1. Determine the objectives of your research.
2. Select a relevant site.
3. Devise a consistent method for recording your observations such as note taking or tape recording.
4. Interpret your findings. Separate *what you actually see* with your own eyes from *your interpretation of what you see.* Remember that another researcher might have a different interpretation of the same observation. You may include multiple interpretations.

A student writer at work: *Observing*

Ayse's field research did not involve observing, but one of her classmates, Roberto Drew-Bear, observed students in a campus cafeteria as part of his own study on differences in communication. Roberto, who is bilingual in Spanish and English, noted that international and U.S.-born students were sitting in separate sections. He then walked along the two sections for 15 minutes each, listened, and took notes.

Here is an excerpt from what Roberto wrote about the native English speakers.

> *Overall, it was a pretty straightforward conversation where there was always a clear understanding of what the person was trying to say.*

In contrast, here is an excerpt from what Roberto wrote about the Spanish speakers.

> *The Spanish speakers had more difficulty understanding one another, even though they were all speaking Spanish. Maybe this is because they were all from different countries.*

■■■▶ Your turn: *Observing*

Using the *Guidelines for Observing*, conduct a systematic observation.

■ Interviewing

Interviewing someone who is knowledgeable about the issue you are investigating gives you access to a source who can provide information, clarify issues, correct misconceptions, make connections, suggest related areas for exploration, or provide research sources. Alternatively, that person may be the subject of your interview, for example, if you aim to learn about that person's career.

Guidelines for Interviewing

1. Contact the person you wish to interview, explain your research project, and ask for an appointment. Set a specific time length and place for the interview.
2. Prepare an interview guide: a list of questions related to your research project.
3. Be flexible with your questions. One good general opening question may be all you need. Let the interviewee talk.
4. Use a tape recorder, if you have permission to do so, take notes, or do both.
5. Ask permission for a follow-up phone call or interview if you find you need further information.
6. Immediately after the interview, reflect on what you have just learned. Spend some time writing and adding to your notes.
7. Thank the interviewee by mail, e-mail, or telephone.

A student writer at work: *Interviewing*

Ayse made an appointment to meet with the director of the International Center, and they discussed issues of importance related to the international student population on campus. The director suggested some research approaches Ayse could take. As a result of the interview, Ayse decided to develop a questionnaire in order to investigate the social relationships between international and U.S.-born students at her college.

■■➡ **Your turn:** *Interviewing*

Using the *Guidelines for Interviewing*, interview at least one person who is knowledgeable about your topic.

■ Conducting a Survey

Conducting a survey is an efficient way of obtaining information from many different people. To accomplish that goal, you first need to construct a questionnaire and distribute it to a large number of people (respondents). For such research to be meaningful, you should plan the questions carefully, choose respondents who are as representative as possible of the group you want to study, and analyze the responses systematically.

Guidelines for Conducting a Survey

1. Create a survey questionnaire.
   - Begin with spaces for respondents to write or check off objective information about themselves, for example, their age, gender, and level of education.
   - Create questions that allow respondents to check off an answer such as *agree* or *disagree*, open-ended questions that allow respondents to provide their own answers, or both types of questions.
2. Test the questionnaire on a small sample group. Determine whether your questions have produced useful answers, and revise the questionnaire accordingly.
3. Decide the best way to distribute the questionnaire.
4. After you have collected the completed questionnaires, analyze the data.
   - Number the questionnaires for easy reference.
   - Total the objective data, for example, the number of females, and create percentages such as "Ten percent say that the social life is different." You may find it helpful to enter the data into a spreadsheet.
   - Look for patterns in the responses to the open-ended questions. You might want to highlight, underline, or copy what you perceive to be significant comments.
   - Create categories to label emerging themes.
   - Create a chart or outline to organize the categories and the responses that illustrate them.

A student writer at work: *Conducting a survey*

With feedback from her instructor and classmates, Ayse designed a questionnaire for international students and then distributed it on campus. Twenty-nine respondents completed the questionnaires. Ayse underlined what she perceived to be key words or phrases, and, in the left-hand margin of each questionnaire, she wrote words to categorize what the respondents had said. She then could look down the margins quickly to see repeated or similar themes to begin her analysis of the open-ended questions.

Two samples of Ayse's completed questionnaire, with her marginal notes and underlining, are on the following pages.

	QUESTIONNAIRE FOR INTERNATIONAL STUDENTS

Gender: Male _✓_ Female ___
Level of education: _1 year of college_
Are you living on campus? (check one) Yes _✓_ No ___
Age: _19_
How long have you been in the U.S.? _____ 3 months _____
What country do you come from? _____ Hong Kong _____

Diversity
Speed

1. How does the life in your home country differ from life at college?

   We have a _more diverse_ ~~choose~~ *choice* of everything, food, clothes, etc. Since Hong Kong is a very small place, we go from 1 place to another a lot _faster_ than in here.

Values

2. What kinds of problems do you face regarding your background, your values, your customs?

   The difference between our _moral values_ is very big. Well, at least my own ~~culture~~ moral.

"Nice"
Cultural
differences

Make fun

3. What are the attitudes of American-born undergraduate students toward you?

   Some of them are really _nice_ but some could _not understand the cultural difference_ and sometimes they _make fun_ of me.

Internat'l
easier
"depends"

4. How easy do you feel when you are with Americans? Is it easier to get along with international students? Why or why not?

   I think it's _easier to get along with some international students,_ but it _depends on our background, our values, our customs._ I get along with some local students just fine.

No contact

5. What do you think the International Club accomplishes?

   I don't have any contact with I. club.

Clubs

6. What should you and other students (American and international) do to understand each other better?

   I was looking for an answer to that question too, but I couldn't find one. Well, at least by _joining different culture club_ would help.

	QUESTIONNAIRE FOR INTERNATIONAL STUDENTS
	Gender: Male ✓ Female ___ Level of education: *3 years of college* Are you living on campus? (check one) Yes ___ No ✓ Age: *22* How long have you been in the U.S.? ___ *2 years* ___ What country do you come from? ___ *Russia* ___
Completely different	1. How does the life in your home country differ from life at college? *Completely, nothing in common.*
Values Differences (meaning, education)	2. What kinds of problems do you face regarding your background, your values, your customs? *Difference attitudes to life and its values. Sometime do no understand people, because of different meanings about the same subject, totally difference system of education.*
No clue	3. What are the attitudes of American-born undergraduate students toward you? *I have no clue! I hope it is alright.*
"Never relax" Internat'l easier "Common language"	4. How easy do you feel when you are with Americans? Is it easier to get along with international students? Why or why not? *I do not feel at ease with Americans, I ~~feel~~, never relax. It is easy for me to find understanding and get along with international students, because we all from different background and in our relations we are trying to find "common language" in understanding.*
Understanding/ Relationships	5. What do you think the International Club accomplishes? *Each other understanding ~~more~~ better relationships between students of different backgrounds.*
Meeting friends	6. What should you and other students (American and international) do to understand each other better? *More intercultural meetings, trying to find more friends among international and American students.*

▪▪▪➤ **Your turn:** *Conducting a survey*

Using the *Guidelines for Conducting a Survey* on page 188, design, distribute, collect, and analyze the data from a survey questionnaire.

■ Focusing Ideas

To fulfill the goal of *focusing ideas* for your readers, you need to determine the questions that your research results answer and write a sentence or two that can serve as the focal point of your essay.

A student writer at work: *Focusing ideas*

As she looked over her completed survey questionnaires, Ayse saw a pattern in the responses and stated her focal point in the form of two questions that her essay would answer.

> • *How do international students think they are perceived by the undergraduate American-born students?*
> • *How do they think they can help the entire college community to understand their background and culture better?*

Ayse also decided it was important to create and distribute a separate questionnaire designed for U.S.-born students in order to gain another perspective on the topic. The new questions she generated were

> • *What are your feelings about studying in college with international students?*
> • *What are the advantages?*
> • *What are the disadvantages?*

➤ **Your turn:** *Focusing ideas*

Using the *Guidelines for Focusing Ideas* on page 61, create a focal point for your essay.

■ Structuring the Essay

Structuring the essay that is drawn from field research involves moving readers toward an answer to a question. Such essays typically have a five-part organizational framework: *introduction, methods, results, discussion,* and *appendix.*

The flow chart on page 192 may help you visualize an overall structure for an essay drawn from field research.

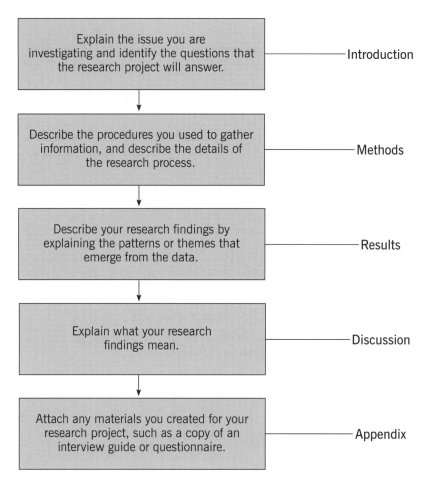

Explain the issue you are investigating and identify the questions that the research project will answer.	Introduction
Describe the procedures you used to gather information, and describe the details of the research process.	Methods
Describe your research findings by explaining the patterns or themes that emerge from the data.	Results
Explain what your research findings mean.	Discussion
Attach any materials you created for your research project, such as a copy of an interview guide or questionnaire.	Appendix

Introduction

The *introduction* to an essay drawn from field research explains the significance of the issue that has been investigated and provides a focal point that states or implies the questions that the research project is designed to answer. (See also *Guidelines for Writing the Introduction* on page 101.)

Activity: *Evaluating introductions*

The passages on the following pages are introductions to student essays drawn from field research. Evaluate two or more of the introductions by answering the following questions.

1 Does the introduction involve you in the topic and make you want to read the rest of the essay? Explain.

2 Can you tell, at the beginning of the essay, which issue the student writer has investigated and why?

3 Can you tell what research question or questions the essay will answer?

4 If you think the introduction should be revised, what suggestions do you have for the student writer?

Student A

> International students like myself generally enjoy studying abroad, even though we face problems. We know that people can have problems wherever they are. Fortunately, on this campus, The International Center is involved with the lives of international students and tries to help us experience as few difficulties as possible. As a way of assisting students further, the center director asked our class to research the international students who attend the college and the variables that affect their adjustment. This paper is based on two questions: How do students from other countries think they are perceived by the undergraduate U.S.-born students? How can the entire college community learn to understand their background and culture better?
>
> The answers to these questions can provide insight into the problems that international students face and the reasons for these problems. They also can lead The International Center to find different ways to welcome future international students in a more congenial atmosphere, to make them feel more at ease in college, and to improve conditions for them. – **Ayse**

Student B

> Our university opens its doors to a relatively high number of international students. International students constitute approximately 13% to 15% of the student body. The school has a diverse and liberal atmosphere, which makes life easier for the international students. Furthermore, the school's academic community is conscious of their presence and is tolerant toward them. The International Center organizes an international orientation before the beginning of the academic year, in order to speed up the transition period.
>
> Nevertheless, in spite of all this help, the international community, because of its diverse background, has many problems in adapting easily to the college social life. According to the director of the International Center, students have to face many difficulties as a result of the different values and morals of a new environment. In response to a request by the director, research was undertaken by members of our English composition class to provide a more specific idea about international students' problems and their adjustment to the social life here. This report is one of four prepared for the International Center. – **Yesim**

Student C

> Although the "American Dream" may mean different things to different people, the underlying hope that it instills in each person is very real. Whether the desire is simply to gain wealth, own a home, or be a star or to fulfill a much deeper yearning like the desire for freedom, America offers the opportunity for it all. Many people have been blessed enough, with a little luck and hard work, to achieve their dream here in the United States. It is this belief in the "American Dream" and the realization that many people have attained it that most often draws thousands of immigrants to this great country each year.

continued

Unfortunately, although the dream is the first step in realizing one's desires, it does not guarantee anything to anyone. The United States offers a vast amount of opportunities but there are also a lot of obstacles, such as the English language and the requirements for U.S. citizenship. The three immigrants I interviewed – Carmen, Houdzie, and Natalie – came to America in search of the "American Dream," and along the way have had to discover that this dream is much more difficult to obtain than they originally thought. Although their journey to America in search of their dreams may have been different for each person, today they have all ended up in the same lower-end job trying to learn English language in order to improve their place in society. All three of them are taking classes at the agency where I am a volunteer tutor. Every Tuesday and Thursday they give two and half hours of their time in order to learn the language. The tutors play a significant role in the program and, because they are in such close contact with the students, it is beneficial for them to know and realize the vast differences and heritages all of the students carry with them. **– Isabel**

Methods

The *methods* section of an essay drawn from field research describes the type of field research you have undertaken and provides specific details about the data-gathering process.

Guidelines for Describing Methods

1. Explain which procedures you used to gather information, for example, observing, interviewing, or conducting a survey.
2. Describe the details of the research process, for example, the time period in which the research took place, how many and which places or people you observed, or how many and which people you interviewed or surveyed.

A student writer at work: *Describing methods*

Ayse made a list of the items that she planned to include in the Methods section of her essay.

Major sources: questionnaires for 29 international students and 6 U.S.-born students
International students:
- *from Asia (14), Europe (9), South America (4), West Indies (2)*
- *20 males, 9 females*
- *17 freshmen, 5 sophomores, 4 juniors, 3 seniors*
- *time in U.S. = 3 months to 16 years (average = $2\frac{1}{3}$ years)*
- *83% live on campus*

Results

The *results* section, which covers several paragraphs of the essay, presents your research findings: the data that you have collected through observation, interview, or survey.

Guidelines for Presenting Results
1. Explain the patterns or themes that have emerged from your analysis of the research data.
2. Provide evidence to support your analysis in the form of details, examples, statistics, and quotations.

The following suggestions offer three possibilities for structuring the section of the essay that presents results. You can use the drafting process to experiment with the organization of the results section; your early efforts can be revised later (see Drafting, pages 274–275, and Revising, pages 278–282).

1. Discuss ideas that have emerged from the data in order of importance, according to your view of what is important. You may begin with what you think is the least important idea and end with the most important, or vice versa.
   a. State the idea that you will discuss.
   b. Provide evidence such as examples, statistics, or quotations to develop the idea.
   c. Repeat this process for each idea you want to discuss.

2. Discuss your research findings according to categories that emerge from the data. For example, your categories may reflect repeated patterns of behavior, phrases, or ways of thinking. Analyze the data where appropriate.
   a. Identify a category of responses or observations.
   b. Provide evidence to show that this category reflects a pattern.
   c. Identify another category and provide evidence to show that this category reflects a pattern.
   d. Repeat this process for each category you want to present.

3. Present the data in chronological order. This organizational pattern will work only with events or activities that you have observed or that someone has described in an interview.
   a. Begin with what happened first.
   b. Continue to tell the story, analyzing the data where appropriate.

Activity: *Evaluating paragraphs that present results*

The passages on the following pages (196–197) are body paragraphs taken from student essays drawn from field research. Evaluate two or more of the paragraphs by answering the following questions.

1 Can you determine, at the beginning of the paragraph, the point the student writer is making?

2 Does the student writer provide sufficient evidence to support the point?

3 If you think the paragraph should be revised, what suggestions do you have for the student writer?

Student A

The general opinion about the relationship between American and international students is that it is easier for the internationals to become friends with other international students. Fifty percent explain that internationals are more alike since they have more things in common such as being abroad, facing the same problems due to their different backgrounds, being more open-minded to differences in others, and being "used to making adjustments." The language is the major problem in hanging out with Americans: it is hard for them to participate in a conversation when they cannot speak as fast. Finding friends from their native countries prevents internationals from making an effort to communicate with Americans. Unfortunately, clinging to friends from their native countries prevents these internationals from making an effort to communicate with Americans. – **Ayse**

Student B

The answers show that half of the international students are enrolled in activities such as the International Club, Cultural Exchange Circle, UNICEF, Italian Club, Korean Students Association, and so on, but these organizations don't satisfy their needs at all. Some of them expected this result at the beginning; the others didn't go to meetings any more. The rest didn't participate in anything. The most striking answer for this question came from a Russian female telling that she had no experience of being a member of any student organization before in her country because they spend their time for other purposes. Most of the students don't feel ready for an active role in these organizations because they have been here for a really short time. But only 2% to 3% are very positive about it. – **Yesim**

Student C

Once she and her cousin reached California, Carmen stayed there for three months living with some family friends. At this point Carmen did not know any English, but her belief in the "America Dream" did not fade. "I was told that America is the land where dreams come true, that's why I came here." Her first years in America were very difficult and she worked hard cleaning, babysitting and working at a candy factory. After two years she realized that she needed to take English classes in order to get a better job and make more money. She also realized that she needed a green card. This was much tougher than she expected and after many denials, she finally moved to Spain and got her citizenship there. While in Spain she got her passport to America and now every three months she has to travel back to Spain in order to remain in the U.S. Overall, Carmen feels that America is what she expected. "I like that older people can go to school to improve life in different ways." One difference she notes is her belief that family is much closer in Guatemala than in the United States. Families often live together, and often when the parents get old they move in with one of the children. Today, seven of her family members are living in the United States and this is very much a blessing. Overall, Carmen says she "loves it here." – **Isabel**

Discussion

The *discussion* section, or conclusion, explains what the research findings mean and examines the implications of what you have written.

Ayse made notes for the ideas that she planned to include in the conclusion of her essay.

> <u>General point</u>: What is needed for intercultural communication = tolerance, open-mindedness, and patience.
>
> <u>Recommendations for the International Center</u>:
> - Organize more intercultural meetings and activities
> - Provide wide exposure of multiple cultures for everyone
> - Teach how to accept difference
> - Address issues that would bring the two groups together

Guidelines for Writing the Discussion Section

1. Interpret your research findings by stating a generalization or theory that ties everything together.
2. Discuss the implications of your research findings by making recommendations based on what you learned or by raising a question or a series of questions that emerge from the research.

Your turn: *Structuring the essay*

Using the *Guidelines for Writing the Introduction* on page 101 and the *Guidelines for Describing Methods*, the *Guidelines for Presenting Results*, and *the Guidelines for Writing the Discussion Section* on pages 194–197, create a flow chart such as the one on page 192 to show what ideas and specifics you might include in your essay.

■ Writing the Essay

Writing the essay can be accomplished most effectively by going through the processes of drafting, receiving feedback, and revising (see Section II of A Handbook for Writing, pages 274–284). Use the following checklist to see if your essay fulfills readers' expectations for an essay drawn from field research. The checklist may be used for self-evaluation or for evaluation of your essay by another reader.

Evaluative Criteria for Writing from Field Research

YES	NO	
☐	☐	**1 Does the introduction to the essay make clear what issue is being investigated?** If yes, what issue does the essay investigate? If no, what information is needed to make the topic clear?
☐	☐	**2 Does the introduction to the essay make clear why this issue is being investigated?** If yes, why is this issue being investigated? If no, how might the purpose of the investigation be clarified?
☐	☐	**3 Does the introduction to the essay raise a question that the research is designed to answer?** If yes, what is the research question? If no, what questions might fit the research findings?
☐	☐	**4 Does the essay provide a detailed methods section?** If yes, what procedures were used? If no, what details are needed?
☐	☐	**5 Does the essay present and analyze the research results?** If yes, which evidence illustrates the patterns or themes that emerged from the research data? If no, what kind of evidence could be added or changed?
☐	☐	**6 Does the conclusion to the essay interpret the data by stating a generalization or theory that ties everything together?** If yes, what do the research findings mean? If no, what might the interpretation be?
☐	☐	**7 Is the essay logically structured?** If yes, what makes the structure logical? If no, how could the essay be more logically structured?

▪▪▶ Activity: *Applying evaluative criteria*

Apply the *Evaluative Criteria for Writing from Field Research* to the following student essay written by Ayse Yeyinmen to fulfill an assignment for a college course.

The Relationship Between International and U. S.-Born Students: Two Perspectives
Ayse Yeyinmen

International students like myself generally enjoy studying abroad, even though we face problems. We know that people can have problems wherever they are. Fortunately, on this campus, The International Center is involved with the lives of international students and tries to help us experience as few difficulties as possible. As a way of assisting students further, the center director asked our class to research the international students who attend the college and the variables that affect their adjustment. This paper is based on two questions: How do students from other countries think they are perceived by the undergraduate U.S.-born students? How can the entire college community learn to understand their background and culture better?

The answers to these questions can provide insight into the problems that international students face and the reasons for these problems. They also can lead The International Center to find different ways to welcome future international students in a more congenial atmosphere, to make them feel more at ease in college, and to improve conditions for them.

More than 475,000 students from other countries are in the United States to get a college education. Despite that large number of students, there are not many accessible articles concerning these students and their problems. My major source for this research was a questionnaire given to twenty-nine international (see Appendix A) and six U.S.-born students (see Appendix B).

RESPONSES OF INTERNATIONAL STUDENTS

The twenty-nine international students who completed the questionnaire are from Asia (14), Europe (9), South America (4), and the West Indies (2). Nine are female and twenty are male. There are seventeen freshmen, five sophomores, four juniors, and three seniors. Their time spent in the United States ranges from three months to sixteen years, averaging two and one-third years. Eighty-three percent of the students live on campus.

Among the differences students notice are the weather, the food, the dinner time, the quantity of work, and a more competitive atmosphere. Twenty percent of the students say that the education, moral values, and attitudes are totally different in their countries and that these differences are the source of misunderstandings and disagreements. However, 16 percent of them say that their life differs only in meeting people from all of the world. Independence is the newest experience for 13 percent of these students. Ten percent think that the social life is limited, and another 10 percent find everything the same as in their country.

Most of the internationals agree that they do not face many serious problems. The reason for this could be that most of them hang out with people speaking their native language. They complain mostly about the different

continued

version of friendship that the Americans[1] conceive. They notice that everybody is friendly with each other while keeping a distance, without a classification of best friend, treating everyone equally. This makes them feel that friendship is less important in the United States because they are not used to calling someone a friend when they just say "hi" to her or him. Internationals have a much deeper concept of friendship.

The general opinion about the relationship between American and international students is that it is easier for the internationals to become friends with other international students. Fifty percent explain that internationals are more alike since they have more things in common such as being abroad, facing the same problems due to their different backgrounds, being more open-minded to differences in others, and being "used to making adjustments." The language is the major problem in hanging out with Americans: it is hard for them to participate in a conversation when they cannot speak as fast. Finding friends from their native countries prevents internationals from making an effort to communicate with Americans. Unfortunately, clinging to friends from their native countries prevents these internationals from making an effort to communicate with Americans.

Twenty percent of internationals say that making friendships depend on the personality, regardless of nationality and native language. Twenty-three percent consider that the Americans are friendly and nice towards them and treat them as any U.S.-born student. International students who have a lot of American friends, 16 percent, think that Americans are open-minded and interested in different cultures. Ten percent agree on the preference of U.S.-born friends among the Americans. Another 10 percent think that Americans are "nice" but at the same time say they can be "indifferent" and "intolerant" toward them. "Focused on their rights," "liberal," "respectful to others," and "outgoing" are some of the other descriptive words given by the international students for Americans. Thus, there is no single, common description of U.S.-born students.

RESPONSES OF U.S.-BORN STUDENTS

Of the six U.S.-born students who completed the questionnaire, all are female; five are freshmen, one is a sophomore; and all live on campus.

The six opinions given by these U.S.-born students about studying with international students shows that they are open-minded and interested in different cultures. They enjoy studying in a cosmopolitan atmosphere. They do not see any disadvantages. However, they think internationals segregate themselves. These Americans want to have more connection between themselves and students from other countries. All of them like learning about others' lives and appreciate cultural opportunities at the college due to its diversity. Like internationals, they agree that misunderstandings may occur because of the language and the lack of a common background.

---

[1] The word *Americans* here refers to U.S.-born citizens.

CONCLUSION

Just as LaRay Barna suggests in her article, "Intercultural Communication Stumbling Blocks," tolerance, open-mindedness, and patience are the key words to a better relationship between international and U.S.-born students. More intercultural meetings and activities can help to make life easy for us. Wide exposure of multiple cultures is necessary to break walls between students. Doing more things together, sharing, and accepting that others can be different are important factors in the adjustment issue. To make everything better and easier, both international and U.S.-born students should make an attempt to take people as they are. In order for these friendships to form, The International Center should sponsor more activities and address issues that would bring the two groups together.

Works Cited

Barna, LaRay M. "Intercultural Communication Stumbling Blocks." In *Guidelines: A Cross-Cultural Reading/Writing Text*. Ruth Spack. New York: Cambridge UP, 2006. 66–74.

APPENDIX A: QUESTIONNAIRE FOR INTERNATIONAL STUDENTS

Gender: Male ___ Female ___
Level of education: _____
Are you living on campus? (check one) Yes ___ No ___
Age: ___
How long have you been in the U.S.? _____
What country do you come from? _____

1. How does the life in your home country differ from life at college?

2. What kinds of problems do you face regarding your background, your values, your customs?

3. What are the attitudes of American-born undergraduate students toward you?

4. How easy do you feel when you are with Americans? Is it easier to get along with international students? Why or why not?

5. What do you think the International Club accomplishes?

6. What should you and other students (American and international) do to understand each other better?

	APPENDIX B: QUESTIONNAIRE FOR U.S.-BORN STUDENTS
	Gender: Male ___ Female ___ Year of graduation from college: _____ Are you living on campus? (check one) Yes ___ No ___ Age: ___ 1. What are your feelings about studying in college with international students? 2. What are the advantages? What are the disadvantages?

▧ Completing the Essay

Completing the essay involves proofreading and editing your final draft as well as preparing a clear final copy to hand in to your instructor for evaluation. See Sections II and III of A Handbook for Writing, pages 282–288.

Chapter 7

Writing from Library and Web-Based Research

Writing an essay drawn from library and Web-based research involves gathering information primarily through written texts. One of the challenges of composing such an essay is to synthesize material from multiple sources.

Chapter 7 includes guidelines that are designed to help you conduct library and Web-based research and develop your essay. Various stages of research are presented one step at a time, for clarity. In the course of doing the research, however, you will discover that the stages often overlap. At each stage, you will have a better understanding of what you have already found and a better idea of what you still need to discover.

Library and Web-Based Research

Essay Assignment

Write an essay in which you draw from library and Web-based research to investigate an issue that is addressed in this book, such as cross-cultural communication, racial and cultural discrimination, legal and illegal immigration, educational opportunities for disadvantaged learners, or grading practices in schools and colleges. Alternatively, you may investigate another issue that you want to learn more about. Consult multiple sources in order to discover a variety of perspectives on your chosen topic. Your purpose is to answer a question or offer a solution to a problem. To accomplish this goal, you will need to build on the existing research by incorporating material from published sources, including scholarly articles and books (see Section I of A Handbook for Writing, pages 236–273). You may also incorporate your own field research, as explained in Chapter 6: *Writing from Field Research*. The exploratory writing of one student, Kristyn Marasca, is included in the following guidelines to show how she developed ideas for an essay drawn from library and Web-based research. Her completed essay, "Get in Line: The Shortage of ESL Classes," appears on pages 228–231.

■ Selecting a Library and Web-Based Research Topic

Selecting a library and Web-based research topic that you want to explore provides the opportunity to find an answer to a question or discover a solution to a problem. Your first task is to decide which issue to investigate.

Guidelines for Selecting a Library and Web-Based Research Topic

1. Skim this book to remind yourself of issues that have been addressed, or use some of the exploratory writing strategies described in Chapter 2, on pages 52–61, to discover an issue of interest to you.

2. Consider whether the issue lends itself to library and Web-based research. Ask yourself: "Is the topic so broad that there will be too much information on it for a research essay? Is the topic so narrow that I will have difficulty finding enough published material to provide multiple perspectives on the topic?"

A student writer at work: *Selecting a library and Web-based research topic*

At first Kristyn struggled to find a topic and stated: "I honestly have no idea where I would like to go in terms of a final project."

But then she began to think about the readings that made the greatest impression on her and decided to focus on the issue of educating English language learners. This subject was of particular interest because Kristyn was a volunteer tutor at a community agency, the Power Program, which provides English as a second language (ESL) classes for adults.

> *In class, my favorite discussion has been on the struggles immigrants must face when coming to America. I wonder if the people I am tutoring had to overcome these obstacles to get to where they are today. . . . I also wonder how efficiently the Power Program is run and where students go once they have completed the program itself. I am also interested in other places where classes are offered, and I would like to inform people about the importance of helping immigrants.*

Your turn: *Selecting a library and Web-based research topic*

Using the *Guidelines for Selecting a Library and Web-Based Research Topic*, choose an issue to investigate.

■ Writing a Research Proposal

Writing a research proposal provides the opportunity to describe to your instructor the research project you want to undertake. In your proposal, you can explain why you want to investigate a particular issue, what you already know about the issue, what you need to learn, and what kinds of answers or solutions you seek.

Guidelines for Writing a Research Proposal

1. Identify your research topic.
2. Explain the purpose of the research project. Answer such questions as: "What do I already know about this issue?" "What do I want to learn?" "What question do I want to answer?" "What problem do I want to solve?"
3. If you have conducted a preliminary search for published sources that are relevant to your proposed topic, describe the material you have found.

A student writer at work: *Writing a research proposal*

As Kristyn began to conduct research on ESL programs for adult learners, she learned that there are long wait lists for such courses. She decided to narrow her topic to the issue of the shortage of classes. Excerpts from the research proposal Kristyn submitted to her instructor are on page 208.

Immigrants have become part of the American identity, and in order to become further immersed in our culture, many try to enroll in ESL classes. Too often, however, they are denied this experience simply because the demand for these classes exceeds the supply. . . .

With the expanding role of English in our culture, it is imperative that there be sufficient resources for immigrants to develop their English skills. Therefore, I am interested in examining the short supply of ESL classes and what we as citizens can do to improve the situation. I spoke to Kathy Chlapowski, the director of Waltham's Power Program, and she said that the program began with 40 students, and now there is a waiting list of 250 students. . . .

I found an article in the May 30, 2002 edition of the *Boston Globe*. This article, "Word of Mouth Keeps Language Classes Filled" by Cynthia Cantrell, reinforces many of the facts that Kathy spoke about [and states that] it is imperative that to receive donations and volunteers. . . .

The next article I read, by Suzanne Sataline, is entitled "English Language Classes in Short Supply, Immigrant Surge Means Waiting Lists" which appeared in the *Boston Globe* on August 15, 2002. This article discusses the extreme shortage of ESL classes in the United States, more specifically in the Northeast. . . .

This article gave many important figures, which I think will add to my paper. For instance, it says that over 14,000 residents in Massachusetts have enrolled in government sponsored ESL classes, but there are 15,500 more waiting for instruction.

Your turn: *Writing a research proposal*

Using the *Guidelines for Writing a Research Proposal* on page 207, write a proposal for your research project.

■ Conducting Library Research

Conducting library research begins with learning where materials are located in the library and how to use them. You should take advantage of opportunities to tour the library and to attend workshops on how to access sources. Much of your research may be conducted on the library's electronic network, so it is especially important to become familiar with the technology. You should also learn who the reference librarians are, for they are trained to assist researchers.

To achieve a thoughtful and fair analysis of your topic, search for scholarly materials. Authors of scholarly books and articles characteristically research academic subjects in depth, view topics from multiple angles, and document sources systematically. Furthermore, their manuscripts undergo careful review by other scholars even before they are published. Such sources are thus especially valuable for college-level investigations.

Determining Subject Headings

Determining subject headings, or how your topic might be listed in the various reference sources in the library, can save you time in finding relevant information.

Guidelines for Determining Subject Headings

One or more of the following suggestions may be helpful:

1. With the assistance of your instructor or a reference librarian, make a list of potential subject headings for your topic.
2. Consult the reference book *Library of Congress: Subject Headings* for headings that may fit your topic.
3. Consult the library's online computer manual for descriptors, or subject headings, that may fit your topic.

A student writer at work: *Determining subject headings*

Kristyn made a preliminary list of subject headings related to her research topic.

> *English as a second language*
> *English language learners*
> *ESL classes*
> *Adult ESL*
> *Literacy*
> *Immigrants – United States*

Your turn: *Determining subject headings*

Using the *Guidelines for Determining Subject Headings*, make a list of subject headings related to your research topic.

Finding Books in the Library

As you begin *finding books in the library*, remember that the most valuable book-length resources for college-level research are those written by scholars or experts and published by academic presses. In addition to searching for books in a library catalog, you may also search on Web sites that host links to online books.

Guidelines for Finding Books in the Library

1. Using your subject headings, search the library catalog to find books that relate to your topic. Use two descriptors if needed, for example, "Literacy – United States."

2. Write down the name of the author, title, and call number, which indicates where the book is located in the library. For example, if the call number is

LC

151.K68

the book is shelved with books on special aspects of education (**LC**) that deal with literacy or illiteracy (any number between **149** and **161**). Books on similar topics are shelved together.

3. Determine whether the author has carefully researched the topic, for example, by checking for footnotes or bibliography. Skim the book to see if its information is useful for your particular project, for example, by checking the table of contents and reading the preface or introduction.

4. Keep a list of books that you may use in your research. Record the author, title, publisher, year of publication, and call number.

A student writer at work: *Finding books in the library*

Using the subject heading, "Literacy – United States," Kristyn conducted a keyword search in the library's online catalog to find books related to her research topic (see Figure 7.1).

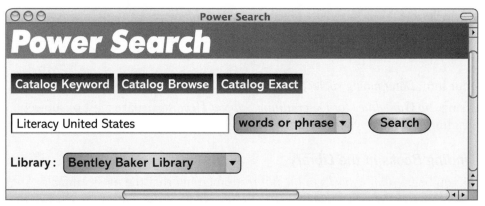

FIGURE 7.1

The keyword search led Kristyn to a list of books related to her chosen topic. She scrolled through the list to find available books of interest. Each item provided the call number, title, author, date of publication, availability, and location of the book (see, for example, Figure 7.2). Kristyn wrote down the call numbers and found the books in the library stacks.

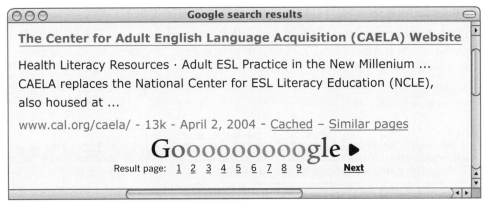

FIGURE 7.2

▪▸ **Your turn:** *Finding books in the library*

Using the *Guidelines for Finding Books in the Library*, search for books that might be useful for your research.

Finding Journal and Magazine Articles

As you begin *finding journal and magazine articles*, remember that the most valuable article-length resources for college-level research are those written by scholars or experts in the field. Such articles appear in journals published by academic organizations, but they may also be found in nonacademic magazines.

Guidelines for Finding Journal and Magazine Articles

1. Using your subject headings, search one or more of the following sources:
   - A general periodical index such as *Reader's Guide to Periodical Literature*
   - A specialized periodical index that lists articles published in your field of interest such as *Education Index*, *Historical Abstracts*, or *Social Sciences Index*
   - An electronic database in your library's network such as *INFOTRAC: Expanded Academic ASAP*; *ProQuest: Research Library*; or *EBSCOhost: Academic Search Premier*
   - The World Wide Web (see pages 214–215)
2. If you use a printed index, check the library catalog to determine whether the library holdings include the journal or magazine you are seeking. If so, find the call number, locate the journal or magazine on the library bookshelves, and look for the article by date and page number; or search for the article in an electronic database.
3. If you use an electronic database, select the options for full texts and for scholarly, peer-reviewed, or refereed articles whenever possible.
4. Keep a list of articles that you may use in your research. Record the author, title, journal name, volume number, date of publication, and page numbers.
5. Photocopy, download and print, or e-mail to yourself whichever articles seem most useful for your research.

A student writer at work: *Finding journal and magazine articles*

Kristyn used various databases to find scholarly articles, including *INFOTRAC: Expanded Academic ASAP*. In the example below (see Figure 7.3), she entered the search terms "volunteers and ESL" and then checked the boxes titled "to articles with text" and "to refereed publications" to be sure that she would find complete scholarly articles.

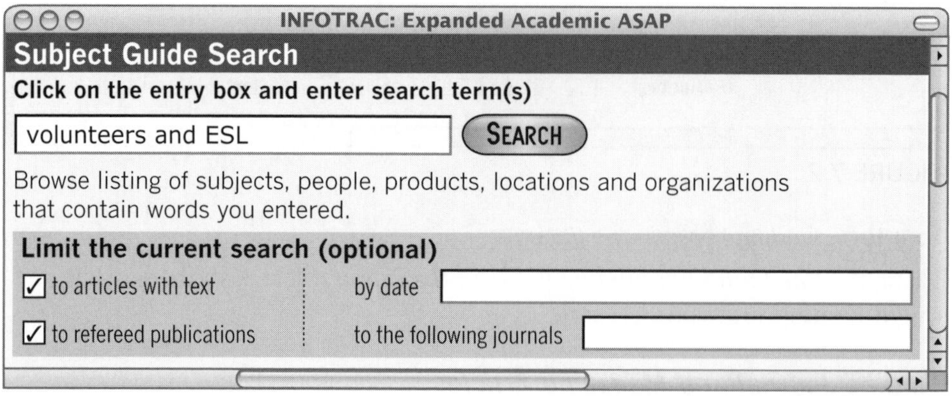

FIGURE 7.3

When Kristyn hit the Search button, she was led to several categories related to the word *volunteers*. She chose the category "Volunteer Workers in Education" because it seemed to be most closely related to her topic. This choice led her to another choice of categories (see Figure 7.4).

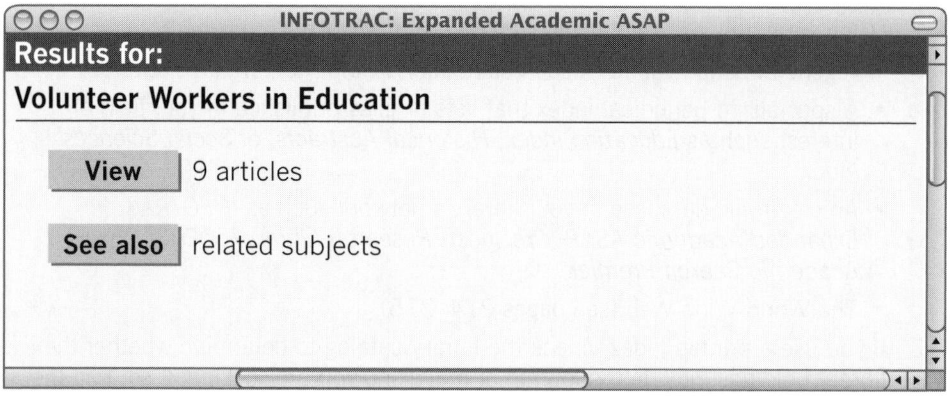

FIGURE 7.4

Kristyn hit the View button and was led to a list of nine articles on volunteering. She selected the article that seemed to be most closely related to her topic, clicked the link titled "Text with graphics" (see Figure 7.5), and found the entire article.

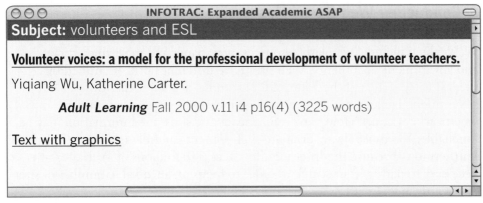

FIGURE 7.5

➡️ **Your turn:** *Finding journal and magazine articles*

Using the *Guidelines for Finding Journal and Magazine Articles* on page 211, locate articles relevant to your research topic.

Finding Newspaper Articles

Finding newspaper articles that are relevant to your research can also help you develop your ideas. Newspapers not only report facts but also include opinion-editorial, or op-ed, columns that analyze issues of the day.

Guidelines for Finding Newspaper Articles

1. Using your subject headings, search one or more of the following sources:
   - A printed newspaper index such as *New York Times Index* or *Index to Black Newspapers*
   - An electronic database in the library's network such as *LexisNexis*, *Newsbank*, or *ProQuest Newspapers*
   - The World Wide Web (see pages 214–215)
2. Check the library catalog to determine whether the library holdings include the newspaper you are seeking. If so, locate a current article in the periodical room and an earlier article on microfilm or in an electronic database.
3. If you use an electronic database, select the option for full texts.
4. Keep a list of articles that you may use in your research. Record the author, if there is one, the title, newspaper name, date of publication, and page numbers.
5. Photocopy or download and print whichever articles seem most useful for your research.

➡️ **Your turn:** *Finding newspaper articles*

Using the *Guidelines for Finding Newspaper Articles*, locate newspaper articles or editorials relevant to your research topic.

■ Conducting Web-Based Research

Conducting Web-based research involves accessing materials on the World Wide Web, which includes scholarly resources, newspaper and magazine articles, and government documents. Web sites have different hosts, identified by the last three letters of the address, for example, academic institution (.edu), government agency (.gov), nonprofit organization (.org), or commercial organization (.com). However, even in academic sites, the information may be unreliable. You must always evaluate such sources carefully (see pages 215–216). Furthermore, because the Internet offers access to millions of Web sites, it is necessary to narrow your search in order to focus on a workable number of sites.

Guidelines for Conducting Web-Based Research

1. Use a search engine, such as *Google, Yahoo,* or *AltaVista,* to find lists of Web sources related to your topic.
2. Perform a keyword search using subject headings related to your topic, or search specific Web sites such as *newspapers.com* or *CNN.com*; magazine articles like *NewsDirectory.com*; ebooks like *Bartleby.com* or *Project Gutenberg (gutenberg.com)*; or federal, state, and city government documents like *FedWorld.gov*, *Mass.gov*, or *cityofboston.gov*.
3. Click on links to Web sites that seem to be relevant to your topic.
4. Skim sources to determine whether they relate to your research topic, and narrow your search to address a particular aspect of your topic.
5. Add useful Web sites to your Favorites list, or print these sources, because Web sites often are hard to find again or later become unavailable.

A student writer at work: *Conducting Web-based research*

Using the search term "adult ESL literacy," Kristyn conducted a search using the Google search engine (see Figure 7.6).

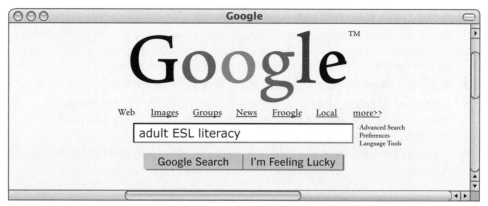

FIGURE 7.6

The search led Kristyn to a list of thousands of Web sites. She could have narrowed her search with a more specific term, but she decided to begin with the first site, which seemed promising (see Figure 7.7), and clicked on the link.

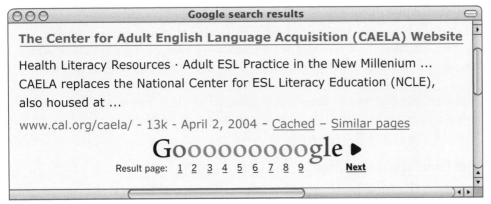

FIGURE 7.7

The link to the Center for Adult English Language Acquisition contained numerous articles, several of which Kristyn found useful for her research.

Your turn: *Conducting Web-based research*

Using the *Guidelines for Conducting Web-Based Research*, find sources relevant to your research topic.

■ Evaluating Sources

Evaluating sources to determine their reliability is a wise investment of time. You can eliminate sources that do not fit accepted evaluative criteria and spend your time only on trustworthy sources.

Guidelines for Evaluating Sources

Answers to the following questions can help you determine if you have found a reliable source:

1. **Is the information up-to-date?** Older publications or Web sites may provide useful background or historical information, but they may be outdated, that is, some of the information may no longer be valid. Check the date of publication.

2. **Is the source biased?** Some publications and Web sites are produced by special-interest groups and have a particular bias. Check the purpose and intended audience of a source by using a reference book that evaluates periodicals, for example, *Magazines for Libraries* or *Standard Periodical Directory*; by reading a Web site home page; or by asking your instructor or a reference librarian.

3. **What is the author's expertise on the subject?** Check the expertise of the author by reading a description of the author, if there is one; by consulting an index that discusses authors' achievements and credentials, for example, *Biographical Index* or *Current Biography*; by reading the author's home page; or by asking your instructor or a reference librarian. Note that papers written by students are not appropriate resources.

4. **Is the source well-researched?** Skim the source to find evidence that the author has conducted well-documented research, with footnotes or a bibliography, and has considered multiple viewpoints.

A student writer at work: *Evaluating sources*

Kristyn made an effort to select research material that represented reliable sources. Because she was doing her research on a current topic (in 2004), she aimed to find articles that were published in the 1990s or later (see her list of Works Cited on page 231). She read Web-site home pages to learn about the organizations that were publishing the articles she had found. And she made sure that her research included sources that contained bibliographies: a sign that the authors were serious researchers.

Your turn: *Evaluating sources*

Using the *Guidelines for Evaluating Sources* on page 215, assess the sources you have gathered for your research. Eliminate any sources that do not fit your evaluative criteria.

■ Taking Notes on Research Sources

The goal of *taking notes on research sources* is to record specific information and ideas that you might use in your research essay. As with all other aspects of research, the way you take notes is dependent on your material and your working style. For example, you may take notes in a notebook, on your computer, or on lined index cards.

Guidelines for Taking Notes on Research Sources

1. Identify the source accurately and completely, including all of the information that would be needed to cite and document the source (see Citing and Documenting Sources, pages 258–271).
2. Indicate the page number from which information is taken.
3. Summarize or outline an entire article, or paraphrase a particular section, to capture the key points and important figures.
4. Copy or highlight any passages that you may refer to in your own essay. Use quotation marks whenever you copy exact wording.

A student writer at work: *Taking notes on research sources*

Kristyn printed several online sources and book chapters and then highlighted information and quotations that she wanted to use in her essay. Here is an article that she found in the *Boston Globe* (November 23, 2003, page A15), with the information she highlighted. Note that "Question 2" in the article refers to a law declaring that all public school children, with limited exceptions, must be taught in English only.

Mastering English for Economic Reasons

LAWRENCE K. FISH

The recent vote in favor Question 2 by Massachusetts voters underscores the importance an overwhelming number of voters place on making our school children proficient in English. But what of their parents?

While English proficiency is seen as one of the leading determinants in students' success in school, proficiency in English is often the first rung on the ladder for the thousands of non-English speakers who come here searching for economic opportunity. These first generation Americans have become a critically important part of the economy of our Commonwealth.

Immigrant workers are in every occupation and every industrial sector in Massachusetts. From the mid-1980s through 1997, immigrants from virtually every land were responsible for 82 percent of the net growth in the Commonwealth's labor force, according to a report authored by Northeastern University labor economist Andrew Sum.

According to Sum, 337,000 immigrants arrived in Massachusetts during the 1990s. Immigrants make up 45 percent of the state's blue collar workforce, 27 percent of the service jobs, 14 percent of the professional positions, 10 percent of companies' support staff, and nearly 10 percent of managers and executives.

Talk to a businessperson, and he or she will underscore the findings of the Northeastern study of the significant contributions immigrants make to our workforce.

At Citizens Bank, more than 10 percent of our employees have English as their second language, and we speak 42 different languages in our branches.

However, while a considerable number of immigrants have at least a bachelor's degree enabling them to get high-skilled jobs soon after they arrive on our shores, on average they have less education than native-born workers. The study showed that 59 percent of newcomers had a high school education or less, compared to 43 percent of native-born residents. Compounding the lack of education is a language barrier that adds to the difficulty they face in getting into the economic mainstream that will carry them to higher paying jobs.

How important is English proficiency? Immigrants who are proficient in English are likely to earn about 20 percent more than those who are not.

This Commonwealth, the birthplace of public education and bilingual education, has long understood the importance of giving children the tools they need to excel in school, go on to college if they choose, and get better paying jobs than their parents were able to get.

Even so, the demand has far outpaced the supply of courses in bilingual and English as a second language.

That's why a number of organizations, including The Boston Foundation, Citizens Bank, the State Street Foundation, Fleet, Verizon, and the New England Regional Council of Carpenters, answered Boston Mayor Thomas Menino's call nearly three years ago to provide ESL courses to their employees and members of the communities where they did business.

And yet, collectively we have barely made a dent in the demand. Earlier this year, more than 40 of our employees and community residents completed the ESL course we offer at our operations center in Medford. A recent *Globe* story noted that more than 14,000 Massachusetts residents have enrolled in government-funded ESL courses, but the waiting list, often stretching to two or three years, totals 15,500. In Boston alone, Menino has pegged the waiting list at nearly 2,000. Clearly, more needs to be done. And with the budget crisis facing the governor-elect and the Legislature, it is wishful thinking to hope that publicly funded ESL programs will be able to keep up with the demand.

That means the business community, organized labor, and nonprofit groups, which understand the contributions of immigrants to our economy, need to do more.

One place to start is by putting the state's business and labor leaders together with the heads of the major nonprofits and the experts at the state Department of Education to update our commitments for meeting the exploding demand for ESL courses.

The battle over Question 2 was contentious. But the battle is over. The opportunity now is to leverage the public support behind Question 2 to help not only the next generation of immigrant children, but their parents as well, who are key contributors to our economy. It is a worthy investment with a high return.

Your turn: *Taking notes on research sources*

Using the *Guidelines for Taking Notes on Research Sources* on page 216, take notes on your own research sources.

■ Writing a Progress Report

Writing a progress report provides the opportunity to stop and assess what you have accomplished. Your report, which can be written as a journal entry or letter to your instructor, should both summarize what you have done since you submitted your research proposal and explain what you still need to do.

Guidelines for Writing a Progress Report

1. Discuss what you have done and learned up to this point about your research topic. Include a description of your library and Web-based searches.
2. Include key bibliographical information for each source you have found: author, title, publication, date of publication, page numbers, Web-site address.
3. Discuss what you still need to discover or what you plan to do to complete the project.
4. Raise any questions or concerns that you may have about the progress of your project.

A student writer at work: *Writing a progress report*

Here are excerpts from the progress report Kristyn submitted to her instructor.

I am writing a paper on the high demand for ESL classes. . . . Since the last time we spoke, I have made considerable progress. . . .

I have emailed Kathy Chlapowski, the director of the Power Program and I have found numerous articles through the library databases and through general Google searches. . . .

I have not had a chance to read them all yet and I am worried as to whether I will be able to write a solid draft by our conference next week. . . .

Whether or not I use all these articles in my final paper remains to be seen, but I feel like I can finally start to organize my thoughts and ideas to form a coherent argument.

Here is a partial list of Kristyn's annotated bibliography.

1. Kozol, Jonathan. *Illiterate America*. Garden City, NY: Anchor, 1985. One of the chapters in this book discusses the many simple activities that depend on being able to read and write in English. This lack of literacy often places immigrants and other non-native speakers in humiliating and degrading situations.

2. McFarlane, Clive. "Adults Learn to Wait; Too Few Classes to Meet Demand." *Telegram & Gazette* 24 Nov. 2003: B1. This article talks about how the city of Worcester, Massachusetts, cannot meet the high demand for ESL classes. The article also discusses the importance of community involvement to help meet the high demand.

3. McKay, Sandra Lee, and Gail Weinstein-Shr. "English Literacy in the U.S.: National Policies, Personal Consequences." *TESOL Quarterly* 27.3 (1993): 91–107. This article states that the shortage of ESL classes results primarily from a lack of sufficient funds.

4. Swerdlow, Joel L. "Changing America." *National Geographic* 200.3 (2001): 42. This article reveals the growing number of immigrants in the United States and their reasons for coming here.

Your turn: *Writing a progress report*

Using the *Guidelines for Writing a Progress Report*, discuss the progress you have made thus far on your research.

■ Focusing Ideas

To fulfill the goal of *focusing ideas* for your readers, you need to determine the major point, question, or problem that your research addresses, and write a sentence or two that can serve as the focal point of your essay.

A student writer at work: *Focusing ideas*

Kristyn decided to present her research study as a problem that needs to be solved. Her preliminary focal point consisted of two sentences.

> With the expanding role of English in our culture, it is imperative that there be sufficient resources for immigrants to develop their English skills. My research focuses on the short supply of ESL classes and what we as citizens can do to improve this situation.

Your turn: *Focusing ideas*

Using the *Guidelines for Focusing Ideas* on page 61, create a focal point for your essay.

■ Writing a Preliminary Outline

Writing a preliminary outline can help you to organize the information you have gathered. You may change the order or content of the outline as you continue to work on your essay.

Guidelines for Writing a Preliminary Outline
1. Reread your research notes.
2. Find the major areas of the topic that you want to present in your essay.
3. Create categories to label those areas.
4. Organize the categories into headings for a preliminary outline.

A student writer at work: *Writing a preliminary outline*

Kristyn looked over her research notes and outlined the different areas of the issue that her essay would cover.

> I. Introduction
> II. Why ESL Classes Are Important
> III. Why There Is a Shortage of ESL Classes
> IV. What Solutions Exist to Solve This Problem
> V. Conclusion

Your turn: *Writing a preliminary outline*

Using the *Guidelines for Writing a Preliminary Outline*, prepare an outline of your research essay.

■ Structuring the Essay

Structuring the essay that is drawn from library and Web-based research involves moving readers toward an understanding of the topic from multiple perspectives. Such essays have a basic, three-part organizational framework: an *introduction*, a *body*, and a *conclusion*.

The following flow chart may help you visualize an overall structure for writing an essay drawn from library and Web-based research.

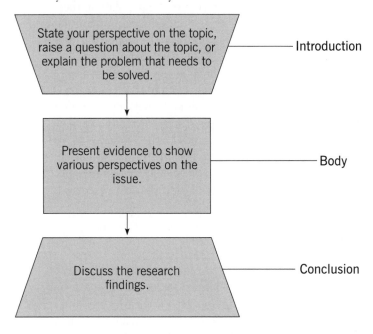

State your perspective on the topic, raise a question about the topic, or explain the problem that needs to be solved. —— Introduction

Present evidence to show various perspectives on the issue. —— Body

Discuss the research findings. —— Conclusion

The Introduction

The *introduction* to an essay drawn from library and Web-based research explains the significance of the issue that you have investigated and provides a focal point that states your perspective toward the issue, raises a question about the issue, or explains the problem that needs to be solved. (See also *Guidelines for Writing the Introduction* on page 101.)

▪▪▪▶ **Activity:** *Evaluating introductions*

The passages on the following pages (222–223) are introductions to student essays drawn from library and Web-based research. Evaluate two or more of the introductions by answering the following questions.

1 Does the introduction involve you in the topic and make you want to read the rest of the essay? Explain.

2 Can you tell, at the beginning of the essay, which issue the student writer has investigated and why?

3 Can you determine the student writer's perspective on the issue, the question the student writer is raising about the issue, or the problem the student writer would like to solve?

4 If you think the introduction should be revised, what suggestions do you have for the student writer?

Student A

> With 30.5 million immigrants, almost 11 percent of the population, the United States is an increasingly diverse society, "a multiethnic, multicultural nation. . . . racially mixed" (Ramos, 33). In fact, in the 1990s some 13.2 million immigrants arrived in the United States; 347,000 in Massachusetts alone (Sataline, "English,"A3). Immigrants leave their countries for many reasons – including unemployment, poor educational systems, or political repression – and come to America looking for new opportunities and a better way of life for themselves and their families. In this land of opportunity, they often become an integral part of America, contributing significantly to the economy. As part of the American identity, many immigrants try to become further immersed in the country's culture by learning English. Too often, however, immigrants are denied this chance simply because the demand for ESL classes exceeds the supply. – **Kristyn**

Student B

> Bilingual education is currently one of the hottest topics among politicians, educators, parents, and students. The debate over what is the best way to teach English to non-native speakers is one that has not yet come to an actual answer. This paper will take an in-depth look into Proposition 227, the landmark law passed in California to input English Immersion, and Chapter 71A, the Massachusetts law passed based upon the findings of Proposition 227. Each of the laws will be analyzed, compared, and suggestions will be made as to what should be done to improve the law to make sure it is in the best interest of all students. – **Richard**

Student C

> The treatment of immigrants in this country has always been controversial. To some people, they are seen as imposers and as a threat to the country. However, being an immigrant myself, I am extra sensitive to the way that immigrants are viewed and many times misunderstood. They have left their lives behind them in hope of a brighter future, and I feel that restricting them and not accepting them is a big crime. How can you deny the rights of a happier and a more hopeful future to people who are so oppressed that are willing to leave everything they know, start at the bottom, and one day maybe rise to achieve goals they only could dream of in their native countries? – **Victoria**

> "It's no secret that America's public schools are failing," said Chester Finn, former assistant secretary for research and improvement in the United States Department of Education (Madaus 229). The entire nation recognizes that public education is in trouble. The students of this generation have so little knowledge about so much that is important. The standards of the schools are not high enough, and they have to be raised in order to improve the system. It is not only that students do not do well on standardized tests, but that they simply are not graduating with the skills they need to contribute to society after they graduate. There are several proposed solutions to help our public education and to professionalize teaching, such as providing adequate funding for schools, eliminating poor teachers and students, and creating a new nationwide examination. But will these solutions really help to improve the poor position we are in now? – **Janet**

The Body

The *body* of an essay based on library and Web-based research integrates ideas and information from different sources. Each paragraph, or set of paragraphs, provides at least one supporting point that relates to and expands on the focal point of your introduction. Each paragraph also includes evidence in the form of ideas, examples, and quotations from research sources to illustrate or substantiate the supporting point. Furthermore, each quotation is accompanied by comments that clarify its meaning and make its significance clear. Finally, each of the research sources is properly cited (see Section 1 of A Handbook for Writing, pages 236–273).

The following suggestions offer three possibilities for structuring the body paragraphs of an essay based on library and Web-based research. You can use the drafting process to experiment with organization; your early efforts can be revised later (see Drafting, pages 274–275, and Revising, pages 278–282).

1. Present one perspective at a time.
   a. In one paragraph, or set of paragraphs, present and explain one aspect of or perspective on the issue and provide evidence to illustrate or support that aspect or perspective.
   b. In one paragraph, or set of paragraphs, present and explain another aspect or perspective and provide evidence to illustrate or support that aspect or perspective.
   c. Continue this process for each aspect or perspective you want to discuss.
2. Present and evaluate opposing viewpoints, one at a time.
   a. In the first section, present and explain what you perceive to be the weaker set of viewpoints.
   b. In the second section, evaluate this weaker set of viewpoints by discussing its strengths and weaknesses.

c. In the third section, present and explain what you perceive to be the stronger set of viewpoints.

d. In the fourth section, evaluate this stronger set of viewpoints by explaining why you believe this is the stronger view.

3. Present and evaluate viewpoints, together.

a. In one paragraph or set of paragraphs, discuss one aspect of the issue, showing opposing viewpoints toward that aspect and evaluating the strengths and weaknesses of each side.

b. Repeat this process for each aspect of the issue that you want to discuss.

Activity: *Evaluating body paragraphs*

The following passages are body paragraphs from student essays drawn from library and Web-based research. Evaluate two or more of the paragraphs by answering these questions.

1 Can you determine, at the beginning of the paragraph, the point the student writer is making?

2 Does the student writer provide sufficient and relevant evidence to develop the point?

3 Does the student writer clarify the meanings of selected quotations and make their significance clear?

4 Does the student writer smoothly and logically integrate material from different research sources?

5 Does the student writer properly cite the research sources?

6 If you think the paragraph should be revised, what suggestions would you have for the writer?

Student A

> The overwhelming demand for ESL classes is a problem in a number of states. In many areas the tremendous need for adult literacy instruction results in waiting lists that are months, or even years, long. For instance, in a study done in El Paso, Texas, it was discovered that "very large numbers of non-English speakers are taking advantage of every opportunity to learn English," but there are not enough classes to accommodate such a high demand (McKay and Weinstein-Shr, 95). In cities such as Los Angeles, New York, and Albuquerque, "officials report too few classes for too many students" (96). In fact, in Los Angeles alone there are as many as 40,000 adults in search of ESL classes (96). There are thousands of people across Massachusetts who desperately need ESL classes (Sataline, "English" A3). Massachusetts has historically been able to meet just 3 to 4 percent of the ESL demand (Franklin, 1). As of May 29, 2002 the Massachusetts Department of Education counted 14,467 people on waiting lists for programs they fund (Rosen). **– Kristyn**

Student B

Laws in both Massachusetts and California have waiver policies, which allow parents to apply for permission for their children to continue in bilingual education classes for one year. The issue that Massachusetts is facing right now that each city and town is deciding on its own whether or not to offer waivers to parents. Cities like Framingham and Brockton have advertised heavily to parents that waivers are available, while Marlborough and Lowell did not inform parents about waivers. For cities that do offer waivers, the demand varies. For example, in Boston, immediately after the school year when Question 2 was passed, over 1,000 waiver applications were completed, although only 470 have been issued so far (Adam). In Brockton, more than 350 students have been granted waivers, while 850 continue to wait for theirs to be approved (Vaishnav). In Chelsea, over 600 students are classified as English learners, but no parents have applied for waivers (Vaishnav). – **Richard**

Student C

There are several requirements that have to be met in order to gain a visa for entry. A request by an immediate relative that is a citizen or a legal alien in the United States must be made. There are different levels of this "family preference system." The first preference is for the unmarried sons and daughters of U.S. citizens, for whom 226,000 visas are granted per year. The second preference is for the spouses and unmarried children of lawful permanent residents. The third preference goes to the married sons or daughters of U.S. citizens, which involves 23,400 visas yearly. Brothers and sisters of U.S. citizens make up the fourth preference with 65,000 visas granted. On top of all this, visas are also subject to "per country ceilings." – **Victoria**

Student D

Another major area of change is the need to eliminate the "uninterested, uncooperative and unresponsive student who is disruptive to the learning atmosphere" (Kraft 192). Today there are drugs and gangs and violence and so many other distractions that influence the students. Many teachers feel that they have less authority and prestige while the students have more rights. School rules are often ignored. For example, "a teacher is threatened by a student in the classroom and nothing is done to assure that teacher's safety." And then "a principal is sent to the hospital by injuries sustained while attempting to break up a fight in his own school" (Kusky 184). Many of best teachers are leaving education or retiring as soon as possible just because they feel they get no respect from their students at all. There are students who are unwilling or unable to learn but are allowed to destroy the environment for learning. Those disruptive students should really be eliminated if they abuse the privilege. But "the state legislature has mandated that every child remain

continued

in school through a certain age and the courts have interpreted this to mean that every student is entitled to the same educational rights regardless of the negative effects upon other students" (Kraft 192). And in order to lower the dropout rate, school boards have removed most of the authority that teachers had to modify disruptive behavior. – **Janet**

The Conclusion

The *conclusion* to an essay drawn from library and Web-based research emphasizes your perspective on the issue you have investigated. Having presented ideas and information from multiple sources, you can now evaluate the various perspectives if you have not already done so; answer your research question; offer a solution to a problem; make a recommendation; predict a future possibility or consequence; suggest a future area of exploration; or apply the insight you gained from your research to your own experience. (See also *Guidelines for Writing the Conclusion* on page 108.)

Your turn: *Structuring the essay*

Using the *Guidelines for Writing the Introduction* on page 101, the *Guidelines for Structuring the Body Paragraphs* on page 105, and the *Guidelines for Writing the Conclusion* on page 108, create a flow chart such as the one on page 221 to show what ideas and specifics you might include in your essay.

▨ Presenting an Oral Research Report

Presenting an oral research report to your entire class or to a small group may help you shape your ideas. A good time to present orally is after you have written a draft. By then you will have done substantial research but can still benefit from comments and questions from your audience.

Guidelines for Presenting an Oral Research Report

Prepare a short oral presentation of your research topic by following these suggestions:

1. Prepare a one-page outline. Plan to explain these points to your listeners:
   - General background information on the topic you are researching
   - The research question or problem
   - Various perspectives on the issue
   - Explanation of your own perspective on the issue
2. Rehearse your presentation.
3. On the day of your presentation, take notes on audience comments and suggestions.

·············▶ Your turn: *Presenting an oral research report*

Using the *Guidelines for Presenting an Oral Research Report*, prepare an oral report of your research.

■ Writing the Essay

Writing the essay can be accomplished most effectively by going through the processes of drafting, receiving feedback, and revising (see Section II of A Handbook for Writing, pages 274–284). Use the following checklist to see if your essay fulfills readers' expectations for an essay drawn from library and Web-based research. The checklist may be used for self-evaluation or for evaluation of your essay by another reader.

	Evaluative Criteria for Writing from Library and Web-Based Research
YES NO	
☐ ☐	**1 Does the introduction to the essay make clear what issue has been investigated?** If yes, what issue does the essay investigate? If no, what information is needed to make the topic clear?
☐ ☐	**2 Does the introduction to the essay make clear why this issue has been investigated?** If yes, why has this issue been investigated? If no, how could the purpose of the investigation be clarified?
☐ ☐	**3 Does the introduction to the essay make a point, raise a question, or address a problem related to the topic?** If yes, what is the point, question, or problem? If no, what point, question, or problem emerges from the evidence in the body of the essay?
☐ ☐	**4 Does the body of the essay include sufficient and relevant evidence from research sources that presents multiple perspectives on the topic?** If yes, what are the different perspectives? If no, where could additional perspectives be added?
☐ ☐	**5 Does the essay properly cite and document the research sources?** If yes, where are these sources cited and documented? If no, how should the citations and documentation be corrected?
☐ ☐	**6 Does the essay provide the student writer's perspective on the topic?** If yes, what is the student writer's perspective? If no, where could the perspective be added?
☐ ☐	**7 Is the essay logically structured?** If yes, what makes the structure logical? If no, how could the essay be more logically structured?

Apply the *Evaluative Criteria for Writing from Library and Web-Based Research* to the following student essay written by Kristyn Marasca to fulfill an assignment for a college course.

Get in Line: The Extreme Shortage of ESL Classes
Kristyn Marasca

With 30.5 million immigrants, almost 11 percent of the population, the United States is an increasingly diverse society, "a multiethnic, multicultural nation. . . . racially mixed" (Ramos, 33). In fact, in the 1990s some 13.2 million immigrants arrived in the United States; 347,000 in Massachusetts alone (Sataline, "English" A3). Immigrants leave their countries for many reasons – including unemployment, poor educational systems, or political repression – and come to America looking for new opportunities and a better way of life for themselves and their families. In this land of opportunity, they often become an integral part of America, contributing significantly to the economy. As part of the American identity, many immigrants try to become further immersed in the country's culture by learning English. Too often, however, immigrants are denied this chance simply because the demand for ESL classes exceeds the supply.

In a country where English is the dominant language, it is imperative that one know English in order to survive, both economically and socially, and immigrants themselves "recognize that English is the key to better jobs, to getting ahead and building a better life" (Sataline, "English" A3). Thus they look to ESL classes to develop speaking, writing, reading, and pronunciation skills. What's more, effective ESL classes are necessary because illiteracy in America has many costs; for example, people who do not read must learn to trust those with whom they may not even be able to communicate, may be unable to access many government services, and cannot participate fully in their children's education (Kozol). In addition, a lack of English skills prevents many workers from advancing to higher-skilled and consequently higher-paid jobs. Moreover, "immigrants who are proficient in English are likely to earn as much as 20 percent more than those who are not" (Fish A15). Thus, students register for ESL classes to "strengthen their literacy skills so they can create a better life for themselves and for their children" (Wrigley 4).

The overwhelming demand for ESL classes is a problem in a number of states. In many areas the tremendous need for adult literacy instruction results in waiting lists that are months or even years long. For instance, in a study done in El Paso, Texas, it was discovered that "very large numbers of non-English speakers are taking advantage of every opportunity to learn English," but there are not enough classes to accommodate such a high demand (McKay and Weinstein-Shr 95). In cities such as Los Angeles, New York, and Albuquerque, "officials report too few classes for too many students" (96). In fact, in Los

Angeles alone there are as many as 40,000 adults in search of ESL classes (96). There are thousands of people across Massachusetts who desperately need ESL classes (Sataline, "English" A3). Massachusetts has historically been able to meet just 3 to 4 percent of the ESL demand (Franklin 1). As of May 29, 2002 the Massachusetts Department of Education counted 14,467 people on waiting lists for programs they fund (Rosen, par. 1).

This short supply of ESL classes can be attributed primarily to insufficient funds, and even though state legislatures have increased funding over the past few years, there is also a lack of qualified teachers (Franklin 2). ESOL is a low-paying field, which quite often affects the ability to attract the best teachers. Those who do teach, however, "work part time, without contract or benefits. Often they are volunteers [and] many receive only the most limited professional preparation and then leave the field after a short period of time" (Crandall 2).

So one question remains, what can be done to help reduce the number of immigrants waiting for ESL classes? The first, and obvious, choice is to increase federal and state funding so programs have the necessary resources to accommodate immigrants in need. In addition, many ESL programs depend on short-term funding (1 to 3 years), which jeopardizes their stability. Most funding for ESL classes comes from federal and state supplies, corporations, foundations, or individual sponsors, and as programs depend on these multiple sources, different components run on different schedules and require their own final and interim reports. Consequently, program funds are most often strained, for administrators spend too much time filling out necessary forms or writing new proposals (Wrigley 3). What's more, even though Congress set aside $70 million for English literacy and civics education in 2002, "21.3 million . . . foreign-born residents reported in the 2000 Census that they do not speak English well" (Sataline, "English" A3). Increased funding can be used to secure ESL classrooms, pay teachers, and buy workbooks and other classroom resources. It is also important to create more "programs that charge adults a minimal fee" (McFarlane B1). Many immigrants are poor and work multiple jobs and simply cannot afford ESL classes. Part of the success of Waltham's Power Program is the fact that it is free. If there were more programs like this, more students would be able to participate in ESL classes.

Furthermore, as programs attempt to provide needed service with diminishing funds, the role of volunteers in teaching adult ESL may become more important. For example, volunteers in the Power Program are an important asset in the ESL classroom. Here, volunteers help personalize instruction, tutor students on a one-on-one basis, and in general enhance the classroom experience. Furthermore, "some community members and former students volunteer once a week to facilitate a small ESOL group session for some on the wait list" (Chlapowski, e-mail). Wu and Carter emphasize that effective volunteer programs need to encourage professionalism, providing ongoing supervision and continual training for the volunteers. However, such programs require additional funding.

continued

Several companies are providing language assistance for their employees. "Frustrated that their employees do not understand one another and don't have time for classes after work, some firms have contracted with teaching organizations to bring training right into the workplace," according to Suzanne Sataline ("Immigrants" 18). For instance, Richard T. Downey, president of Hypertronics Inc. in Hudson, Massachusetts, said his firm has found that ESL training had made "an 85 percent improvement in job retention and substantial reduction in absenteeism" (Franklin 1). In addition, Lawrence K. Fish, chairman, president, and chief executive officer of Citizens Financial Group Inc., recognizes the importance of immigrants in our society and their need for English proficiency. Immigrant workers are in every occupation in Massachusetts, making up "45 percent of the state's blue-collar workforce, 27 percent of the service jobs, 14 percent of the professional positions, 10 percent of companies' support staff, and nearly 10 percent of managers and executives" (A15). Thus, Citizens Bank and several other organizations such as The Boston Foundation, Fleet, and Verizon are providing ESL courses for their employees and members of the communities they serve. If other companies followed this example and took the initiative to offer ESL tutoring for their employees, both the workers and the companies would greatly benefit. As Fish says, "it is a worthy investment with a high return" (A15).

Finally, it is important to find imaginative ways to strengthen ESL programs. For example, the Take-and-Give (TAG) program of the Boston Chinese Neighborhood has creatively reduced the wait from approximately 1,000 to 350 people (Downs C2). The TAG program uses volunteer tutors who have recently graduated from ESL classes, and not only does this program benefit students, but it also enables tutors to improve their English skills. Furthermore, the program only costs about $280 per student per year, a significant reduction from other ESL classes which can cost more than 10 times that amount (Downs C2). This creative approach should be followed by other cities and states looking to reduce the number of immigrants who are looking for English as a Second Language classes.

"In 2000, 1.1 million adults studied in federally funded English as a second language programs" (Sataline, "English" A3), but this number could be significantly higher with proper funding and the expanded role of volunteers in the ESL classroom. Through learning English, immigrants can create a better life for both themselves and their families. They can communicate better in a society that relies heavily on English and can become fully integrated in this culture, for it can transform immigrants from foreigners to vital components of American culture. It is clear that there is a growing need for ESL classes. With the expanding role of English in our culture, it is imperative that there be sufficient resources for immigrants to develop their English skills. Implementing ESL classes can provide learners with the opportunity to communicate better and consequently to achieve a better life.

Works Cited

Chlapowski, Kathleen. Personal interview. 27 Mar. 2004.

————. E-mail interview. 15 Apr. 2004.

Crandall, JoAnn. "Creating a Professional Workforce in Adult ESL Literacy."
    Digest. Apr. 1994. National Center for ESL Literacy Education. 2 Apr. 2004
    <http://www.cal.org/caela/digests/CRANDALL.HTM>.

Downs, Andreae. "From Student to Tutor in English-Language Classes."
    Boston Globe 16 Mar. 2003: C2. ProQuest. 2 Apr. 2004
    <http://www.proquest.umi.com>.

Fish, Lawrence K. "Mastering English for Economic Reasons." Opinion.
    Boston Globe 23 Nov. 2003: A15.

Franklin, James L. "English Joins Immigrants' Core Curriculum, Waiting List
    Grows as Newer Arrivals, Firms Seek Classes." *Boston Globe* 11 Oct. 1998:
    1. ProQuest. 14 Apr. 2004 <http://www.proquest.umi.com>.

Kozol, Jonathan. *Illiterate America*. Garden City, NY: Anchor, 1985.

McFarlane, Clive. "Adults Learn to Wait: Too Few Classes to Meet Demand."
    Telegram & Gazette 24 Nov. 2003: B1. ProQuest. 29 Mar. 2004
    <http://www.proquest.umi.com>.

McKay, Sandra Lee, and Gail Weinstein-Shr. "English Literacy in the U.S.:
    National Policies, Personal Consequences." *TESOL Quarterly* 27.3 (1993):
    91-107.

Ramos, Jorge. *The Other Face of America: Chronicles of the Immigrants
    Shaping Our Future*. Trans. Patricia J. Duncan. New York: HarperCollins,
    2002.

Rosen, David J. "The Wait for Services in Massachusetts Is Growing!" 5 Feb.
    2003. 12 Apr. 2004 <http://www.alri.org/waitlists.html>.

Sataline, Suzanne. "English Language Classes in Short Supply, Immigrant
    Surge Means Waiting List." *Boston Globe* 15 Aug. 2002: A3. 29 Mar. 2004
    <http://www.asu.edu/educ/epsl/LPRU/newsarchive/Art867.txt>.

————."Immigrants' First Stop: The Line for English Classes." *The Christian
    Science Monitor* 27 Aug. 2002: 18. 9 Apr. 2004
    <http://www.csmonitor.com/2002/0827/p18s02-lecl.htm>.

Wrigley, Heide Spruck. "Adult ESL Literacy: Findings from a National Study."
    ERIC Digest. 1994. 12 Apr. 2004 <http://www.ericdigests.org/1994/adult.

Wu, Yiqiang, and Katharine Carter. "Volunteer Voices: A Model for the
    Professional Development of Volunteer Teachers." *Adult Learning* 11.4
    (2000): 16 (4). EBSCOHost. 6 Apr. 2004. <http://www.epnet.com>.

■ Completing the Essay

Completing the essay involves proofreading and editing your final draft as well
as preparing a clear final copy to hand in to your instructor for evaluation. See
Sections II and III of A Handbook for Writing, pages 282–288.

A HANDBOOK FOR WRITING

A Handbook for Writing is divided into four sections. Section I, Citing, Incorporating, and Documenting Sources, provides guidelines for citing, summarizing, paraphrasing, quoting, synthesizing, and documenting your reading and research sources; Section II, Drafting, Exchanging Feedback, and Revising, offers guidelines for testing out your ideas on paper and reshaping those ideas in response to comments you receive from other readers and writers; Section III, Locating Errors, provides guidelines for finding errors in your own writing; and Section IV, Correcting Errors, provides guidelines for correcting your errors. Throughout the handbook, excerpts from student writing illustrate ways to fulfill the guidelines, and various activities provide opportunities for practice.

Contents

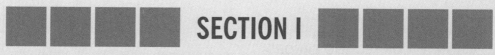
SECTION I

CITING, INCORPORATING, AND DOCUMENTING SOURCES

Whenever you incorporate material from another source into your own text, you have an obligation to acknowledge the source through a citation within your own essay. By summarizing, paraphrasing, or quoting other writers' ideas and synthesizing those ideas with your own, you show that you are borrowing from previous thinking on a subject and that your own work builds on this existing base of knowledge. By documenting your sources accurately – providing bibliographic information such as author, title, and date of publication – you legitimize your use of the material.

Citing Ideas

Citing ideas from another writer involves identifying the source within your essay and presenting the author's ideas fairly and accurately.

Guidelines for Citing Ideas

1. Select an idea from a reading that you want to refer to in your own essay.
2. Identify the source, for example, by naming the author and title.
3. Make clear whose ideas you are presenting by distinguishing your own ideas from the other writer's.
4. Indicate the author's purpose or point of view (see Summarizing, pages 238–241, Paraphrasing, pages 241–244, Quoting, pages 245–254, and the sample list of verbs that follow these guidelines).
5. Use the present tense to discuss an author's ideas. This use of the present tense acknowledges that the author's ideas continue to exist even though the author has finished writing about them.

The following verbs and verbal phrases, listed alphabetically, are among those most commonly used to cite an author and at the same time reflect an author's purpose or point of view. Check a thesaurus or a dictionary, if needed, to determine which verb or verb phrase is most appropriate.

admit	bring to light	convey
advise	caution	declare
affirm	claim	disclose
argue	concentrate on	discuss
ask	conclude	emphasize
assert	confess	establish
believe	contend	examine

explain	maintain	say
feel	note	show
find	observe	state
focus on	point out	suggest
give credence to	propose	support
identify	question	uncover
illustrate	reason	underline
imply	recommend	underscore
indicate	remark	voice
insist	reveal	write

The following sentences show a variety of ways student writers have cited the ideas of other writers. Note that the student writers make clear whose ideas they are citing, that they use verbs or expressions that reflect the author's point of view, and that they use the present tense to discuss the author's idea.

> In his essay, "We Should Cherish Our Children's Freedom to Think," Kie Ho argues that the American system of education, though flawed, is better than any other.

> However, as Barna points out, language is not the only problem an international student will face.

> According to Ernest L. Boyer, there is a "mismatch between faculty and student expectations" (p. 82).

Activity: *Citing ideas*

Using the *Guidelines for Citing Ideas*, create your own sentences by incorporating ideas from the following passages.

1 "When I would describe in English certain concepts and objects enmeshed in Korean emotion and imagination, I became slowly aware of nuances, of differences between two languages even in simple expression." *Kim, page 42*

2 "What we found in many classrooms was a mismatch between faculty and student expectations, a gap that left both parties unfulfilled." *Boyer, page 82*

3 "But I do think that the language spoken in the family, especially in immigrant families which are more insular, plays a large role in shaping the language of the child." *Tan, page 49*

4 "Another deterrent to an understanding between persons of differing cultures or ethnic groups is the *tendency to evaluate*, to approve or disapprove, the statements and actions of the other person or group rather than to try to completely comprehend the thoughts and feelings expressed." *Barna, page 70*

Summarizing

Summarizing involves condensing a text by restating only the text's key concepts. A summary should be written in your own words and yet preserve the original meaning of the text.

■ Summarizing Nonfiction

The primary purpose of *summarizing nonfiction* is to extract the points that you perceive to be most important for your analysis. You thus need to distinguish between key ideas and secondary details.

<table>
<tr><td colspan="1">

Guidelines for Summarizing Nonfiction

1. Reread the text carefully in order to understand its purpose and structure, observing the way ideas and examples are linked to other ideas or examples.
2. Consider the significance of each idea and example, and decide what you are going to include in your summary and what you are going to omit.
3. Group the essential information, ideas, and details that you have selected in an order that shows the relationships among the ideas and facts. This grouping does not necessarily have to be the order in which they are presented in the reading selection.
4. In your own words, create a sentence – or several sentences, as long as the summary is considerably shorter than the original – that reveals what the entire selection is about. You might try to do this orally first, as if you were telling a friend what you have just read.
5. Check to make sure that the summary includes only the author's ideas, not your reactions to the author's ideas.

</td></tr>
</table>

In some reading selections, a main idea may be clearly stated, and summarizing simply involves putting that idea into your own words. More often, several ideas are embedded in a text. To summarize, you need to combine those ideas in order to establish the point of the entire reading. Sometimes you can be fooled by a sentence that appears to be the main idea of a text, but careful reading will reveal that another idea emerges later on. This may happen, for example, with the following paragraph from Kie Ho's "We Should Cherish Our Children's Freedom to Think."

> There's no doubt that American education does not meet high standards in such basic skills as mathematics and language. And we realize that our youngsters are ignorant of Latin, put Mussolini in the same category as Dostoevski, cannot recite the Periodic Table by heart. Would we, however, prefer to stuff the developing little heads of our children with hundreds of geometry problems, the names of rivers in Brazil and 50 lines from *The Canterbury Tales*? Do we really want to retard their impulses, frustrate their opportunities for self-expression? (page 113)

The first sentence suggests that Ho's point is that American education does not meet high standards in certain basic skills. He includes details in the second sentence to support this idea. But in the third sentence, he questions the alternatives. And in the final sentence, he suggests that an alternative educational program might prevent opportunities for self-expression. If only the first sentence were used to summarize this passage, the meaning of the passage would be distorted. By combining the idea in the first sentence with the idea in the last sentence, a one-sentence summary that preserves the meaning could be as follows:

> Although American education does not meet high standards in certain basic skills, it does provide valuable opportunities for self-expression.

This summary, one of many possible sentences, presents two ideas: (1) that Ho acknowledges the weak standards of American education and (2) that Ho nonetheless approves of the values of American education. The summary is carefully constructed to show the relationship between the ideas. The first clause is a dependent (subordinate) clause (subordinated by the word *Although*), showing that this idea is less important to the author. The second clause is an independent (main) clause, showing that the student believes this is the main point Ho wishes to make. Note that other details in the paragraph are omitted in the summary: ignorance of Latin, names of rivers in Brazil, and so on. These details support what Ho means, but they are secondary to the main idea of the paragraph.

■ Summarizing Fiction

Summarizing fiction involves describing the plot: the series of events and thoughts that is arranged to reveal some meaning or significance in the story. To summarize the plot, you need to identify the key events, the main conflict, and the resolution or outcome. The conflict may be internal, involving a character's inner psychological struggle, or it may be external, involving a struggle between characters or between characters and their physical, social, political, economic, or spiritual environment.

Guidelines for Summarizing Fiction

1. Briefly retell the key events of the story.
2. Briefly explain the story's main conflict and its outcome.

Activity: *Summarizing nonfiction*

Using the *Guidelines for Summarizing Nonfiction* on page 239, summarize one or more of the following passages, which are excerpted from reading selections in this book.

Passage A: Levine and Wolff, page 75

> *"If a man does not keep pace with his companions, perhaps it is because he hears a different drummer."* This thought by Thoreau strikes a chord in so many people that it has become part of our language. We use the phrase "the beat of a different drummer" to explain any pace of life unlike our own. Such colorful vagueness reveals how informal our rules of time really are. The world over, children simply "pick up" their society's time concepts as they mature. No dictionary clearly defines the meaning of "early" or "late" for them or for strangers who stumble over the maddening incongruities between the time sense they bring with them and the one they face in a new land.

Passage B: Barna, page 66

> There are many viewpoints regarding the practice of intercultural communication but a familiar one is that "people are people," basically pretty much alike; therefore increased interaction through travel, student exchange programs, and other such ventures should result in more understanding and friendship between nations. Others take a quite different view, particularly those who have done research in the field of speech communication and are fully aware of the complexities of interpersonal interaction, even *within* cultural groups. They do not equate contact with communication, do not believe that the simple experience of talking with someone insures a successful transfer of meanings and feelings. Even basic commonalities of birth, hunger, family, death, are perceived and treated in vastly different ways by persons with different backgrounds. If there *is* a universal, it might be that each has been so subconsciously influenced by his own cultural upbringing that he assumes that the needs, desires, and basic assumptions of others are identical to his own.

Passage C: Boyer, page 82

> What we found in many classrooms was a mismatch between faculty and student expectations, a gap that left both parties unfulfilled. Faculty, concerned with scholarship, wanted to share ideas with students, who were expected to appreciate what professors do. This appreciation might exist in graduate or upper-division courses, where teachers and students have overlapping interests, but we found that often this was not the case in lower-division courses.

Activity: *Summarizing fiction*

Using the *Guidelines for Summarizing Fiction* on page 239, summarize one of the short stories in Chapter 5.

Paraphrasing

Paraphrasing involves clarifying a passage by restating its meaning while preserving its tone. Like a summary, a paraphrase should be written in your own words. Unlike a summary, a paraphrase does not condense the original text; instead, a paraphrase closely matches the text's length and content. For that reason, you should choose only short passages to paraphrase.

Guidelines for Paraphrasing

After selecting a short passage that you plan to refer to in your own essay, use these suggestions as a guide:

1. Look up the definitions of any unfamiliar words.
2. Decide what you perceive to be the author's meaning.
3. Use one of these strategies to find your own words to rephrase the passage:
   - Cover up the passage, and write from memory.
   - Take notes on the passage, then write the paraphrase from your notes.
   - Write word-by-word substitutions, then rewrite the substitute passage so that it makes sense.
4. Reread the original passage to make sure that you have preserved its meaning and tone. Revise your paraphrase if necessary.
5. Incorporate the paraphrase into your own sentence, making clear whose ideas are discussed in your sentence. Be sure to give credit to the original source and to distinguish your ideas from the other writer's ideas.

■ Putting Ideas into Your Own Words

Paraphrasing is not a simple matter of substituting every word. *Putting ideas into your own words* involves retaining some basic words, for example, proper names, pronouns, and prepositions. Furthermore, using a thesaurus or dictionary to substitute words can sometimes create sentences that are nonsensical or more difficult to understand than the original.

The following examples illustrate unacceptable and acceptable paraphrases.

Original sentence. The following sentence comes from LaRay M. Barna's "Intercultural Communication Stumbling Blocks."

> Learning the language, which most foreign visitors consider their only barrier to understanding, is actually only the beginning. (page 69)

Unacceptable paraphrase. Here is a word-by-word, unintelligible paraphrase of Barna's sentence.

> Acquisition of knowledge of human or written speech, which the majority of alien guests or newcomers think their alone of its kind obstacle to comprehension, is in fact but the commencement.

Acceptable paraphrase. The following would be a clearer paraphrase of Barna's sentence.

> In spite of what most international travelers think, language is not the only factor preventing full communication.

■ Capturing the Meaning and Tone

Capturing the meaning of a passage involves thinking about what the author is really saying and observing how the passage fits with the author's main idea or argument. *Capturing the tone* of a passage involves determining the author's attitude toward the subject matter. This attitude is conveyed primarily through the language the author uses. If you perceive that the author is sarcastic or funny or angry or compassionate, your paraphrase should reflect that sarcasm, humor, anger, or compassion.

The following example illustrates an unacceptable and an acceptable paraphrase.

Original sentence. The following sentence comes from May Sarton's "The Rewards of Living a Solitary Life." (*New York Times* Op-Ed, 8 April 1974)

> For him it proved to be a shock nearly as great as falling in love to discover that he could enjoy himself so much alone.

Unacceptable paraphrase. In the following paraphrase, the student writer does not capture the tone and meaning of Sarton's sentence. Sarton's expression, "a shock nearly as great as falling in love," has a positive connotation, whereas the student writer's expression, "a stroke," has a negative connotation.

> He nearly had a stroke when he realized that he liked being by himself.

Acceptable paraphrase. In the following paraphrase, the student writer captures the positive tone and meaning of Sarton's sentence with the words "delighted" and "pleasure."

> He was surprised and delighted when he realized that he could find pleasure in solitude.

The following analysis illustrates an acceptable paraphrase and how a student writer incorporated the paraphrase into his own sentence.

Original sentence. The following sentence comes from LaRay M. Barna's "Intercultural Communication Stumbling Blocks." The words "stumbling block" are added in brackets to show what the word "first" refers to.

> The first [stumbling block] is so obvious it hardly needs mentioning – *language*. (page 69)

Acceptable paraphrase. In the following paraphrase, the student writer (1) preserved the order of the sentence; (2) substituted the word "basic" for "first," allowing for the deletion of the phrase "so obvious it hardly needs mentioning"; (3) substituted the word "problem" for the implied "stumbling block"; and (4) incorporated the paraphrase into his own sentence. Note that the student was careful to indicate that this idea came from Barna's essay by mentioning Barna's name. By using the expression "correctly," the student writer made his own point of view clear, showing that he agrees with Barna.

> The basic problem that an international student faces, as Barna correctly says, is the language.

•••▶ **Activity:** *Analyzing paraphrases*

Using the sample analysis of the acceptable paraphrase above as a guide, analyze these student paraphrases of sentences from "Intercultural Communication Stumbling Blocks" by LaRay M. Barna. Determine what changes were made to the original sentence.

1 Barna's sentence: *Learning the language, which most foreign visitors consider their only barrier to understanding, is actually only the beginning.* (page 69)

   Student's paraphrase: *However, as Barna points out, language is not the only problem a foreigner will face.*

2 Barna's sentence: *Stereotypes are stumbling blocks for communicators because they interfere with objective viewing of stimuli.* (page 70)

   Student's paraphrase: *According to Barna, stereotypes create communication barriers because they cause people to make biased judgments about each other.*

•••▶ **Activity:** *Evaluating paraphrases*

Each of the following sentences is taken from a reading selection in this book and is followed by a student paraphrase. Evaluate each paraphrase by answering the following questions. If the answer to any of these questions is no, rewrite the paraphrase.

- Is the paraphrase written primarily in the student writer's own words?
- Does the paraphrase preserve the original meaning?
- Does the paraphrase maintain the author's tone?
- Does the paraphrase give credit to the original source?

1   Original sentence: *What was my little sorrow to the centuries of pain which those stars had watched?* (Yezierska, page 41)

Student's paraphrase: *My unhappiness was unimportant when compared with the suffering that the world has always known.*

2   Original sentence: *People from different cultures inhabit different nonverbal sensory worlds.* (Barna, page 69)

Student's paraphrase: *There are diverse ways of speaking in other countries.*

3   Original sentence: *When I would describe in English certain concepts and objects enmeshed in Korean emotion and imagination, I became slowly aware of nuances, of differences between the two languages even in simple expression.* (Kim, page 42)

Student's paraphrase: *English and Korean have differences in basic ways of expressing ideas.*

4   Original sentence: *If faculty and students do not see themselves as having important business to do together, prospects for effective learning are diminished.* (Boyer, page 83)

Student's paraphrase: *Knowledge is unattainable if teachers and learners do not take the educational process seriously.*

Activity: *Paraphrasing*

Using the *Guidelines for Paraphrasing* on page 241, paraphrase the following passages. Refer back to the reading selections to see the passages in their original context.

1   "When people of different cultures interact, the potential for misunderstanding exists on many levels." *Levine and Wolff, page 77*

2   "The belief that self-esteem is a precondition to learning is now dogma that few teachers question." *Moore, page 119*

3   "Compounding the problem is a reliance on the sort of instruction that treats children as passive receptacles into which knowledge or skills are poured." *Kohn, page 122*

4   "There are many viewpoints regarding the practice of intercultural communication but a familiar one is that 'people are people,' basically pretty much alike; therefore increased interaction through travel, student exchange programs, and other such ventures should result in more understanding and friendship between nations. Others take a quite different view, particularly those who have done research in the field of speech communication and are fully aware of the complexities of interpersonal interaction, even *within* cultural groups." *Barna, page 66*

Activity: *Incorporating a paraphrase into your own sentence*

Incorporate one of the four paraphrases you created in the previous activity into your own sentence. Remember to give credit to the original source and to distinguish your ideas from the other writer's ideas.

Quoting

Quoting involves repeating an author's words exactly as they appear in the original text. If you borrow any uniquely expressed phrases or recognizable expressions from the author, even just two words, you need to make clear that the words are quoted.

■ Selecting a Quotation

The purpose of *selecting a quotation* is to take material from a reading to introduce or support a point you want to discuss in your own essay. Quoting also enriches your writing by adding the distinctive flavor of the author's language. Too many quotations can break the flow of your discussion, however. Because readers are primarily interested in learning how you make sense of the reading, most of your essay should be written in your own words. For that reason, you need to select quotations carefully.

Guidelines for Selecting a Quotation

Before you decide to quote rather than to paraphrase, ask yourself questions such as these:

1. Are the author's words so moving or so clever that to put them in my own words would lessen their impact?
2. Are the author's words so precise that to put them in my own words would change their meaning?
3. Are the author's words so concise that I would need twice as many words to paraphrase the passage?

The following sentence is taken from Sophia's essay, "Is Creativity Suppressed by Knowledge?" (pages 283–284), in which she analyzes Kie Ho's "We Should Cherish Our Children's Freedom to Think" (pages 112–114). Sophia wanted to capture the flavor of Kie Ho's writing style, so she decided to quote a line that shows the unique way he expresses his attitude toward an educational system based on memorizing.

> Ho wonders if we would "prefer to stuff the developing little heads of our children with hundreds of geometry problems, the names of rivers in Brazil and 50 lines from *The Canterbury Tales*" (p. 113).

■ Incorporating a Quotation

Incorporating a quotation involves smoothly integrating an author's words into your own essay in such a way that the purpose of the quotation is clear and that your own writing does not have a choppy, unnatural rhythm.

Guidelines for Incorporating a Quotation

1. Introduce the quotation.
2. Comment on the quotation.
3. Insert *ellipses* (spaced periods . . .) if you delete any words from the original quotation.
4. Use *brackets* [ ] to add words to or to substitute words for those in the original quotation.
5. Check to see that the grammar and syntax of your sentence makes sense.
6. Follow rules and conventions for punctuating quotations (see pages 249–251).
7. Include the page number on which a quotation appears.

The following excerpt from Sophia's essay shows how she incorporated quotations from Kie Ho's "We Should Cherish Our Children's Freedom to Think" (pages 112–114).

Sophia introduced quotations by making clear that they represent Ho's questions and beliefs. She then commented on the quotations by explaining her position toward Ho's ideas. Note that she uses quotation marks for the quoted lines and includes the page number on which each quotation appears.

> However, I don't agree that this is the best way to educate students. Ho wonders if we would "prefer to stuff the developing little heads of our children with hundreds of geometry problems, the names of rivers in Brazil and 50 lines from *The Canterbury Tales*" (p. 113). He believes that by asking them to acquire much knowledge and take memorization seriously, we really "retard" the impulses of students and "frustrate their opportunities for self-expression" (p. 113). While I agree that experimentation, free expression of one's self and creativity, and innovations are important, I don't think that by learning geography, history, and math or by studying literature, students underdevelop their impulses. I think that these impulses develop in life by themselves and that knowledge, even that boring, awful memorizing of cities and names of rivers, helps expand one's horizons and enlarge one's perspectives. Besides this, there are some things students have to learn the way they are because, otherwise, they are misunderstood and mixed up. It is not flattering at all for America that "our youngsters . . . put Mussolini in the same category as Dostoevski" (p. 113).

Introducing Quotations

An introductory phrase should make clear whose words are being quoted and why the quotation is included in your essay. The following approaches suggest several ways to introduce a quotation.

1. Establish the author's point of view.

> *According to the author, ". . . ."*
>
> *As the author says, ". . . ."*
>
> *The author claims that ". . . ."*

2. Show your agreement with the author's point of view.

   I agree with the author's point that ". . . ."

   It is true, as the author states, that ". . . ."

   My own experience has shown that ". . . ."

3. Show your disagreement with the author's point of view.

   I disagree with the author's idea that ". . . ."

   It is not a question of ". . . ." but of ". . . ."

   The author's reasoning is flawed when he argues that ". . . ."

4. Show your mixed position toward the author's point of view.

   I agree with the author's point that ". . . ." but not with the idea that ". . . ."

   The author's argument that ". . . ." has some merit but is not convincing.

   To say, as the author does, that ". . . ." is true, but the point is irrelevant to the issue.

Commenting on Quotations

Commentary on quotations should clarify their meaning and make their significance clear. The following approaches suggest several ways to comment.

1. Explain what the quotation means by paraphrasing it.
2. Expand on the quotation by adding details or facts or ideas that reveal its truth or significance.
3. Explain the connection between the quotation and what has already been said.
4. Refer to one important word or phrase in the quotation and explain its significance.
5. Explain your position in relation to the quotation, for example, agree or disagree or take a mixed position toward the point made in the quotation.

Using Ellipses to Delete Words

Ellipses can be used to delete words from a quoted passage as long as you preserve the author's meaning. Use three spaced periods (. . .) to indicate deleted words in the middle of a sentence. Use four spaced periods (. . . .) if the deleted words include a period at the end of a sentence. The following instructions and examples show the primary ways to use ellipses.

1. Use ellipses to delete words from a quotation to make the quotation shorter, or to select the part of the quotation that makes the point you want to emphasize.

   Original sentence. The following sentence comes from Alfie Kohn's "Confusing Harder with Better."

   > Part of the problem is that the enterprise of raising standards in practice means little more than raising scores on standardized tests, many of which are norm-referenced, multiple-choice, and otherwise flawed. (page 121)

Altered sentence. To get right to Kohn's key point, the student writer deleted the words "norm-referenced, multiple-choice, and otherwise" from the selected quotation and replaced them with ellipses.

> Kohn makes the point that "raising standards in practice means little more than raising scores on standardized tests, many of which are . . . flawed" (p. 121).

2. Use ellipses to delete words to make a quotation fit logically into your own sentence.

Original sentence. The following sentence comes from Randy Moore's "Grades and Self-Esteem."

> We'll improve students' self-esteem most by helping and motivating our students to exceed higher standards. (page 120)

Altered sentence. To write from a third-person perspective, the student writer deleted the word "our" and replaced it with ellipses.

> Moore argues that teachers can "improve students' self-esteem most by helping and motivating . . . students to exceed higher standards" (p. 120).

3. Use ellipses only if you omit words from the *middle* of a quotation you have selected. It is not necessary to use ellipsis if you omit words from the beginning or from the end of the sentence containing the quotation you have just selected.

Original sentence. The following sentence comes from Ernest L. Boyer's "Creativity in the Classroom."

> What we found in many classrooms was a mismatch between faculty and student expectations, a gap that left both parties unfulfilled. (page 82)

Altered sentence. The student writer selected the middle of the original passage and placed it between quotation marks, with no ellipses.

> Boyer identified "a mismatch between faculty and student expectations" (p. 82).

Using Brackets to Add Words

If you need to add words or substitute words in a quotation, you can put additional or changed words within brackets as long as you preserve the meaning of the passage. Remember to use brackets [ ], not parentheses ( ), for this purpose. The following instructions and examples show the two primary reasons for using brackets to substitute words.

1. Use brackets to add words to help clarify a potentially confusing quotation.

Original sentence. The following sentence comes from LaRay M. Barna's "Intercultural Communication Stumbling Blocks."

> In a foreign land they increase our feeling of security. . . . (page 70)

Altered sentence. To make clear what the word *they* refers to, the student writer added the word "stereotypes" in brackets.

> Barna explains that "in a foreign land they [stereotypes] increase our feeling of security" (p. 70).

2. Use brackets to substitute words in order to make a quotation fit smoothly into your own sentence. You may use brackets, for example, to change verb tenses or to change pronouns to nouns.

Original sentence. The following sentence comes from Robert Levine's "Social Time: The Heartbeat of Culture."

> Our final measurement, the average time it took postal clerks to sell one stamp, turned out to be less straightforward than we expected. (page 80)

Altered sentence. To write from a third-person perspective, the student writer deleted the word "we" and replaced it with the word "they" in brackets.

> The final measurement of Levine's research team "turned out to be less straightforward than [they] expected" (p. 80).

Punctuating Quotations

Writers indicate they have borrowed exact wording from another source by using quotation marks for short passages and by blocking off lengthy passages. The following rules and conventions are accepted practice in the United States.

1. **Titles.** Use double quotation marks (" ") to enclose titles of essays, articles, stories, poems, and chapters.

> In "What True Education Should Do," Sydney J. Harris argues for an educational approach that builds on a student's background knowledge.

2. **Direct quotations.** Use double quotation marks (" ") to enclose a direct quotation.

> According to Harris, students "are more like oysters than sausages" (p. 5).

3. **Quotations within quotations.** Use single quotation marks (' ') to enclose a quotation within a quotation.

> Robert Levine tells of his experience in Brazil when he rushed to be on time to teach a class, only to hear "gentle calls of 'Hola, professor' and 'Tudo bem, professor?' from unhurried students" (p. 75).

4. **Page numbers.** Place a period *after* the parenthesis when the page number is included within parentheses at the end of a sentence.

> According to Harris, students "are more like oysters than sausages" (p. 5).

Note: Place a period *before* the end quotation mark if there is no need for the page number (for example, when the title of an essay is mentioned at the end of the sentence).

> Sydney J. Harris expresses sympathy toward college students in his essay, "What True Education Should Do."

5. **End of quotation.** Place a comma *before* the end quotation mark.

> America "is still the country of innovation," insists Ho (p. 113).

6. **Introduction of short quotation.** Use a comma to introduce a short quotation.

> As Moore says, "self-esteem is *earned*" (p. 119).

Note: Do not use a comma if the quoted statement follows the word *that*.

> Moore argues that "self-esteem is *earned*" (p. 119).

7. **Explanatory interruption.** Use commas to set off explanatory phrases that interrupt a quotation; include an extra set of quotation marks.

> "The job of teaching," Harris argues, "is not to stuff them [students] and then seal them up, but to help them open and reveal the riches within" (p. 5).

8. **A quoted question or exclamation.** Place question marks (?) and exclamation points (!) *before* the end quotation marks if the quotation itself is a question or an exclamation.

> Kie Ho asks, "If American education is so tragically inferior, why is it that this is still the country of innovation?" (p. 113).

Note: If your own words follow a quotation that ends in a question mark or exclamation point, you do not need to add a comma after the quotation.

> "If American education is so tragically inferior, why is it that this is still the country of innovation?" asks Kie Ho (p. 113).

9. **A quotation within your question or exclamation.** Place question marks and exclamation points *after* the end quotation mark when your own sentence (which includes the quotation) is a question or exclamation.

> Is it really true, as Moore argues on page 119, that the emphasis on self-esteem "cheats students out of a quality education"?

10. **Long quotations.** Block off a lengthy quotation (more than four or five lines) with a colon, and with no quotation marks (unless there is a quotation within the quotation), by indenting five spaces from the left margin. Double-space throughout.

> LaRay M. Barna offers an insightful explanation of why stereotypes are barriers to intercultural communication:
>
>> Unfortunately, [stereotypes] are not easy to overcome in others or in ourselves by demonstrations of the "truth." . . . They persist because they sometimes rationalize prejudices or are firmly established as myths or truisms by one's own national culture. They are also sustained and fed by the tendency to perceive selectively only those pieces of new information that correspond to the image. (p. 70)
>
> What is interesting about Barna's analysis is that she explains why it is so difficult to eliminate stereotypes even within ourselves.

11. **Lines of dialogue.** Quote multiple lines of dialogue as they appear on the page. Begin a new line of dialogue (with a new speaker) on a new line. Indent the beginning of each new line of dialogue. Double-space throughout.

> In Paul Laurence Dunbar's story, "The Ingrate," Mrs. Leckler objects to her husband's plan to help a slave become literate, as the following conversation reveals:
>
> > "Just here. If Josh knew how to read and write and cipher – "
> >
> > "Mr. Leckler, are you crazy!"
> >
> > "Listen to me, my dear, and give me the benefit of your judgment. This is a very momentous question. As I was about to say, if Josh knew these things, he could protect himself from cheating when his work is at too great a distance for me to look after it for him."
> >
> > "But teaching a slave – " (p. 143)

Note: If multiple lines of dialogue include narration, place double quotation marks at the beginning of each new paragraph but only at the end of the entire quotation. Use single quotation marks to enclose lines of dialogue.

> > " 'Well, of course, it's just as you think best,' said his wife.
> >
> > " 'I knew you would agree with me,' he returned. 'It's such a comfort to take counsel with you, my dear!' And the generous man walked out onto the veranda, very well satisfied with himself and his wife, and prospectively pleased with Josh." (p. 143)

Activity: *Selecting a quotation*

The following statements were written by students about Sydney J. Harris's "What True Education Should Do" (page 5). Read the three student statements, and then search through the opening paragraphs of the source text on page 252 to find at least one quotation that could introduce or verify each statement.

1 Harris creates an unusual analogy to explain how most people view education.

2 According to many people, the purpose of education is to fill students with knowledge.

3 Some scholars' concept of education has focused on the student rather than the teacher.

Source text: Harris, page 5

> When most people think of the word "education," they think of a pupil as a sort of animate sausage casing. Into this empty casing, the teachers are supposed to stuff "education."
>
> But genuine education, as Socrates knew more than two thousand years ago, is not inserting the stuffings of information *into* a person, but rather eliciting knowledge *from* him; it is the drawing out of what is in the mind.
>
> "The most important part of education," once wrote William Ernest Hocking, the distinguished Harvard philosopher, "is this instruction of a man in what he has inside of him."
>
> And, as Edith Hamilton has reminded us, Socrates never said, "I know, learn from me." He said, rather, "Look into your own selves and find the spark of truth that God has put into every heart, and that only you can kindle to a flame."

Activity: *Using ellipses and brackets*

Incorporate the following quotations into your own sentences, using ellipses to delete words and brackets to add or substitute words (see pages 247–249). You may use a combination of ellipses and brackets in a sentence. Remember to make clear whose words you are quoting.

1 "Faculty, concerned with scholarship, wanted to share ideas with students, who were expected to appreciate what professors do." *Boyer, page* 82

2 "To judge schools by how demanding they are is rather like judging an opera on the basis of how many notes it contains that are hard for singers to hit. In other words, it leaves out most of what matters." *Kohn, page* 122

3 "And it was perhaps the first time she had heard me give a lengthy speech, using the kind of English I have never used with her. I was saying things like, 'The intersection of memory upon imagination' and 'There is an aspect of my fiction that relates to thus-and-thus' – a speech filled with carefully wrought grammatical phrases, burdened, it suddenly seemed to me, with nominalized forms, past perfect tenses, conditional phrases, all the forms of standard English that I had learned in school and through books, the forms of English I did not use at home with my mother." *Tan, page* 47

4 "Because there's no consistency in what children were taught in previous grades, teachers have to make a disastrous compromise: either they fill in knowledge gaps for all students in the class, making progress excruciatingly slow, or they go forward at a pace suited to the more prepared students, leaving others behind." *Hirsch, page* 116

QUOTING

■■■➤ **Activity:** *Incorporating quotations*

Incorporate a quotation from each source text into the student paragraph that follows it.

- Select an appropriate quotation.
- Give credit to the original source of the quotation.
- Incorporate the source logically.
- Punctuate correctly (see pages 249–251).

1 Source text: Barna, page 71

> The fifth stumbling block is *high anxiety*, separately mentioned for the purpose of emphasis. Unlike the other four (language, illusive nonverbal cues, preconceptions and stereotypes, and the practice of immediate evaluation), the stumbling block of anxiety is not distinct but underlies and compounds the others. The presence of high anxiety/tension is very common in cross-cultural experiences because of the uncertainties present.

Student paragraph

> Anxiety is the last problem that Barna mentions in her article. Many foreign students get scared because they don't know what to expect. During my first month in America, I did not dare talk to anybody. I often had a stomachache before I went to school. Every time a teacher asked me a question, my legs got so shaky and my voice cracked. I was afraid that other students might laugh at my English when I mispronounced some words. Everyday I tried to figure out what other people were saying, but it seemed so hopeless. By the end of the day when I got home, I felt so exhausted; I felt like I had been jogging for ten miles or more.

2 Source text: Ho, page 113

> When I was 12 in Indonesia, where education followed the Dutch system, I had to memorize the names of all the worlds' major cities, from Kabul to Karachi. At the same age, my son, who was brought up a Californian, thought that Buenos Aires was Spanish for good food – a plate of tacos and burritos, perhaps. However, unlike his counterparts in Asia and Europe, my son had studied *creative* geography. When he was only 6, he drew a map of the route that he traveled to get to school, including the streets and their names, the buildings and traffic signs and the houses that he passed.
>
> Disgruntled American parents forget that in this country their children are able to experiment freely with ideas; without this they will not really be able to think or to believe in themselves.

Student paragraph

> Some societies value creativity; they encourage and fertilize their children's thinking. In their schools, teachers don't tell students what to think but rather let them create their own ideas and provide them with opportunities to express them. As a result of this system, children are like pumpkins that are free to carve themselves as they imagine. Each pumpkin is completely different. However, there is a danger to this approach.

Activity: *Correcting punctuation errors in quotations*

Applying the rules and conventions for punctuating quotations (see pages 249–251), correct the punctuation errors in the following sentences, taken from student essays.

1 Kie Ho said in his article "We Should Cherish Our Children's Freedom to Think" that while studying in Indonesia he "simply didn't have a choice, to make a decision whether to memorize or not "Hamlet's "To be or not to be soliloquy flawlessly." [The original quotation appears on page 113.]

2 Students feel that they are being stuffed with miscellaneous facts. Because of this they feel that they don't have enough time "to draw on his own resources, to use his own mind for analyzing and synthesizing and evaluating this material." (p. 5)

3 One evidence of this is that many students complain of being stuffed with miscellaneous facts, with such indigestible mass of material, that they had no time (and was given no encouragement) to draw on their own resources, to use their own mind for analyzing and synthesizing and evaluating this material. [The original quotation appears on page 5.]

Activity: *Selecting and incorporating a quotation*

Using the *Guidelines for Selecting a Quotation* on page 245, select a quotation from one of the reading selections in this book that you plan to refer to in an assigned essay. Using the *Guidelines for Incorporating Quotations* on page 246, incorporate the quotation into your own sentence.

Synthesizing

Synthesizing involves combining two or more sources that cover the same subject. This process enables you both to demonstrate your understanding of how the different sources view the subject and to develop your own point of view.

Guidelines for Synthesizing

1. Select two or more readings that deal with the same general subject, such as education or immigration.

2. List the similarities between the readings, for example, similar details and facts, or points on which the authors agree.

3. List the differences between the readings, for example, different details and examples, or points on which the authors disagree.

4. Examine your lists of similarities and differences to identify a pattern in the readings' treatment of the subject.

5. Decide what points you want to make about the subject, and select ideas and details from the readings to illustrate or support each of your points.

6. Decide how you will structure the body paragraphs of your essay. Here are three organizational possibilities.

   • Make a point about the subject and explain in the same paragraph what each author says or shows about that point. In the next paragraph, make a new point and explain what each author says or shows about this new point. Repeat this procedure for each point you want to make.

   • Discuss the first reading and explain how the author treats the subject. In the next paragraph or set of paragraphs, begin with a transition to the second reading and then explain how that author treats the subject. Make a connection to the first reading. Repeat this procedure for each reading you want to discuss.

   • Divide the body into two sections, discussing the readings' similarities first and then their differences, or vice versa.

7. Use appropriate transitional phrases to show the connections between the ideas in one reading to the ideas in another (see "Transitions" in Correcting Errors, pages 295–297).

8. Identify your sources clearly (see pages 258–271).

The first paragraph on page 256 shows how a student writer synthesized ideas from two readings. The first sentence presents the student writer's point. The next sentences support that point, using material from Kie Ho's essay, "We Should Cherish Our Children's Freedom to Think" (pages 112–114), and Sydney J. Harris's essay, "What True Education Should Do" (page 5). The underlined sentence shows the transition from one reading to the other, indicating the connection between the readings' ideas.

Schools should encourage intellectual creativity and not just memorization. As Kie Ho says in his essay, "We Should Cherish Our Children's Freedom to Think," children will not be able to think critically unless they have the opportunity to play with ideas. Ho claims that if students spend too much time memorizing mathematics, geography, and literature, schooling will "retard their impulses" and prevent the full expression of their ideas (p. 113). In "What True Education Should Do," Sydney J. Harris makes the same point. According to Harris, the best way to educate is to elicit ideas, not "stuff" them into a person's head (p. 5). Spending too much time memorizing massive amounts of information can keep students from using their minds to analyze what they are studying.

The following paragraph, taken from Kristyn Marasca's research essay, "Get in Line: The Extreme Shortage of ESL Classes" (pages 228–231), shows how Kristyn synthesized ideas from multiple research sources. The first sentence presents a question. The next sentences answer the question, using evidence from the different sources. The underlined phrases show the transition from one source to another, indicating the connection between the sources' ideas and information.

So one question remains, what can be done to help reduce the number of immigrants waiting for ESL classes? The first, and obvious, choice is to increase federal and state funding so programs have the necessary resources to accommodate immigrants in need. In addition, many ESL programs depend on short-term funding (1 to 3 years), which jeopardizes their stability. Most funding for ESL classes comes from federal and state supplies, corporations, foundations, or individual sponsors, and as programs depend on these multiple sources, different components run on different schedules and require their own final and interim reports. Consequently, program funds are most often strained, for administrators spend too much time filling out necessary forms or writing new proposals (Wrigley 3). What's more, even though Congress set aside $70 million for English literacy and civics education in 2002, "21.3 million . . . foreign-born residents reported in the 2000 Census that they do not speak English well" (Sataline, "English" A3). Increased funding can be used to secure ESL classrooms, pay teachers, and buy workbooks and other classroom resources. It is also important to create more "programs that charge adults a minimal fee" (McFarlane B1). Many immigrants are poor and work multiple jobs and simply cannot afford ESL classes. Part of the success of Waltham's Power Program is the fact that it is free. If there were more programs like this, more students would be able to participate in ESL classes.

Activity: *Synthesizing two sources*

Using the *Guidelines for Synthesizing* on page 255, create a paragraph of synthesis that uses details from the following two passages to support a point or answer a question about the subject of writing or writing instruction.

Passage A: Esmeralda Santiago[1]

> "Today," Sra. Leona said, "we will write a composition using the words you were assigned."
>
> She wrote the words on the blackboard. Someone asked if we were supposed to use all ten words, and she laughed and said that would be impossible.
>
> "Use as many as you can, but not less than five."
>
> It was a stupid assignment. I hated her.
>
> I wrote the words at the top of the page. Sra. Leona walked up and down the aisles between our seats, and stopped and hovered over me.
>
> "Esmeralda, try to form those letters better. I always have trouble reading your handwriting."
>
> The point on my pencil broke. She looked at me though her thick glasses, and I wished I were bigger and could punch her.
>
> "Go sharpen your pencil."
>
> She treated me like I had a disease. If I died and never came back to school, she'd probably be happy. But not for long. I'd come back to haunt her. I'd fill her inkwell with glue. I'd put hot peppers in her face cream. I'd curl a snake under her pillow.
>
> I sat down to write the stupid composition using her ten stupid words. I would use all of them, just because she thought I couldn't. *Incandescent* and *Carmelize* must go together somehow. *Bannister* and *Delimitation*. *Boundary*. "A Cartographer draws the Delimitation of Boundaries in maps." There, I'd even given her a word bigger than the assigned ones. What else could I say about cartographers? I had to think.
>
> The door of the classroom was open. Across the hall, someone recited a poem I knew by heart.
>
> "Esmeralda, is there something in the hall you'd like to share with us?"
>
> Kids laughed. Sra. Leona hated it when my mind went elsewhere than her classroom.
>
> "I was just thinking, Sra. Leona."
>
> She curled her lip.
>
> "Well. This is not the time for daydreaming. You're supposed to be writing, not thinking."

Passage B: Alvarez, page 34

> In sixth grade, I had one of the first in a lucky line of great English teachers who began to nurture in me a love of language, a love that had been there since my childhood of listening closely to words. Sister Maria Generosa did not make our class interminably diagram sentences from a work-book or learn a catechism of grammar rules. Instead, she asked us to write little stories imagining we were snowflakes, birds, pianos, a stone in the pavement, a star in the sky. What would it feel like to be a flower with roots in the ground? If the clouds could talk, what would they say? She had an expressive, dreamy look that was accentuated by the wimple that framed her face.

[1] From Esmeralda Santiago's *When I Was Puerto Rican* (NY: Vintage, 1994).

continued

SYNTHESIZING

Supposing, just supposing . . . My mind would take off, soaring into possibilities, a flower with roots, a star in the sky, a cloud full of sad, sad tears, a piano crying out each time its back was tapped, music only to our ears.

Sister Maria stood at the chalkboard. Her chalk was always snapping in two because she wrote with such energy, her whole habit shaking with the swing of her arm, her hand tap-tap-tapping on the board. "Here's a simple sentence: 'The snow fell.'" Sister pointed with her chalk, her eyebrows lifted, her wimple poked up. Sometimes I could see wisps of gray hair that strayed from under her headdress. "But watch what happens if we put an adverb at the beginning and a prepositional phrase at the end: 'Gently, the snow fell on the bare hills.'"

I thought about the snow. I saw how it might fall on the hills, tapping lightly on the bare branches of trees. Softly, it would fall on the cold, bare fields. On toys children had left out in the yard, and on cars and on little birds and on people out late walking on the streets. Sister Marie filled the chalk board with snowy print, on and on, handling and shaping and moving the language, scribbling all over the board until English, those verbal gadgets, those tricks and turns of phrases, those little fixed units and counters, became a charged, fluid mass that carried me in its great fluent waves, rolling and moving onward, to deposit me on the shores of my new homeland. I was no longer a foreigner with no ground to stand on. I had landed in the English language.

Activity: *Synthesizing two or more sources*

Using the *Guidelines for Synthesizing* on page 255, find passages in two or more readings in this book that deal with the same subject matter, and create a paragraph of synthesis that uses details from the readings to show how the authors view a particular aspect of the subject. Make your own point of view clear.

Documenting Sources

Properly *documenting sources* legitimizes your use of the material and shows readers where the material originally appeared. A selected number of citation and documentation guidelines are presented here in two different formats, one recommended by the American Psychological Association (APA) and the other by the Modern Language Association (MLA). For additional guidelines, consult a style manual or visit the APA Web site: www.apastyle.org, the MLA Web site: www.mla.org, or the Online Writing Lab at Purdue University: http://owl.english.purdue.edu.

■ APA Formats for Citation and Documentation

The *American Psychological Association (APA) formats for citation and documentation* are widely used in the social sciences. The following APA guidelines cover instructions for (1) citing research sources within your own text and (2) documenting research sources in a list of references at the end of your text.

■ APA In-Text Citation

Identifying your research sources within your own essay is the accepted way to give credit to another writer's work. The following guidelines and examples illustrate various ways to cite sources in your own sentences. Carefully follow the punctuation in the examples.

Guidelines for APA In-Text Citation
1. Identify the author or authors by last name only.
2. Provide the year of publication.
3. Include page numbers for quotations. If no page numbers are listed, use paragraph numbers.
4. Match the citation to a list of References, attached at the end of the essay.

1. **Author named in your own sentence.** If your sentence contains the author's name, put the year of publication within parentheses.

> According to Vaishnav (2003), some school systems did not inform parents of the option to apply for a waiver.

2. **Author not named in your own sentence.** If your sentence does not contain the author's name, put the author's last name and year of publication within parentheses. Place a comma between the name and year, and place a period after the parenthetic reference if it appears at the end of a sentence.

> Some school systems did not inform parents of the option to apply for a waiver (Vaishnav, 2003).

3. **Two authors.** If a source has two authors, join the two names using *and* (in your own sentence) or & (in the parenthetical reference). If the source has more than two authors, and you have repeated references to the source, use only the first author's name for the repeated references, followed by *et al.* ("and others"), for example, *Johnson et al.*

> Zamel and Spack (2004) emphasize the role that supportive classrooms across the curriculum play in promoting students' second language acquisition.

> Supportive classrooms across the curriculum play a significant role in promoting students' second language acquisition (Zamel & Spack, 2004).

4. **No author listed.** If your source does not have an author, place all or part of the title within parentheses, along with the year of publication.

> Bilingual education continues to be offered in California because many parents request waivers so that their children can be educated in two languages ("English Learners," 2003).

5. **Quotation from a printed source.** If you use a quotation from a printed source, include the page number or numbers in parentheses. Use a p. for one page; use pp. for more than one page; for example, (p. 23), (pp. 23–24), or (pp. 256–57).

> Rossell insists that "there is no unequivocal research demonstrating that bilingual education is the educational disaster that some of its critics claim" (2002, p. iii).

> Rossell (2002) insists that "there is no unequivocal research demonstrating that bilingual education is the educational disaster that some of its critics claim" (p. iii).

6. **No page number available in electronic source.** If you use a quotation from an electronic source that does not provide page numbers, use the paragraph number, preceded by the paragraph symbol ¶, or the abbreviation *para*. Alternatively, include a heading, if available, with the paragraph number.

> One Boston public school official expressed "both his intent to carry out the law and his disagreement with its goal of cutting back native-language support for English-language learners (Zehr, 2003, ¶ 2).

> The petition states that the requirement to educate all students in English can be waived if parents or legal guardians "personally visit the school to apply for the waiver" (Tamayo, 2001, Section 5: Parental waivers, para. 1).

7. **Same point, multiple sources.** If the same point or statistic appears in more than one source, place the sources within the same parentheses, in alphabetical order, separated by a semicolon.

> Experts agree that language is acquired most efficiently when students have the opportunity to engage in meaningful communication and interaction (Auerbach, 1992; Krahnke & Christison, 1983).

8. **Reprinted source.** If your entire source was reprinted from an earlier date, include both dates of publication, beginning with the earliest date.

> In "Mother Tongue," Tan contends that immigrant families' use of spoken language greatly influences their children's language development (1990/2006).

9. **Indirect source.** If you repeat the statement of a person who is quoted in one of your sources, indicate where you found the quotation by using the term *cited in*.

> Ron Unz, who financed the anti-bilingual education initiative, says he believes that "the parents and voters of Massachusetts should have the right to decide whether their children should be taught in English" (cited in Sutner, 2001).

10. **Personal communications.** If you quote or paraphrase someone you interviewed or corresponded with by letter or e-mail, identify the type of communication along with the date, within parentheses. Cite personal communications in text only, not in the reference list.

According to the director of the International Center, the college needs to strengthen cross-cultural relationships on campus (personal communication, September 15, 2004).

11. **Content note.** If you need to add an explanatory note, type a superscript numeral after the word or phrase in the text you wish to comment on. Then create a footnote at the bottom of the page or an endnote at the end of the essay, as the example shows.

[1]I learned this information in high school, but I can no longer recall the source.

APA List of References

Identifying your research sources in a detailed list at the end of your essay is the accepted way to give credit to the authors whose work you have consulted. The list also enables readers to evaluate how recent, reliable, and thorough your research is. The following guidelines and list of References explain how to use APA formats to create a list of references. If you need to reference a type of source that is not listed here, consult a style manual or choose an example that is most like your source and follow that format.

Guidelines for APA List of References

1. Start the reference list on a new page at the end of your essay.
2. Type the word **References** at the top of the page, centered.
3. Double-space throughout.
4. Start the first line at the margin; indent subsequent lines.
5. Put the author's last name first, followed by a comma and then the first initial of the author's first name.
6. Put the list in alphabetical order, according to the last name of the author. If there is no author, alphabetize according to the first letter of the title. If the title begins with *A*, *An*, or *The*, alphabetize according to the second word in the title.

References

Abraham, Y. (2005, June 19). Immigrant labor force booming. *Boston Globe*, pp. A1, A22.

Commission on Minority Participation in Education and American Life. (1988). *One-third of a nation: A report of the Commission on Minority Participation in Education and American Life.* Washington, D.C.: American Council on Education.

Fish, L. K. (2003, November 23). Mastering English for economic reasons. [Opinion]. *Boston Globe*, p. A15.

Hiding the refugee problem offshore. (2004, October 20). [Editorial]. *New York Times*, p. A26.

Kolbert, E. (2005, June 6). Last words: A language dies. *New Yorker*, 46–59.

Ramos, J. (2002). *The Other Face of America: Chronicles of the Immigrants Shaping Our Future*. (P.J. Duncan, Trans.). New York: HarperCollins. (Original work published 2001)

Sataline, S. (2002, August 27). Immigrants' first stop: The line for English classes. *The Christian Science Monitor*. Retrieved April 9, 2004, from http://www. csmonitor.com/ 2002/0827/p18s02-lecl.htm

Sieber, T. (2004). Excelling in the critical study of culture: The multilingual-multicultural student advantage. In V. Zamel & R. Spack (Eds.), *Crossing the curriculum: Multilingual learners in college classrooms* (pp. 129–44). Mahwah, NJ: Erlbaum.

Zamel, V., & Spack, R. (Eds.). (2004). *Crossing the curriculum: Multilingual learners in college classrooms*. Mahwah, NJ: Erlbaum.

APA Formats for Books

The following guidelines and examples illustrate APA formats for specific types of books. Carefully follow the indentation, punctuation, and capitalization in the examples, as well as the order in which the information is given.

Guidelines for APA Formats for Books

Bibliographic information can be found in the opening pages of a book. APA bibliographic entries for books follow this order:

1. *Author(s)*, last name first, then first initial
2. *Year of publication*, in parentheses
3. *Book title*, underlined or in italics; capitalize only the first word, the first word after a colon, and proper nouns
4. *City of publication*, plus state, if city is not well known
5. *Publisher*

---

1. **A book by one author**

   Spack, R. (2002). *America's second tongue: American Indian education and the ownership of English, 1860–1900*. Lincoln: University of Nebraska Press.

2. **A book by two or more authors**

   Kaplan, J., & Bernays, A. (1997). *The language of names: What we call ourselves and why it matters*. New York: Simon & Schuster.

3. **A book with an editor**

   Lesser, W. (Ed.). (2005). *The genius of language: Fifteen writers reflect on their mother tongue.* New York: Anchor.

4. **A book with two or more editors**

   Zamel, V., & Spack, R. (Eds.). (2004). *Crossing the curriculum: Multilingual learners in college classrooms.* Mahwah, NJ: Erlbaum.

5. **A book other than the first edition**

   Spack, R. (2005). *Teaching writing for ESL students.* (4th ed.). Upper Saddle River, NJ: Pearson, 2005.

6. **A book with a corporate (agency, association) author**

   Commission on Minority Participation in Education and American Life. (1988). *One-third of a nation: A report of the Commission on Minority Participation in Education and American Life.* Washington, D.C.: American Council on Education.

7. **A translation**

   Ramos, J. (2002). *The other face of America: Chronicles of the immigrants shaping our future.* (P. J. Duncan, Trans.). New York: HarperCollins. (Original work published 2001)

8. **An article or chapter in a book**

   Sieber, T. (2004). Excelling in the critical study of culture: The multilingual-multicultural student advantage. In V. Zamel & R. Spack (Eds.), *Crossing the curriculum: Multilingual learners in college classrooms* (pp. 129–44). Mahwah, NJ: Erlbaum.

9. **A speech published in a book**

   Esquivel, R. (1992). Bilingual education helps minority children. In C. P. Cozic (ed.), *Education: Opposing viewpoints* (pp. 170–76). San Diego, CA: Greenhaven Press. (Original speech delivered 1991)

APA Formats for Articles in Periodicals

The following guidelines and examples illustrate APA formats for specific types of periodicals. Carefully follow the indentation, punctuation, and capitalization in the examples, as well as the order in which the information is given.

Guidelines for APA Formats for Articles in Periodicals

Bibliographic information can be found on the first page of the journal article or on the front page of the journal itself. APA bibliographic entries for articles follow this order:

1. *Author's name* (if there is one), last name first, then first initial
2. *Date of publication*, in parentheses:
   - full date: year, month, and day for weekly magazines and for newspapers
   - month and year for monthly magazines
   - year only for quarterly and monthly journals
3. *Title of the article*
4. *Name of the periodical*, underlined or in italics
5. *Volume of a journal*, underlined or in italics
6. *Inclusive page numbers of the article*

1. **A journal article**

   Spack, R. (2000). English, pedagogy, and ideology: A case study of the Hampton Institute, 1878–1900. *American Indian Culture and Research Journal, 24,* 1–24.

2. **A book review**

   Moreland, K. (2003). [Review of the book *America's Second Tongue: American Indian Education and the Ownership of English, 1860–1900*]. *Southern Humanities Review, 37,* 294–98.

3. **An article from a weekly magazine**

   Kolbert, E. (2005, June 6). Last words: A language dies. *New Yorker,* 46–59.

4. **An unsigned article from a weekly magazine**

   The ghosts of Vietnam. (1993, June 5). *Economist,* p. 32.

5. **An article from a monthly magazine**

   Levine, R. (with Wolff, E.). (1985, March). Social time: The heartbeat of culture. *Psychology Today, 19,* 29–30; 32; 34–35.

6. **An article from a newspaper**

   Abraham, Y. (2005, June 19). Immigrant labor force booming. *Boston Globe,* pp. A1, A22.

7. **An unsigned article from a newspaper**

   Bitter reminder of a lethal World War II tragedy. (1994, July 18). *New York Times,* p. A10.

8. **A signed newspaper editorial [Op-ed]**

   Fish, L. K. (2003, November 23). Mastering English for economic reasons. [Opinion]. *Boston Globe,* p. A15.

9. **An unsigned editorial**

Hiding the refugee problem offshore. (2004, October 20). [Editorial]. *New York Times*, p. A26.

10. **A letter to the editor**

McCarron, P. (2005, June 13). A bad lesson for children [Letter to the Editor]. *Boston Globe*, p. A14.

11. **A motion picture**

Estes, L. (Producer), & Eyre, C. (Director). (1998). *Smoke signals* [Motion picture]. United States: Miramax Films.

12. **An electronic copy of a journal article, retrieved from a database**

Wu, Y., & Carter, K. (2000). Volunteer voices: A model for the professional development of volunteer teachers. *Adult Learning*, 11, 16 (4). Retrieved April 6, 2004, from the INFOTRAC database.

13. **An electronic copy of a newspaper article, retrieved from a search**

Sataline, S. (2002, August 27). Immigrants' first stop: The line for English classes. *Christian Science Monitor*. Retrieved April 9, 2004, from http://www.csmonitor.com/2002/0827/p18s02-lecl.htm

■ MLA Formats for Citation and Documentation

The *Modern Language Association (MLA) formats for citation and documentation* are used primarily in the humanities. The following MLA guidelines cover instructions for (1) citing research sources within your text and (2) documenting research sources in a list of references at the end of your text.

■ MLA In-Text Citation

Identifying your research sources within your own essay is the accepted way to give credit to another writer's work. The following guidelines and examples illustrate various ways to cite sources in your own sentences. Carefully follow the punctuation in the examples.

Guidelines for MLA In-Text Citation

1. Include the author's or authors' full name or names on first mention. In subsequent references and in parenthetical references, use only the last name or names.

2. Identify the page numbers, paragraph numbers, or section headings for any ideas or information, quoted or paraphrased, that you borrow from printed or electronic sources.

3. Match the citation to a reference in a list of Works Cited, attached at the end of the paper.

---

1. **Author named in your own sentence.** If your sentence contains the author's name, put the page number or numbers in parentheses, for example, (7) or (23–24) or (256–57).

> Michelle Adam reports that one positive result of the bilingual education initiative was that it forced the schools to focus on English language learners (7).

2. **Author not named in your own sentence.** If your sentence does not contain the author's name, put the author's last name and the page number or numbers in parentheses.

> One positive result of the bilingual education initiative was that it forced the schools to focus on English language learners (Adam 7).

3. **Two or more authors.** If the source has two or three authors, list all authors, joining the (last) two names using *and*. If the source has more than three authors, cite only the first author's last name followed by *et al.* ("and others"), for example, *Johnson* et al.

> Zamel and Spack emphasize the role that supportive classrooms across the curriculum play in promoting students' second language acquisition (xi).

> Supportive classrooms across the curriculum play a significant role in promoting students' second language acquisition (Zamel and Spack xi).

4. **No page number available.** If no page number is available, put the paragraph number or numbers within parentheses, using the abbreviation *par.* or *pars.*, for example, (par. 5) or (pars. 5–6); put the section heading within parentheses, for example, (Introduction); or cite the work in your sentence rather than in a parenthetical reference.

> According to Vaishnav, some school systems did not inform parents of the option to apply for a waiver (par. 9).

> The petition states that the requirement to educate all students in English can be waived if parents or legal guardians "personally visit the school to apply for the waiver" (Tamayo, Section 5: Parental waivers).

> In his article, "Bilingual Education: The Controversy," Richard Rothstein argues that different approaches to teaching language may suit different immigrant groups or individuals.

5. **No author listed.** If your source does not have an author, place all or part of the title within parentheses, along with the page number or paragraph number or numbers.

> Bilingual education continues to be offered in California because a substantial number of parents request waivers so that their children can be educated in two languages ("English Learners" par. 2).

6. **Same point, multiple sources.** If the same point or statistic appears in more than one source, you can place both sources within the same parentheses, separated by a semicolon.

Experts agree that language is acquired most effectively when students have the opportunity to engage in meaningful communication and interaction (Auerbach 280; Krahnke and Christison 244).

7. **Indirect source.** If you repeat the statement of a person who is quoted in one of your sources, indicate where you found the quotation by using the abbreviation *qtd. in.*

> Ron Unz, who financed the anti-bilingual education initiative, said he believes "the parents and voters of Massachusetts should have the right to decide whether their children should be taught in English" (qtd. in Sutner, par. 3).

8. **Personal communication.** If you quote or paraphrase someone you interviewed or corresponded with by letter or e-mail, provide that person's name in the text. The person's name should also appear on your list of Works Cited, with the type of communication identified.

> According to Kathleen Chlapowski, director of the Power Program in Waltham, participants in the ESL classes come from 54 countries and speak 40 languages.

9. **Content note.** If you need to add an explanatory note, type a superscript numeral after the word or phrase in the text you wish to comment on. Then create a footnote at the bottom of the page or an endnote at the end of the essay, as the example shows.

> [1]I learned this information in high school, but I can no longer recall the source.

■ MLA List of Works Cited

Identifying your research sources in a detailed list at the end of your essay is the accepted way to give credit to the authors whose work you have consulted. The list also enables readers to evaluate how recent, reliable, and thorough your research is. The following guidelines and list of Works Cited explain how to use MLA formats to create a list of works cited. If you need to reference a type of source that is not listed here, consult a style manual or choose an example that is most like your source and follow that format.

Guidelines for MLA List of Works Cited

1. Put the list on a separate page at the end of your essay.
2. Type the words **Works Cited** at the top of the page.
3. Double-space throughout.
4. Start the first line at the margin; indent subsequent lines.
5. Put the author's last name first, followed by a comma and then first name.
6. Put the list in alphabetical order, according to the last name of the author. If there is no author, alphabetize according to the first letter of the title. If the title begins with *A*, *An*, or *The*, alphabetize according to the second word in the title.

Works Cited

Abraham, Yvonne. "Immigrant Labor Force Booming." *Boston Globe* 19 June 2005: A1, A22.

Commission on Minority Participation in Education and American Life. *One-Third of a Nation: A Report of the Commission on Minority Participation in Education and American Life*. Washington, D.C.: American Council on Education, 1988.

Fish, Lawrence K. "Mastering English for Economic Reasons." Opinion. *Boston Globe* 23 Nov. 2003: A15.

"Hiding the Refugee Problem Offshore." Editorial. *New York Times* 20 October 2004: A26.

Kolbert, Elizabeth. "Last Words: A Language Dies." *The New Yorker* 6 June 2005: 46–59.

Ramos, Jorge. *The Other Face of America: Chronicles of the Immigrants Shaping Our Future*. Trans. Patricia J. Duncan. New York: HarperCollins, 2002.

Sataline, Suzanne. "Immigrants' First Stop: The Line for English Classes." *Christian Science Monitor* 27 Aug. 2002: 18.2. 9 Apr. 2004. <http://www.csmonitor.com/2002/0827/p18s02-lecl.htm>.

Sieber, Tim. "Excelling in the Critical Study of Culture: The Multilingual-Multicultural Student Advantage." In *Crossing the Curriculum: Multilingual Learners in College Classrooms*. Eds. Vivian Zamel and Ruth Spack. Mahwah, NJ: Erlbaum, 2004. 129–44.

Zamel, Vivian, and Ruth Spack, eds. *Crossing the Curriculum: Multilingual Learners in College Classrooms*. Mahwah, NJ: Erlbaum, 2004.

MLA Formats for Books

The following guidelines and examples illustrate MLA formats for specific types of books. Carefully follow the indentation, punctuation, and capitalization in the examples, as well as the order in which the information is given.

DOCUMENTING SOURCES

> ## Guidelines for MLA Formats for Books
>
> Bibliographic information can be found in the opening pages of a book. MLA bibliographic entries for books follow this order:
>
> 1. *Author(s)*, last name first. If there is more than one author, put first name first for subsequent authors.
> 2. *Book title*, underlined or italicized. Capitalize all words, except prepositions, conjunctions, and articles.
> 3. *City of publication*, plus state, if city is not well known.
> 4. *Publisher*, shortened form. Use just the first surname of companies such as *Harcourt* for *Harcourt Brace Jovanovich, Inc.*, or *Norton* for *W.W. Norton and Co., Inc.* Use *UP* for *University Press*, such as *Cambridge UP*.

1. **A book by one author**

   Spack, Ruth. *America's Second Tongue: American Indian Education and the Ownership of English, 1860–1900*. Lincoln: U of Nebraska P, 2002.

2. **A book by two or more authors**

   Kaplan, Justin, and Anne Bernays. *The Language of Names: What We Call Ourselves and Why It Matters*. New York: Simon & Schuster, 1997.

3. **A book with an editor**

   Lesser, Wendy, ed. *The Genius of Language: Fifteen Writers Reflect on Their Mother Tongue*. New York: Anchor, 2005.

4. **A book with two or more editors**

   Zamel, Vivian, and Ruth Spack, eds. *Crossing the Curriculum: Multilingual Learners in College Classrooms*. Mahwah, NJ: Erlbaum, 2004.

5. **A book other than the first edition**

   Spack, Ruth. *Teaching Writing for ESL Students*. 4th ed. Upper Saddle River, NJ: Pearson, 2005.

6. **A book with a corporate (agency, association) author**

   Commission on Minority Participation in Education and American Life. *One-Third of a Nation: A Report of the Commission on Minority Participation in Education and American Life*. Washington, D.C.: American Council on Education, 1988.

7. **A translation**

   Ramos, Jorge. *The Other Face of America: Chronicles of the Immigrants Shaping Our Future*. Trans. Patricia J. Duncan. New York: HarperCollins, 2002.

DOCUMENTING SOURCES

8. **An article or chapter in a book**

Sieber, Tim. "Excelling in the Critical Study of Culture: The Multilingual-Multicultural Student Advantage." In *Crossing the Curriculum: Multilingual Learners in College Classrooms*. Eds. Vivian Zamel and Ruth Spack. Mahwah, NJ: Erlbaum, 2004. 129–44.

9. **A speech published in a book**

Esquivel, Rita. "Bilingual Education Helps Minority Children." *Education: Opposing Viewpoints*. Charles P. Cozic (ed). San Diego, CA: Greenhaven Press, 1992. 170–76. (Original speech delivered 1991)

MLA Formats for Articles in Periodicals

The following guidelines and examples illustrate MLA formats for specific types of periodicals. Carefully follow the indentation, punctuation, and capitalization in the examples, as well as the order in which the information is given.

Guidelines for MLA Formats for Articles in Periodicals

Bibliographic information can be found on the first page of the journal article or on the front page of the journal itself. MLA bibliographic entries for articles follow this order:

1. *Author's name* (if there is one), last name first (for successive authors, put first name first)
2. *Title of the article*, within quotation marks
3. *Name of the periodical*, underlined or in italics
4. *Date of publication*
   - full date: day, month, and year for weekly magazines and for newspapers
   - month and year for monthly magazines
   - volume, number, and year (in parentheses) for quarterly and monthly journals
5. *Page numbers* of the entire article. Exception: When the article is not printed on consecutive pages, write only the first page number and a plus sign, for example, 22+.

---

1. **A journal article**

Spack, Ruth. "English, Pedagogy, and Ideology: A Case Study of the Hampton Institute, 1878–1900." *American Indian Culture and Research Journal* 24.1 (2000): 1–24.

2. **A book review**

Moreland, Kim. Rev. of *America's Second Tongue: American Indian Education and the Ownership of English, 1860–1900*, by Ruth Spack. *Southern Humanities Review* 37.2 (2003): 294–98.

3. **An article from a weekly magazine**

   Kolbert, Elizabeth. "Last Words: A Language Dies." *New Yorker* 6 June 2005: 46–59.

4. **An unsigned article from a weekly magazine**

   "The Ghosts of Vietnam." *Economist* 5 June 1993: 32.

5. **An article from a monthly magazine**

   Levine, Robert (with Ellen Wolff). "Social Time: The Heartbeat of Culture." *Psychology Today*, 19.3 (Mar. 1985): 29+.

6. **An article from a newspaper**

   Abraham, Yvonne. "Immigrant Labor Force Booming." *Boston Globe* 19 June 2005: A1+.

7. **An unsigned article from a newspaper**

   "Bitter Reminder of a Lethal World War II Tragedy." *New York Times* 18 July 1994: 10.

8. **A signed newspaper editorial [Op-ed]**

   Fish, Lawrence K. "Mastering English for Economic Reasons." Opinion. *Boston Globe* 23 Nov. 2003: A15.

9. **An unsigned editorial**

   "Hiding the Refugee Problem Offshore." Editorial. *New York Times* 20 October 2004: 26.

10. **A letter to the editor**

    McCarron, Patricia. Letter. *Boston Globe* 13 June 2005: A14.

11. **A film or video recording**

    Smoke Signals. Screenplay by Sherman Alexie. Dir. Chris Eyre. Perf. Adam Beach, Evan Adams, Gary Farmer, Tantoo Cardinal, Irene Bedard. Miramax, 1998.

12. **A personal communication**

    Chlapowski, Kathleen. Personal Interview. 27 Mar. 2004.

    Chlapowski, Kathleen. E-mail Interview. 15 Apr. 2004.

13. **An electronic copy of a journal article, retrieved from a database**

    Wu, Yiqiang, and Katharine Carter. "Volunteer Voices: A Model for the Professional Development of Volunteer Teachers." *Adult Learning* 11.4 (2000): 16 (4). INFOTRAC. 6 Apr. 2004 <http://infotrac.galegroup.com>.

14. **An electronic copy of a newspaper article, retrieved from a search**

    Sataline, Suzanne. "Immigrants' First Stop: The Line for English Classes." *Christian Science Monitor* 27 Aug. 2002: 18.2. 9 Apr. 2004 <http://www.csmonitor.com/2002/0827/p18s02-lecl.htm>.

Academic Integrity[1]

Academic integrity is the responsibility of every member of the academic community. Students are expected to take advantage of the opportunity for intellectual development and, in doing so, to conduct themselves in a manner consistent with high standards of academic honesty. When standards are violated or compromised, individuals and the entire college community suffer. Students who engage in acts of academic dishonesty not only face university censure but also may harm their future educational and employment opportunities.

Guidelines for Academic Integrity

1. **Manage your time effectively.** Prepare early for deadlines to avoid the temptation to use someone else's writing without attribution.

2. **Distinguish another person's ideas and words from your own.** Make clear when you borrow ideas by following accepted conventions for citing sources within your own writing.

3. **Learn how to document sources.** Follow accepted formats for creating footnotes and a bibliography.

4. **Prepare your own work.** If you need help to fulfill assignments, seek aid *only* from sources approved by your instructor. Never have anyone write any part of your paper. Never hand in a paper written by someone else and represent it as your own work.

5. **Prepare work that is original to the course.** Submit work completed for one course to satisfy the requirements of another course only with written permission from both instructors.

■ Avoiding Plagiarism

Plagiarism is the act of dishonestly presenting someone else's material as your own. Using another person's words or ideas fraudulently is a serious violation of academic honesty. *Avoiding plagiarism* is a mark of integrity. Students who do not fully understand the rules and conventions for borrowing, citing, and documenting sources may unintentionally violate these rules or conventions. Instructors understand that an inadvertent violation may occur. However, it is your responsibility to learn the conventions of academic writing to avoid plagiarism in the first place.

[1] The wording of this section is drawn from Bentley College's Academic Integrity Policy (www.bentley.edu), co-authored by Ruth Spack.

The following examples illustrate some acceptable and unacceptable ways to cite a source.

Original sentence. The following sentence comes from LaRay M. Barna's "Intercultural Communication Stumbling Blocks."

> Another deterrent to an understanding between persons of differing cultures or ethnic groups is the *tendency to evaluate*, to approve or disapprove, the statements and actions of the other person or group rather than to try to completely comprehend the thoughts and feelings expressed. (page 70)

Acceptable citation. The following sentence uses a direct quotation. The student writer identified the original source, put the author's exact words within quotation marks, and included the page number on which the quotation appears.

> In her article, "Intercultural Communication Stumbling Blocks," LaRay M. Barna explains that the habit of judging others is a "deterrent to an understanding between persons of differing cultures or ethnic groups" (p. 70).

Acceptable citation. The following sentence is a paraphrase. The student writer correctly identified the original source and restated the passage in his own words while preserving the meaning and tone of the original.

> According to LaRay M. Barna, one reason that people from different ethnic and cultural backgrounds have difficulty communicating is that they tend to judge one another.

Acceptable citation. The following sentence uses a quotation and a paraphrase. The student writer identified the original source, put the author's exact words within quotations marks, included the page number for the quotation, and paraphrased the rest of the author's idea.

> According to Barna, the *"tendency to evaluate"* (p. 70) creates a communication barrier between people of different ethnic and cultural backgrounds.

Unacceptable citation. The following sentence is an example of plagiarism. The student writer did not include quotation marks to identify the quoted words: "deterrent to an understanding between persons of differing cultures or ethnic groups."

> Barna believes that the habit of judging others is a deterrent to an understanding between persons of differing cultures or ethnic groups.

Unacceptable citation. The following sentence is another example of plagiarism. The student writer did not acknowledge that the idea comes from another source.

> I believe that one reason that people from different cultural and ethnic backgrounds have difficulty communicating is that they tend to judge rather than try to understand one another.

SECTION II
DRAFTING, EXCHANGING FEEDBACK, AND REVISING

The processes of drafting, exchanging feedback, and revising provide an opportunity to test out your ideas and to reshape those ideas in response to advice from other readers and writers. The writing of one student, Sophia Skoufaki, is included in this section to show how she drafted and revised an essay in response to the feedback she received from her instructor and classmates. Her completed essay, "Is Creativity Suppressed by Knowledge?" appears on pages 283–284.

Drafting

Drafting involves testing out the ideas you generated during the exploratory stage of writing to see how they will work together. Without the pressure to write a perfect essay at this stage, you can treat your writing as a work in progress, to be completed over time.

■ Writing a Trial Draft

You can begin working toward completing an assigned essay by *writing a trial draft*. At this stage, you do not need to be concerned with grammatical correctness.

Guidelines for Writing a Trial Draft

1. Don't try to write a perfect paper at this stage.
2. Focus on the development of ideas rather than on grammar, spelling, or punctuation.
3. If you can't think of a beginning, start in the middle.
4. If you can't think of an ending, just stop.

In her trial draft analyzing Kie Ho's "We Should Cherish Our Children's Freedom to Think" (pages 112–114), Sophia wrote only one paragraph, but it was enough to give her a sense that she could write a longer essay:

> This is one of the most successful essays I've read till today. The essay is mainly personal experiences of Ho – experiences that he had as a student in Indonesia and as a father of a student in California. What I like most in this essay is that it talks about a specific difference between educational systems that is probably the most important. I have heard a lot of times complaints of foreign people and natives about school here. All of them concern the exact same problems of American students compared to international students. None

DRAFTING

of the essays I had read before Ho's had so specifically and correctly pointed out the difference of the high school education between the U.S. and other countries.

If you need a more structured approach to drafting, follow the *Guidelines for Writing an Interim Draft* below.

■ Writing an Interim Draft

Writing an interim draft involves writing between the first and final stages of composing. During this process you are likely to be pausing to reread, rethink, cross out, or rewrite certain sections before you reach the end.

Guidelines for Writing an Interim Draft

1. **Analyze the assignment.** Determine its purpose, its requirements, and the needs and expectations of your readers.

2. **Set aside some uninterrupted time and start to write.** You may have to force yourself to begin, but once you get started, your writing will probably begin to flow.

3. **Devise a tentative organizational plan for the essay.** Try to follow the organizational pattern you have planned, but be flexible in your approach. If the plan doesn't work, allow another organizational pattern to emerge from your material.

4. **Build evidence to develop ideas.** Include details, examples, statistics, or quotations where appropriate.

5. **Identify any sources you have consulted.** Use the appropriate formats for citing and documenting sources (see pages 258–271).

6. **Create a title.** The title should reflect the subject matter or point of view of the essay.

Writing an interim draft was a challenging process for Sophia as she tried to match her intentions with her concern for making her ideas understandable to readers. Part of her interim draft appears on pages 279–282.

Exchanging Feedback

Exchanging feedback on writing provides an opportunity for you to learn ways to strengthen the draft of your essay. By sharing your work in progress with others, you can become aware of how readers react to what you have written. At the same time, the process of responding to other writers' drafts can lead you to internalize the kinds of questions that will help you become a critical reader of your own work.

Guidelines for Exchanging Feedback

Feedback can be provided in pairs, groups, or with the whole class.

1. Exchange drafts and read silently, or take turns reading your own drafts aloud.
2. Use the Feedback Form on page 277 and the relevant Evaluative Criteria checklist in Chapters 2–7, or raise your own questions. Your instructor will help you decide whether to provide written as well as oral feedback.
3. Discuss the responses to each draft, helping the writer understand what is effective in the draft and what might be done to strengthen it.
4. After the discussion of your own draft, write a note to yourself or to your instructor, explaining what you may do to strengthen your writing.

To prepare for exchanging feedback, read the recommendations below, titled "How to Criticize Painlessly" and "How to Accept Criticism," which are taken verbatim from a book on problem solving titled *The Revised All New Universal Traveler.* The authors refer to problem solving as a journey, and they give advice in the form of tips for travelers. The recommendations are followed by a feedback form that can guide you as you respond to someone else's writing.

How to Criticize Painlessly

The need for assertive criticism often emerges in the realm of conscious problem-solving.

Here is a fool-proof method for telling yourself or someone else that something is wrong without fear of losing a friendship or starting a battle.

The trick is to place the criticism within a context of positive reinforcements . . . just simple diplomacy.

1. BEGIN WITH POSITIVE REINFORCEMENTS.
   You really are a well-seasoned traveler.
   You have all the best gear for hiking.

2. INSERT YOUR CRITICISM.
   I wish we could stay in step when we hike together.

3. ADD ONE MORE POSITIVE REINFORCEMENT.
   I notice that you can adapt easily to most things.

4. FINISH WITH A RAY OF HOPE.
   If we work on this together, I'm sure we'll be able to get harmony on our stride.

Now you try it!

How to Accept Criticism

It is easier to feel a discontent than it is to accept the challenge of constructively improving the situation. And it is also easier, as the old saying goes, "to give criticism than it is to receive it." Being "defensive" of our position, which we imagine to be under attack from outside, is wasted motion. But it is also far more normal than an outlook of receptive self-improvement.

Be *abnormal.* Instead of wasting time with defenses and soothing self-inflicted, imaginary hurts, get procedural. *Accept* the comments for further analysis and definition. If the criticism then seems appropriate, "try it on for size." If not, discard it as irrelevant and the matter is finished.

Reprinted, with permission, from *The Universal Traveler* by Don Koberg and Jim Bagnall. Copyright © 1981 by William Kaufmann, Inc. Los Altos, CA 94022. All rights reserved.

FEEDBACK FORM

Writer's name: _____ Reader's name: _____

Directions: Your goal in providing feedback is to help the writer discover what works and what doesn't work and to find ways of strengthening the essay. Read for meaning only, ignoring error, unless an error interferes with your ability to understand what the writer is saying.

1. *Begin with positive reinforcement.* Tell the writer what you like about the essay and what you think should not be changed.

2. *Insert your criticism.* Tell the writer what confused you, misled you, bothered you, or left you wanting more. Be specific.

3. *Finish with a ray of hope.* Give the writer helpful suggestions. Be specific. If you were the writer of this essay, what would you do to strengthen it?

EXCHANGING FEEDBACK

Activity: *Giving feedback*

Using the *Feedback Form* above, practice giving feedback on the student essay written by Sophia Skoufaki, on page 283, which fulfilled an assignment for a college course.

Revising

Revising involves more than just rewriting a draft. The revising process enables you to think about your writing, to take a new look, to reshape and refine your thoughts. After you receive feedback on your draft, you can revise it to meet your readers' needs and expectations and your own goals. Guidelines are provided first for examining the entire interim draft and then for closely examining the body paragraphs.

■ Revising the Interim Draft

Revising the interim draft provides an opportunity to gain an overall perspective on what you have written. By now, one or more students or your instructor has commented on your draft. If you have followed the recommendations for accepting criticism (see page 277), you have accepted the comments for further analysis. You can now determine which comments can best lead you to strengthen your writing.

Guidelines for Revising the Interim Draft

The following questions may help you sift through the feedback you have received:

1. **What Should I Keep?** Reread your reviewers' comments or your own notes on the feedback you received to remember what your readers like about your draft. Keep their positive impressions in your mind as you rewrite.

2. **What Should I Add?** Reread your reviewers' comments or your own notes on the feedback you received to discover whether more details and examples or other evidence are needed to illustrate or support the points you have made. If so, make note of the places where your readers want to know more. It might be helpful at this point to look at some passages of the reading selections to see how the published authors achieved detailed writing. Try using some of the exploratory writing described in Chapter 2 (see pages 52–61) to generate new points or examples.

3. **What Should I Delete?** A reader might suggest that you used too much detail or included too much information. This is especially difficult criticism to hear because this reviewer may be recommending deletion of some of your favorite parts. Before you take anything out, remember that this is one reader's reaction. As with all feedback, you might determine that the suggestion is not appropriate and decide to include the material in your revision. However, if another reader has made the same comment, you might want to follow this advice.

4. **What Should I Change?** If a reader expresses confusion, make note of the section or sections of your draft that caused the problem. You may be able to solve the problem just by explaining what you meant to say. As you rewrite the confusing section, you may want to experiment with one or two versions. Read the new versions aloud to yourself, or show them to someone who can help you determine which version is clearer.

---

5. **What Should I Rearrange?** If a reader says that your draft needs a more logical structure, it might be a good idea to outline your draft briefly, paragraph by paragraph, summarizing each paragraph. Then look at your outline to see where the logic of the organization breaks down. Revise the outline to reflect a better organization. Then rearrange the material in your draft.

6. **What Should I Rethink?** A reader may think you may not have clearly expressed your point of view about the topic. Reconsider what you have written. Try an exploratory strategy, such as looping, to generate new ideas (see page 54), or discuss your topic with a friend to find what is important to you about this topic.

After receiving feedback from two of her classmates and her instructor, Sophia reviewed her interim draft and considered what to keep, add, delete, change, rearrange, or rethink. Among her many revisions, she made a change in her introduction to create a clear focal point that indicated her position toward the author's argument.

Here is the interim draft of Sophia's introduction.

> One of the most successful essays I have ever read is "We Should Cherish Our Children's Freedom to Think" by Kie Ho, whose purpose is to compare the education of the United States with that of Indonesia and other places in the world. The essay consists mainly of personal experiences of Ho, experiences that he had as a student in Indonesia and as a father of a student in California. What I like most in this essay is that it is about a specific difference between educational systems. I have often heard complaints about the schools in the States. All of them concern the problems of American students as compared to international students. None of the essays I had read before Ho's had so specifically and correctly pointed out the difference of the education between the U.S. and other countries.

— Title
Author's name and purpose

Sophia's reason for liking the reading

In her revision, Sophia eliminated the discussion of why she liked the reading and instead clarified her position toward Ho's idea.

Here is Sophia's revised introduction.

> In his essay, "We Should Cherish Our Children's Freedom to Think," Kie Ho supports the American system of education. He expresses disappointment with the Indonesian way of teaching that he had experienced. As he points out, American schools tend to teach students how to develop their creativity more, rather than try to "stuff" their heads with knowledge. Ho always had to memorize things and to acquire as much knowledge as he could from books, while his son in California learned practical things through experience. Ho admires the approach of his son's school. But I hesitate to endorse it.

Title
Author's name and main idea

Illustration of the author's idea

Sophia's position toward the author's idea

■ Revising Body Paragraphs

To engage successfully in the process of *revising body paragraphs*, you need to understand how paragraphing works. The paragraph is an important signaling system. The presence of a new paragraph in the body of an academic essay sends a message to readers that you are introducing a different aspect of the topic or shifting emphasis. The first sentence of a new paragraph should link what you just said in the previous paragraph to what you are about to say. The rest of the sentences in the paragraph provide explanations and examples to expand on the new idea.

Guidelines for Revising Body Paragraphs

1. Rewrite the first sentence of the paragraph if it does not link what has just been said to what is about to be said.
2. Rewrite the beginning of the paragraph if it does not state an idea that will be developed in the rest of the paragraph.
3. Rewrite the rest of the paragraph if it does not provide relevant and sufficient evidence to develop the idea.

The body paragraphs of Sophia's interim draft did not have clearly articulated ideas supported by sufficient evidence. When she revised the draft, she restructured the body by beginning each paragraph with an idea and then providing evidence to explain that idea. In each of these revised body paragraphs (below and on page 282), Sophia begins with a sentence (highlighted) that contains an idea that refers back to the previous paragraph. Each paragraph then continues by providing explanations and examples to develop the idea.

Ho connects this focus on creativity and practicality with the country's strength. He asks why so many people complain about the American education system, since America is "the country of innovation" (p. 113). This innovativeness is tied to the fact that the public schools provide children with the opportunity to be creative:

> I think I found the answer on an excursion to the Laguna Beach Museum of Art, where the work of school children was on exhibit . . . they had transformed simple paper lunch bags into, among other things, a waterfall with flying fish (p. 113).

I have to agree that Ho's observation is true. The opportunity for creativity impressed me, too, when I first went to an American high school. I admired how much attention the teachers gave to students' work and talents. I was impressed by the programs the school offered, the many different opportunities they gave students to do whatever they wanted, no matter how different and unique it was. I noticed that the students were always involved in activities, competitions, and exhibitions that are connected with their classes at school. That is a way of learning that Ho supports.

First sentence links to the previous paragraph and states the author's idea

Explanation of author's idea provided through paraphrase and quotation

Agreement

Evidence provided from personal experience

However, I don't agree that this is the best way to educate students. Ho wonders if we would *"prefer to stuff the developing little heads of our children with hundreds of geometry problems, the names of rivers in Brazil, and 50 lines from <u>The Canterbury Tales</u>"* (p. 113). He believes that by asking them to *acquire* much knowledge and take memorization seriously, we really *"retard"* the impulses of the students, *"frustrate their opportunities for self-expression"* (p. 113). While I agree that experimentation, free expression of one's self and creativity, and innovation are important, I don't think that by learning geography, history, and math or by studying literature, students underdevelop their impulses. I think that these impulses develop in life by themselves and that knowledge, even that boring, awful memorizing of cities and names of rivers, helps expand one's horizons and enlarge one's perspectives. Besides this, there are some things students have to learn the way they are because, otherwise, they are misunderstood and mixed up. It is not flattering at all for America that *"our youngsters . . . put Mussolini in the same category as Dostoevski"* (p. 113).

Transition to
disagreement

Explanation of
author's view
provided through
paraphrase and
quotation

Reasons for
disagreement

Preparing a Final Copy

Once you have drafted and revised your essay, you can begin the process of *preparing a final copy* for evaluation. Handing in an essay that is clear and readable is a sign of respect for the reader.

Guidelines for Preparing a Final Copy

1. Proofread and edit your essay (see Section III of A Handbook for Writing, pages 285–288).
2. Use good quality ink and paper.
3. At the top of the first page, include the course name and number, your instructor's name, the due date, the title of your essay, and your name.
4. Number the pages.
5. Create margins of at least one inch.
6. Double-space throughout.
7. Staple the pages together.

Is Creativity Suppressed by Knowledge?
Sophia Skoufaki

In his essay, "We Should Cherish Our Children's Freedom to Think," Kie Ho supports the American system of education. He expresses disappointment with the Indonesian way of teaching that he had experienced. As he points out, American schools tend to teach students how to develop their creativity more, rather than try to "stuff" their heads with knowledge. Ho always had to memorize things and to acquire as much knowledge as he could from books, while his son in California learned practical things through experience. Ho admires the approach of his son's school. But I hesitate to endorse it.

Ho connects this focus on creativity and practicality with the country's strength. He asks why so many people complain about the American education system, since America is "the country of innovation" (p. 113). This innovativeness is tied to the fact that the public schools provide children with the opportunity to be creative:

> I think I found the answer on an excursion to the Laguna Beach Museum of Art, where the work of school children was on exhibit . . . they had transformed simple paper lunch bags into, among other things, a waterfall with flying fish. (p. 113)

I have to agree that Ho's observation is true. The opportunity for creativity impressed me, too, when I first went to an American high school. I admired how much attention the teachers gave to students' work and talents. I was impressed by the programs the school offered, the many different opportunities they gave students to do whatever they wanted, no matter how different and unique it was. I noticed that the students were always involved in activities, competitions, and exhibitions that are connected with their classes at school. That is a way of learning that Ho supports.

However, I don't agree that this is the best way to educate students. Ho wonders if we would "prefer to stuff the developing little heads of our children with hundreds of geometry problems, the names of rivers in Brazil and 50 lines from *The Canterbury Tales*" (p. 113). He believes that by asking them to acquire much knowledge and take memorization seriously, we really "retard" the impulses of students and "frustrate their opportunities for self-expression" (p. 113). While I agree that experimentation, free expression of one's self and creativity, and innovation are important, I don't think that by learning geography, history, and math or by studying literature, students underdevelop their impulses. I think that these impulses develop in life by themselves and that knowledge, even that boring, awful memorizing of cities and names of rivers, helps expand one's horizons and enlarge one's perspectives. Besides this, there are some things students have to learn the way they are because, otherwise, they are misunderstood and mixed up. It is not flattering at all for America that "our youngsters . . . put Mussolini in the same category as Dostoevski" (p. 113).

continued

Nevertheless, Ho believes that the knowledge his son got in school was more useful than what he himself got in the Indonesian school. He writes:

> [U]nlike his counterparts in Asia and Europe, my son had studied *creative* geography. When he was only 6, he drew a map of the route that he traveled to get to school, including the streets and their names, the buildings and traffic signs and the houses that he passed. (p. 113)

What Ho names "creative geography," I would call development of common sense, which is, of course, important. But wouldn't students have a better sense of orientation if they studied world maps and knew where their country is located and where other countries, which they hear about every day, are in respect to their country? Isn't it sad that Ho's son thought that "Buenos Aires was Spanish for food – a plate of tacos and burritos, perhaps" (p. 113) and that that doesn't sound strange to Ho? If students know history, if they memorize names, places, and facts, they give themselves material with which to think, criticize, evaluate, and draw conclusions about social and economic conditions. For example, the invasion of Iraq into Kuwait had a lot of impact on other countries. If someone does not know the geography or the history of these places and the relationship of the rival countries with other nations, that person cannot fully understand the influence the event had on the world and on his or her own country at the same time. The focus on using imagination can have negative consequences. In my Chemistry class in an American high school, for example, our teacher gave us a limited number of instructions and expected us to do everything else needed to conduct the experiment. Students who had never had Chemistry before did the chemical experiments with more ease than I did, due to their imagination and previous experience in other experimental classes. However, they did not know why things happened the way they did, because they did not have enough chemistry background to understand and interpret the results of the experiments. If all classes were like that, then the only thing students would gain is a lot of dispersed, unorganized, and superficial information and not real knowledge.

Ho was raised by having to memorize things and learn by heart information that he may never have used in his life. His son grew up in a school system where practical information is more desirable than any other kind of information. "Our public education certainly is not perfect, but it is a great deal better than any other" is the conclusion of Ho's essay (p. 114). It is clear that Ho has a definite opinion about the system he prefers. I am not able to do that. On the one hand, I believe in memorizing things, in having to learn history, in having to know geography and literature, because these not only serve as the tools people need to face life in a more spherical way, but they also sharpen the mind and expand points of view. On the other hand, I think that schools should provide students with challenges, competition, and opportunities for creativity. Schools that lack these stimuli should develop them; students need opportunities to get involved in things they may be good at but they never had the chance to discover.

SECTION III

LOCATING ERRORS

Errors are a natural part of the language acquisition process. Most errors have logical causes, and you can learn from your mistakes by examining why you have made them. But errors can shift a reader's attention away from meaning, so you need to work toward eliminating errors that might interfere with a reader's comprehension. This section of A Handbook for Writing provides guidelines for proofreading, determining the causes of errors, and editing your own writing. Because these processes require attention to errors rather than to ideas, it is best to focus on them at a later stage in writing, after you have developed and organized your thoughts.

Proofreading

Proofreading is the process of searching for errors. Your instructor may locate some of your errors, but as the semester progresses, you should take increased responsibility for your own proofreading.

Guidelines for Proofreading

One or more of the following suggestions may be helpful:

1. Silently search your essay to find error, reading word by word.
2. Search only for errors that you know you commonly make.
3. Read your essay aloud to yourself or to someone else to hear any errors.
4. Check to see that you have copied quotations *exactly* as they were originally written and that you have provided a page number for each quotation.
5. Check to see that you have properly documented all sources (see pages 258–271).

Activity: *Proofreading*

Using the *Guidelines for Proofreading*, proofread your assigned essay.

Causes of Error

Understanding the *causes of error* can help you make decisions about how to address error in your own writing. Some errors are simply mistakes made through carelessness and can be located through careful proofreading. But other errors have more complex causes.

■ Interlingual Transfer

Errors resulting from *interlingual transfer* occur when writers apply a rule or sound of another language in place of the correct rule or sound in English, as the following student examples illustrate.

1. **Rolando's error:** *Even so, I am giving it a <u>tray</u>.*

   Rolando's explanation: *This is a problem of pronunciation. I wrote "tray" instead of* try *because I was trying to get the right English sound [the long vowel sound ī]. To get that sound in Spanish, you need to write "ay." So when I looked at the word "tray," a voice inside my head said "try."*

   Rolando's correction: *Even so, I am giving it a <u>try</u>.*

2. **Rolando's error:** *<u>Is</u> hurting my pride.*

   Rolando's explanation: *I forgot to put "It" at the beginning of the sentence. That's because in Spanish, you don't always have to use the subject pronoun. You can tell by the verb form what the subject is.*

   Rolando's correction: *<u>It is</u> hurting my pride.*

■ Overgeneralization

Errors resulting from *overgeneralization* occur when writers apply an English language rule they have learned to the wrong situation, as the following student examples illustrate.

1. **Angela's error:** *It does not <u>solves</u> or <u>prevents</u> any problems.*

   Angela's explanation: *I was thinking that the word "It" is third person singular and so it needed a third person singular verb. I added "s" to "solve" and "prevent" to make them third person singular. I forgot that "does" already had the "s" ending.*

   Angela's correction: *It does not <u>solve</u> or <u>prevent</u> any problems.*

2. **Ida's error:** *Neusner believes that in college we are trained to think that, "failure leaves no record" (p. 125).*

   Ida's explanation: *I didn't use the correct rule to punctuate the quotation. I used the rule that says a comma is used to introduce a quotation. When I looked up the rules to discover why the teacher marked the error, I realized that a comma should not follow the word "that."*

   Ida's correction: *Neusner believes that in college we are trained to think that "failure leaves no record" (p. 125).*

■ Reliance on Incorrect Patterns

Errors resulting from *reliance on incorrect patterns* occur when writers repeatedly use words, phrases, or sentence patterns without realizing that they are incorrect, nonexistent, or inappropriate in a particular context, as the following student examples illustrate.

1. **Efrat's error:** *When I get to a point where I am stuck and don't know how to go on with the work, I use the following strategy: Since usually I am too close, physically and emotionally, to the work, I try to get away from it, and to do something else like go for a walk or visit an art show. After a while I know <u>what is the best way I want to continue</u>.*

   Efrat's explanation: *I used the forms <u>what is the best way</u> and <u>I want to continue</u> together in my sentence. I didn't know that it couldn't be used in this way. It sounded fine because I always use it when I speak.*

   Efrat's correction: *After a while I know the best way to continue.*

2. **Al's error:** *Pressure is like a <u>tumid</u> in the brain.*

   Al's explanation: *I was surprised that the teacher underlined this error. I thought the word "tumid" was correct. But the problem was that I never pronounced the word correctly.*

   Al's correction: *Pressure is like a <u>tumor</u> in the brain.*

■ Appeal to Authority

Errors resulting from *appeal to authority* occur when writers seek help from an outside source, such as a bilingual dictionary or a thesaurus, and make an incorrect or inaccurate choice, as the following student examples illustrate.

1. **Sam's error:** *I agree with as well as <u>contradict</u> some of his ideas.*

   Sam's explanation: *I didn't want to keep using the same words,* agree *and* disagree, *again and again in my paper. So I looked up the word* disagree *in the thesaurus. I used the synonym "contradict," but it wasn't the correct substitute.*

   Sam's correction: *I agree with some of his ideas but <u>reject</u> others.*

2. **George's error:** *I was a little bit frightened in the beginning that I would flunk out of school, but my grades quickly <u>reassured</u> my confidence.*

   George's explanation: *I wanted to say that my grades made me feel better. But I didn't know how to say it in a sophisticated way. My roommate told me I could say, "my grades were reassuring." But when I wrote the sentence, I wanted to express the idea that my confidence had changed quickly. I used a form of my roommate's word, but I used it incorrectly.*

   George's correction: *I was a little bit frightened in the beginning that I would flunk out of school, but my grades quickly <u>bolstered</u> my confidence.*

■ Risk Taking

Errors resulting from *risk taking* can occur when writers take risks at guessing at or inventing rules, forms, or expressions that they have not learned or mastered, as the following student examples illustrate.

1. **Angela's error:** *These complaints have <u>brought up</u> the attention of social scientists and researchers.*

   Angela's explanation: *I used the expression "brought up" because I just couldn't think of the correct expression in English.*

   Angela's correction: *These complaints have <u>come to</u> the attention of social scientists and researchers.*

2. **Milto's error:** *I couldn't believe that the author was right in what he was saying, so I started analyzing his points to find where his reasoning <u>leaked</u>.*

   Milto's explanation: *I was thinking that the author's argument had holes in it. I mean, that his reasoning leaked out like water leaks out of a pail with holes in it. I wasn't sure if it was the right word, but I decided to try it and see.*

   Milto's correction: *I couldn't believe that the author was right in what he was saying, so I started analyzing his points to find where his reasoning <u>failed</u>.*

Activity: *Searching for causes of error*

Search your essay for an error, and then try to determine the cause of that error.

Editing

Editing, the process of correcting error, contributes to the preparation of a clearly expressed and comprehensible essay.

Guidelines for Editing

1. After you or your instructor has located errors in your writing, correct every error you can without asking for help.
2. Attempt to understand the causes of your error (see pages 286–288).
3. Use Section IV, *Correcting Errors* (pages 289–327), or another grammar resource, to help you correct errors that you cannot correct on your own.
4. Ask for help if you do not know how to correct an error even after consulting a grammar handbook.

Activity: *Editing*

Using the *Guidelines for Editing*, edit your assigned essay.

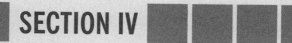

SECTION IV
CORRECTING ERRORS

Correcting errors depends not only on grammar rules and principles but also on how much knowledge the writer and reader share. Furthermore, the writer's intention plays an important role in determining which forms to use. This section of A Handbook for Writing addresses selected items for correcting errors. You can consult a more comprehensive grammar book to learn other rules and principles.

Sentence Boundaries

To help readers understand your ideas, your writing should have clear *sentence boundaries*, that is, clear indications of where each sentence begins and ends. The following information covers some basic structures for written sentences.

■ The Basic Sentence

The fundamental unit of communication in English is the sentence, and it has at least two parts: *subject*[1] and *verb*[2] (**S + V**). The first three words of James Thomas Jackson's essay "Waiting in Line at the Drugstore" (page 16) constitute a sentence.

Subject	Verb	
I	*am*	black.

Note that a sentence begins with a capital letter and ends with punctuation (a sentence must end in a period, question mark, or exclamation point).

■ The Independent Clause

Every sentence you write should have at least one *independent clause*, which has a subject-verb combination. A sentence can contain more than one independent clause, as in James Thomas Jackson's second sentence.

> I am black. I am a writer and I want to place full credit where it belongs for the direction my life has taken: on a photography studio and a drugstore on Main Street in Houston, Texas. (page 16)

---

[1] An exception to this rule is a command, in which the subject is understood but not always stated. For example, the command *Be still* (Yezierska, page 36) omits the understood subject *You: (You) be still.*

[2] The verb must be complete. For example, the word *going* is part of a complete verb only when it is combined with an auxiliary form: *am going, have been going*, etc.

SENTENCE
BOUNDARIES

Note that the two clauses are connected by the word *and* (see list of other coordinating words on page 295).

Subject	Verb		Coordinator	Subject	Verb
I	*am*	a writer	*and*	*I*	*want . . .*

The independent clause may be part of a larger sentence, but if it is removed from the sentence, it can stand alone (be independent) as a complete sentence.

Subject	Verb	
I	*am*	a writer.

Subject	Verb	
I	*want*	to place full credit where it belongs. . . .

■ The Dependent Clause

A *dependent clause* has a subject and verb combination (S + V) but is introduced by a subordinating word, such as *when* or *if* (see list of other subordinating words on pages 297–299). The following sentence begins with a dependent clause that is followed by an independent clause.

> When people of different cultures interact, the potential for misunderstanding exists on many levels. (*Levine and Wolff, page 77*)

The subordinating word ("When") signals that the dependent clause needs to be attached to an independent clause in order to be part of a complete sentence. The dependent clause alone is not considered a complete sentence.

<table>
<tr><th colspan="3">Dependent Clause</th></tr>
<tr><th>Subordinator</th><th>Subject</th><th>Verb</th></tr>
<tr><td>*When*</td><td>*people of different cultures*</td><td>*interact,*</td></tr>
<tr><th colspan="3">Independent Clause</th></tr>
<tr><td></td><th>Subject</th><th>Verb</th></tr>
<tr><td>*the potential for misunderstanding*</td><td>*exists*</td><td>*on many levels.*</td></tr>
</table>

When the order of these clauses is reversed, no comma is needed between them.

> The potential for misunderstanding exists on many levels when people of different cultures interact.

■ Sentence Fragments

A *sentence fragment* is a group of words that is punctuated like a sentence but does not qualify as a sentence because it lacks an independent clause or a subject-verb combination. Sentence fragments are sometimes used deliberately by experienced writers for emphasis or to express a theme. A sentence fragment is an error only when a writer creates one unintentionally.

The following guidelines and examples show several ways to turn fragments into complete sentences.

Guidelines for Turning Fragments into Sentences

1. Add a subject or a verb to create a subject-verb combination if it is missing.
2. Connect a fragment to an independent clause.
3. Integrate a fragment into the sentence that precedes or follows it.

---

1. Add a subject or a verb to create a subject-verb combination if it is missing.

    Sentence fragment. The following fragment lacks a subject-verb combination.

    > All the while going to the drugstore each morning.

    Complete sentence. The following complete sentence has a subject-verb combination ("I kept").

    > All the while I kept going to the drugstore each morning. *(Jackson, page 18)*

2. Connect a fragment to an independent clause.

    Sentence fragment. The following fragment, underlined, is a dependent clause. The sentence that precedes it is an independent clause.

    > She pointed out my place in the line. <u>Where I had to stand with the rest like a lot of wooden soldiers.</u>

    Complete sentence. In the following complete sentence, the fragment is connected to the independent clause.

    > She pointed out my place in the line, where I had to stand with the rest like a lot of wooden soldiers. *(Yezierska, page 39)*

3. Integrate a fragment into the sentence that precedes or follows it.

    Sentence fragment. The following fragment is underlined. The sentence that follows it is an independent clause.

    > <u>For example, the guy across the hall.</u> Yesterday he asked me to turn down my stereo.

Complete sentence. In the following complete sentence, the fragment is integrated into the independent clause.

> Yesterday, for example, the guy across the hall asked me to turn down my stereo. *(Niella, page 14)*

■ Run-on Sentences and Comma Faults

Some sentence boundary errors are the result of faulty punctuation. One common error is the *run-on sentence*, an error that occurs when a writer uses no punctuation between independent clauses. Another common punctuation error is the *comma fault*, an error that occurs when a writer connects two long independent clauses with only a comma. Such sentences need punctuation that provides readers with clues as to how the ideas in the clauses relate to one another and how the words in the sentence are grouped together.

The following guidelines and examples illustrate several ways for combining and punctuating two independent clauses to avoid run-on sentences or comma faults.

Guidelines for Correcting Run-On Sentences and Comma Faults

1. To correct a run-on sentence, add punctuation between the independent clauses.
2. To correct a comma fault, replace the comma between the independent clauses with stronger punctuation such as a semicolon or period.
3. In both cases, you may also add a transitional word between the clauses.

The following two independent clauses are used in the examples below. IC refers to *independent clause*, and DC refers to *dependent clause*.

- I expected to find a lot of new friends in this country.
- I soon realized that this would not be so easy.

1. **IC. IC.** To give equal emphasis to both statements, place a *period* between the two independent clauses.

   > I expected to find a lot of new friends in this country. I soon realized that this would not be so easy.

2. **IC; IC.** To show a close link between the two statements, place a semicolon between the two clauses.

   > I expected to find a lot of new friends in this country; I soon realized that this would not be so easy.

3. **IC, coordinator IC.** To give relatively equal emphasis to both statements, place a comma and then a *coordinator* (see page 295) between the two clauses.

   > I expected to find a lot of new friends in this country, but I soon realized that this would not be so easy.

4. **DC, IC.** To indicate the relationship between the clauses and to emphasize the second statement, use a *subordinator* (see pages 297–300) to turn the first independent clause into a dependent clause, and then place a *comma* before the second clause.

> <u>Although</u> I expected to find a lot of new friends in this country, I soon realized that this would not be so easy.

5. **IC DC.** To indicate the relationship between the clauses and to emphasize the first statement, use a *subordinator* (see pages 297–300) to turn the second independent clause into a dependent clause.

> I expected to find a lot of new friends in this country although I soon realized that this would not be so easy.

6. To indicate the relationship between the two independent clauses, use a transition (see pages 295–297) in one of the following ways.

   a. **IC; transition, IC.** Place a *semicolon*, then a *transition*, and then a *comma* between the clauses.

   > I expected to find a lot of new friends in this country; <u>however</u>, I soon realized that this would not be so easy.

   b. **IC. Transition, IC.** Place a *period* between the two clauses. Begin the second clause with a *transition*, followed by a *comma*.

   > I expected to find a lot of new friends in this country. <u>However</u>, I soon realized that this would not be so easy.

   c. **IC. IC, transition.** Place a *period* between the two clauses. Place a *comma*, and then a *transition*, at the end of the second clause.

   > I expected to find a lot of new friends in this country. I soon realized that this would not be so easy, <u>however</u>.

   d. **IC. IC, transition, DC.** Place a *period* between the two clauses. Place a *transition*, with *commas* on each side, between the independent and dependent clauses in the second sentence.

   > I expected to find a lot of new friends in this country. I soon realized, <u>however</u>, that this would not be so easy.

Activity: *Analyzing sentence fragments*

Find the two sentence fragments in the following passage from *Flight to Arras* by Antoine de Saint Exupéry (translated by L. Galantière) and discuss what you perceive to be the author's purpose in using the fragments.

> Looking down on those swarming highways I understood more clearly than ever what peace meant. In time of peace the world is self-contained. The villagers come home at dusk from their fields. The grain is stored up in the barns. The folded linen is piled up in the cupboards. In time of peace each thing is in its place, easily found. Each friend is where he belongs, easily

continued

SENTENCE BOUNDARIES

reached. All men know where they will sleep when night comes. Ah, but peace dies when the framework is ripped apart. When there is no longer a place that is yours in the world. When you know no longer where your friend is to be found. Peace is present when man can see the face that is composed of things that have meaning and are in their place. Peace is present when things form part of a whole greater than their sum, as the divers minerals on the ground collect to become the tree.

But this is war.

Activity: *Turning sentence fragments into sentences*

Find the sentence fragments in the following excerpts taken from student essays. Then, using the *Guidelines for Turning Fragments into Sentences* on page 291, turn the fragments into complete sentences.

1 I was pleased by the warm greeting I received from my American sponsor. Whom I had also known from my previous job in Vietnam.

2 I disagree with Moore's argument that instructors' focus on self-esteem is connected to the problem of under-prepared students. Is much more complex than that.

3 Neusner and Harris both discuss college students, but they reveal different attitudes toward them. Especially when it comes to the issue of how hard they work.

4 According to Barna, because the process of communicating across cultures can result in serious misunderstandings, the solution being to have an open mind.

5 Ho argues that freedom to think is an important component of education. And that creativity is crucial as well.

Activity: *Correcting run-on sentences and comma faults*

Using the *Guidelines for Correcting Run-on Sentences and Comma Faults* on page 292, correct the errors in the following sentences taken from student essays.

1 He would break everything down into pieces and start from scratch he would then build on that slowly so that I would understand.

2 In the past, Americans had a tendency to think that English was the only language worth knowing and that foreigners were forced to learn it so they did not even try to learn another language.

3 However, the fact is that I am not a supernatural being, I could not take the stress.

4 My decision to apply early to college was meant to lighten the burden, unfortunately the three essays and several short questions added to my unbearable load.

Activity: *Identifying sentence fragments in your own writing*

Look through the draft of your assigned essay to see if you have unintentionally created a sentence fragment. If you find a fragment, turn it into a complete sentence.

▸▸▸ **Activity:** *Punctuating your own clauses*

Look through the draft of your assigned essay to determine if you have properly combined and punctuated clauses. Add or change punctuation where necessary.

Connecting Clauses

Writers use three kinds of linking words when *connecting clauses*: coordinators, transitions, and subordinators. Coordinators and transitions show how the idea discussed in one independent clause is related to the idea discussed in another independent clause. Subordinators turn independent clauses into dependent clauses.

■ Coordinators

Coordinators are words that link independent clauses, making them equal in importance.

Coordinator	Purpose
and	to indicate the *addition* of an idea or example
but } *yet*	to indicate the *difference*, or *contrast*, between one thing and another
for	to indicate the *cause*, or *reason*, for something
or } *nor*	to indicate an *alternative* or a *condition*
so	to indicate the *effect*, or *result*, of something

The following sentences include examples of coordinators.

Most students are quite satisfied with the teaching on their campus, <u>but</u> the pressure to get good grades diminishes their enthusiasm. *(Boyer, page 84)*

To be sure, learning often requires sustained attention and effort. <u>But</u> there's a vital difference between that which is rigorous and that which is merely onerous. *(Kohn, page 123)*

This advice obviously is unacceptable, so it is fortunate that a few paths are being laid around the obstacles. *(Barna, page 72)*

■ Transitions

Transitions are words or phrases that move readers from one independent clause to another, enabling them to refer back to what has just been said and to predict what will follow.

Function	Sample transitional words and phrases
To indicate the *addition* of an idea or example	*also; in addition; furthermore; moreover; besides; in fact*
To supply an *example* to support a generalization	*for example; for instance; e.g.*
To indicate the *order* in which events occur or ideas are presented	*first; next; then; lastly; finally; in conclusion; initially; at first; earlier; subsequently; later; meanwhile*
To indicate the *cause*, or *reason*, for something	*the reason is that; for this reason*
To indicate the *effect*, or *result*, of something	*therefore; thus; as a result; consequently; accordingly; then*
To indicate the *difference*, or *contrast*, between one thing and another	*however; nevertheless; on the contrary; in contrast; on the other hand*
To indicate the *similarity* between one thing and another thing that was already mentioned	*similarly; likewise; in the same manner; in the same way; along the same lines*
To indicate the *continuation* of an idea or experience	*still*
To indicate the *consequence* of not doing something	*otherwise*
To indicate a *restatement* or *clarification* of an idea	*in other words; that is; i.e.*
To indicate *concession to* or *agreement with* an idea	*admittedly; of course*
To indicate *emphasis* on a certain idea	*indeed; certainly; above all; after all*
To indicate an *explanation* of something	*in this case*

The following sentences include two examples using the same transitional word, *however*. Note the difference in punctuation for *however* in these two sentences.

> The belief that self-esteem is a precondition to learning is now dogma that few teachers question. <u>However</u>, this confuses cause and effect. *(Moore, page 119)*

> People who attend to nuance have long been at a disadvantage in politics, where spin is out of control. Never before, <u>however</u>, has the same been quite so true of the public conversation about education, which is distinguished today by simplistic demands for "accountability" and "raising the bar." *(Kohn, page 121)*

■ Subordinators in Adverbial Clauses

Subordinators are words or phrases that turn independent clauses into dependent clauses, giving the independent clause in the sentence more importance or emphasis, and enabling the subordinate (dependent) clause to explain the independent clause. A subordinate (dependent) adverbial clause typically answers a question about the independent clause.

Relationship of independent and dependent clause	Subordinating words
TIME (When?)	*after* (subsequent to the time)
	as (at the same time; when; while)
	as long as (for all the time)
	as soon as (quickly after)
	before (prior to the time)
	by the time (just before a specific time)
	once (after; quickly after)
	since (from that time to now)
	so long as (during all that time)
	until (up to the time)
	when (at the time)
	whenever (every time; at any time that)
	while (during the time)
	the first / second / last / next time

continued

CONNECTING CLAUSES

Relationship of independent and dependent clause	Subordinating words
PLACE (Where?)	*where* (at *or* in the place) *wherever* (anywhere that)
CONDITION (Under what circumstances?)	*as long as* (only if) *even if* (whether or not) *except that* (if it were not for the fact that) *in case* (if this circumstance should happen) *in the event that* (if this circumstance should happen) *if* (under this circumstance; on condition that; whether) *on condition that* (under only one circumstance) *once* (under this circumstance) *only if* (under only one circumstance) *provided that* (only if) *so long as* (only if) *unless* (if . . . not) *when* (under this circumstance; on condition that) *whenever* (under this circumstance; on condition that) *whether or not* (regardless of circumstances)
UNEXPECTED RESULT (In spite of what?)	*although* *even if* *even though* *despite the fact that* (contrary to expectation) *in spite of the fact that* *regardless of the fact that* *though*

Relationship of independent and dependent clause	Subordinating words
OPPOSITION (In contrast to what?)	*whereas* (in opposition to) *while*
REASON (Why? Because of what?)	*because* (for the reason that) *as* *as long as* *because of the fact that* *due to the fact that* *inasmuch as* (because) *since* *so long as* *in view of the fact that* *now that* (because now)
PURPOSE (Why? For what?)	*in order that* *so that* (to fulfill this purpose) *in the hope that*
DEGREE (To what extent?)	*as far as* *insofar as* (to the extent that) *so far as*
MANNER (How?)	*as if* *as though* (in such a way as to suggest that)

The following sentences include examples of subordinating words in adverbial clauses.

<u>As soon as</u> I comprehended part of what was said and done, a mischievous spirit of revenge possessed me. (*Zitkala-Ša, page 29*)

After that, <u>whenever</u> I returned to the butcher, the package of meat seemed to grow even larger but the price was still twenty cents. (*Kim, page 45*)

<u>If</u> our students are memorizing more forgettable facts than ever before, <u>if</u> they are spending their hours being drilled on what will help them ace a standardized test, then we may indeed have raised the bar – and more's the pity. (*Kohn, page 124*)

CONNECTING CLAUSES

Critics of American education cannot grasp one thing, something that they don't truly understand <u>because</u> they are never deprived of it: freedom. *(Ho, page 113)*

Because the rules for clauses are complex, writers sometimes make errors when creating sentences that include adverbial clauses. The following sentences show typical adverbial clause errors (underlined) and their corrected forms (underlined).

1. **Unnecessary *but* in an independent clause**

   Error: *While the college teaching we observed was often uninspired, <u>but</u> we still found exciting examples of outstanding teaching at many institutions.*

   Correction: *While the college teaching we observed was often uninspired, we still found exciting examples of outstanding teaching at many institutions.* (Boyer, page 87)

2. **Unnecessary *of* following *despite***

   Error: *<u>Despite of</u> our familiarity with these homegrown differences in tempo, problems with time present a major stumbling block to Americans abroad.*

   Correction: *<u>Despite</u> our familiarity with these homegrown differences in tempo, problems with time present a major stumbling block to Americans abroad.* (Levine & Wolff, page 77)

   Alternative correction: *<u>In spite of</u> our familiarity with these homegrown differences in tempo, problems with time present a major stumbling block to Americans abroad.*

■ Split Subordinators in Adverbial Clauses

The expressions *so . . . that, such . . . that,* and *such a . . . that* indicate that something expressed in the independent clause leads to or should lead to the result expressed in the *that* clause.

1. Use *so . . . that* with adjectives or adverbs and with the quantity words *much, many, few,* and *little,* for example, *so <u>funny</u> that, so <u>foolishly</u> that, so <u>many</u> that.*
2. Use *such . . . that* with plural and uncountable singular nouns, for example, *such <u>problems</u> that, such <u>trouble</u> that.*
3. Use *such a . . . that* with singular nouns, for example, *such a big <u>difference</u> that.*

The following sentences include examples of split subordinators in adverbial clauses. Note that the word *that* can be omitted, as in the second example.

Once in America, I wanted to write <u>so</u> much <u>that</u> I refused to accept the fact that my English was far from being adequate to write a novel. *(Kim, page 42)*

For a minute when I entered the dean's grand office, I was <u>so</u> confused I couldn't even see. *(Yezierska, page 39)*

CONNECTING CLAUSES

■ Subordinators in Adjective Clauses

Adjective clauses provide information about a noun or pronoun in another clause.

Noun or pronoun	Subordinating word	Sample sentence
PERSON	*who*	"I like the professors <u>who</u> have a sense of humor." *(student quoted in Boyer, page 84)*
	whom	I would be like those people from the Bible we had studied in religion class, <u>whom</u> I imagined standing at the foot of an enormous tower. . . . *(Alvarez, page 34)*
	whose	There is such a thing as the affinity of spirits, and among the authors of ancient and modern times, one must try to find an author <u>whose</u> spirit is akin to his own. *(Lin, page 93)*
	that	"The best teachers are those <u>that</u> really care about their students." *(student quoted in Boyer, page 84)*
THING	*that*	The language problem <u>that</u> I was attacking loomed larger and larger as I began to learn more. *(Kim, page 42)*
	which	Learning the language, <u>which</u> most foreign visitors consider their only barrier to understanding, is actually only the beginning. *(Barna, page 69)*
	whose	At Abbot Academy, <u>whose</u> school song was our lullaby as babies . . . she had become quite Americanized. *(Alvarez, page 32)*
TIME	*when*	During a holiday season <u>when</u> I was hired by the library to wax some leather-bound books, for fifty cents an hour, I often daydreamed. . . . *(Kim, page 43)*
PLACE	*where*	This appreciation might exist in graduate or upper-division courses, <u>where</u> teachers and students have overlapping interests, but we found that often this was not the case in lower-division courses. *(Boyer, page 82)*

continued

Noun or pronoun	Subordinating word	Sample sentence
REASON	*why*	"The reason <u>why</u> certain foreigners may think that Americans are superficial – and they are, Americans even recognize this – is that they talk and smile too much." (*student quoted in Barna, page 67*)

■ Punctuating Adjective Clauses to Reflect Meaning

Punctuation can change the meaning of a sentence containing adjective clauses.

> Americans who remember the "good old days" are not alone in complaining about the educational system in this country. (*Ho, page 112*)

Observe the independent clause in Ho's sentence from "We Should Cherish Our Children's Freedom to Think" (page 112).

> Americans . . . are not alone in complaining about the educational system in this country.

This part of the sentence suggests that all Americans complain about the educational system in this country. But Ho has included a dependent clause in the sentence that specifically identifies which Americans he is referring to (underlined).

> Americans <u>who remember "the good old days"</u> are not alone in complaining about the educational system in this country.

By adding this clause, Ho indicates that he is not talking about all Americans, but only about those Americans who remember the "good old days." Note what happens, however, if commas separate the dependent clause from the independent clause.

> Americans, who remember "the good old days," are not alone in complaining about the educational system in this country.

By using commas to set off the dependent clause from the independent clause, the independent clause states that *all* Americans complain about the educational system (and all of them remember "the good old days"), which is not what Ho intended to say.

Because the rules for adjective clauses are complex, writers sometimes make errors when creating sentences that include these clauses. The following sentences show typical adjective clause errors and their corrected forms.

1. **Unnecessary pronoun**

   Error: *Americans who remember "the good old days" <u>they</u> are not alone in complaining about the educational system in this country.*

   Correction: *Americans who remember "the good old days" are not alone in complaining about the educational system in this country.* (Ho, page 112)

2. **Unnecessary preposition**

   Error: *There was in them that sure, settled look of those who belong to the world <u>in</u> which they were born <u>in</u>.*

   Correction: *There was in them that sure, settled look of those who belong to the world <u>in</u> which they were born.* (Yezierska, page 37)

3. **Missing prepositional phrase**

   Error: *We have many prepackaged excuses for our failures, <u>which some</u> are partly valid and others that are self-delusion.*

   Correction: *We have many prepackaged excuses for our failures, <u>some of which</u> are partly valid and others that are self-delusion.* (Moore, page 118)

4. **Unnecessary comma before clause introduced by *that***

   Error: *Each language has a vocabulary of time, that does not always survive translation.*

   Correction: *Each language has a vocabulary of time that does not always survive translation.* (Levine & Wolff, page 78)

■ Subordinators in Noun Clauses

Noun clauses function like nouns.

Subordinating word	Function of clause	Sample sentence
that	Subject	<u>That</u> Jackson benefited from a discriminatory situation is ironic. *(excerpt from student essay)*
	Subject after *It*	It is only this kind of reading, this discovery of one's favorite author, <u>that</u> will do one any good at all. *(Lin, page 93)*
	Object of verb	I believed <u>that</u> her English reflected the quality of what she had to say. *(Tan, page 48)*
	Restated subject or object	The belief <u>that</u> self-esteem is a precondition to learning is now dogma that few instructors question. *(Moore, page 119)*

continued

CONNECTING CLAUSES

Subordinating word	Function of clause	Sample sentence
how, what, when, where, who, which, why, however, whatever, whenever, wherever, whoever, whichever, whether	Subject	<u>How</u> a country paces its social life is a mystery to most outsiders, one that we're just beginning to unravel. (*Levine & Wolff, page 77*)
	Object of verb	I knew <u>what</u> the tests were asking, but I could not block out of my mind the images already created by the first pair. . . . (*Tan, page 50*)
	Object of preposition	When you tossed on our desks writing upon <u>which</u> you had not labored, we read it and even responded, as though you earned a response. (*Neusner, page 126*)

Activity: *Identifying clauses*

Identify the independent and dependent clauses in each of the following sentences.

1 "There's no doubt that American education does not meet high standards in such basic skills as mathematics and language." *Ho, page 113*

2 "When I was 12 in Indonesia, where education followed the Dutch system, I had to memorize the names of all the world's major cities, from Kabul to Karachi." *Ho, page 113*

3 "I got so wild with rage that I seized the hurdle and right before their eyes I smashed it to pieces." *Yezierska, page 39*

4 "The most discouraging comment came from a professor who said he *liked* the passivity of students." *Boyer, page 83*

5 "I felt I was making some progress in mastering the English language even if my collection of rejection slips seemed to shout otherwise." *Kim, page 43*

Activity: *Correcting errors in clauses*

Locate and correct errors in the following sentences.

1 The few who achieve complete insight and acceptance, they are outstanding by their rarity. (See Barna, page 66, for the correct sentence.)

2 Though we rode several days inside of the iron horse, but I do not recall a single thing about our luncheons. (See Zitkala-Ša, page 25, for the correct sentence.)

3 I believed, that her English reflected the quality of what she had to say. (See Tan, page 48, for the correct sentence.)

4 This was the beauty for which I had always longed for. (See Yezierska, page 37, for the correct sentence.)

5 Despite of your fantasies, it was not even that we wanted to be liked by you. (See Neusner, page 126, for the correct sentence.)

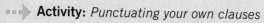

Activity: *Punctuating your own clauses*

Look through the draft of your assigned essay to determine if you have properly combined and punctuated clauses. Add or change punctuation where necessary.

Agreement

Agreement refers to a grammatical match between different parts of a sentence, for example, the match between the subject and its verb or the match between a pronoun and the noun to which it refers.

■ Subject-Verb Agreement

There is *subject-verb agreement* if both the subject and verb are singular or if both the subject and verb are plural.

Singular Subject	Singular Verb	
Language	*is*	the tool of my trade. *(Tan, page 47)*
Plural Subject	Plural Verb	
Pupils	*are*	more like oysters than sausages. *(Harris, page 5)*

Making verbs agree with their subjects is not as easy as it may first appear. The grammatical singular or plural form of the subject is not the only factor. The intention of the writer and current usage may also play a role. The following examples may help you decide whether to use a singular or plural verb in these cases.

1. The subject is *everybody, everyone, anybody, anyone, somebody, someone, nobody, no one, every + noun, each (+ noun), one of the + plural noun.*

   Use a singular verb.

   > Everyone <u>is</u> right! *(Moore, page 118)*

   > One of the biggest problems <u>is</u> to make friends . . . *(Niella, page 55)*

2. The subject is *who, which,* or *that.*

   Use a singular verb if the word it refers to is singular.

   > Anyone who <u>reads</u> a book with a sense of obligation does not understand the art of reading. *(Lin, page 91)*

   Use a plural verb if the word it refers to is plural.

   > Thus, high scores are often a sign of *lowered* standards – a paradox rarely appreciated by those who <u>make</u>, or <u>report</u> on, education policy. *(Kohn, pages 121–122)*

   Current usage allows for a choice of singular or plural verb when the expression *one of* is involved.

   > He is one of those professors who <u>prefers</u> (<u>prefer</u>) to lecture.

AGREEMENT

3. The subject is a collective noun.

Use a singular verb if you think of the people as one unit.

> The faculty <u>takes</u> pride in its achievements.

Use a plural verb if you think of the people as separate individuals.

> We the faculty <u>take</u> no pride in our educational achievements with you. (*Neusner, page 125*)

Nouns that fit into this category include *audience, class, committee, couple, crowd, faculty, family, government, group, party, public, staff,* and *team.*

4. The subject is composed of two or more nouns joined by *either . . . or, neither . . . nor,* or *not only . . . but also.*

Use a singular verb if the subject closest to it is singular.

> Neither the students nor the professor <u>is</u> to blame.

Use a plural verb if the subject closest to it is plural.

> Neither the professor nor the students <u>are</u> to blame.

5. The subject is *enough* or *none.*

Use a singular verb if the reference is to one item.

> Enough <u>has</u> been said.

Use a plural verb if the reference is to more than one item or person.

> Enough <u>were</u> there to start the meeting.

Current usage allows for a choice of singular or plural verb when *none* is followed by *of.*

> None of the students <u>is</u> (<u>are</u>) ready to take the exam.

6. The subject is *there.*

Use a singular verb if the reference is singular.

> There <u>was</u> new knowledge to be conveyed, and it became more difficult to call on all students in the enlarged classes. (*Boyer, page 85*)

Use a plural verb if the reference is plural.

> There <u>are</u> times, of course, when lecturing is necessary to convey essential issues and ideas and also to handle large numbers of students. (*Boyer, page 86*)

7. The subject is an expression of quantity with the word *of.*

Use a singular verb if it is followed by an uncountable noun. (See list of uncountable nouns on page 317.)

> Some of the advice he gave <u>is</u> inadequate.

Use a plural verb if it is followed by a plural noun.

> Yet some of my friends <u>tell</u> me they understand 50 percent of what my mother says. (*Tan, page 48*)

8. The subject includes the expression *number of*.

Use a singular verb if the expression is *the number of*.

The number of adult immigrants who need ESL classes <u>is</u> 14,000.

Use a plural verb if the expression is *a number of* (meaning *some* or *several*).

However, while a considerable number of immigrants <u>have</u> at least a bachelor's degree enabling them to get high-skilled jobs soon after they arrive on our shores, on average they have less education than native-born workers. *(Fish, page 217)*

9. The subject is an infinitive (*to* + verb), gerund (simple form of verb + *-ing*), or dependent noun clause (see pages 303–304).

Use a singular verb.

Infinitive: Now to be able to live two hours out of twelve in a different world and take one's thoughts off the claims of the immediate present <u>is</u>, of course, a privilege to be envied by people shut up in their bodily prison. *(Lin, pages 90–91)*

Gerund: Compounding the problem <u>is</u> a reliance on the sort of instruction that treats children as passive receptacles into which knowledge or skills are poured. *(Kohn, page 122)*

Dependent noun clause: How a country paces its social life <u>is</u> a mystery to most outsiders, one that we're just beginning to unravel. *(Levine & Wolff, page 77)*

10. The subject is a book or essay title.

Use a singular verb.

"Intercultural Communication Stumbling Blocks" by LaRay Barna <u>includes</u> students' own testimonies.

11. The subject combines an expression of quantity or amount + a plural noun referring to time, money, weight, or distance.

Use a singular verb.

Six months <u>is</u> a long time to be away from home.

12. The subject is a noun that ends in *-s* but is considered singular. For example, nouns that fit into this category are countries (e.g., *the Netherlands*), stores (e.g., *Sears*), institutions (e.g., *the United Nations*), and fields of study that end in *-ics* (e.g., *Economics*).

Use a singular verb.

With 30.5 million immigrants (almost 11 percent of the population), the United States <u>is</u> an increasingly diverse society. . . . *(Marasca, page 228)*

13. The subject is a percentage + *of*.

Use a plural verb.

More than 30% of U.S. 17-year-olds <u>don't know</u> that Abraham Lincoln wrote the Emancipation Proclamation. *(Moore, page 118)*

AGREEMENT

Activity: *Identifying errors of subject-verb agreement*

Look through a draft of your assigned essay to search for and correct any errors of subject-verb agreement.

■ Pronoun Agreement

There is *pronoun agreement* if the pronoun and the noun it refers to are both singular, both plural, both masculine, both feminine, or both neuter.

> Americans who remember "the good old days" are not alone in complaining about the educational system in this country. Immigrants, too, complain, and with more up-to-date comparisons. Lately I have heard a Polish refugee express dismay that his daughter's high school has not taught her the difference between Belgrade and Prague. A German friend was furious when he learned that the mathematics test given to his son on his first day as a freshman included multiplication and division. A Lebanese boasts that the average high-school graduate in his homeland can speak fluently in Arabic, French and English. Japanese businessmen in Los Angeles send their children to private schools staffed by instructors imported from Japan to learn mathematics at Japanese levels, generally considered at least a year more advanced than the level here. *(Ho, page 112)*

> Our public education certainly is not perfect, but it is a great deal better than any other. *(Ho, page 114)*

The following examples show nouns and pronouns taken from the passages by Kie Ho above.

Singular Noun   Singular Pronoun

A German *friend* was furious when *he* learned . . .

Plural Noun   Plural Pronoun

Japanese *businessmen* in Los Angeles send *their* children . . .

Masculine Noun   Masculine Pronoun

. . . test given to his   *son*   on   *his*   first day as a freshman . . .

Feminine Noun   Feminine Pronoun

. . . his *daughter*'s high school has not taught *her* the difference . . .

Neuter Noun   Neuter Pronoun

. . . *education* certainly is not perfect, but *it* is a great deal better . . .

Pronoun Agreement with Collective Nouns

With collective nouns, selecting the correct pronoun is dependent on the writer's intended meaning. Collective nouns include words such as *audience, class, committee, couple, crowd, faculty, family, government, group, party, public, staff,* and *team.*

The following sentences show two examples of pronoun choice with the same noun.

1. The collective noun refers to the individuals in the unit.

    We the <u>faculty</u> take no pride in <u>our</u> educational achievements with you. *(Neusner, page 125)*

2. The collective noun refers to the unit as a whole.

    The <u>faculty</u> takes pride in <u>its</u> achievements.

Pronoun Agreement When the Subject Is an Indefinite Pronoun

When the subject of a sentence is an indefinite pronoun, selecting the appropriate pronoun involves a writer's knowing whether the subject is masculine, feminine, or either. Indefinite pronouns include the words *each, one, everybody, everyone, somebody, someone, anybody, anyone, nobody,* and *no one.*

The following sentences show three examples of pronoun choice when the subject of the sentence is an indefinite noun. In each case, the writer knows whether the indefinite pronoun refers to a man, a woman, or both.

1. Everyone in the group is male.

    <u>Each</u> expressed <u>his</u> ideas.

2. Everyone in the group is female.

    <u>Each</u> expressed <u>her</u> ideas.

3. The group is a mix of males and females.

    <u>Each</u> person expressed ideas.

Deciding Whether the Pronoun Should Be Singular or Plural

Selecting a pronoun can be challenging because the choice can depend upon other words in the sentence or upon how closely situated the pronoun is to the word it refers to. The following examples may help you decide whether a pronoun should be singular or plural.

1. The words the pronoun refers to are joined by *and*.

    Use a plural pronoun.

    If Jacob Neusner <u>and</u> Sidney J. Harris were to meet, <u>they</u> would have an interesting debate about college life.

AGREEMENT

2. The words the pronoun refers to are joined by *or* or *nor*.

   Use a singular pronoun.

   > If Ernest Boyer <u>or</u> Alfie Kohn were to enter our classroom, <u>he</u> would probably discuss <u>his</u> views on education.

3. The subject consists of two or more nouns joined by *either . . . or, neither . . . nor*, or *not only . . . but also*.

   Use a singular pronoun if the noun located closest to the pronoun is singular.

   > Not only the students but also <u>the professor</u> found <u>his</u> attention wandering.

   Use a plural pronoun if the noun closer to the pronoun is plural.

   > Not only the professor but also <u>the students</u> found <u>their</u> attention wandering.

Avoiding Use of Sexist Language

Using the masculine pronoun to refer to human beings in general was common practice before the 1980s. The use of the masculine pronoun to refer to all human beings is now considered sexist by most readers and editors. The following examples show several ways to avoid a sexist pronoun.

1. Use the alternatives *he or she, him or her, his or hers*.

   > Previous practice: *Each person's culture, <u>his</u> own way of life, always seems right, proper, and natural.* (Barna, page 70)

   > Current practice: *Each person's culture, <u>his or her</u> own way of life, always seems right, proper, and natural.*

2. Turn the reference into a plural form.

   > Previous practice: <u>*The reader*</u> *cannot be told to love this one or that one, but when <u>he has</u> found the author <u>he loves</u>, <u>he knows</u> it <u>himself</u> by a kind of instinct.* (Lin, page 93)

   > Current practice: <u>*Readers*</u> *cannot be told to love this one or that one, but when <u>they have</u> found the author <u>they love</u>, <u>they know</u> it <u>themselves</u> by a kind of instinct.*

3. Rewrite the sentence to avoid pronouns with gender.

   > Previous practice: *Each sees, hears, feels, and smells only that which has some meaning or importance for <u>him</u>.* (Barna, page 69)

   > Current practice: *Each sees, hears, feels, and smells only that which has some <u>personal</u> meaning or importance.*

▸▸▸ **Activity:** *Identifying errors of pronoun agreement*

Look through a draft of your assigned essay to search for and correct any errors of pronoun agreement.

Verb Tenses

Tense is concerned with time, but not in any simple way. It is possible, for instance, to use a present tense to express a future time, as the following example shows.

> If we <u>are</u> to avoid misreading issues that involve time perceptions, we need to understand better our own cultural biases and those of others. *(Levine and Wolff, page 77)*

■ The Presents

The Simple Present

The simple present is used primarily in four ways.

1. It refers to states of being (as opposed to actions) that exist at the moment of writing.

    > I <u>think</u> my mother's English almost had an effect on limiting my possibilities in life as well. *(Tan, page 49)*

    Verbs that fit into this category of states of being include *appreciate, believe, care, desire, dislike, doubt, envy, fear, hate, imagine, know, like, love, mean, mind, need, prefer, recognize, remember, seem, suppose, think, trust, understand,* and *want.*

2. It refers to habits or routines.

    > There are people who <u>adopt</u> a self-important posture at the desk when they are about to do some reading, and then <u>complain</u> they are unable to read because the room is too cold, or the chair is too hard, or the light is too strong. *(Lin, page 94)*

3. It refers to universal truths or permanent situations.

    > Even within our own country, of course, ideas of time and punctuality <u>vary</u> considerably from place to place. *(Levine & Wolff, page 77)*

4. It refers to an author's ideas (see also page 236).

    > In "Grades and Self-Esteem," Randy Moore <u>argues</u> that self-esteem is not a "prepackaged handout" but must be earned (p. 119). *(Excerpt from student essay)*

The Present Progressive

The present progressive tense is formed by *be (am, is, are)* + verb +*-ing*.

1. It refers to temporary activities or situations that are in progress at the present moment.

    > The ship is <u>docking</u>; I <u>am setting</u> my foot on the new world. *(Schnitzler, page 156)*

2. It refers to activities or situations that are in progress at the present moment and will probably continue.

> Educators and linguists <u>are improving</u> methods of learning a second language. (*Barna, page 72*)

The Present Perfect

The present perfect tense is formed by *has* or *have* + past participle.

1. It refers to an activity or situation repeated in the past that still affects the present and is likely to be repeated in the future.

> Even so, the demand <u>has</u> far <u>outpaced</u> the supply of courses in bilingual and English as a second language. (*Fish, page 217*)

2. It refers to an activity or situation recently completed that still affects the present moment.

> Many teachers <u>have lowered</u> their standards so far that most of their students – the same ones we claim cannot think critically and who employers know are unprepared for entry-level jobs – are A or B students. (*Moore, page 119*)

3. It refers to a completed activity or situation that occurred at an unspecified time in the past and that might continue.

> My mother <u>has</u> long <u>realized</u> the limitations of her English as well. (*Tan, page 48*)

Note: The words *since* and *for* are often used with present perfect or past perfect forms to indicate the beginning point or span of an event. Use *since* to indicate the beginning point of the event.

> Five moons or five months <u>had gone</u> by <u>since</u> the day he had passed with Lae Choo through the Golden Gate; but the great Government of Washington still delayed sending the answer which would return him to his parents. (*Sui Sin Far, page 152*)

Use *for* to indicate the entire span of an event. The word *for* (not *since*) is always used with words referring to quantity of time (e.g., *for a long time*, *for many years*, *for five weeks*).

> The tired slogans <u>have dominated</u> U.S. educational discourse <u>for over 40 years</u>, and are a chief cause of the curricular chaos. (*Hirsch, page 116*)

The Present Perfect Progressive

The present perfect progressive tense is formed by *has* or *have been* + verb + *-ing*.

It refers to an activity in progress over a period of time in the past and continuing into the present.

> Lately, <u>I've been giving</u> more thought to the kind of English my mother speaks. (*Tan, page 48*)

Note: The present perfect (*have given*) could be used in this case without changing the writer's intended meaning, but it would not emphasize that the activity is still going on, as the progressive form does.

■ The Pasts

The Simple Past

The simple past tense for regular verbs is formed by the simple form of the verb + *-ed*. Irregular verbs have many different past tense endings.

1. It refers to activities or situations completed in the past, which happened only one time.

    A year passed, and I <u>discovered</u> a black library branch at Booker T. Washington High. (*Jackson, page 18*)

2. It refers to activities or situations completed in the past.

    I <u>was</u> eighteen then and a drop-out, but I was deep into the wonderful world of literature and life. (*Jackson, page 18*)

The Past Progressive

The past progressive tense is formed by *was* or *were* + verb + *-ing*.

It refers to an unfinished, temporary activity in progress in the past that overlapped with another past activity.

    The language problem that I <u>was attacking</u> loomed larger and larger as I began to learn more. (*Kim, page 42*)

The Past Perfect

The past perfect tense is formed by *had* + past participle.

It refers to an activity or situation completed in the past prior to another past event or condition.

    I was filled with self-doubt and wondered how in the world I <u>had acquired</u> the fantastic idea that I could write the drama of human emotion in fiction in a second language – no, in my third. (*Kim, page 44*)

Note: The past perfect is the form used for the action that happened first.

The Past Perfect Progressive

The past perfect progressive is formed by *had been* + verb + *-ing*.

1. It refers to a completed activity or situation that was in progress over a period of time in the past.

    In my purse was the money I <u>had been saving</u> from my food, from my clothes, a penny to a penny, a dollar to a dollar, for so many years. (*Yezierska, page 36*)

Note: The past perfect form *(had saved)* could have been used in this case without changing the writer's essential meaning, but it would not emphasize that the activity had <u>just</u> ended, as the progressive form does.

2. It refers to an activity in progress over a period of time in the past that overlapped with another past activity.

> In 1953 when I enrolled in the Writers Workshop of the University of Iowa, I <u>had been writing</u> fiction for six years and had completed one novel. *(Kim, page 43)*

Note: The past perfect form *(had written)* would not be appropriate here because it would relate to a single moment in time and not reflect the writer's meaning that the activity had been in progress.

■ The Futures

There are many ways to express the future in English.

1. The present progressive can be used to describe a plan of action for the future.

> He <u>is taking</u> a train to Washington, D.C., tomorrow.

2. The simple present can be used to describe an anticipated or scheduled event.

> The class <u>meets</u> at six o'clock this evening.

Note: This simple present form is used with verbs such as *start, begin, finish* and *arrive, depart, leave,* for example.

3. *Be going to* can be used to describe an intention or plan.

> I <u>am going to</u> take a long walk.

4. *Be to* can be used to describe a future obligation.

> He <u>is to</u> be in class at 2:30 sharp.

5. *Be about to* can be used to describe an action on the verge of happening.

> He <u>is about to</u> start the class.

The Simple Future

The simple future tense is formed by *will* + the simple form of a verb.

It refers to an activity or situation that will take place in the future in response to some prior activity or situation.

> Recently, my own state introduced a test that students <u>will</u> soon <u>have to</u> pass in order to receive a high school diploma. *(Kohn, page 123)*

The Future Progressive

The future progressive tense is formed by *will be* + verb + *-ing*.

It refers to a temporary action that will be in progress in the near future.

> They <u>will be driving</u> to work at 8 a.m. tomorrow.

The Future Perfect

The future perfect tense is formed by *will have* + past participle.

It refers to an action that will be completed prior to a specific future time.

> We'll improve students' self-esteem most by helping and motivating our students to exceed *higher* standards. Only then <u>will</u> our students <u>have accomplished</u> something meaningful and <u>will</u> we <u>have excelled</u> at our work. *(Moore, page 120)*

The Future Perfect Progressive

The future perfect progressive is formed by *will have been* + verb + *-ing*.

It refers to an activity in progress until another time or event.

> I <u>will have been writing</u> for three hours by the time the class starts.

Activity: *Examining verb tenses in your own writing*

Create a chart to show the time line for the events and ideas you are writing about in your essay. Then examine the verb tenses in your essay in relation to the time at which you are currently writing, and determine whether each tense accurately reflects what you want to say. You may find Figure 1 below helpful in determining which verb tenses to use.

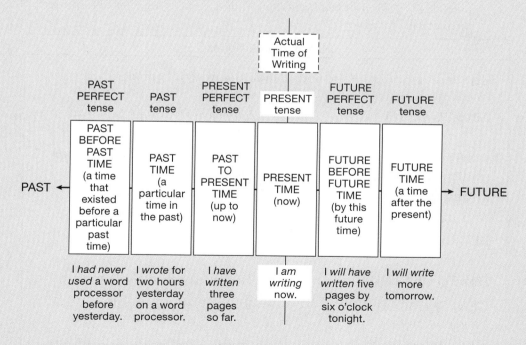

FIGURE 1: The Relationship of Several Tenses on a Time Line.

VERB TENSES

Articles

Each time you write a noun in English, you must make a decision concerning the use of articles. Should I include an article? Should I write *a, an,* or *the*? Answers to the following questions can help you determine the use of articles.

1. Is the noun countable or uncountable?
2. Is the noun singular or plural?
3. Does the writer believe the noun refers to something that is familiar or unfamiliar to the reader?
4. Is the statement that contains the noun general or specific?
5. Does the noun have a modifier (a word that describes or limits the meaning of the noun)?
6. Does the noun act to classify a person or thing, or is it representative of the category it is in?
7. Is the noun part of an idiom?

Because there are so many factors, it is impossible to memorize all the rules for using articles. Two basic rules may be easy to remember.

*   Plural nouns never take *a* or *an*.

*   A singular, countable noun must have an article, even if an adjective precedes the noun (*a beautiful day*), unless there is another determiner[1] rather than the article.

Uncountable Nouns	
Here are a few categories of uncountable nouns with examples. Note: Uncountable nouns typically do not form plurals.	
GROUPS OF ITEMS	*equipment, furniture, homework, machinery, money*
SUBSTANCES (without a fixed shape)	*air, blood, coffee, grass, meat, milk, smoke, steam, tea, water*
ABSTRACTIONS	*advice, confidence, happiness, information, knowledge, news*
RECREATIONS	*baseball, chess, football, soccer, tennis*
FIELDS OF STUDY	*biology, economics, history*
GENERAL ACTIVITIES (in gerund form)	*driving, studying, traveling*
NATURAL PHENOMENA	*darkness, fog, sunshine, weather*

[1]Determiners, other than articles, can be possessives such as *his* or *Maria's*; demonstratives such as *that* or *those*; indefinite quantity words such as *any, each, more* or *some*; and numerals such as *two* or *fifty*.

■ Article Usage in Context

To show how articles can function in context, the following sections analyze the opening paragraphs of James Thomas Jackson's essay, "Waiting in Line at the Drugstore" (pages 16–18). Each of Jackson's sentences is numbered. On pages 317–320, nouns taken from the passage are matched with the sentence number (in parentheses). Note: Although many categories emerge, they do not represent all possible uses of articles.

---

¹I am black. ²I am a writer and I want to place full credit where it belongs for the direction my life has taken: on a photography studio and a drugstore on Main Street in Houston, Texas.

³When I was thirteen, I dropped out of school, bought a bike for $13 (secondhand and innately durable) and went to work as a messenger for the Owl Foto Studio. ⁴Each day we processed film which I picked up as raw rolls on my three routes. ⁵That was great: a bike and job are supreme joys to a thirteen-year-old.

⁶The Owl Studio, on a nondescript street name Brazos (very Texan), was located in a white stucco building that blended unobtrusively into the rest of the neighborhood, which was mostly residential. ⁷The area was predominantly white, and though it did not smack of affluence, it was not altogether poverty stricken either. ⁸Six blocks away was the drugstore, where I had to go first thing each morning for coffee, cakes, doughnuts, jelly rolls, milk, cigarettes, whatever– anything the folks at the Owl wanted. ⁹My trip amounted to picking up "breakfast" for a crew of six: three printer-developers, one wash-dry man, the roll-film man and the foreman. ¹⁰The drugstore was the biggest challenge of my young life. ¹¹Being thirteen is doubtless bad enough for white male youths, but for blacks – me in particular – it was pure dee hell. ¹²Going to the drugstore each morning was part of my job; it was required of me. ¹³With my dropping out of school and all, my parents would have whipped my behind till it roped like okra if I had tried to supply them with reasons for not wanting to go. ¹⁴So, I gritted my teeth and, buoyed by the power of my Western Flyer, rode on down there.

No Article

1. Use no article with a noun that, in the context of the passage, has an uncountable sense.

film (4)	affluence (7)
coffee (8)	milk (8)
picking up (9)	breakfast (9)
hell (11)	okra (13)
wanting (13)	

Note: Uncountable nouns sometimes can be used with *the*, if the noun has a modifier or is followed by *of* + noun. In the following example taken from the first two sentences of an essay, the author uses the word *language* in its uncountable sense, both with and without an article.

> What would I be without <u>language</u>? My existence has been determined by <u>language</u>, not only <u>the</u> spoken but <u>the</u> unspoken, <u>the</u> language of speech and <u>the</u> language of motion. *(from Simon Ortiz, "The Language We Know,"* I Tell You Now: Autobiographical Essays by Native American Writers, *University of Nebraska Press, 1987.)*

2. Use no article with a plural, countable noun that the writer uses to represent a general category of things or people.

rolls (4)	joys (5)
cakes (8)	doughnuts (8)
jelly rolls (8)	cigarettes (8)
white male youths (11)	blacks (11)
reasons (13)	

Note: Plural, countable nouns can be used with *the* if the writer makes a specific reference or modifies the noun. In the following example taken from a research article, the authors use a plural countable noun without an article when the reference is general and with an article when the reference is specific. *(from Milton Miller et al., "The Cross-Cultural Student: Lessons in Human Nature,"* Bulletin of the Menninger Clinic, 1971.)

> Many East Asians we interviewed had come to feel that <u>Americans</u> lacked spiritual values [and] <u>the Americans in Taiwan</u> expressed approximately the same sentiment about their hosts.

3. Use no article with a singular or plural noun that has another determiner.

Each day (4)	my three routes (4)
Six blocks (8)	each morning (8, 12)
My trip (9)	three printer-developers (9)
one wash-dry man (9)	my behind (13)
my parents (13)	my dropping out (13)
my teeth (14)	my Western Flyer (14)

In cases where the noun is known to the reader or has been referred to previously by the writer, a numeral such as six can be preceded by the article *the*. For example, if Jackson were to refer to the distance between the studio and the drugstore <u>again</u>, he could refer to it as <u>*the*</u> *six blocks* (e.g., *I walked the six blocks to the drugstore every day*).

4. Use no article with a noun used in certain idioms.

place full credit where (2)
drop out of school (3, 13)
go to work (3)

Other common idioms that lack an article include the following.

at college, at school, at work, at home
by bus, by train, by plane
go to school, go to church, go to bed
have faith in
have fun
make friends with
play soccer (or any other ball game)
take advantage of
take care of
take notice of
take part in
take pride in

A or An

1. Use *a* or *an* when you use a singular, countable noun to refer to something or someone that you did not previously refer to, if you know or assume that the reader cannot know which thing or person you are referring to.

a photography studio (2)   a drugstore (2)
a bike (3)   a nondescript street (6)
a white stucco building (6)   a crew (9)

2. Use *a* or *an* when you use a singular, countable noun to classify a person or thing or to represent a whole group of which the noun is a member.

a writer (2)   a messenger (3)
a bike (3, 5)   a bike and a job (5)
a thirteen-year-old (5)

Note: A singular, countable noun can also be used with *the* when the writer's intention is to classify or to make the noun representative of other members of its group. In the following example, the writer is not referring to specific people that she knows or has previously introduced but rather is generalizing about the types of people she mentions.

The foreign visitor to the United States nods, smiles, and gives affirmative comments, which the straightforward, friendly American confidently translates as meaning that he has informed, helped, and pleased the newcomer. *(Barna, page 68)*

The

1. Use *the* when you use a singular or plural noun to refer to something that you previously referred to (not necessarily with the exact same word) and that you know is now familiar to the reader.

the neighborhood (6)
The area (7)
the drugstore (8, 10, 12)

Note: The article *the* can also be used in situations where the writer has not previously referred to what the noun represents but knows or assumes the reader is familiar with it. In the following example, the writer of a *Boston Globe* editorial assumes his Massachusetts readers know about the vote in favor of Question 2:

> The recent vote in favor of Question 2 by Massachusetts voters underscores the importance an overwhelming number of voters place on making our school children proficient in English. *(Fish, page 217)*

2. Use *the* when you use a singular or plural, countable or uncountable noun that is followed by a modifier. You may or may not have previously referred to this noun.

> the direction my life has taken (2)
> the rest of the neighborhood (6)
> the power of my Western Flyer (14)

Note: A countable noun followed by *of* + noun can take *a*, *an*, or *the*, depending on the writer's intention. In the following example, the writer chooses *an* to indicate that the noun is not the only one of its kind.

> In other words, we wanted to devise an objective study of a controversial issue on which almost everyone has an opinion. *(Catharine Krupnick, "Women and Men in the Classroom: Inequality and Its Remedies," in On Teaching and Learning: Journal of the Harvard Danforth Center, 1985.)*

If the author had used *the* in this case, she would have been saying that they wanted to devise the only or the most important objective study.

3. Use *the* when you use a singular or plural countable noun that you know is unique (the only one that exists).

> the Owl Foto Studio (3)
> The Owl Foto Studio (6)
> the folks at the Owl (8)
> the roll-film man (9)
> the foreman (9)

Note: A singular countable noun that is unique to the writer can also be used with *a*.

4. Use *the* with a singular or plural, countable or uncountable noun that is preceded by a superlative.

> the biggest challenge (10)

Activity: *Locating errors in the use of articles*

Check each noun in the draft of your assigned essay to try to determine whether it needs *a*, *an*, *the*, or no article.

Punctuation

Punctuation is a tool writers use to help their readers understand how to read their sentences. Many principles govern punctuation, but how a sentence is punctuated is often dependent on a writer's style or intended meaning. For example, read this sentence and then consider its meaning:

> A woman without her man is lost.

Now notice how the meaning of the sentence can change when the punctuation is changed.

> A woman: without her, man is lost.

Punctuation can be changed further to reflect the writer's style or emphasis. Consider the effect of the following changes.

> A woman without her man is lost.
>
> A woman, without her man, is lost.
>
> A woman without her man is lost!
>
> A woman without her man is lost?

> A woman: without her, man is lost.
>
> A woman: Without her, man is lost!
>
> A woman – without her, man is lost.
>
> A woman. Without her, man is lost.

Many punctuation marks are actually pause or stop symbols, telling the reader when to rest. These rest symbols represent progressively longer pauses.

,	–	;	:	.
comma	dash	semicolon	colon	period

Many of the following guidelines for punctuation exist to help readers avoid the misreading of sentences. Your guiding principle in determining which mark of punctuation to choose should be to find a way to transmit your ideas as clearly as possible to your readers. (See also information about punctuating quotations on pages 249–251.)

■ The Period .

A period is used in the following situations.

1. It comes at the end of statements and commands or requests.

    > I pressed my face against the earth. *(Yezierska, page 41)*

2. It can come after deliberate sentence fragments.

    > Worse than being an outcast. *(Yezierska, page 40)*

3. It can come after abbreviations.

    > Mr. Leckler was a man of high principle. *(Dunbar, page 142)*

■ The Question Mark   ?

A question mark is used in the following situations.

1. It comes after direct questions.

> What do our time judgments say about our attitude toward life? *(Levine & Wolff, page 78)*

2. It comes after deliberate sentence fragments that imply a question.

> And my waits at the counter? *(Jackson, page 18)*

■ The Exclamation Point   !

An exclamation point is used after emphatic or emotional statements, phrases, words, or expressions.

> That burning day when I got ready to leave New York and start out on my journey to college! *(Yezierska, page 36)*

■ The Comma   ,

A comma is used to indicate a natural division or slight pause in a sentence and can be used in many situations.

1. It can separate three or more items (words, phrases, or clauses) in a series.

> In another newspaper I wrapped up my food for the journey: a loaf of bread, a herring, and a pickle. *(Yezierska, page 36)*

a. The comma before the word *and* may be omitted if the writer feels the sentence is easy to read without it.

> We complain endlessly that students don't know anything, don't *want* to know anything, can't write well and can't think critically. *(Moore, page 118)*

b. The word *and* may be omitted from the end of the series, usually when the writer wants to create a more dramatic effect.

> And we realize that our youngsters are ignorant of Latin, put Mussolini in the same category as Dostoevski, cannot recite the Periodic Table by heart. *(Ho, page 113)*

2. It can come between two independent clauses linked by a coordinator: *and, but, for, or, nor, so, yet.*

> Most students are quite satisfied with the teaching on their campus, but the pressure to get good grades diminishes their enthusiasm. *(Boyer, page 84)*

a. The comma before the coordinator may be omitted if the writer feels the sentence is easy to read without it.

> I am a writer and I want to place full credit where it belongs for the direction my life has taken: on a photography studio and a drugstore on Main Street in Houston, Texas. *(Jackson, page 16)*

b. A semicolon may be used instead of a comma if the writer feels it is necessary for clarity or emphasis.

> The communication cut-off caused by immediate evaluation is heightened when feelings and emotions are deeply involved; yet this is just the time when listening with understanding is most needed. *(Barna, page 70)*

3. It can follow introductory elements.

   a. It can follow dependent clauses.

   > As I entered the classroom, I saw young men and girls laughing and talking to one another without introductions. *(Yezierska, page 38)*

   b. It can follow phrases.

   > Back home in California, I never need to look at a clock to know when the class hour is ending. *(Levine & Wolff, page 76)*

Note: The comma may be omitted if the writer feels the sentence is clear without it.

> All the while I kept going to the drugstore each morning. *(Jackson, page 18)*

   c. It can follow introductory transitional words.

   > However, this confuses cause and effect. *(Moore, page 119)*

4. It can set off interrupting transitional expressions.

   > There are times, of course, when lecturing is necessary to convey essential issues and ideas and also to handle large numbers of students. *(Boyer, page 86)*

5. It can set off phrases of explanation or expansion of ideas.

   > We have to look at the whole method of instruction, the underlying theory of learning, rather than just quibbling about how hard the assignment is or how much the students must strain. *(Kohn, page 123)*

6. It can set off ending phrases.

   > Lectures were, however, a talking textbook as instructors read slowly and students copied down what was said, word for word. *(Boyer, page 85)*

■ The Semicolon ;

A semicolon links two closely related clauses. It also indicates a major division in a sentence, marking a stronger pause than is indicated by a comma.

1. It can come between two independent clauses.

   > Almost two thirds say they are under great pressure to get high grades; about one third feel it is difficult to get good grades and still "really learn something." *(Boyer, page 84)*

2. It can come between two independent clauses joined by a transitional or adverbial expression.

> One part of them feels obligated to fulfill their parents' expectations; after all, their parents are older and presumably wiser. (*William K. Zinsser, "College Pressures,"* Blair & Ketchum's Country Journal, *1979.*)

Note: The transitional expression is usually followed by a comma, as in the previous example. The comma after the transitional expression may be omitted if the writer feels the sentence is clear without it.

> There are many viewpoints regarding the practice of intercultural communication but a familiar one is that "people are people," basically pretty much alike; therefore increased interaction through travel, student exchange programs, and other such ventures should result in more understanding and friendship between nations. (*Barna, page 66*)

3. It can come between independent clauses, if one or both clauses contain a comma.

> On the matter of classroom participation, we found that 81 percent of liberal arts college students feel they are encouraged to "discuss their feelings about important issues"; but that's true for only 66 percent of the total sample. (*Boyer, page 84*)

■ The Colon :

A colon introduces explanatory items and lists. It marks a major break in a sentence and directs attention to what follows it. A colon can be used in at least three situations.

1. It can link independent clauses when the subsequent clause explains or expands on the first.

> As a result, we are facing a situation in this country that can be described without exaggeration as an educational emergency: The intellectual life is being squeezed out of classrooms, schools are being turned into giant test-prep centers, and many students — as well as some of our finest educators — are being forced out. (*Kohn, page 121*)

2. It can set off a listing or series of items.

> In another newspaper I wrapped up my food for the journey: a loaf of bread, a herring, and a pickle. (*Yezierska, page 36*)

3. It can introduce a full-sentence quotation.

> Robert T. Oliver phrases it thus: "If we would communicate across cultural barriers, we must learn what to say and how to say it in terms of the expectations and predispositions of those we want to listen." (*Barna, page 73*)

■ The Apostrophe '

An apostrophe indicates (1) possession or (2) the omission of one or more letters in a word.

1. To indicate possession, add an apostrophe.

   a. Add 's to form the possessive of singular nouns and pronouns.

      As you envision tomorrow's international society, do you wonder who will set the pace? *(Levine & Wolff, page 81)*

      Everyone's opinion has equal value! *(Moore, page 118)*

   b. Add 's to form the possessive of plural nouns that do not end in -s.

      They had none of that terrible fight for bread and rent that I always saw in New York people's eyes. *(Yezierska, page 37)*

   c. Add an apostrophe to form the possessive of plural nouns ending in -s or -es.

      Contrary to proponents' claims, emphasizing all-purpose mental skills to "prepare children for the 21st century" is not new. *(Hirsch, page 116)*

   d. Add 's to form the possessive of a gerund (noun + -ing).

      This type of reading with a business purpose is in no way different from a senator's reading up on files and reports before he makes a speech. *(Lin, page 91)*

   e. Add 's to the last word in a compound noun or pronoun.

      James Thomas Jackson tells his story from a thirteen-year-old's perspective.

   f. Add 's to the last item to indicate joint possession (one item shared by two people).

      Levine and Wolff's article is titled "Social Time: The Heartbeat of Culture."

   g. Add 's to each item to indicate individual possession (two separate items).

      Kohn's and Moore's essays deal with the subject of educational standards.

2. To indicate omission of a letter, insert the apostrophe where the letter is missing.

   There's [contraction of *There is*] no doubt that American education does not meet high standards in such basic skills as mathematics and language. *(Ho, page 113)*

■ Parentheses ( )

Parentheses may be used for several purposes.

1. They can enclose comments or explanations that interrupt the main thought.

   There appears to be a very strong relationship (see charts) between the accuracy of clock time, walking speed and postal efficiency across the countries we studied. *(Levine & Wolff, page 79)*

2. They can expand on an idea.

> By this time, he knew that Korean was my mother tongue; Japanese my second (I had learned this under the Japanese occupation) and English my third (I started to learn English during my high school days in Korea). *(Kim, page 43)*

3. They can indicate documentation of sources.

> Isn't it sad that Ho's son thought that "Buenos Aires was Spanish for food – a plate of tacos and burritos, perhaps (page 113) and that that doesn't sound strange to Ho? (Skoufaki, page 283)

■ The Hyphen   -

A hyphen is used for the following purposes.

1. It can divide multi-syllable words when there is no more room on the line.

> Many of the readings have made me reconsider what ed-
> ucation should be.

2. It can join compound words.

> That was great: a bike and job are supreme joys to a thirteen-year-old. *(Jackson, page 16)*

■ The Dash   –

A dash marks an emphatic or abrupt break. It can replace a colon, semicolon, comma, or parentheses in some of their uses.

1. It can expand on an idea or add details.

> If you were making a list of what counts in education – that is, the criteria to use in judging whether students would benefit from what they were doing – the task's difficulty level would be only one factor among many, and almost certainly not the most important. *(Kohn, page 122)*

2. It can set off a final item, for emphasis.

> I simply went in a store, picked up the food and wheeled back to the studio – slowly. *(Jackson, page 17)*

Note: A dash typed on a keyboard consists of two consecutive hyphens.

■ Underlining or *Italics*

Underline or put in italics titles of newspapers, magazines, films, and books. One way to remember whether to underline or to use quotation marks is this rule of thumb: Underline or italicize the longer works; use quotation marks with the shorter works.

> The essay "The Rewards of Living a Solitary Life" was originally published in the New York Times.

The article "Social Time: The Heartbeat of Culture" was originally published in <u>Psychology Today</u>, a monthly magazine that makes research findings accessible to a nonprofessional audience.

"College" is the title of a chapter in Anzia Yezierska's book *The Bread Givers*.

"Don't Worry, Be Happy" is a song on the album entitled *Simple Pleasures*.

Activity: *Punctuating sentences*

Punctuate each of the following sentences two times, so that two meanings emerge. Then use various forms of punctuation on each sentence to reflect a different writing style or emphasis (see example on page 321). Refer to a dictionary to look up vocabulary words, if necessary.

1 See the elephant eat Maria
2 Give the bird to my cousin Sylvia
3 She said hold it softly
4 I can can can but I cant cant can you

Activity: *Identifying and correcting punctuation errors*

Locate punctuation errors in your own essay and correct them.

Credits

The author and publisher would like to thank the following for permission to reproduce copyright material. Every effort has been made to track down rightsholders of third-party material to clear permissions. If any rightsholder has concerns about any such material, Cambridge University Press would be pleased to hear from them.

Text Credits

Page 5, Sydney J. Harris, "What True Education Should Do." Copyrighted by and used with the permission of *Chicago Sun-Times, Inc.* Copyright © 1994. *Chicago Sun-Times, Inc.* All rights reserved. Reproduction prohibited.

Page 16, James Thomas Jackson, "Waiting in Line at the Drugstore." From *Waiting in Line at the Drugstore and Other Writings of James Thomas Jackson*, published by the University of North Texas Press, 1993. Reprinted by permission.

Page 30, Julia Alvarez, "My English." From *Something to Declare*, published by Plume, an imprint of Penguin Group (USA), in 1999 and originally in hardcover by Algonquin Books of Chapel Hill. Copyright © 1998 by Julia Alvarez. Reprinted by permission of Susan Bergholz Literary Services, New York. All rights reserved.

Page 35, Anzia Yezierska, "College." From Pages 209–220 of *Bread Givers* by Anzia Yezierska. Copyright © 1925 by Doubleday, renewed 1952 by Anzia Yezierska, transferred to Louise Levitas Henriksen 1970.

Page 42, Kim Yong Ik, "A Book-Writing Venture." From *The Writer*. Currently in *Visions of America: Personal Narratives from the Promised Land*. Reprinted by permission of Faith Leigh, 340 Haverstraw Rd., Suffern, NY 10901-3137.

Page 46, Amy Tan, "Mother Tongue." First appeared in *The Threepenny Review*. Copyright © 1990 by Amy Tan. Reprinted by permission of the author and the Sandra Dijkstra Literary Agency.

Page 66, LaRay M. Barna, "Intercultural Communication Stumbling Blocks." From *Intercultural Communication: 2nd Edition* by Samovar/Porter. Copyright © 1976. Reprinted with permission of Wadsworth, a division of Thomson Learning: www.thomsonrights.com. Fax 800 730 2215. Reprinted by permission.

Page 75, Robert Levine with Ellen Wolff, "Social Time: The Heartbeat of Culture." From *Psychology Today* magazine. Copyright © 1985. (Sussex Publishers, Inc.).

Page 82, Ernest L. Boyer, "Creativity in the Classroom." From *College: The Undergraduate Experience in America*. Copyright © 2005. The Carnegie Foundation for the Advancement of Teaching. Reprinted with permission.

Page 90, Lin Yu'Tang, "The Art of Reading." From *Importance of Living* (1960). Ayer Company Publishers, 400 Bedford St., Suite 322, Manchester, NH 03101. Fax (603) 922-3348. Reprinted with permission.

Page 112, Kie Ho, "We Should Cherish Our Children's Freedom to Think." Copyright © 1983. Reprinted by permission of the author.

Page 115, E.D. Hirsch, "Teach Knowledge, Not Mental Skills." From *The New York Times*. Copyright © 1993 by *The New York Times*. Reprinted by permission.

Page 117, Randy Moore, "Grades and Self-Esteem." From *The American Biology Teacher*, vol. 55, no. 7 (October 1993). Reprinted by permission of Randy Moore.

Page 121, Alfie Kohn, "Confusing Harder with Better." Copyright © 1999. From *Education Week* reprinted with the author's permission. For more information, please see www.alfiekohn.org.

Page 125, Jacob Neusner, "The Commencement Speech You'll Never Hear." From *The Daily Herald* (1981). Brown University campus newspaper. Reprinted with permission.

Page 156, Arthur Schnitzler, "America." Translation by Tom J. Lewis and Robert E. Jungman. Copyright © 1986 from *On Being Foreign: Culture Shock in Short Fiction*. Yarmouth, ME: Intercultural Press.

Page 158, Cristina Garcia, "Tito's Good-bye." From *Iguana Dreams: New Latino Fiction*. Copyright © 1992. Reprinted by permission of Ellen Levine Literary Agency/Trident Media Group.

Page 162, Frances Khirallah Noble, "Albert and Esene." From *The Situe Stories*. Copyright © 2000. Syracuse University Press. Reprinted with permission.

Page 217, Lawrence K. Fish, "Mastering English for Economic Reasons." From *The Boston Globe*. Reprinted by permission of the author.

Page 276, Don Koberg, " How to Criticize Painlessly . . . How to Accept Criticism." From Crisp: *Universal Traveler* 3rd edition by Don Koberg. Copyright © 2004. Reprinted with permission of Course Technology, a division of Thomson Learning: www.thomsonrights.com. Fax 800 730-2215.

Art Credits

Page 27: © Hampton University. Courtesy of Hampton University Archives.

Page 28: © Hampton University. Courtesy of Hampton University Archives.

Page 77: *Main photo:* © Roe DiBona; *Inset illustration:* © Michael Witte

Page 78: *Main photo:* © Robert Levine; *Inset illustration:* © Michael Witte

Page 79: *Main photo:* © Lester Goodman; *Inset illustration:* © Michael Witte

Page 80: *Main photo:* © Robert Levine; *Inset illustration:* © Michael Witte

Page 236: © Punchstock

Index

plot, *170*

point of view, *170, 236–37, 246–47*

present perfect progressive tense, *312–13*

present perfect tense, *312, 315*

present progressive tense, *311–12*

present tense, *311–13, 315*

progress reports, *218–19*

pronouns

    agreement, *308–10*

    indefinite pronouns, *309*

    sexist language, *310*

    singular vs. plural, *309–10*

proofreading, *285*

punctuation, *321–27*

    adjective clauses, *302–303*

    apostrophe, *325*

    brackets, *248–49, 252*

    colon, *321, 324*

    comma, *292–93, 294, 321, 322–23*

    dash, *321, 326*

    ellipses, *247–48, 252*

    exclamation point, *250, 322*

    hyphen, *326*

    parentheses, *325–26*

    period, *292, 293, 321*

    question mark, *250, 322*

    quotation mark, *249–50, 254*

    semicolon, *292, 293, 321, 323–24*

Purdue University Online Writing Lab, *258*

question mark, *250, 322*

questionnaires, *187–90, 202–203*

quotation marks, *249–50, 254*

quotations, *236*

    added word to, *248–49, 252*

    commentary on, *247*

    deleted words in, *247–48, 252*

    dialogue, *251*

    documentation of, *260*

    incorporating, *245–51, 253–54*

    introductory phrases for, *246–47*

    in journal entries, *11*

    long, *250–51*

    punctuation for, *249–50, 254*

    selecting, *245, 251–52*

reading critically, strategies for, *4–10*

readings

    experiences that relate to, *98–100*

    note taking on, *9, 10, 97–98, 129–30*

    selecting, *96–97, 128–29, 169*

"Relationship Between International and U.S.-Born Students" (Yeyinmen), *184, 199–201*

research. *See* field research; library and Web-based research

research proposals, *207–208*

results section, *195–97*

Revised All New Universal Traveler, *276*

revising process, *278–82*

"Rewards of Living a Solitary Life" (Sarton), *242*

risk taking, *288*

run-on sentences, *292–93, 294*

Sarton, Mary, *242*

Schnitzler, Arthur, *156–58*

scholarly books and articles, *206, 208, 212*

"School Days of an Indian Girl" (Zitkala-Ša), *24–30, 175–76, 178*

semicolon, *292, 293, 323–24*

sentence boundaries, *289–95*

setting, *170*

sexist language, *310*

simple future tense, *314*

simple past tense, *313*

simple present tense, *311*

Skoufaki, Sophia, *279–82, 283–84*

"Social Time" (Levine and Wolff), *75–82, 103, 240*

sources

    acknowledgement of, *236, 244*

    citing ideas from, *236–37*

    documentation of, *217, 236, 258–71*

    evaluation of, *215–16*

    note taking on, *216–18*

    paraphrasing ideas from, *236, 241–44*

    quotations from, *236, 245–54*

    summarizing ideas from, *236, 238–41*

    synthesizing ideas from, *255–58*

Index of Guideline Boxes